THE

DE CORONA

OF

DEMOSTHENES.

WITH ENGLISH NOTES,

BY THE

REV. ARTHUR HOLMES, M. A.,
SENIOR FELLOW OF CLARE COLLEGE, CAMBRIDGE, AND PREACHER AT THE CHAPEL ROYAL, WHITEHALL.

Revised Edition,

BY W. S. TYLER,
WILLISTON PROFESSOR OF GREEK IN AMHERST COLLEGE.

BOSTON:
JOHN ALLYN, PUBLISHER.
1874.

University Press: Welch, Bigelow, & Co.,
Cambridge.

PREFACE.

The text of this edition is almost an exact reprint of that in the Catena Classicorum, edited by Rev. Arthur Holmes of Cambridge, and Rev. Charles Bigg of Oxford. In revising the Notes of that edition, at the request of the publisher, it has been my single aim to produce, as nearly as possible within the same limits, a text-book of the De Corona adapted to meet the wants of students in our American colleges. With this end in view, I have omitted not a few of the English editor's superabundant citations from Greek authors, and whatever else in his Notes seemed to me to be superfluous or sure to be neglected by even the better scholars in a college class, and have filled the place with such grammatical references, exegetical annotations, and exact yet idiomatic translations of difficult passages, as the experience of many years in teaching Demosthenes has shown to be best calculated to lead students to a right method of studying the great Athenian orator.

When the English editor has fallen into manifest errors and misapprehensions, I have not hesitated to correct them, or to supersede his Notes by my own or those of other editors. In this revision I have had constantly before me the editions of Reiske, Schäfer, Dindorf, Dissen, Bremi, Westermann, Drake, Whiston, and others, and have derived from them many useful hints and suggestions. The Notes of

Whiston are so scholarly and judicious, and his renderings so just and happy, that I have adopted them pretty freely. If in any instance I have failed to give due credit for borrowed materials, the failure has been unintentional.

To the Introduction of the English edition, which is reprinted entire as a concise statement of the history of the De Corona, I have added an Analysis of the Argument, which, it is hoped, will aid the student in understanding the skilful arrangement of the orator and possessing himself of his masterly reasoning. So far from sympathizing with the depreciatory remarks which occur too frequently in the English edition, and which I have taken the liberty to abridge, I scarcely fall below Lord Brougham in my admiration of this matchless and almost faultless piece of rhetoric; and I could wish that not only students of Greek, but orators and students of oratory, would study and repeat the oration as his Lordship did, and as he advised the youthful Macaulay to do, so as "to enter into the spirit of the speech, thoroughly know the positions of the parties, follow each turn of the argument, and make the absolutely perfect and most chaste and severe composition familiar to his mind." And I venture to urge upon teachers and pupils such a repeated reading and reading aloud of the oration, as so inspired the Leyden Greek Professor Wyttenbach in his youth, that he fancied himself "to be Demosthenes standing before the assembly, delivering the oration, and exhorting the Athenians to emulate the bravery and glory of their ancestors," and thus gave him the first genuine impulse to an enthusiastic study of the language and literature of the Greeks.

W. S. TYLER.

AMHERST COLLEGE, January 1, 1874.

INTRODUCTION.

I.

The Speech on the Crown was made in defence of an accusation for παράνομα, which legal term we may paraphrase as a "Breach of the Constitution." Æschines had laid the charge and conducted the accusation. The accused was Ctesiphon, son of Leosthenes, an Athenian citizen belonging to the deme Anaphlystus. The ground of the action was as follows: Ctesiphon had proposed a decree, that, according to common Athenian usage, the state should bestow a crown of gold on Demosthenes, as one who had proved himself to be a public benefactor, not merely by his general policy, but also by his special liberality on two recent occasions. As member of the Fortifications Commission, appointed just after Chæronea, Demosthenes gave to the Building Fund no less a donation than three talents. At the same time, as trustee to the fund for theatrical and similar expenses, he gave to that fund a hundred minas as a voluntary contribution. These two instances seemed to supply an immediate opportunity for recognizing his general as well as his special merits. The decree further proposed expressly, that proclamation of this grant of honor should be made in the theatre of Athens, at the time of the Great Dionysia, when the new tragedies were coming on; that is, at a time and place where crowds of strangers, as well as citizens, were certain to be assembled. Thus the honor conferred by the state would be at once of the most public as well as the most complimentary kind.

We cannot but think the proposal of this decree had further objects than merely to honor the orator. We may well suppose it included a strong political move on the side of the Constitutional party, who had always opposed and (so far as they could) resisted the power of Macedon. To laud Demosthenes and his policy was really to censure Philip; nor was it only to censure Philip, but also to stigmatize the whole Macedonian party, whose numbers were very strong in the Public Assembly of Athens, of which party Æschines may be called the political leader. Ctesiphon, it is to be noticed, was quite an unknown man. And yet his name is attached to this important decree. How can this be explained except by the supposition that he was put forward by other men of greater power and distinction? The Constitutional party, in fact, were throwing down a challenge to their opponents; and their action would certainly lead to a public trial and contest. Now the fact that Ctesiphon was an unknown and insignificant person would be useful to them in two ways for fighting their battle of politics. First, it would look as if the merits of Philip's chief antagonist were such as to call forth the most disinterested praises, uttered by an humble voice in the ranks with honest, untaught enthusiasm. Next, in attacking this decree, the prosecutor could get no hold on the character of its proposer. He would not be able to denounce the decree as proposed by a well-known demagogue, by a man of notorious character, whose very advocacy was enough to condemn his cause.

At the actual date of Ctesiphon's measure, the numbers

of the Macedonian party were probably weak in the Council, however strong they may have been in the body of the Assembly. The decree was passed by the Council, so far as we know, without opposition. It was then deposited among the public records, to await its confirmation by the vote of the next Assembly. At this stage it was merely a bill (*προβούλευμα*); it required the vote of the Assembly to make it an act (*ψήφισμα*). The month in which it passed the Council, we are told, was Pyanepsion (corresponding to the second half of October and the first half of November) in the year 337. No step was taken to bring it before the Assembly, its supporters probably waiting for a favorable crisis to do so. But the fortunes of Macedon continued to be on the ascendant; Philip had realized his full ambition, and was making his preparations to invade the Persian empire as commander-in-chief of Greece. The Macedonian party at Athens were accordingly stronger and bolder than ever. On the sixth day of Elaphebolion, five months after Ctesiphon's measure had received the sanction of the Council, Æschines laid a charge against him, before the Archons of the year, as having been guilty of *παράνομα* on three distinct grounds: (1) that he had proposed to honor with a public vote of thanks a commissioner and trustee whose accounts had yet to pass the ordeal of the public audit; (2) that he had moved for a proclamation to be made in a place distinctly forbidden by law; (3) that he had caused a document false in substance to be deposited among the public records. These first and second points were, of course, purely technical. The third was the main issue; whether it were true or false that Demosthenes had proved himself to be a public benefactor.

In order to stop Ctesiphon's measure from coming before the Assembly, it was quite sufficient for Æschines to have given the above notice of action. Matters would rest in abeyance until the case was tried; the state of the law on this point is incidentally mentioned in the course of our present speech.* In an action whose issue was so doubtful, neither party would be very anxious to hurry matters on; each would be interposing delays till a favorable crisis came for their own particular object. The death of Philip, the revolts and confusion which followed, the prospects of Alexander's reign, whose success or failure no one could predict, these and the like variations of fortune kept the fickle Democracy of Athens in a constant state of excitement. As the fortunes of Macedon waxed or waned for the moment, so for that moment the Macedonian party would have the Athenian mob at their back or else at their throat. Until it was clear beyond all question what Alexander was equal to doing, any attempt to precipitate matters was warily to be avoided by the Constitutional party no less than by their opponents. In the depth of degradation which Athenian politics had reached, statesmanship had come to be merely a game played for the paltry stake of personal wealth and distinction. We entirely exempt Demosthenes himself from this imputation; and a few eminent names might be mentioned as being exceptions also. But the general run of leading politicians were animated by nothing else than the greed of personal advantage and interest. And the men composing the public Assembly were either puppets in the hands of a strong unscrupulous clique, or else a feeble *fainéant* set of obstructives, without the courage or honesty to open their lips and speak the truth. Hence the policy of Athens wavered like a reed in the wind. Let the news have been received from Asia of "another great Macedonian vic-

* § 102, p. 36.

tory," and all Athens would be on its knees to worship the youthful and rising sun. Next day let a fiery piece of rhetoric burst from the lips of an independent member, and behold the "vulgus infidum" turning their backs on the luminary of yesterday's adoration. Men and parties being such at Athens, it is easy to see how the great question, which Ctesiphon's case would really raise, was allowed to lie in abeyance for some six years or more. At last, early in 330, when the arms of Macedon were thoroughly triumphant, Alexander a few months before having crushed Darius at Arbela, and Antipater having done the same to the Peloponnesian league in Greece, Æschines thought they were strong enough to command a majority in the Assembly, and that any body of dikasts appointed to try the case would reflect public opinion and give their verdict accordingly. So he hurried his action on, to get Demosthenes censured and ruined before some change of fortune should intervene in his favor.

A case so exciting as this insured a crowded court. From all parts of Greece, it is said,* they flocked to Athens to hear the trial. Æschines, speaking for the prosecution, dwells first on his two strong points, the technical breaches of the law. He then proceeds to make a withering analysis of all the public and private life of Demosthenes, showing him up in such a light that, if it were true, his proper portion would be, instead of public honor, public infamy and exile. He divides his analysis into four chapters : the first denounces the orator as accomplice of Philocrates, in making the fatal peace of 346 ; the second imputes to the orator's Eubœan policy the final breach of that peace with Philip, and all the war and disorder belonging to the whole period ; the third

* Cicero, de Opt. Gen. Orat. 7.

includes subsequent charges connected with the war against Amphissa, the alliance with Thebes, and the last conflict with Philip; the fourth is confined to the reign of Alexander, taxing the orator with being Alexander's secret friend, whence three opportunities, it is alleged, have been allowed to slip, in any one of which the fortunes of Athens might fairly have been restored. Then there follows the famous picture of the perfect ideal politician, and a caricature of Demosthenes, to be viewed in strong contrast. The caricature is, of course, embellished with the grossest personality. And so concludes what we may call the first part of the oration, containing the separate arguments in support of the three distinct pleas. The second part is a warning to the Court on no account to allow Demosthenes to have this honor paid him. The present abuse of public laudation is contrasted bitterly with the ancient practice, when such honors were rare instead of common, and given only to men of merit, not to the worthless and venal. To remedy this, let them now revive the old severity of the Court in dealing with breaches of the Constitution. For instance, let them compel Demosthenes to reply to the charges in the order in which they were actually laid, taking the special illegalities first and the general topic after. Æschines then anticipates the line of his opponent's reply, and does his best to refute it, in detail as well as in general, specially explaining the reason why he had not brought forward these accusations sooner. He protests against the immorality, as well as the bad example to the young, of a man receiving a grant of honor who is not only undistinguished by any public service, but who has been also the cause of so many public disasters. Let them beware of styling such as the benefactors of the state; let them think of their country and its laws, and their own famous forefathers. The rest of his speech is merely a brilliant peroration.

Ctesiphon now rose to reply, but we do not possess the smallest record of what his answer was. Probably it only amounted to a formal denial of the charge. He might safely leave Demosthenes to deal with the whole matter. How the orator discharged this duty we see in the speech itself. It only remains to notice its general merit and value.

He vindicates with the greatest success his *honesty* as a politician. Whether his policy was wise, — whether the freedom of Athens could not have been better secured by making Philip their friend than by driving him into hostility, — this is another question. But the course which the orator advised the state to take was certainly honest and brave, if it did verge on desperate. And when we compare him with the other leaders of the same age and time, his courage and honesty really shine as beyond description brilliant. It is well to bear this in mind when we read his self-laudation, which entirely lacks the reserve and delicacy one would have preferred to see. But he spoke under strong provocation. Ever since this vote of honor had been proposed by Ctesiphon, accusation after accusation had been brought against Demosthenes by the friends and agents of Macedon. If they could once have secured a conviction, of course the decree of the Crown would have been ignominiously cancelled. Their attacks, in short, amounted to an organized persecution; and this persecution had lasted for something like six years. But the spirit of law and right was not entirely dead at Athens, although it was moribund. What with the strength of his character, and what with the strength of his party, the orator passed unscathed through this protracted ordeal. But the iron must indeed have entered into his soul. And hence we can make a great allowance for the bitterness of his recrimination and the rather glaring colors of his eulogies on himself. He speaks like a man whose honest anger has been aggravated into passion, and like one whose consciousness of innocence has been aggravated into self-worship. We must also, in estimating the moral tone of the speech, allow for the decadence of his age and the low calibre of Athenian courts of justice. To a speaker addressing such an audience, exaggeration was indispensable, and personalities, however coarse, were more impressive than any logic. If we estimated the Speech on the Crown from an objective point of view, we might call its arguments somewhat strained, its veracity sometimes suspicious, and its taste by no means faultless. But defects which belong to an age or a nation can only be viewed apart. Whatever else may be said of the speech, "the greatest effort of the greatest orator," this at least is undeniable, — it won a triumph for right and truth at a very critical moment, and has cleared forever the public character of one who was truly a patriot.

The instances of suspicious veracity are noticed as they occur;* my own theory respecting them is that the orator's statements are just true in the letter, just barely true and no more, anything but explicit, and very likely to convey a false impression to his hearers. Morally they are as indefensible as if they were actual falsehood; but rhetorically they were perfect triumphs of ingenuity and skill. The usual interpretation of them would make Demosthenes guilty not merely of direct misstatements, but also of positive stupidity; the former, I think, is very improbable, the latter quite impossible. To hope to defeat an opponent by flat

* See §§ 22, 24, notes.

contradiction involving palpable falsehood, this would be simply absurd; and Demosthenes of all men would have been the last to attempt it. So with respect to his defence on the two technical points of law, some of the editors impute to him a tissue of pure inventions; and there again it is doubtful whether they do a greater insult to his truthfulness or to his common-sense, or, last of all, to his talent. I should fancy the case to be thus: that Æschines, in his accusations, had raked up clauses of law, existing indeed, but never now enforced, or at any rate very frequently violated by consent; that Demosthenes, on the other hand, raked up clauses of exceptions and exemptions belonging to the same laws, and equally obsolete, or at any rate of equally little importance in point of right. He might as well have stated honestly that this was his line of argument. But such a statement would not have suited Athenian critical ears. Nothing except artifice would ever satisfy them. Æschines had shown superb artifice in getting the legal objections together; it was now for Demosthenes to show the same by the manner in which he would overthrow them. If Ctesiphon's measure had really been so directly in violation of the law, is it likely that the Council would have passed it? or that he himself would not have been warned to amend the measure for his own sake? Again, if Demosthenes's reply on the legal points of the case had been really as convincing as he pretends it to be, is it likely that he would have objected to take those two points first and the general topic after? I believe, in fine, that these two breaches of the law were nominal rather than real; the law in both cases existed, if any one chose to enforce it; the law might be made to apply to the present charge in both cases, if the Court were only disposed to rule in that direction. If they were otherwise disposed, the legal points were entirely worthless. If the Court wished to condemn Ctesiphon, they had a legal justification, although of a feeble kind. If the Court wished to acquit him, they had their justification then in common-sense and in common practice.

The real issue, as we have seen, in the present prosecution, was not an issue of points disputed in national law or national history; the issue was whether Philip's opponents at Athens could or could not be crushed; Demosthenes once overthrown, the rest of his party would prove easy victims. But Æschines had overrated his own ability and influence. The fiery rhetoric of the reply shrivelled the accusation to atoms. The popular Court of Justice at Athens, always notorious for their facility in yielding anything and everything to the eloquence of the moment, always in the hands and at the beck of the person who happened to speak last, had no hesitation whatever in their verdict on this occasion. By the honesty of their political leaders most of them would set but little store; by the talent of their public speakers there was scarcely a man who would not set a store which was the very greatest. And where, as on this rare occasion, honesty and talent fought combined, their force was irresistible, and their triumph perfectly certain. The few who did not care for the orator's eloquence would give him their support as an honest man and a victim; the many who did not care for the orator's honesty would give him their support as a truly glorious speaker. So that Æschines would be reduced to personal friends or bought partisans as his only supporters on the bench. It is little marvel that he failed to obtain even so much as one fifth of the votes, and left the Assembly a ruined man with nothing but exile before him.

The blow he had aimed at Demosthenes was suicidal (to himself.) Nor can we imagine the possibility of any other result than this when we read the rival speeches. The verdict of any who read them will surely be always the same as that of the Court which heard them. True, the speech of Æschines has many points that are brilliant. But it is inferior in vigor, inferior in dexterity, inferior in its indignation, and inferior in its pathos. The one speech has a genuine ring of patriotism and courage about it; the other rings like debased metal, coated over thickly enough with an affectation of high principle, but still transparent to the naked eye as coin that will not pass. We have the two orations to compare in their last, most finished shape, not as they were actually spoken, but as they were corrected and polished, with a view to publication by their authors in permanent manuscript form. They are, therefore, works which embody reflection and logical power, as well as ready eloquence and mere rhetorical talent. The comparison leads to only one conclusion, that Demosthenes, in our common phrase, was the "better man all round." It is really impossible to say that Æschines has the advantage of him at any point whatever, — even on the two legal questions, be their value what it may. Never perhaps in the course of history was defeat in a political duel so decisive, so overwhelming, so irretrievable as this.

To conclude: if we cannot wholly approve the moral tone of the Speech on the Crown, we can praise without reserve or stint the magnificent style of its language. The orator's exquisite choice of words and their still more perfect arrangement, the splendid roll of his long periods, the delicate balance of the antitheta, the superb grammatical finish pervading the whole, — these are unmistakable indeed; there can be but one opinion about them. It is pleasant to know that even in those days the beaten rival could own so freely his victor's superior merit; we agree entirely with Æschines, that a speech so grand to read must have been sublime to hear; we echo his graceful compliment, and add ourselves what his Rhodian friends may perhaps have added then, "O 'si audissemus.'"

II.

The "Phocian War" and the "Peace of Philocrates" are introduced so prominently in the course of the Speech on the Crown that a brief historical notice of both is almost indispensable. But the records we have of this period are so confused and involved that we cannot assign exact dates to each of the several events: we are only able to trace their general sequence and connection. The War took its rise most probably out of the old ill-feeling which had always subsisted between Thebes and Phocis, and a strong wish, on the part of Thebes, to cripple Phocis as a dangerous and ill-affected neighbor. For this purpose they took advantage of the all but defunct Amphictyonic Council, whose meetings for a long period had been little more than formal, and whose decrees had ceased to be looked on as of any political importance. However, the state of Phocis, in the year 357, was prosecuted before this Council as guilty of sacrilege. The ground of the charge was the fact that they had occupied and tilled a part of the land which was dedicated to Apollo as supreme God of Delphi. The prosecution was actually brought by the Thessalian members of the Council; but it is almost certain that Thebes was the prime mover in the case, and Thessaly merely their instrument. Sentence was passed on the Phocians, and a heavy fine imposed. At this time the leading men of Phocis were Philomelus and his two brothers, Onomarchus and Phayllus. At the instigation of Philomelus, the Phocians refused to pay the fine, marched upon Delphi and seized the town and temple, alleging that they were the original presidents of the oracle, and therefore entitled to hold it in their own possession. Of course they intended to use the oracle as the mouthpiece of their own policy, and in fact Philomelus did so on the earliest opportunity. Thus they were able, ostensibly, to condemn and annul the decrees of the Amphictyonic Council by the voice and sentence of the God himself, whose honor and worship that Council was specially appointed to guard. And hence the war, as regarded from the view of either party, was entitled the "Sacred War," and is commonly so referred to.

Two unsuccessful attempts to expel the Phocians from Delphi were made by the neighboring state, the Locrians of Amphissa. After the second defeat the Locrians implored the help of Thebes, appealing to them in the name of the God. Thebes assented, and induced Thessaly to join them in making the attack. On the other hand, Athens and Sparta favored Philomelus, though they could not give him active support; and Achæa sent him a small army of reinforcement. After an irregular campaign and a battle near the town of Neon, the result of which was doubtful, the Phocians retired on Delphi, and the allies went home. Philomelus, who was killed in the last engagement, was succeeded by Onomarchus as commander-in-chief. The latter seems to have been a vicious despot, but an able general. He conducted the war with such success that he laid

Locris and Doris waste, captured Amphissa and other towns, seized Orchomenus in Bœotia, and was actually besieging Chæronea when the Theban army compelled him to fall back on his own territory.

At this point of the war, in the year 352, Onomarchus was appealed to for aid by Lycophron of Pheræ (probably his ally; for Pheræ had refused to join the rest of Thessaly in the attack on Phocis): Pheræ was being besieged by Philip of Macedon, abetted, though little aided, by the northern Thessalians, at whose invitation he had first invaded Thessaly, in order that they might gratify their old grudge against the Pheræans. Onomarchus sent Phayllus with an army to relieve Pheræ, but he was defeated and driven back. Onomarchus then advanced upon Philip himself with the whole of his forces; but after some few partial successes, his army was utterly crushed, and he lost his own life. Pheræ surrendered, and Philip was master of Thessaly.

The remnant of the Phocian army, having returned under the command of Phayllus, seems to have been in a little time reconstituted as a military force. Mercenary troops at this period were easy enough to procure. And the plunder of the sacred treasury at Delphi had supplied the Phocians with ample funds for this and all the expenses of the war. They now seem to have invaded Bœotia with more or less of success; they prolonged the conflict up to the year 346. Meantime, Athens was intriguing to recover Thespiæ and Platea, and, at all events, Oropus; Sparta was trying to annex Megalopolis and Messene. Hence Megalopolis, in 352, solicited the aid of Athens against Sparta; but Athens, after much discussion, resolved to remain neutral. The Thebans, however, sent a strong force, just set at liberty by the defeat of Onomarchus, to assist the Megalopolitans: Argos, Sicyon, Messene, also joined the same side. Sparta, on the other hand, was aided by Phocis and Pheræ: and a series of dubious battles followed, ending in a hollow truce, no decisive results whatever having been attained by either side.

Philip, in the interval, had made secure his ground in Thessaly, and then proceeded to do the same in Thrace. Forming an alliance with one Thracian potentate, Amadocus, he invaded the dominions of another, the famous Cersobleptes, defeated him in battle, and carried away his son as a hostage. Having thus made good his footing in Thrace, he made a demonstration against Heræum on the Propontis, to the great temporary wrath and excitement of the Athenians, who, however, took no action at present, in spite of the urgent appeals addressed to them by Demosthenes. Consequently Philip went on with his plans against the Chalcidian cities. In the year 349 he began the actual attack, having spent the two previous years in sowing the seeds of venal treachery in all their principal towns. Although interrupted by a revolt of Pheræ, and by the Athenian forces sent under Chares and Charidemus to the assistance and relief of Olynthus, Philip succeeded either by treachery or force in capturing all the chief of the Chalcidian cities, and Olynthus finally surrendered, and was razed to the ground in the year 348.

In the course of all these events Demosthenes had maintained the same consistent attitude: we have his speeches which trace the whole history; the speech on behalf of the Megalopolitans, spoken in 353 or 352; the first Philippic, spoken in 351, when Philip had just commenced the siege of Heræum; lastly, the Olynthiac orations in 349. The orator, up to this point, had showed himself as the earnest and bitter antagonist of the king of Macedon, and with rare political foresight had understood from the outset the ulterior aims of Philip regarding the states of Greece.

And now we have come to the "Peace of Philocrates." In November of the year 347 Philocrates passed a resolution in the Assembly at Athens that envoys should be sent to Philip to make terms of peace and alliance. Among the envoys were Demosthenes and Æschines both: Philip met them at Pella. His diplomacy proved completely triumphant over the Athenian politicians; he forced Athenian concessions out of them, one after another; but they failed to elicit from him the slightest promise or arrangement respecting Thrace, Thebes, or Phocis. Yet, strange to say, when the envoys returned to Athens, in March of the year 346, after hot discussion, debate, and reciprocal vilification, the terms of peace were accepted; and Antipater, on Philip's part, actually administered the oath of peace to the Athenians, so that their state was bound to inaction, Philip still remaining at liberty to carry on his operations until he should formally have taken the same oath himself. A second body of envoys from Athens to administer the oath to Philip, after delay and procrastination which makes their conduct most suspicious, find him at last in Thrace, just victorious in a campaign with his old enemy, Cersobleptes, who for the time is utterly crushed and made into a tributary subject. Thus the territory lying between Macedonia and the Athenian property in the Chersonese is entirely in Philip's hands. He can march through it as he pleases, and use its resources at his own discretion. Still the envoys show no haste in binding him down by the oath of peace. More than two months have now been wasted since the oath was taken by Athens; yet Philip beguiles the envoys to come with him southward, as far as Pheræ, before he consents to be sworn: at Pheræ he does at last condescend to confirm the treaty, with this grave exception however, that the Phocians are formally excluded from it. This was the death blow of Phocis. Phalæcus, their commander-in-chief (the son of Onomarchus, who had succeeded to the office on the death of his uncle Phayllus), at first prepared to resist Philip with the aid of Archidamus and a Lacedæmonian force. But he and Archidamus quarrelled as to the plan of the campaign, and the Lacedæmonians withdrew. Phalæcus then turned traitor, and made terms with Philip for himself and his mercenaries. Philip allowed them to retire unharmed, and these soldiers of fortune betook themselves to Crete. Meantime the Macedonian forces were in the heart of Phocis. The Phocians, although deserted by their leader and by their army, made a desperate effort to resist the invading foe. The result was that their cities were stormed and all the inhabitants taken captive.

The Amphictyonic Council met, to decide on the sentence that should be passed upon Phocis. They decreed that all the towns of the state, excepting Abæ, should be destroyed, and that henceforward the Phocians should live in small and scattered villages. It was further decreed that they should pay a fine of ten thousand talents, in annual instalments of sixty; that they should be excluded henceforward from entering the temple of Delphi; and that they should forfeit their seat in the Amphictyonic body. Their seat, with its two votes, was transferred to Macedon.

So concluded the Phocian War after some ten years' duration. It may seem strange that so small a state should have ever been able to hold its own in a conflict thus severe and protracted. The explanation, however, lies in the simple facts of the case: their funds were ample, their leaders a very determined and influential family, their army was easy to raise and recruit with the help of mercenary troops. The cause of the war, and the war itself, is insignificant enough, and would scarcely have left a mark in history, but for the serious results of which it proved the beginning. Phocis, we may say, in point of fact, was Philip's opportunity in Greece, just as Pheræ had been his opportunity in Thessaly, and just as Cersobleptes had been his opportunity in Thrace. Step by step the king of Macedon pursued his southward way. His policy was as consistent and simple as it was unscrupulous and wholly immoral: to take part in a national quarrel with whatever side appeared the stronger, to pursue that quarrel up to its end till the hostile party was vanquished, when the whole nation in consequence would be at his own disposal, either as conquered subjects, or else as friends and allies. So he had dealt with Thessaly and Thrace; so he proceeded to deal with Greece. And wherever the force of arms would have been inadequate for his purpose, there he tried the more deadly forces of bribery and of corruption, until he had so far corroded the strength of the power he wished to assail, that their making any effectual resistance was really out of the question. Nor were his arts of corruption of a merely vulgar kind: they included personal courtesy and friendship, frequent and profuse hospitalities, the exercise of great diplomatic talent, as well as unlimited money. By such policy firmly maintained with immense tenacity of purpose, and carried out in all its details with extraordinary courage and vigor, Philip made his upward career as rapid as it was triumphant. But his aims were always far beyond the narrow limits of Hellas. As Thessaly and Thrace to him were but stepping-stones to Greece, so Greece itself was to him but a stepping-stone to Persia. He could only hope to invade the Persian Empire as leader of the united Greeks, and with all their power to support him. He could only hope to secure their support by bringing them all beneath his own control, either in right of conquest, or else in right of alliance. His direct aim therefore was to be recognized, in the first instance, as one of the Powers of Greece. The Phocian War supplied him the means, and the close of that conflict saw his end attained.

The Peace of Philocrates was imperilled in the very year it was made. Athens omitted to send envoys to represent her, as usual, at the Pythian games that year, where Philip, or at any rate Macedon, had been appointed to preside. Envoys were sent by Philip to Athens to call this conduct in question; but matters seem to have been adjusted. It was at this crisis that Demosthenes delivered his oration on the Peace, and deprecated most strongly the renewal of the hostilities.

The years 345 and 344 have little that is remarkable. Philip, renewing his old course of intrigue, gave the Messenians assistance against the Lacedæmonians, and so obtained for himself a hold on the Peloponnesus; he also achieved a triumphant expedition into Thrace, and on his return he made a redistribution of Thessaly. At this juncture Demosthenes delivered his Second Philippic. He had previously been sent by Athens as envoy to Messene and Argos, in order to caution those states against the designs of Philip.

In the next year, 343, fortune favored to some extent the Athenian undertakings. They baffled Philip in his attacks on Megara, Ambracia, and Leucas. They conducted negotiations with him in a very independent tone respecting Cardia and Halonnesus and other places in dispute. This was the year when Demosthenes and Æschines both delivered their orations about the alleged Misconduct of Embassy. The speech of Demosthenes on Halonnesus, as well as these two speeches, give the very fullest account of the whole political situation.

In the two succeeding years, 342 and 341, the disturbances about Eubœa are the most important feature. Macedonian troops occupied Oreus, and revolutions, both in that town and Eretria, placed a despotic government in both, of course in Philip's interest. The king of Macedon was equally busy in Thrace and in the Propontis, where his action seriously menaced the interests and property of Athens. Demosthenes made his Speech on the Chersonese, and at his instance Athenian forces were sent to Eubœa, in the autumn of the year 341, which expelled the despots of Oreus and Eretria. Demosthenes was honored with the thanks of the state; and in this year he spoke his Third Philippic.

Matters had clearly come to a crisis when peace between Athens and Macedon could no longer be maintained. Philip laid siege to Perinthus as a means to capture Byzantium; finding an unexpected resistance, he blockaded Byzantium simultaneously. And early in 340 he sent a letter to Athens which amounted to a formal complaint of their hostile action in various cases since the conclusion of peace. Finally, it threatened them with speedy punishment, unless they altered their policy. On this challenge being received, Demosthenes urged that it should be accepted at once, and that a fleet from Athens should be sent to relieve Byzantium. War was then formally declared, and so ended the Peace of Philocrates.

ANALYSIS OF THE ARGUMENT.

An oration which, by the unanimous verdict of the best judges in ancient and modern times, has been pronounced not only "the unapproachable masterpiece of Grecian oratory," but "the greatest speech of the greatest orator in the world," and which so candid and capable a critic as David Hume has declared to be "the most perfect production of the human intellect," cannot have been a mere display of subtle logic or splendid rhetoric. It must have possessed more substantial merits. It was, in fact, what all the judicial orations of Demosthenes were, emphatically an *argument* constructed on a well-considered and wisely ordered plan, having a beginning, a middle, and an end. The orator himself, in the opening of his speech, insists on "the order of arrangement" which "he has chosen for himself" as at once his constitutional right and quite indispensable to a successful defence. The student or reader, therefore, who would understand and appreciate the oration, should observe and see clearly what that order is.

The skeleton or frame-work of the argument is concisely as follows: The first eight sections constitute the exordium, or introduction, in which, modestly but earnestly, he claims his right to make his own defence in his own way, and with marvellous skill sweeps away all the cunning contrivances of his prosecutor, and clears the ground for a fair fight. The next forty-four sections (9 – 52) are occupied with some preliminary and extraneous matters in reply to assaults partly on his private character and partly on public measures on which Æschines had dwelt at great length, but for which, being prior to the administration of Demosthenes, he was in no way responsible, or which, in legal terms, were wholly impertinent to the indictment. In the next seventy-three sections (53 – 125) he takes up the charges in the very order of the indictment: first, defending his public policy during the period in which he took a leading part in the affairs of the state; secondly, justifying the proposal of Ctesiphon that he should be crowned for his patriotic services while he was still in office and his accounts had not yet been audited; and, thirdly, showing that it was lawful and proper that the crown should be proclaimed, as Ctesiphon proposed, in the theatre at the Dionysiac festivals. This review of the measures by which he had deserved such public honors and for which, in repeated instances, he had been previously crowned, leads the orator to show up in contrast the character and conduct of his rival. This terrible invective occupies the next thirty-four sections (126 – 159). Having thus disposed, in passing as it were, of some of the strongest points in the argument of Æschines, he returns to a narration, rapid and graphic, of the course of events in the last great struggle of Grecian liberty against the supremacy of Macedon, and puts forth that world-renowned matchless justification or rather glorification of his policy which, though it led to the disaster at Chæronea, was the only policy which Athens could have adopted consistently with her ancestral glory, and of which the Athenians themselves, after their defeat, expressed their unshaken and hearty approval by choosing

Demosthenes to pronounce the funeral oration over those who had fallen in the battle (160 – 290). In the remaining sections (291 – 324), which are of a more general nature, the orator portrays the ideal statesman and statesmanship which Athens required for those times, and shows how he himself had answered to that ideal, in contrast with the baseness and treachery of Æschines and his fellow hirelings and traitors in all the Grecian States, concluding with that magnificent prayer and imprecation which the best translators have confessed their inability to render adequately into any other language.

The commentators all remark the felicity of the general arrangement by which he throws the merely technical and legal points wherein his own weakness and the strength of his opponent lay into the middle of his oration, as Nestor advised Agamemnon to drive into the middle his poorest troops, while the beginning and end and main portion are so ablaze with the glory of his public policy, which his judges and hearers had adopted and still cherished as their own, that if they gave any consideration to these nice points of law, they could not but regard them practically as of no account. A critical examination of the whole structure of the oration, like that of Dissen, discloses a similar felicity in the arrangement of each and all of the several parts. At the same time, there is no appearance of art. It is that perfect art which conceals art, and seems like nature. The topics and arguments succeed each other in the most natural order. The critical reader cannot fail to discern this in the mere skeleton above given, and he will discern it more fully at every step as he advances in the reading and the study of the oration. Nor can he fail to observe with what consummate skill the orator plants a battery on every position of which he takes possession in his argument, and then with what tremendous power he pours the hot shot of his fiery invective upon the character and standing of his rival.

The following remarks of Mr. Kennedy draw a just comparison between the two orators, and furnish a concise and graphic outline of the principal topics in the oration of Demosthenes. "As the speeches of both the orators are preserved to us, we have the means of comparing one with the other and forming our opinion of their respective merits. The world in general have decided as the people of Athens did, not only upon the oratorical merits of the two rivals, but upon the principal questions at issue between them. The accuser, who thought to brand his opponent with eternal infamy, has only added to the lustre of his renown. Independently of the internal evidence furnished by this and other orations of Demosthenes which have carried to most hearts a conviction of his patriotism, we cannot fail to be strongly influenced by the judgment of the Athenians themselves, whom neither their own past misfortunes nor the terror inspired by the late victory of Antipater could deter from giving a verdict, by which, while they acquitted Demosthenes from all blame, they in effect declared their approbation of his measures in opposition to Macedonia.

The reader who carefully examines the speech of Æschines will not fail to observe that he betrays a consciousness of weakness in that part of his case where he attacks the political character of his rival. He seems also to feel that he is speaking in opposition to the general feeling of his hearers. His own character as a politician had been dubious; his conduct so open to suspicion that, while he most bitterly assails his adversary, he is constantly under the necessity of defending himself. On the whole life, public and private, of Demosthenes, he pours a torrent of invective; to this the greater part of his speech is directed; yet he seems to have been impelled to it rather by hate and revenge than by any calculation of advantage. On the other hand, when he deals with the legal part of his case, commenting on those specific violations of law which Ctesiphon's measure was charged with, it is evident that his strength lay there; he handles his subject temperately, skilfully, and carefully, laboring to make every point clear to the jury, and to impress them with the conviction that to uphold the laws was the sure way to maintain constitutional government. On these points he mainly relied, hoping by this measure to secure a verdict which would give him a triumph over his enemy, and carry the general opinion over Greece that the credit and influence of Demosthenes were extinguished.

Demosthenes, feeling his weakness as to the legal questions, dexterously throws them into the middle of his speech and passes rapidly and lightly over them, while he devotes his greatest efforts to the vindication of his own merits as a patriot and a statesman. Refusing to comply with the insidious demand of Æschines that he should take the questions in the same order as his accuser, he insists upon his legal right to conduct his defence as he pleases. Opening with a modest exordium to conciliate the favor of the jury, he launches gradually into the history of his own conduct and measures, presenting first a general view of the condition of Greece when he entered public life, and of the difficulties under which the Athenians labored in their contest with Philip; then setting forth his own views, plans, and objects, and showing that he had advised a course of action which both the circumstances of the time and the honor of the country required. He apologizes for the self-praise mixed up with his speech, on the ground that he was drawn to it by his opponent. Entering on the Sacred War and the Peace of B. C. 346, he labors to exculpate himself from all share in the errors then committed, imputing them chiefly to the negligence of the other ambassadors and to the treachery of Philocrates and Æschines, who, by the false hopes which they excited at Athens, prevented the people from assisting the Phocians. Coming to the events which brought on a renewal of the war, he shows how Philip's ambitious projects and encroachments in every part of Greece made it necessary to oppose him, especially for the Athenians who were menaced at home as well as abroad by his aggressions in Thrace, Eubœa, and Megara. He pursues these topics until he has carried with him the feelings of his hearers, which must have been strongly on his side when he dilated on the glorious issue of the campaigns in Eubœa and the Propontis, and read to them the decrees of the Byzantines, Perinthians, and Chersonesites in honor of Athens, all which were due to the vigorous measures of his own administration. Having thus secured the good-will and sympathy of his judges, he proceeds to discuss the legal charges against Ctesiphon. Dwelling on them but a short time, he plunges into a personal attack upon Æschines, holding up to ridicule the meanness of his birth and parentage, and retorting on him the same coarse and opprobrious language which had been used towards himself. The bitterness of his invective is only to be excused on the ground of strong provocation, added to an assurance that his more grave charges of treason and corruption were well-founded. Those charges, so often advanced before, he here repeats, denouncing more particularly the conduct of Æschines upon his mission to Delphi, B. C. 339, to which the disaster of Chæronea was attributable. The account which Æschines had given of this affair he shows to be false, and enters upon a minute examination of the proceedings which caused Philip to be elected Amphictyonic general, and to march south an invading army, nominally against the Amphissian Ionians, really against Bœotia and Attica. A graphic description is given of the consternation at Athens on hearing that Philip had seized Elatea. The meeting of the people, the advice of Demosthenes to them, his embassy to Thebes, the success of his negotiations, and the conclusion of the alliance between Thebes and Athens are briefly recounted, Demosthenes forcibly pointing out the advantage of his measures, contending that they were not to be judged by the mere event of the battle, and that it was far more glorious for his country to be defeated in a struggle for the independence of Greece than it would have been to keep aloof from the contest. Here he makes that noble adjuration which has in all ages been admired, appealing to his countrymen by the deeds of their ancestors, of whom they would have acted most unworthily, had they without a struggle abandoned the post of honor bequeathed to them. He himself as a statesman would have deserved execration, had he advised such a course. The failure of their arms was not to be imputed to the minister, who had done all he could to insure their success, but rather to the commanders or to evil fortune. As Æschines had said so much about the ill-fortune which attended him, he draws a comparison between the different fortunes of himself and his rival, first of their early life and education, next of their course as public men. Æschines from the beginning had taken a part which put him in opposition to the true interests of Athens, which caused him to rejoice at her disasters, to quail and tremble at her successes. He never came forward to assist her counsels when she needed them, but only to censure others who had given their honest advice because it had not turned out as well as was expected. It was a signal proof of his malignant disposition, that he had expatiated on the late disastrous events as if they were a subject of triumph to him, without shedding a single tear, without any faltering in his voice, without betraying the least emotion or symptom of grief. In reply to the challenge of Æschines to say for what merit he claimed the reward of a crown, Demosthenes boldly declares, for his incorruptibility, by which he was distinguished, not only from Æschines, but from the multitude of venal orators in the Grecian world. Had there been but a few more like himself in other states, Macedonia never could have risen to greatness upon their ruin. He had done all that was possible for a single man; and Athens, while she shared the misfortune of all the Greeks, had the consolation of reflecting that she had striven gallantly and bravely to avert the common calamity. Æschines had lauded the great men of a by-gone age, drawing an invidious contrast between Demosthenes and them. This, says Demosthenes, was not a fair way of judging him: he should be tried by reference to his own acts as compared with those of his contemporaries. Yet even from the former comparison he did not shrink; for he had acted on the same principles as the statesmen of olden time, striving always to maintain the honor and dignity of Athens. Attachment to his country and earnest anxiety for her welfare had been his constant and abiding motives of action: throughout his whole life, in the day of power, in the hour of trial and adversity, those feelings had never deserted him: that was the test of a good and honest citizen; by that he ought to be judged.

Such is, in substance, the argument of this celebrated oration as far as relates to the main question in the cause. The effect produced by the speech upon an Athenian audience can be but faintly imagined by us who read it at this distance of time. Although Athens was not then what she had once been; although she was shorn of her honors, stripped of her empire and dependencies, without allies, without resources, without means of resistance to that iron power under which all Greece had succumbed, there was still the remembrance of the past, not yet extinguished by habitual servitude; there were still vague hopes of future deliverance, and a fire of smothered indignation burning in the hearts of the people, ready to burst into a flame at the first opportunity. That such were their feelings is proved by what occurred seven years afterwards upon the death of Alexander, when Athens made one convulsive effort for freedom, ere she finally submitted to her fate. Demosthenes stood before his countrymen, representing all which remained of Athenian dignity and glory. If any man could help them, it was he. His advice had always been steady and constant; his warnings should have been earlier attended to; but even yet there might be need of him. He was their consolation for the past, their hope for the future. During the progress of his address such thoughts rushed upon their minds with greater and greater force, till they were elevated above themselves, and all the spirit of their ancestors was, for the moment, regenerate within them. They felt that it was impossible for them to find him guilty without passing sentence upon themselves, without condemning the policy which Athens had for a long series of years consistently pursued. The genius of Athens protected her from such disgrace; and by an overwhelming majority, which left the accuser no choice but to retire into exile, a verdict was given for the defendant.

ΥΠΕΡ ΚΤΗΣΙΦΩΝΤΟΣ ΠΕΡΙ ΤΟΥ ΣΤΕΦΑΝΟΥ.

ΠΡΩΤΟΝ μὲν, ὦ ἄνδρες Ἀθηναῖοι, τοῖς θεοῖς
εὔχομαι πᾶσι καὶ πάσαις, ὅσην εὔνοιαν ἔχων ἐγὼ
διατελῶ τῇ τε πόλει καὶ πᾶσιν ὑμῖν, τοσαύτην
ὑπάρξαι μοι παρ' ὑμῶν εἰς τουτονὶ τὸν ἀγῶνα,
ἔπειθ' ὅπερ ἐστὶ μάλισθ' ὑπὲρ ὑμῶν καὶ τῆς ὑμετέρας εὐσεβείας τε καὶ δόξης, τοῦτο παραστῆσαι τοὺς
θεοὺς ὑμῖν, μὴ τὸν ἀντίδικον σύμβουλον ποιήσασθαι
περὶ τοῦ πῶς ἀκούειν ὑμᾶς ἐμοῦ δεῖ (σχέτλιον γὰρ 2
ἂν εἴη τοῦτό γε), ἀλλὰ τοὺς νόμους καὶ τὸν ὅρκον,
ἐν ᾧ πρὸς ἅπασι τοῖς ἄλλοις δικαίοις καὶ τοῦτο
γέγραπται, τὸ ὁμοίως ἀμφοῖν ἀκροάσασθαι. τοῦτο
δ' ἐστὶν οὐ μόνον τὸ μὴ προκατεγνωκέναι μηδὲν,
οὐδὲ τὸ τὴν εὔνοιαν ἴσην ἀμφοτέροις ἀποδοῦναι,
ἀλλὰ καὶ τὸ τῇ τάξει καὶ τῇ ἀπολογίᾳ, ὡς βεβούληται καὶ προῄρηται τῶν ἀγωνιζομένων ἕκαστος,
οὕτως ἐᾶσαι χρήσασθαι.

Πολλὰ μὲν οὖν ἔγωγ' ἐλαττοῦμαι κατὰ τουτονὶ 3
τὸν ἀγῶνα Αἰσχίνου, δύο δ', ὦ ἄνδρες Ἀθηναῖοι,

καὶ μεγάλα, ἓν μὲν ὅτι οὐ περὶ τῶν ἴσων ἀγωνίζο-
μαι· οὐ γάρ ἐστιν ἴσον νῦν ἐμοὶ τῆς παρ' ὑμῶν
εὐνοίας διαμαρτεῖν καὶ τούτῳ μὴ ἑλεῖν τὴν γραφὴν,
ἀλλ' ἐμοὶ μὲν — οὐ βούλομαι δὲ δυσχερὲς εἰπεῖν
οὐδὲν ἀρχόμενος τοῦ λόγου, οὗτος δ' ἐκ περιουσίας
μου κατηγορεῖ. ἕτερον δ', ὃ φύσει πᾶσιν ἀνθρώποις ὑπάρχει, τῶν μὲν λοιδοριῶν καὶ τῶν κατηγοριῶν ἀκούειν ἡδέως, τοῖς ἐπαινοῦσι δ' αὑτοὺς ἄχθεσ-
4 θαι· τούτων τοίνυν ὃ μέν ἐστι πρὸς ἡδονὴν, τούτῳ
δέδοται, ὃ δὲ πᾶσιν ὡς ἔπος εἰπεῖν ἐνοχλεῖ, λοιπὸν
ἐμοί. κἂν μὲν εὐλαβούμενος τοῦτο μὴ λέγω τὰ
πεπραγμένα ἐμαυτῷ, οὐκ ἔχειν ἀπολύσασθαι τὰ
πατηγορημένα δόξω οὐδ' ἐφ' οἷς ἀξιῶ τιμᾶσθαι
δεικνύναι· ἐὰν δ' ἐφ' ἃ καὶ πεποίηκα καὶ πεπολίτευμαι βαδίζω, πολλάκις λέγειν ἀναγκασθήσομαι
περὶ ἐμαυτοῦ. πειράσομαι μὲν οὖν ὡς μετριώτατα
τοῦτο ποιεῖν· ὅ τι δ' ἂν τὸ πρᾶγμα αὐτὸ ἀναγκάζῃ,
τούτου τὴν αἰτίαν οὗτός ἐστι δίκαιος ἔχειν ὁ τοιοῦτον ἀγῶνα ἐνστησάμενος.

5 Οἶμαι δ' ὑμᾶς, ὦ ἄνδρες Ἀθηναῖοι, πάντας ἂν ὁμολογῆσαι κοινὸν εἶναι τουτονὶ τὸν ἀγῶνα ἐμοί τε καὶ Κτησιφῶντι καὶ οὐδὲν ἐλάττονος ἄξιον σπουδῆς 'μοί· πάντων μὲν γὰρ ἀποστερεῖσθαι λυπηρόν ἐστι καὶ χαλεπὸν, ἄλλως τε κἂν ὑπ' ἐχθροῦ τῳ τοῦτο συμβαίνῃ, μάλιστα δὲ τῆς παρ' ὑμῶν εὐνοίας καὶ φιλανθρωπίας, ὅσῳπερ καὶ τὸ τυχεῖν τούτων μέγιστόν ἐστιν. περὶ τούτων δ' ὄντος τουτουὶ τοῦ

ἀγῶνος, ἀξιῶ καὶ δέομαι πάντων ὁμοίως ὑμῶν ἀκοῦ- 6
σαί μου περὶ τῶν κατηγορημένων ἀπολογουμένου
δικαίως, ὥσπερ οἱ νόμοι κελεύουσιν, οὓς ὁ τιθεὶς ἐξ
ἀρχῆς Σόλων, εὔνους ὢν ὑμῖν καὶ δημοτικὸς, οὐ
μόνον τῷ γράψαι κυρίους ᾤετο δεῖν εἶναι, ἀλλὰ καὶ
τῷ τοὺς δικάζοντας ὑμᾶς ὀμωμοκέναι, οὐκ ἀπιστῶν 7
ὑμῖν, ὥς γ' ἐμοὶ φαίνεται, ἀλλ' ὁρῶν ὅτι τὰς αἰτίας
καὶ τὰς διαβολὰς, αἷς ἐκ τοῦ πρότερος λέγειν ὁ
διώκων ἰσχύει, οὐκ ἔνι τῷ φεύγοντι παρελθεῖν,
εἰ μὴ τῶν δικαζόντων ἕκαστος ὑμῶν τὴν πρὸς
τοὺς θεοὺς εὐσέβειαν διαφυλάττων καὶ τὰ τοῦ
λέγοντος ὑστέρου δίκαια εὐνοϊκῶς προσδέξεται,
καὶ παρασχὼν ἑαυτὸν ἴσον καὶ κοινὸν ἀμφοτέροις ἀκροατὴν οὕτω τὴν διάγνωσιν ποιήσεται περὶ
ἁπάντων.

Μέλλων δὲ τοῦ τε ἰδίου βίου παντὸς, ὡς ἔοικε, 8
λόγον διδόναι τήμερον καὶ τῶν κοινῇ πεπολιτευμένων, βούλομαι πάλιν τοὺς θεοὺς παρακαλέσαι, καὶ
ἐναντίον ὑμῶν εὔχομαι πρῶτον μὲν, ὅσην εὔνοιαν
ἔχων ἐγὼ διατελῶ τῇ τε πόλει καὶ πᾶσιν ὑμῖν,
τοσαύτην ὑπάρξαι μοι παρ' ὑμῶν εἰς τουτονὶ τὸν
ἀγῶνα, ἔπειθ' ὅ τι μέλλει συνοίσειν καὶ πρὸς εὐ-
δοξίαν κοινῇ καὶ πρὸς εὐσέβειαν ἑκάστῳ, τοῦτο
παραστῆσαι τοὺς θεοὺς πᾶσιν ὑμῖν περὶ ταυτησὶ
τῆς γραφῆς γνῶναι.

Εἰ μὲν οὖν περὶ ὧν ἐδίωκε μόνον κατηγόρησεν 9
Αἰσχίνης, κἀγὼ περὶ αὐτοῦ τοῦ προβουλεύματος

εὐθὺς ἂν ἀπελογούμην· ἐπειδὴ δ' οὐκ ἐλάττω λόγον
τἄλλα διεξιὼν ἀνήλωκε καὶ τὰ πλεῖστα κατεψεύσατό μου, ἀναγκαῖον εἶναι νομίζω καὶ δίκαιον ἅμα
βραχέα, ὦ ἄνδρες Ἀθηναῖοι, περὶ τούτων πρῶτον
εἰπεῖν, ἵνα μηδεὶς ὑμῶν τοῖς ἔξωθεν λόγοις ἠγμένος
ἀλλοτριώτερον τῶν ὑπὲρ τῆς γραφῆς δικαίων ἀκούῃ
μου.

10 Περὶ μὲν δὴ τῶν ἰδίων ὅσα λοιδορούμενος βε-
βλασφήμηκε περὶ ἐμοῦ, θεάσασθε ὡς ἁπλᾶ καὶ
δίκαια λέγω. εἰ μὲν ἴστε με τοιοῦτον οἷον οὗτος
ᾐτιᾶτο (οὐ γὰρ ἄλλοθί που βεβίωκα ἢ παρ' ὑμῖν),
μηδὲ φωνὴν ἀνάσχησθε, μηδ' εἰ πάντα τὰ κοινὰ
ὑπέρευ πεπολίτευμαι, ἀλλ' ἀναστάντες καταψηφί-
σασθε ἤδη· εἰ δὲ πολλῷ βελτίω τούτου καὶ ἐκ
βελτιόνων, καὶ μηδενὸς τῶν μετρίων, ἵνα μηδὲν
ἐπαχθὲς λέγω, χείρονα καὶ ἐμὲ καὶ τοὺς ἐμοὺς
ὑπειλήφατε καὶ γιγνώσκετε, τούτῳ μὲν μηδ' ὑπὲρ
τῶν ἄλλων πιστεύετε (δῆλον γὰρ ὡς ὁμοίως ἅπαντ'
ἐπλάττετο), ἐμοὶ δ', ἣν παρὰ πάντα τὸν χρόνον
εὔνοιαν ἐνδέδειχθε ἐπὶ πολλῶν ἀγώνων τῶν πρότε-
11 ρον, καὶ νυνὶ παράσχεσθε. κακοήθης δ' ὤν, Αἰσχίνη, τοῦτο παντελῶς εὔηθες ᾠήθης, τοὺς περὶ τῶν
πεπραγμένων καὶ πεπολιτευμένων λόγους ἀφέντα
με πρὸς τὰς λοιδορίας τὰς παρὰ σοῦ τρέψεσθαι.
οὐ δὴ ποιήσω τοῦτο· οὐχ οὕτω τετύφωμαι· ἀλλ'
ὑπὲρ μὲν τῶν πεπολιτευμένων ἃ κατεψεύδου καὶ
διέβαλλες, αὐτίκα ἐξετάσω, τῆς δὲ πομπείας ταύτης

τῆς ἀνέδην οὑτωσὶ γεγενημένης ὕστερον, ἂν βουλομένοις ἀκούειν ᾖ τουτοισὶ, μνησθήσομαι.

Τὰ μὲν οὖν κατηγορημένα πολλὰ καὶ δεινὰ, καὶ 12
περὶ ὧν ἐνίων μεγάλας καὶ τὰς ἐσχάτας οἱ νόμοι
διδόασι τιμωρίας· τοῦ δὲ παρόντος ἀγῶνος ἡ προαίρεσις αὐτὴ ἐχθροῦ μὲν ἐπήρειαν ἔχει καὶ ὕβριν καὶ
λοιδορίαν καὶ προπηλακισμὸν ὁμοῦ καὶ πάντα τὰ
τοιαῦτα· τῶν μέντοι κατηγοριῶν καὶ τῶν αἰτιῶν
τῶν εἰρημένων, εἴπερ ἦσαν ἀληθεῖς, οὐκ ἔνι τῇ πόλει
δίκην ἀξίαν λαβεῖν, οὐδ' ἐγγύς. οὐ γὰρ ἀφαιρεῖ- 13
σθαι δεῖ τὸ προσελθεῖν τῷ δήμῳ καὶ λόγου τυχεῖν,
οὐδ' ἐν ἐπηρείας τάξει καὶ φθόνου τοῦτο ποιεῖν·
οὔτε μὰ τοὺς θεοὺς ὀρθῶς ἔχον οὔτε πολιτικὸν οὔτε
δίκαιόν ἐστιν, ὦ ἄνδρες Ἀθηναῖοι· ἀλλ' ἐφ' οἷς
ἀδικοῦντά με ἑώρα τὴν πόλιν, οὖσί γε τηλικούτοις
ἡλίκα νῦν ἐτραγῴδει καὶ διεξῄει, ταῖς ἐκ τῶν νόμων
τιμωρίαις παρ' αὐτὰ τἀδικήματα χρῆσθαι, εἰ μὲν
εἰσαγγελίας ἄξια πράττοντα ἑώρα, εἰσαγγέλλοντα
καὶ τοῦτον τὸν τρόπον εἰς κρίσιν καθιστάντα παρ'
ὑμῖν, εἰ δὲ γράφοντα παράνομα, παρανόμων γραφό-
μενον· οὐ γὰρ δήπου Κτησιφῶντα μὲν δύναται διώκειν δι' ἐμὲ, ἐμὲ δ', εἴπερ ἐξελέγξειν ἐνόμιζεν, αὐτὸν
οὐκ ἂν ἐγράψατο. καὶ μὴν εἴ τι τῶν ἄλλων ὧν 14
νυνὶ διέβαλλε καὶ διεξῄει ἢ καὶ ἄλλ' ὁτιοῦν ἀδικοῦντά με ὑμᾶς ἑώρα, εἰσὶ νόμοι περὶ πάντων καὶ
τιμωρίαι καὶ ἀγῶνες καὶ κρίσεις πικρὰ καὶ μεγάλα
ἔχουσαι τἀπιτίμια, καὶ τούτοις ἐξῆν ἅπασι χρῆσθαι

κατ' ἐμοῦ, καὶ ὁπηνίκα ἐφαίνετο ταῦτα πεποιηκὼς καὶ
τοῦτον τὸν τρόπον κεχρημένος τοῖς πρὸς ἐμέ, ὡμολο-
15 γεῖτ' ἂν ἡ κατηγορία τοῖς ἔργοις αὐτοῦ. νῦν δ' ἐκστὰς
τῆς ὀρθῆς καὶ δικαίας ὁδοῦ καὶ φυγὼν τοὺς παρ'
αὐτὰ τὰ πράγματα ἐλέγχους, τοσούτοις ὕστερον
χρόνοις αἰτίας καὶ σκώμματα καὶ λοιδορίας συμφορ-
ήσας ὑποκρίνεται· εἶτα κατηγορεῖ μὲν ἐμοῦ, κρίνει
δὲ τουτονί, καὶ τοῦ μὲν ἀγῶνος ὅλου τὴν πρὸς ἐμὲ
ἔχθραν προΐσταται, οὐδαμοῦ δ' ἐπὶ ταύτην ἀπηντη-
κὼς ἐμοὶ τὴν ἑτέρου ζητῶν ἐπιτιμίαν ἀφελέσθαι
16 φαίνεται. καίτοι πρὸς ἅπασιν, ὦ ἄνδρες Ἀθηναῖοι,
τοῖς ἄλλοις δικαίοις οἷς ἂν εἰπεῖν τις ὑπὲρ Κτησιφῶντος ἔχοι, καὶ τοῦτ' ἔμοιγε δοκεῖ καὶ μάλ' εἰκότως ἂν λέγειν, ὅτι τῆς ἡμετέρας ἔχθρας ἡμᾶς ἐφ'
ἡμῶν αὐτῶν δίκαιον ἦν τὸν ἐξετασμὸν ποιεῖσθαι,
οὐ τὸ μὲν πρὸς ἀλλήλους ἀγωνίζεσθαι παραλείπειν,
ἑτέρῳ δ' ὅτῳ κακόν τι δώσομεν ζητεῖν· ὑπερβολὴ
γὰρ ἀδικίας τοῦτό γε.

17 Πάντα μὲν τοίνυν τὰ κατηγορημένα ὁμοίως ἐκ
τούτων ἄν τις ἴδοι οὔτε δικαίως οὔτ' ἐπ' ἀληθείας
οὐδεμιᾶς εἰρημένα· βούλομαι δὲ καὶ καθ' ἓν ἕκαστον
αὐτῶν ἐξετάσαι, καὶ μάλισθ' ὅσα ὑπὲρ τῆς εἰρήνης
καὶ τῆς πρεσβείας κατεψεύσατό μου, τὰ πεπραγμένα ἑαυτῷ μετὰ Φιλοκράτους ἀνατιθεὶς ἐμοί. ἔστι
δ' ἀναγκαῖον, ὦ ἄνδρες Ἀθηναῖοι, καὶ προσῆκον
ἴσως, ὡς κατ' ἐκείνους τοὺς χρόνους εἶχε τὰ πράγματα ἀναμνῆσαι ὑμᾶς, ἵνα πρὸς τὸν ὑπάρχοντα καιρὸν ἕκαστα θεωρῆτε.

Τοῦ γὰρ Φωκικοῦ συστάντος πολέμου, οὐ δι' 18
ἐμὲ (οὐ γὰρ ἔγωγε ἐπολιτευόμην πω τότε), πρῶτον
μὲν ὑμεῖς οὕτω διέκεισθε ὥστε Φωκέας μὲν βού-
λεσθαι σωθῆναι, καίπερ οὐ δίκαια ποιοῦντας ὁρῶν-
τες, Θηβαίοις δ' ὁτιοῦν ἂν ἐφησθῆναι παθοῦσιν,
οὐκ ἀλόγως οὐδ' ἀδίκως αὐτοῖς ὀργιζόμενοι· οἷς
γὰρ ηὐτυχήκεσαν ἐν Λεύκτροις, οὐ μετρίως ἐκέχ-
ρηντο· ἔπειθ' ἡ Πελοπόννησος ἅπασα διειστήκει,
καὶ οὔθ' οἱ μισοῦντες Λακεδαιμονίους οὕτως ἴσχυον
ὥστε ἀνελεῖν αὐτούς, οὔθ' οἱ πρότερον δι' ἐκείνων
ἄρχοντες κύριοι τῶν πόλεων ἦσαν, ἀλλά τις ἦν
ἄκριτος καὶ παρὰ τούτοις καὶ παρὰ τοῖς ἄλλοις
ἅπασιν ἔρις καὶ ταραχή. ταῦτα δ' ὁρῶν ὁ Φίλιπ- 19
πος (οὐ γὰρ ἦν ἀφανῆ) τοῖς παρ' ἑκάστοις προδόταις χρήματα ἀναλίσκων πάντας συνέκρουε καὶ
πρὸς αὐτοὺς ἐτάραττεν· εἶτ' ἐν οἷς ἡμάρτανον ἄλλοι
καὶ κακῶς ἐφρόνουν, αὐτὸς παρεσκευάζετο καὶ κατὰ
πάντων ἐφύετο. ὡς δὲ ταλαιπωρούμενοι τῷ μήκει
τοῦ πολέμου οἱ τότε μὲν βαρεῖς, νῦν δ' ἀτυχεῖς Θηβαῖοι φανεροὶ πᾶσιν ἦσαν ἀναγκασθησόμενοι καταφεύγειν ἐφ' ὑμᾶς, ὁ Φίλιππος, ἵνα μὴ τοῦτο γένοιτο
μηδὲ συνέλθοιεν αἱ πόλεις, ὑμῖν μὲν εἰρήνην, ἐκείνοις δὲ βοήθειαν ἐπηγγείλατο. τί οὖν συνηγωνί- 20
σατο αὐτῷ πρὸς τὸ λαβεῖν ὀλίγου δεῖν ὑμᾶς ἑκόντας
ἐξαπατωμένους; ἡ τῶν ἄλλων Ἑλλήνων, εἴτε χρὴ
κακίαν εἴτ' ἄγνοιαν εἴτε καὶ ἀμφότερα ταῦτ' εἰπεῖν,
οἳ πόλεμον συνεχῆ καὶ μακρὸν πολεμούντων ὑμῶν,

καὶ τοῦτον ὑπὲρ τῶν πᾶσι συμφερόντων, ὡς ἔργῳ φανερὸν γέγονεν, οὔτε χρήμασιν οὔτε σώμασιν οὔτ' ἄλλῳ οὐδενὶ τῶν ἁπάντων συνελάμβανον ὑμῖν· οἷς καὶ δικαίως καὶ προσηκόντως ὀργιζόμενοι ἑτοίμως ὑπηκούσατε τῷ Φιλίππῳ. ἡ μὲν οὖν τότε συγχωρηθεῖσα εἰρήνη διὰ ταῦτ', οὐ δι' ἐμέ, ὡς οὗτος διέβαλλεν, ἐπράχθη· τὰ δὲ τούτων ἀδικήματα καὶ δωροδοκήματα ἐν αὐτῇ τῶν νυνὶ παρόντων πραγμά-
21 των, ἄν τις ἐξετάζῃ δικαίως, αἴτια εὑρήσει. καὶ ταυτὶ πάνθ' ὑπὲρ τῆς ἀληθείας ἀκριβολογοῦμαι καὶ διεξέρχομαι. εἰ γὰρ εἶναί τι δοκοίη τὰ μάλιστα ἐν τούτοις ἀδίκημα, οὐδέν ἐστι δήπου πρὸς ἐμέ, ἀλλ' ὁ μὲν πρῶτος εἰπὼν καὶ μνησθεὶς ὑπὲρ τῆς εἰρήνης Ἀριστόδημος ἦν ὁ ὑποκριτής, ὁ δ' ἐκδεξάμενος καὶ γράψας καὶ ἑαυτὸν μετὰ τούτου μισθώσας ἐπὶ ταῦτα Φιλοκράτης ὁ Ἁγνούσιος, ὁ σός, Αἰσχίνη, κοινωνός, οὐχ ὁ ἐμός, οὐδ' ἂν σὺ διαρραγῇς ψευδόμενος, οἱ δὲ συνειπόντες ὅτου δήποτε ἕνεκα (ἐῶ γὰρ τοῦτό γ' ἐν τῷ παρόντι) Εὔβουλος καὶ Κηφισοφῶν· ἐγὼ δ'
22 οὐδὲν οὐδαμοῦ. ἀλλ' ὅμως, τούτων τοιούτων ὄντων καὶ ἐπ' αὐτῆς τῆς ἀληθείας οὕτω δεικνυμένων, εἰς τοῦθ' ἧκεν ἀναιδείας ὥστ' ἐτόλμα λέγειν ὡς ἄρα ἐγὼ πρὸς τῷ τῆς εἰρήνης αἴτιος γεγενῆσθαι καὶ κεκωλυκὼς εἴην τὴν πόλιν μετὰ κοινοῦ συνεδρίου τῶν Ἑλλήνων αὐτὴν ποιήσασθαι. εἶτ' ὦ — τί ἄν εἰπών σέ τις ὀρθῶς προσείποι; ἔστιν ὅπου σὺ παρὼν τηλικαύτην πρᾶξιν καὶ συμμαχίαν, ἡλίκην

νυνὶ διεξῄεις, ὁρῶν ἀφαιρούμενόν με τῆς πόλεως
ἠγανάκτησας, ἢ παρελθὼν ταῦτα ἃ νῦν κατηγορεῖς
ἐδίδαξας καὶ διεξῆλθες; καὶ μὴν εἰ τὸ κωλῦσαι τὴν 23
τῶν Ἑλλήνων κοινωνίαν ἐπεπράκειν ἐγὼ Φιλίππῳ,
σοὶ τὸ μὴ σιγῆσαι λοιπὸν ἦν, ἀλλὰ βοᾶν καὶ δια-
μαρτύρεσθαι καὶ δηλοῦν τουτοισί. οὐ τοίνυν ἐποίη-
σας οὐδαμοῦ τοῦτο, οὐδ' ἤκουσέ σου ταύτην τὴν
φωνὴν οὐδείς, εἰκότως· οὔτε γὰρ ἦν πρεσβεία πρὸς
οὐδένας ἀπεσταλμένη τότε τῶν Ἑλλήνων, ἀλλὰ
πάλαι πάντες ἦσαν ἐξεληλεγμένοι, οὔθ' οὗτος ὑγιὲς
περὶ τούτων εἴρηκεν οὐδέν. χωρὶς δὲ τούτων καὶ 24
διαβάλλει τὴν πόλιν τὰ μέγιστα ἐν οἷς ψεύδεται·
εἰ γὰρ ὑμεῖς ἅμα τοὺς μὲν Ἕλληνας εἰς πόλεμον
παρεκαλεῖτε, αὐτοὶ δὲ πρὸς Φίλιππον περὶ εἰρήνης
πρέσβεις ἐπέμπετε, Εὐρυβάτου πρᾶγμα, οὐ πόλεως
ἔργον οὐδὲ χρηστῶν ἀνθρώπων διεπράττεσθε. ἀλλ'
οὐκ ἔστι ταῦτα, οὐκ ἔστι· τί γὰρ καὶ βουλόμενοι
μετεπέμπεσθ' ἂν αὐτοὺς ἐν τούτῳ τῷ καιρῷ; ἐπὶ
τὴν εἰρήνην; ἀλλ' ὑπῆρχεν ἅπασιν. ἀλλ' ἐπὶ τὸν
πόλεμον; ἀλλ' αὐτοὶ περὶ εἰρήνης ἐβουλεύεσθε.
οὐκοῦν οὔτε τῆς ἐξ ἀρχῆς εἰρήνης ἡγεμὼν οὐδ'
αἴτιος ὢν ἐγὼ φαίνομαι, οὔτε τῶν ἄλλων ὧν κατεψεύσατό μου οὐδὲν ἀληθὲς ὃν δείκνυται.

Ἐπειδὴ τοίνυν ἐποιήσατο τὴν εἰρήνην ἡ πόλις, 25
ἐνταῦθα πάλιν σκέψασθε τί ἡμῶν ἑκάτερος προείλετο πράττειν· καὶ γὰρ ἐκ τούτων εἴσεσθε τίς ἦν ὁ
Φιλίππῳ πάντα συναγωνιζόμενος, καὶ τίς ὁ πράτ-

των ὑπὲρ ὑμῶν καὶ τὸ τῇ πόλει συμφέρον ζητῶν.
ἐγὼ μὲν τοίνυν ἔγραψα βουλεύων ἀποπλεῖν τὴν
ταχίστην τοὺς πρέσβεις ἐπὶ τοὺς τόπους ἐν οἷς ἂν
ὄντα Φίλιππον πυνθάνωνται, καὶ τοὺς ὅρκους ἀπο-
λαμβάνειν· οὗτοι δὲ οὐδὲ γράψαντος ἐμοῦ ταῦτα
26 ποιεῖν ἠθέλησαν. τί δὲ τοῦτ᾽ ἐδύνατο, ὦ ἄνδρες
Ἀθηναῖοι; ἐγὼ διδάξω. Φιλίππῳ μὲν ἦν συμφέρον
ὡς πλεῖστον τὸν μεταξὺ χρόνον γενέσθαι τῶν ὅρκων,
ὑμῖν δ᾽ ὡς ἐλάχιστον. διὰ τί; ὅτι ὑμεῖς μὲν οὐκ ἀφ᾽
ἧς ὠμόσατε ἡμέρας μόνον, ἀλλ᾽ ἀφ᾽ ἧς ἠλπίσατε τὴν
εἰρήνην ἔσεσθαι, πάσας ἐξελύσασθε τὰς παρασκευὰς
τὰς τοῦ πολέμου, ὁ δὲ τοῦτο ἐκ παντὸς τοῦ χρόνου
μάλιστα ἐπραγματεύετο, νομίζων, ὅπερ ἦν ἀληθές,
ὅσα τῆς πόλεως προλάβοι πρὸ τοῦ τοὺς ὅρκους
ἀποδοῦναι, πάντα ταῦτα βεβαίως ἕξειν· οὐδένα γὰρ
27 τὴν εἰρήνην λύσειν τούτων ἕνεκα. ἃ ἐγὼ προορώμενος, ὦ ἄνδρες Ἀθηναῖοι, καὶ λογιζόμενος τὸ ψήφισμα τοῦτο γράφω, πλεῖν ἐπὶ τοὺς τόπους ἐν οἷς
ἂν ᾖ Φίλιππος, καὶ τοὺς ὅρκους τὴν ταχίστην ἀπολαμβάνειν, ἵν᾽ ἐχόντων τῶν Θρᾳκῶν, τῶν ὑμετέρων
συμμάχων, ταῦτα τὰ χωρία ἃ νῦν οὗτος διέσυρε, τὸ
Σέρρειον καὶ τὸ Μυρτηνὸν καὶ τὴν Ἐργίσκην, οὕτω
γίγνοινθ᾽ οἱ ὅρκοι, καὶ μὴ προλαβὼν ἐκεῖνος τοὺς
ἐπικαίρους τῶν τόπων κύριος τῆς Θρᾴκης κατα-
σταίη, μηδὲ πολλῶν μὲν χρημάτων, πολλῶν δὲ
στρατιωτῶν εὐπορήσας ἐκ τούτων ῥᾳδίως τοῖς λοι-
28 ποῖς ἐπιχειροίη πράγμασιν. εἶτα τοῦτο μὲν οὐχὶ

λέγει τὸ ψήφισμα, οὐδ᾽ ἀναγιγνώσκει· εἰ δὲ βουλεύων ἐγὼ προσάγειν τοὺς πρέσβεις ᾤμην δεῖν, τοῦτό μου διαβάλλει. ἀλλὰ τί ἐχρῆν με ποιεῖν; μὴ προσάγειν γράψαι τοὺς ἐπὶ τοῦθ᾽ ἥκοντας, ἵν᾽ ὑμῖν διαλεχθῶσιν; ἢ θέαν μὴ κατανεῖμαι τὸν ἀρχιτέκτονα αὐτοῖς κελεῦσαι; ἀλλ᾽ ἐν τοῖν δυοῖν ὀβολοῖν ἐθεώρουν ἄν, εἰ μὴ τοῦτ᾽ ἐγράφη. ἢ τὰ μικρὰ συμφέροντα τῆς πόλεως ἔδει με φυλάττειν, τὰ δ᾽ ὅλα, ὥσπερ οὗτοι, πεπρακέναι; οὐ δήπου. λέγε τοίνυν μοι τὸ ψήφισμα τουτὶ λαβών, ὃ σαφῶς οὗτος εἰδὼς παρέβη.

ΨΗΦΙΣΜΑ. 29

[Ἐπὶ ἄρχοντος Μνησιφίλου, ἑκατομβαιῶνος ἔνῃ καὶ νέᾳ, φυλῆς πρυτανευούσης Πανδιονίδος, Δημοσθένης Δημοσθένους Παιανιεὺς εἶπεν, ἐπειδὴ Φίλιππος ἀποστείλας πρέσβεις περὶ τῆς εἰρήνης ὁμολογουμένας πεποίηται συνθήκας, δεδόχθαι τῇ βουλῇ καὶ τῷ δήμῳ τῷ Ἀθηναίων, ὅπως ἂν ἡ εἰρήνη ἐπιτελεσθῇ ἡ ἐπιχειροτονηθεῖσα ἐν τῇ πρώτῃ ἐκκλησίᾳ, πρέσβεις ἑλέσθαι ἐκ πάντων Ἀθηναίων ἤδη πέντε, τοὺς δὲ χειροτονηθέντας ἀποδημεῖν μηδεμίαν ὑπερβολὴν ποιουμένους, ὅπου ἂν ὄντα πυνθάνωνται τὸν Φίλιππον, καὶ τοὺς ὅρκους λαβεῖν τε παρ᾽ αὐτοῦ καὶ δοῦναι τὴν ταχίστην ἐπὶ ταῖς ὡμολογημέναις συνθήκαις αὐτῷ πρὸς τὸν Ἀθηναίων δῆμον, συμπεριλαμβάνοντας καὶ τοὺς ἑκατέρων συμμάχους. πρέσβεις ᾑρέθησαν Εὔβουλος Ἀναφλύστιος, Αἰσχίνης Κοθωκίδης, Κηφισοφῶν Ῥαμνούσιος, Δημοκράτης Φλυεύς, Κλέων Κοθωκίδης.]

Ταῦτα γράψαντος ἐμοῦ τότε καὶ τὸ τῇ πόλει 30 συμφέρον, οὐ τὸ Φιλίππῳ ζητοῦντος, βραχὺ φροντίσαντες οἱ χρηστοὶ πρέσβεις οὗτοι καθῆντο ἐν

Μακεδονίᾳ τρεῖς ὅλους μῆνας, ἕως ἦλθε Φίλιππος ἐκ Θρᾴκης πάντα καταστρεψάμενος τἀκεῖ, ἐξὸν ἡμερῶν δέκα, μᾶλλον δὲ τριῶν ἢ τεττάρων, εἰς τὸν Ἑλλήσποντον ἀφῖχθαι καὶ τὰ χωρία σῶσαι, λαβόντας τοὺς ὅρκους πρὶν ἐκεῖνον ἐξελεῖν αὐτά· οὐ γὰρ ἂν ἥψατ' αὐτῶν παρόντων ἡμῶν, ἢ οὐκ ἂν ὡρκίζομεν αὐτὸν, ὥστε τῆς εἰρήνης ἂν διημαρτήκει καὶ οὐκ ἂν ἀμφότερα εἶχε, καὶ τὴν εἰρήνην καὶ τὰ χωρία.

31 Τὸ μὲν τοίνυν ἐν τῇ πρεσβείᾳ πρῶτον κλέμμα
μὲν Φιλίππου, δωροδόκημα δὲ τῶν ἀδίκων τούτων
ἀνθρώπων καὶ θεοῖς ἐχθρῶν τοιοῦτον ἐγένετο· ὑπὲρ
οὗ καὶ τότε καὶ νῦν καὶ ἀεὶ ὁμολογῶ πολεμεῖν καὶ
διαφέρεσθαι τούτοις. ἕτερον δ' εὐθὺς ἐφεξῆς ἔτι
32 τούτου μεῖζον κακούργημα θεάσασθε. ἐπειδὴ γὰρ
ὡμολόγησε τὴν εἰρήνην ὁ Φίλιππος προλαβὼν τὴν
Θρᾴκην διὰ τούτους οὐχὶ πεισθέντας τῷ ἐμῷ ψηφίσματι, πάλιν ὠνεῖται παρ' αὐτῶν ὅπως μὴ ἀπίω-
μεν ἐκ Μακεδονίας, ἕως τὰ τῆς στρατείας τῆς ἐπὶ
τοὺς Φωκέας εὐτρεπῆ ποιήσαιτο, ἵνα μὴ, δεῦρ'
ἀπαγγειλάντων ἡμῶν ὅτι μέλλει καὶ παρασκευάζεται πορεύεσθαι, ἐξέλθοιτε ὑμεῖς καὶ περιπλεύ-
σαντες ταῖς τριήρεσιν εἰς Πύλας ὥσπερ πρότερον
κλείσαιτε τὸν πορθμὸν, ἀλλ' ἅμ' ἀκούοιτε ταῦτα
ἀπαγγελλόντων ἡμῶν κἀκεῖνος ἐντὸς εἴη Πυλῶν καὶ
33 μηδὲν ἔχοιθ' ὑμεῖς ποιῆσαι. οὕτω δ' ἦν ὁ Φίλιππος
ἐν φόβῳ καὶ πολλῇ ἀγωνίᾳ, μὴ καὶ ταῦτα προειλη-

φότος αὐτοῦ, εἰ πρὸ τοῦ τοὺς Φωκέας ἀπολέσθαι
ψηφίσαισθε βοηθεῖν, ἐκφύγοι τὰ πράγματ' αὐτὸν,
ὥστε μισθοῦται τὸν κατάπτυστον τουτονὶ, οὐκέτι
κοινῇ μετὰ τῶν ἄλλων πρέσβεων, ἀλλ' ἰδίᾳ καθ'
αὑτὸν, τοιαῦτα πρὸς ὑμᾶς εἰπεῖν καὶ ἀπαγγεῖλαι δι'
ὧν ἅπαντ' ἀπώλετο. ἀξιῶ δὲ ὑμᾶς, ὦ ἄνδρες 34
'Αθηναῖοι, καὶ δέομαι τοῦτο μεμνῆσθαι παρ' ὅλον
τὸν ἀγῶνα, ὅτι μὴ κατηγορήσαντος Αἰσχίνου μηδὲν
ἔξω τῆς γραφῆς οὐδ' ἂν ἐγὼ λόγον οὐδένα ἐποιού-
μην ἕτερον, πάσαις δ' αἰτίαις καὶ βλασφημίαις ἅμα
τούτου κεχρημένου ἀνάγκη κἀμοὶ πρὸς ἕκαστα τῶν
κατηγορημένων μικρὰ ἀποκρίνασθαι. τίνες οὖν 35
ἦσαν οἱ παρὰ τούτου λόγοι τότε ῥηθέντες, καὶ δι'
οὓς ἅπαντ' ἀπώλετο; ὡς οὐ δεῖ θορυβεῖσθαι τῷ
παρεληλυθέναι Φίλιππον εἴσω Πυλῶν· ἔσται γὰρ
ἅπανθ' ὅσα βούλεσθ' ὑμεῖς, ἂν ἔχηθ' ἡσυχίαν, καὶ
ἀκούσεσθε δυοῖν ἢ τριῶν ἡμερῶν, οἷς μὲν ἐχθρὸς
ἥκει, φίλον αὐτὸν γεγενημένον, οἷς δὲ φίλος, τοὐναντίον ἐχθρόν. οὐ γὰρ τὰ ῥήματα τὰς οἰκειότητας
ἔφη βεβαιοῦν, μάλα σεμνῶς ὀνομάζων, ἀλλὰ τὸ
ταὐτὰ συμφέρειν· συμφέρειν δὲ Φιλίππῳ καὶ Φωκεῦσι καὶ ὑμῖν ὁμοίως ἅπασι τῆς ἀναλγησίας καὶ
τῆς βαρύτητος ἀπαλλαγῆναι τῆς τῶν Θηβαίων.
ταῦτα δ' ἀσμένως τινὲς ἤκουον αὐτοῦ διὰ τὴν τόθ' 36
ὑποῦσαν ἀπέχθειαν πρὸς τοὺς Θηβαίους. τί οὖν
συνέβη μετὰ ταῦτ' εὐθὺς, οὐκ εἰς μακράν; τοὺς μὲν
Φωκέας ἀπολέσθαι καὶ κατασκαφῆναι τὰς πόλεις

αὐτῶν, ὑμᾶς δ' ἡσυχίαν ἀγαγόντας καὶ τούτῳ πεισθέντας μικρὸν ὕστερον σκευαγωγεῖν ἐκ τῶν ἀγρῶν,
τοῦτον δὲ χρυσίον λαβεῖν, καὶ ἔτι πρὸς τούτοις τὴν
μὲν ἀπέχθειαν τὴν πρὸς Θηβαίους καὶ Θετταλοὺς τῇ
πόλει γενέσθαι, τὴν δὲ χάριν τὴν ὑπὲρ τῶν πεπραγ-
37 μένων Φιλίππῳ. ὅτι δ' οὕτω ταῦτ' ἔχει, λέγε μοι
τό τε τοῦ Καλλισθένους ψήφισμα καὶ τὴν ἐπιστολὴν τὴν τοῦ Φιλίππου, ἐξ ὧν ἀμφοτέρων ταῦθ'
ἅπανθ' ὑμῖν ἔσται φανερά. λέγε.

ΨΗΦΙΣΜΑ.

[Ἐπὶ Μνησιφίλου ἄρχοντος, συγκλήτου ἐκκλησίας ὑπὸ
στρατηγῶν καὶ πρυτάνεων [καὶ] βουλῆς γνώμῃ, μαιμακτηριῶνος
δεκάτῃ ἀπιόντος, Καλλισθένης Ἐτεονίκου Φαληρεὺς εἶπε μηδένα Ἀθηναίων μηδεμιᾷ παρευρέσει ἐν τῇ χώρᾳ κοιταῖον γίγνεσθαι, ἀλλ' ἐν ἄστει καὶ Πειραιεῖ, ὅσοι μὴ ἐν τοῖς φρουρίοις
εἰσὶν ἀποτεταγμένοι· τούτων δ' ἑκάστους ἣν παρέλαβον τάξιν
38 διατηρεῖν μήτε ἀφημερεύοντας μήτε ἀποκοιτοῦντας. ὃς δ' ἂν
ἀπειθήσῃ τῷδε τῷ ψηφίσματι, ἔνοχος ἔστω τοῖς τῆς προδοσίας
ἐπιτιμίοις, ἐὰν μή τι ἀδύνατον ἐπιδεικνύῃ περὶ ἑαυτὸν ὄν· περὶ
δὲ τοῦ ἀδυνάτου ἐπικρινέτω ὁ ἐπὶ τῶν ὅπλων στρατηγὸς καὶ ὁ
ἐπὶ τῆς διοικήσεως καὶ ὁ γραμματεὺς τῆς βουλῆς. κατακομίζειν
δὲ καὶ τὰ ἐκ τῶν ἀγρῶν πάντα τὴν ταχίστην, τὰ μὲν ἐντὸς
σταδίων ἑκατὸν εἴκοσιν εἰς ἄστυ καὶ Πειραιᾶ, τὰ δὲ ἐκτὸς
σταδίων ἑκατὸν εἴκοσιν εἰς Ἐλευσῖνα καὶ Φυλὴν καὶ Ἄφιδναν
καὶ Ῥαμνοῦντα καὶ Σούνιον. εἶπε Καλλισθένης Φαληρεύς.]

Ἆρ' ἐπὶ ταύταις ταῖς ἐλπίσι τὴν εἰρήνην ἐποιεῖ-
σθε, ἢ ταῦτ' ἐπηγγέλλεθ' ὑμῖν οὗτος ὁ μισθωτός;
39 Λέγε δὴ τὴν ἐπιστολὴν ἣν δεῦρ' ἔπεμψε Φίλιππος μετὰ ταῦτα.

ΕΠΙΣΤΟΛΗ.

[Βασιλεὺς Μακεδόνων Φίλιππος Ἀθηναίων τῇ βουλῇ καὶ τῷ δήμῳ χαίρειν. ἴστε ἡμᾶς παρεληλυθότας εἴσω Πυλῶν καὶ τὰ κατὰ τὴν Φωκίδα ὑφ' ἑαυτοὺς πεποιημένους, καὶ ὅσα μὲν ἑκουσίως προσετίθετο τῶν πολισμάτων, φρουρὰς εἰσαγηοχότας, τὰ δὲ μὴ ὑπακούοντα κατὰ κράτος λαβόντες καὶ ἐξανδραποδισάμενοι κατεσκάψαμεν. ἀκούων δὲ καὶ ὑμᾶς παρασκευάζεσθαι βοηθεῖν αὐτοῖς γέγραφα ὑμῖν, ἵνα μὴ ἐπὶ πλέον ἐνοχλῆσθε περὶ τούτων. τοῖς μὲν γὰρ ὅλοις οὐδὲν μέτριόν μοι δοκεῖτε ποιεῖν, τὴν εἰρήνην συνθέμενοι καὶ ὁμοίως ἀντιπαρεξάγοντες, καὶ ταῦτα οὐδὲ συμπεριειλημμένων τῶν Φωκέων ἐν ταῖς κοιναῖς ἡμῶν συνθήκαις. ὥστε ἐὰν μὴ ἐμμένητε τοῖς ὡμολογημένοις, οὐδὲν προτερήσετε ἔξω τοῦ ἐφθακέναι ἀδικοῦντες.]

Ἀκούετε ὡς σαφῶς δηλοῖ καὶ διορίζεται ἐν τῇ 40
πρὸς ὑμᾶς ἐπιστολῇ πρὸς τοὺς ἑαυτοῦ συμμάχους,
ὅτι "ἐγὼ ταῦτα πεποίηκα ἀκόντων Ἀθηναίων καὶ
λυπουμένων, ὥστ' εἴπερ εὖ φρονεῖτε, ὦ Θηβαῖοι
καὶ Θετταλοί, τούτους μὲν ἐχθροὺς ὑπολήψεσθε,
ἐμοὶ δὲ πιστεύσετε," οὐ τούτοις τοῖς ῥήμασι γράψας, ταῦτα δὲ βουλόμενος δεικνύναι. τοιγαροῦν ἐκ
τούτων ᾤχετ' ἐκείνους λαβὼν εἰς τὸ μηδ' ὁτιοῦν
προορᾶν τῶν μετὰ ταῦτα μηδ' αἰσθάνεσθαι, ἀλλ'
ἐᾶσαι πάντα τὰ πράγματα ἐκεῖνον ὑφ' ἑαυτῷ ποιήσασθαι· ἐξ ὧν ταῖς παρούσαις συμφοραῖς οἱ ταλαίπωροι κέχρηνται. ὁ δὲ ταύτης τῆς πίστεως αὐτῷ 41
συνεργὸς καὶ συναγωνιστὴς καὶ ὁ δεῦρ' ἀπαγγείλας
τὰ ψευδῆ καὶ φενακίσας ὑμᾶς οὑτοσὶ ὁ τὰ Θηβαίων
ὀδυρόμενος νῦν πάθη καὶ διεξιὼν ὡς οἰκτρά, καὶ τούτων καὶ τῶν ἐν Φωκεῦσι κακῶν καὶ ὅσ' ἄλλα πεπόν-

θασιν οἱ Ἕλληνες ἁπάντων αὐτὸς ὢν αἴτιος. δῆλον γὰρ ὅτι σὺ μὲν ἀλγεῖς ἐπὶ τοῖς συμβεβηκόσιν, Αἰσχίνη, καὶ τοὺς Θηβαίους ἐλεεῖς, κτήματ' ἔχων ἐν τῇ Βοιωτίᾳ καὶ γεωργῶν τὰ ἐκείνων, ἐγὼ δὲ χαίρω, ὃς εὐθὺς ἐξῃτούμην ὑπὸ τοῦ ταῦτα πράξαντος.

42 Ἀλλὰ γὰρ ἐμπέπτωκα εἰς λόγους, οὓς αὐτίκα μᾶλλον ἴσως ἁρμόσει λέγειν. ἐπάνειμι δὴ πάλιν ἐπὶ τὰς ἀποδείξεις, ὡς τὰ τούτων ἀδικήματα τῶν νυνὶ παρόντων πραγμάτων γέγονεν αἴτια.

Ἐπειδὴ γὰρ ἐξηπάτησθε μὲν ὑμεῖς ὑπὸ Φιλίππου διὰ τούτων τῶν ἐν ταῖς πρεσβείαις μισθωσάντων ἑαυτοὺς καὶ οὐδὲν ἀληθὲς ὑμῖν ἀπαγγειλάντων,
43 ἐξηπάτηντο δὲ οἱ ταλαίπωροι Φωκεῖς καὶ ἀνῄρηντο αἱ πόλεις αὐτῶν, τί ἐγένετο; οἱ μὲν κατάπτυστοι Θετταλοὶ καὶ ἀναίσθητοι Θηβαῖοι φίλον, εὐεργέτην, σωτῆρα τὸν Φίλιππον ἡγοῦντο· πάντ' ἐκεῖνος ἦν αὐτοῖς· οὐδὲ φωνὴν ἤκουον, εἴ τις ἄλλο τι βούλοιτο λέγειν. ὑμεῖς δὲ ὑφορώμενοι τὰ πεπραγμένα καὶ δυσχεραίνοντες ἤγετε τὴν εἰρήνην ὅμως· οὐ γὰρ ἦν ὅ τι ἂν ἐποιεῖτε. καὶ οἱ ἄλλοι δὲ Ἕλληνες, ὁμοίως ὑμῖν πεφενακισμένοι καὶ διημαρτηκότες ὧν ἤλπισαν, ἦγον τὴν εἰρήνην ἄσμενοι, καὶ αὐτοὶ τρόπον τινὰ ἐκ
44 πολλοῦ πολεμούμενοι. ὅτε γὰρ περιιὼν Φίλιππος Ἰλλυριοὺς καὶ Τριβαλλούς, τινὰς δὲ καὶ τῶν Ἑλλήνων κατεστρέφετο, καὶ δυνάμεις πολλὰς καὶ μεγάλας ἐποιεῖθ' ὑφ' ἑαυτῷ, καί τινες τῶν ἐκ τῶν πόλεων

ἐπὶ τῇ τῆς εἰρήνης ἐξουσίᾳ βαδίζοντες ἐκεῖσε διεφθεί-
ροντο, ὧν εἷς οὗτος ἦν, τότε πάντες, ἐφ' οὓς ταῦτα
παρεσκευάζετ' ἐκεῖνος, ἐπολεμοῦντο. εἰ δὲ μὴ ᾐσθά-
νοντο, ἕτερος λόγος οὗτος, οὐ πρὸς ἐμέ. ἐγὼ μὲν 45
γὰρ προὔλεγον καὶ διεμαρτυρόμην καὶ παρ' ὑμῖν ἀεὶ
καὶ ὅποι πεμφθείην· αἱ δὲ πόλεις ἐνόσουν τῶν μὲν
ἐν τῷ πολιτεύεσθαι καὶ πράττειν δωροδοκούντων καὶ
διαφθειρομένων ἐπὶ χρήμασι, τῶν δὲ ἰδιωτῶν καὶ
πολλῶν τὰ μὲν οὐ προορωμένων, τὰ δὲ τῇ καθ' ἡμέραν ῥᾳστώνῃ καὶ σχολῇ δελεαζομένων, καὶ τοιουτονί
τι πάθος πεπονθότων ἁπάντων, πλὴν οὐκ ἐφ' ἑαυτοὺς
ἑκάστων οἰομένων τὸ δεινὸν ἥξειν, ἀλλὰ διὰ τῶν
ἑτέρων κινδύνων τὰ ἑαυτῶν ἀσφαλῶς σχήσειν, ὅταν
βούλωνται. εἶτ' οἶμαι συμβέβηκε τοῖς μὲν πλήθε- 46
σιν ἀντὶ τῆς πολλῆς καὶ ἀκαίρου ῥᾳθυμίας τὴν ἐλευθερίαν ἀπολωλεκέναι, τοῖς δὲ προεστηκόσι καὶ τἄλλα
πλὴν ἑαυτοὺς οἰομένοις πωλεῖν πρώτους ἑαυτοὺς
πεπρακόσιν αἰσθέσθαι· ἀντὶ γὰρ φίλων καὶ ξένων, ἃ
τότε ὠνομάζοντο, ἡνίκα ἐδωροδόκουν, νῦν κόλακες καὶ
θεοῖς ἐχθροὶ καὶ τἄλλ' ἃ προσήκει πάντ' ἀκούουσιν.
εἰκότως· οὐδεὶς γάρ, ὦ ἄνδρες Ἀθηναῖοι, τὸ τοῦ 47
προδιδόντος συμφέρον ζητῶν χρήματ' ἀναλίσκει,
οὐδ' ἐπειδὰν ὧν ἂν πρίηται κύριος γένηται, τῷ
προδότῃ συμβούλῳ περὶ τῶν λοιπῶν ἔτι χρῆται·
οὐδὲν γὰρ ἂν ἦν εὐδαιμονέστερον προδότου. ἀλλ'
οὐκ ἔστι ταῦτα· πόθεν; πολλοῦ γε καὶ δεῖ. ἀλλ'
ἐπειδὰν τῶν πραγμάτων ἐγκρατὴς ὁ ζητῶν ἄρχειν

καταστῇ, καὶ τῶν ταῦτα ἀποδομένων δεσπότης ἐστὶ,
τὴν δὲ πονηρίαν εἰδὼς τότε δὴ, τότε καὶ μισεῖ καὶ
48 ἀπιστεῖ καὶ προπηλακίζει. σκοπεῖτε δέ. καὶ γὰρ
εἰ παρελήλυθεν ὁ τῶν πραγμάτων καιρὸς, ὁ τοῦ γε
εἰδέναι τὰ τοιαῦτα καιρὸς ἀεὶ πάρεστι τοῖς εὖ φρονοῦσι. μέχρι τούτου Λασθένης φίλος ὠνομάζετο
Φιλίππου, ἕως προὔδωκεν Ὄλυνθον· μέχρι τούτου
Τιμόλαος, ἕως ἀπώλεσε Θῆβας· μέχρι τούτου Εὔ-
δικος καὶ Σῖμος οἱ Λαρισαῖοι, ἕως Θετταλίαν ὑπὸ
Φιλίππῳ ἐποιήσαν. εἶτ' ἐλαυνομένων καὶ ὑβριζο-
μένων καὶ τί κακὸν οὐχὶ πασχόντων πᾶσα ἡ οἰκουμένη μεστὴ γέγονε προδοτῶν. τί δ' Ἀρίστρατος
49 ἐν Σικυῶνι, καὶ τί Περίλαος ἐν Μεγάροις; οὐκ
ἀπερριμμένοι; ἐξ ὧν καὶ σαφέστατ' ἄν τις ἴδοι ὅτι
ὁ μάλιστα φυλάττων τὴν ἑαυτοῦ πατρίδα καὶ πλεῖστα ἀντιλέγων τούτοις, οὗτος ὑμῖν, Αἰσχίνη, τοῖς
προδιδοῦσι καὶ μισθαρνοῦσι τὸ ἔχειν ἐφ' ὅτῳ δωροδοκήσετε περιποιεῖ, καὶ διὰ τοὺς πολλοὺς τουτωνὶ
καὶ τοὺς ἀνθισταμένους τοῖς ὑμετέροις βουλήμασιν
ὑμεῖς ἐστὲ σῷ καὶ ἔμμισθοι, ἐπεὶ διά γε ὑμᾶς αὐτοὺς
πάλαι ἂν ἀπολώλειτε.

50 Καὶ περὶ μὲν τῶν τότε πραχθέντων ἔχων ἔτι
πολλὰ λέγειν, καὶ ταῦτα ἡγοῦμαι πλείω τῶν ἱκανῶν
εἰρῆσθαι. αἴτιος δ' οὗτος, ὥσπερ ἑωλοκρασίαν τινά
μου τῆς πονηρίας τῆς ἑαυτοῦ καὶ τῶν ἀδικημάτων
κατασκεδάσας, ἣν ἀναγκαῖον ἦν πρὸς τοὺς νεωτέρους
τῶν πεπραγμένων ἀπολύσασθαι. παρηνώχλησθε

δὲ καὶ ὑμεῖς ἴσως, οἱ καὶ πρὶν ἐμὲ εἰπεῖν ὁτιοῦν
εἰδότες τὴν τούτου τότε μισθαρνίαν. καίτοι φιλίαν 51
γε καὶ ξενίαν αὐτὴν ὀνομάζει, καὶ νῦν εἶπέ που λέγων "ὁ τὴν Ἀλεξάνδρου ξενίαν ὀνειδίζων ἐμοί."
ἐγώ σοι ξενίαν Ἀλεξάνδρου; πόθεν λαβόντι ἢ πῶς
ἀξιωθέντι; οὔτε Φιλίππου ξένον οὔτ' Ἀλεξάνδρου φίλον εἴποιμ' ἂν ἐγώ σε, οὐχ οὕτω μαίνομαι, εἰ μὴ καὶ
τοὺς θεριστὰς καὶ τοὺς ἄλλο τι μισθοῦ πράττοντας
φίλους καὶ ξένους δεῖ καλεῖν τῶν μισθωσαμένων. ἀλλ' 52
οὐκ ἔστι ταῦτα· πόθεν; πολλοῦ γε καὶ δεῖ. ἀλλὰ μι-
σθωτὸν ἐγώ σε Φιλίππου πρότερον καὶ νῦν Ἀλεξάνδρου καλῶ, καὶ οὗτοι πάντες. εἰ δ' ἀπιστεῖς, ἐρώτησον
αὐτούς, μᾶλλον δ' ἐγὼ τοῦθ' ὑπὲρ σοῦ ποιήσω. πότερον ὑμῖν, ὦ ἄνδρες Ἀθηναῖοι, δοκεῖ μισθωτὸς Αἰσχίνης
ἢ ξένος εἶναι Ἀλεξάνδρου; ἀκούεις ἃ λέγουσιν.

Βούλομαι τοίνυν ἤδη καὶ περὶ τῆς γραφῆς αὐτῆς 53
ἀπολογήσασθαι καὶ διεξελθεῖν τὰ πεπραγμέν' ἐμαυτῷ, ἵνα καίπερ εἰδὼς Αἰσχίνης ὅμως ἀκούσῃ δι' ἅ
φημι καὶ τούτων τῶν προβεβουλευμένων καὶ πολλῷ
μειζόνων ἔτι τούτων δωρεῶν, δίκαιος εἶναι τυγχάνειν.
καί μοι λέγε τὴν γραφὴν αὐτὴν λαβών.

ΓΡΑΦΗ.

['Επὶ Χαιρώνδου ἄρχοντος, ἐλαφηβολιῶνος ἕκτῃ ἱσταμένου, 54
Αἰσχίνης Ἀτρομήτου Κοθωκίδης ἀπήνεγκε πρὸς τὸν ἄρχοντα
παρανόμων κατὰ Κτησιφῶντος τοῦ Λεωσθένους Ἀναφλυστίου,
ὅτι ἔγραψε παράνομον ψήφισμα, ὡς ἄρα δεῖ στεφανῶσαι Δημοσθένην Δημοσθένους Παιανιέα χρυσῷ στεφάνῳ, καὶ ἀναγο-

ρεῦσαι ἐν τῷ θεάτρῳ Διονυσίοις τοῖς μεγάλοις, τραγῳδοῖς καινοῖς, ὅτι στεφανοῖ ὁ δῆμος Δημοσθένην Δημοσθένους Παιανιέα
χρυσῷ στεφάνῳ ἀρετῆς ἕνεκα, καὶ εὐνοίας ἧς ἔχων διατελεῖ
εἴς τε τοὺς Ἕλληνας ἅπαντας καὶ τὸν δῆμον τὸν Ἀθηναίων,
καὶ ἀνδραγαθίας, καὶ διότι διατελεῖ πράττων καὶ λέγων τὰ βέλτιστα τῷ δήμῳ καὶ πρόθυμός ἐστι ποιεῖν ὅ τι ἂν δύνηται ἀγα-
55 θόν, πάντα ταῦτα ψευδῆ γράψας καὶ παράνομα, τῶν νόμων οὐκ
ἐώντων πρῶτον μὲν ψευδεῖς γραφὰς εἰς τὰ δημόσια γράμματα
καταβάλλεσθαι, εἶτα τὸν ὑπεύθυνον στεφανοῦν (ἔστι δὲ Δημοσθένης τειχοποιὸς καὶ ἐπὶ τῷ θεωρικῷ τεταγμένος), ἔτι δὲ
μὴ ἀναγορεύειν τὸν στέφανον ἐν τῷ θεάτρῳ Διονυσίοις τραγῳδῶν τῇ καινῇ, ἀλλ' ἐὰν μὲν ἡ βουλὴ στεφανοῖ, ἐν τῷ βουλευτηρίῳ ἀνειπεῖν, ἐὰν δὲ ἡ πόλις, ἐν πυκνὶ ἐν τῇ ἐκκλησίᾳ. τίμημα τάλαντα πεντήκοντα. κλητῆρες Κηφισοφῶν Κηφισο-
φῶντος Ῥαμνούσιος, Κλέων Κλέωνος Κοθωκίδης.]

56 Ἃ μὲν διώκει τοῦ ψηφίσματος, ὦ ἄνδρες Ἀθηναῖοι, ταῦτ' ἐστιν. ἐγὼ δ' ἀπ' αὐτῶν τούτων πρῶτον οἶμαι δῆλον ὑμῖν ποιήσειν ὅτι πάντα δικαίως
ἀπολογήσομαι· τὴν γὰρ αὐτὴν τούτῳ ποιησάμενος
τῶν γεγραμμένων τάξιν περὶ πάντων ἐρῶ καθ'
57 ἕκαστον ἐφεξῆς καὶ οὐδὲν ἑκὼν παραλείψω. τοῦ
μὲν οὖν γράψαι πράττοντα καὶ λέγοντα τὰ βέλ-
τιστά με τῷ δήμῳ διατελεῖν καὶ πρόθυμον εἶναι
ποιεῖν ὅ τι ἂν δύνωμαι ἀγαθόν, καὶ ἐπαινεῖν ἐπὶ
τούτοις, ἐν τοῖς πεπολιτευμένοις τὴν κρίσιν εἶναι
νομίζω· ἀπὸ γὰρ τούτων ἐξεταζομένων εὑρεθήσεται
εἴτε ἀληθῆ περὶ ἐμοῦ γέγραφε Κτησιφῶν ταῦτα καὶ
58 προσήκοντα εἴτε καὶ ψευδῆ· τὸ δὲ μὴ προσγρά-
ψαντα "ἐπειδὰν τὰς εὐθύνας δῷ" στεφανοῦν, καὶ

ἀνειπεῖν ἐν τῷ θεάτρῳ τὸν στέφανον κελεῦσαι, κοινωνεῖν μὲν ἡγοῦμαι καὶ τοῦτο τοῖς πεπολιτευμένοις,
εἴτε ἄξιός εἰμι τοῦ στεφάνου καὶ τῆς ἀναρρήσεως τῆς
ἐν τούτοις εἴτε καὶ μή, ἔτι μέντοι καὶ τοὺς νόμους
δεικτέον εἶναί μοι δοκεῖ, καθ' οὓς ταῦτα γράφειν
ἐξῆν τούτῳ. οὑτωσὶ μὲν, ὦ ἄνδρες Ἀθηναῖοι, δικαίως καὶ ἁπλῶς τὴν ἀπολογίαν ἔγνωκα ποιεῖσθαι,
βαδιοῦμαι δ' ἐπ' αὐτὰ ἃ πέπρακταί μοι. καί με 59
μηδεὶς ὑπολάβῃ ἀπαρτᾶν τὸν λόγον τῆς γραφῆς, ἐὰν
εἰς Ἑλληνικὰς πράξεις καὶ λόγους ἐμπέσω· ὁ γὰρ
διώκων τοῦ ψηφίσματος τὸ λέγειν καὶ πράττειν τὰ
ἄριστά με καὶ γεγραμμένος ταῦτα ὡς οὐκ ἀληθῆ,
οὗτός ἐστιν ὁ τοὺς περὶ ἁπάντων τῶν ἐμοὶ πεπολιτευμένων λόγους οἰκείους καὶ ἀναγκαίους τῇ γραφῇ
πεποιηκώς. εἶτα καὶ πολλῶν προαιρέσεων οὐσῶν
τῆς πολιτείας τὴν περὶ τὰς Ἑλληνικὰς πράξεις
εἱλόμην ἐγὼ, ὥστε καὶ τὰς ἀποδείξεις ἐκ τούτων
δίκαιός εἰμι ποιεῖσθαι.

Ἃ μὲν οὖν πρὸ τοῦ πολιτεύεσθαι καὶ δημηγορεῖν 60
ἐμὲ προὔλαβε καὶ κατέσχε Φίλιππος, ἐάσω· οὐδὲν
γὰρ ἡγοῦμαι τούτων εἶναι πρὸς ἐμέ· ἃ δ' ἀφ' ἧς
ἡμέρας ἐπὶ ταῦτα ἐπέστην ἐγὼ διεκωλύθη, ταῦτα
ἀναμνήσω καὶ τούτων ὑφέξω λόγον, τοσοῦτον ὑπειπών. πλεονέκτημα, ὦ ἄνδρες Ἀθηναῖοι, μέγα 61
ὑπῆρξε Φιλίππῳ. παρὰ γὰρ τοῖς Ἕλλησιν, οὐ
τισὶν, ἀλλὰ πᾶσιν ὁμοίως, φορὰν προδοτῶν καὶ
δωροδόκων καὶ θεοῖς ἐχθρῶν ἀνθρώπων συνέβη

γενέσθαι τοσαύτην ὅσην οὐδείς πω πρότερον μέμνηται γεγονυῖαν· οὓς συναγωνιστὰς καὶ συνεργοὺς
λαβὼν καὶ πρότερον κακῶς τοὺς Ἕλληνας ἔχοντας
πρὸς ἑαυτοὺς καὶ στασιαστικῶς ἔτι χεῖρον διέθηκε,
τοὺς μὲν ἐξαπατῶν, τοῖς δὲ διδούς, τοὺς δὲ πάντα
τρόπον διαφθείρων, καὶ διέστησεν εἰς μέρη πολλὰ
ἑνὸς τοῦ συμφέροντος ἅπασιν ὄντος, κωλύειν ἐκεῖνον
62 μέγαν γίγνεσθαι. ’ν τοιαύτῃ δὲ καταστάσει καὶ ἔτι
ἀγνοίᾳ τοῦ συνισταμένου καὶ φυομένου κακοῦ τῶν
ἁπάντων Ἑλλήνων ὄντων δεῖ σκοπεῖν ὑμᾶς, ὦ ἄνδρες Ἀθηναῖοι, τί προσῆκον ἦν ἑλέσθαι πράττειν καὶ
ποιεῖν τὴν πόλιν, καὶ τούτων λόγον παρ' ἐμοῦ λα-
βεῖν· ὁ γὰρ ἐνταῦθα ἑαυτὸν τάξας τῆς πολιτείας
63 εἰμί ἐγώ. πότερον αὐτὴν ἐχρῆν, Αἰσχίνη, τὸ φρόνημα ἀφεῖσαν καὶ τὴν ἀξίαν τὴν αὑτῆς ἐν τῇ Θετταλῶν καὶ Δολόπων τάξει συγκατακτᾶσθαι Φιλίππῳ
τὴν τῶν Ἑλλήνων ἀρχὴν καὶ τὰ τῶν προγόνων
καλὰ καὶ δίκαια ἀναιρεῖν; ἢ τοῦτο μὲν μὴ ποιεῖν,
δεινὸν γὰρ ὡς ἀληθῶς, ἃ δ' ἑώρα συμβησόμενα, εἰ
μηδεὶς κωλύσει, καὶ προῃσθάνεθ', ὡς ἔοικεν, ἐκ
64 πολλοῦ, ταῦτα περιιδεῖν γιγνόμενα; ἀλλὰ νῦν
ἔγωγε τὸν μάλιστα ἐπιτιμῶντα τοῖς πεπραγμένοις
ἡδέως ἂν ἐροίμην, τῆς ποίας μερίδος γενέσθαι τὴν
πόλιν ἐβούλετ' ἄν, πότερον τῆς συναιτίας τῶν συμβεβηκότων τοῖς Ἕλλησι κακῶν καὶ αἰσχρῶν, ἧς ἂν
Θετταλοὺς καὶ τοὺς μετὰ τούτων εἴποι τις, ἢ τῆς
περιεορακυίας ταῦτα γιγνόμενα ἐπὶ τῇ τῆς ἰδίας

πλεονεξίας ἐλπίδι, ἧς ἂν Ἀρκάδας καὶ Μεσσηνίους
καὶ Ἀργείους θείημεν. ἀλλὰ καὶ τούτων πολλοί, 65
μᾶλλον δὲ πάντες, χεῖρον ἡμῶν ἀπηλλάχασιν. καὶ
γὰρ εἰ μὲν ὡς ἐκράτησε Φίλιππος ᾤχετ' εὐθέως
ἀπιὼν καὶ μετὰ ταῦτ' ἦγεν ἡσυχίαν, μήτε τῶν αὑτοῦ
συμμάχων μήτε τῶν ἄλλων Ἑλλήνων μηδένα μηδὲν
λυπήσας, ἦν ἄν τις κατὰ τῶν ἐναντιωθέντων οἷς
ἔπραττεν ἐκεῖνος μέμψις καὶ κατηγορία· εἰ δὲ
ὁμοίως ἁπάντων τὸ ἀξίωμα, τὴν ἡγεμονίαν, τὴν
ἐλευθερίαν περιείλετο, μᾶλλον δὲ καὶ τὰς πολιτείας,
ὅσων ἐδύνατο, πῶς οὐχ ἁπάντων ἐνδοξότατα ὑμεῖς
ἐβουλεύσασθε ἐμοὶ πεισθέντες;

Ἀλλ' ἐκεῖσε ἐπανέρχομαι. τί τὴν πόλιν, Αἰσχί- 66
νη, προσῆκε ποιεῖν ἀρχὴν καὶ τυραννίδα τῶν Ἑλλήνων ὁρῶσαν ἑαυτῷ κατασκευαζόμενον Φίλιππον;
ἢ τί τὸν σύμβουλον ἔδει λέγειν ἢ γράφειν τὸν
Ἀθήνησιν ἐμὲ (καὶ γὰρ τοῦτο πλεῖστον διαφέρει),
ὃς συνῄδειν μὲν ἐκ παντὸς τοῦ χρόνου μέχρι τῆς
ἡμέρας ἀφ' ἧς αὐτὸς ἐπὶ τὸ βῆμα ἀνέβην, ἀεὶ περὶ
πρωτείων καὶ τιμῆς καὶ δόξης ἀγωνιζομένην τὴν
πατρίδα, καὶ πλείω καὶ χρήματα καὶ σώματα ἀνη-
λωκυῖαν ὑπὲρ φιλοτιμίας καὶ τῶν πᾶσι συμφερόντων ἢ τῶν ἄλλων Ἑλλήνων ὑπὲρ αὑτῶν ἀνηλώκασιν
ἕκαστοι, ἑώρων δ' αὐτὸν τὸν Φίλιππον, πρὸς ὃν ἦν 67
ἡμῖν ὁ ἀγών, ὑπὲρ ἀρχῆς καὶ δυναστείας τὸν ὀφθαλμὸν ἐκκεκομμένον, τὴν κλεῖν κατεαγότα, τὴν χεῖρα,
τὸ σκέλος πεπηρωμένον, πᾶν ὅ τι βουληθείη μέρος

ἡ τύχη τοῦ σώματος παρελέσθαι, τοῦτο προϊέμενον,
68 ὥστε τῷ λοιπῷ μετὰ τιμῆς καὶ δόξης ζῆν· καὶ μὴν
οὐδὲ τοῦτό γε οὐδεὶς ἂν εἰπεῖν τολμήσαι, ὡς τῷ μὲν
ἐν Πέλλῃ τραφέντι, χωρίῳ ἀδόξῳ τότε γε ὄντι καὶ
μικρῷ, τοσαύτην μεγαλοψυχίαν προσῆκεν ἐγγενέσθαι
ὥστε τῆς τῶν Ἑλλήνων ἀρχῆς ἐπιθυμῆσαι καὶ τοῦτ'
εἰς τὸν νοῦν ἐμβαλέσθαι, ὑμῖν δ' οὖσιν Ἀθηναίοις
καὶ κατὰ τὴν ἡμέραν ἑκάστην ἐν πᾶσι καὶ λόγοις
καὶ θεωρήμασι τῆς τῶν προγόνων ἀρετῆς ὑπομνήμαθ'
ὁρῶσι τοσαύτην κακίαν ὑπάρξαι ὥστε τῆς τῶν Ἑλλήνων ἐλευθερίας αὐτεπαγγέλτους ἐθελοντὰς παρα-
69 χωρῆσαι Φιλίππῳ. οὐδ' ἂν εἷς ταῦτα φήσειεν.
λοιπὸν τοίνυν ἦν καὶ ἀναγκαῖον ἅμα πᾶσιν οἷς ἐκεῖνος ἔπραττεν ἀδικῶν ὑμᾶς ἐναντιοῦσθαι δικαίως.
τοῦτ' ἐποιεῖτε μὲν ὑμεῖς ἐξ ἀρχῆς εἰκότως καὶ προσηκόντως, ἔγραφον δὲ καὶ συνεβούλευον καὶ ἐγὼ καθ'
οὓς ἐπολιτευόμην χρόνους. ὁμολογῶ. ἀλλὰ τί
ἐχρῆν με ποιεῖν; ἤδη γάρ σ' ἐρωτῶ, πάντα τἄλλ'
ἀφείς, Ἀμφίπολιν, Πύδναν, Ποτίδαιαν, Ἁλόννησον·
70 οὐδενὸς τούτων μέμνημαι· Σέρρειον δὲ καὶ Δορίσκον
καὶ τὴν Πεπαρήθου πόρθησιν καὶ ὅσ' ἄλλα τοιαῦτα
ἡ πόλις ἠδίκητο, οὐδ' εἰ γέγονεν οἶδα. καίτοι σύ
γ' ἔφησθά με ταῦτα λέγοντα εἰς ἔχθραν ἐμβαλεῖν
τουτουσί, Εὐβούλου καὶ Ἀριστοφῶντος καὶ Διοπεί-
θους τῶν περὶ τούτων ψηφισμάτων ὄντων, οὐκ ἐμῶν,
71 ὦ λέγων εὐχερῶς ὅ τι ἂν βουληθῇς. οὐδὲ νῦν περὶ
τούτων ἐρῶ. ἀλλ' ὁ τὴν Εὔβοιαν ἐκεῖνος σφετε-

ριζόμενος καὶ κατασκευάζων ἐπιτείχισμα ἐπὶ τὴν
Ἀττικὴν, καὶ Μεγάροις ἐπιχειρῶν, καὶ καταλαμβά-
νων Ὠρεὸν, καὶ κατασκάπτων Πορθμὸν, καὶ καθισ-
τὰς ἐν μὲν Ὠρεῷ Φιλιστίδην τύραννον, ἐν δ' Ἐρε-
τρίᾳ Κλείταρχον, καὶ τὸν Ἑλλήσποντον ὑφ' ἑαυτῷ
ποιούμενος, καὶ Βυζάντιον πολιορκῶν, καὶ πόλεις
Ἑλληνίδας ἃς μὲν ἀναιρῶν, εἰς ἃς δὲ τοὺς φυγάδας
κατάγων, πότερον ταῦτα πάντα ποιῶν ἠδίκει καὶ
παρεσπόνδει καὶ ἔλυε τὴν εἰρήνην ἢ οὔ; καὶ πότερον φανῆναί τινα τῶν Ἑλλήνων τὸν ταῦτα κωλύσοντα
ποιεῖν αὐτὸν ἐχρῆν ἢ μή; εἰ μὲν γὰρ μὴ ἐχρῆν, ἀλλὰ 72
τὴν Μυσῶν λείαν καλουμένην τὴν Ἑλλάδα οὖσαν
ὀφθῆναι ζώντων καὶ ὄντων Ἀθηναίων, περιείργασμαι
μὲν ἐγὼ περὶ τούτων εἰπὼν, περιείργασται δ' ἡ πόλις
πεισθεῖσα ἐμοὶ, ἔστω δὲ ἀδικήματα πάντα ἃ πέπρακται καὶ ἁμαρτήματα ἐμά. εἰ δὲ ἔδει τινὰ τούτων
κωλυτὴν φανῆναι, τίνα ἄλλον ἢ τὸν Ἀθηναίων δῆμον
προσῆκε γενέσθαι; ταῦτα τοίνυν ἐπολιτευόμην ἐγὼ,
καὶ ὁρῶν καταδουλούμενον πάντας ἀνθρώπους ἐκεῖνον ἠναντιούμην, καὶ προλέγων καὶ διδάσκων μὴ
προΐεσθαι ταῦτα Φιλίππῳ διετέλουν.

Καὶ μὴν τὴν εἰρήνην γ' ἐκεῖνος ἔλυσε τὰ πλοῖα 73
λαβὼν, οὐχ ἡ πόλις, Αἰσχίνη. Φέρε δ' αὐτὰ τὰ
ψηφίσματα καὶ τὴν ἐπιστολὴν τὴν τοῦ Φιλίππου,
καὶ λέγε ἐφεξῆς· ἀπὸ γὰρ τούτων ἐξεταζομένων τίς
τίνος αἴτιός ἐστι γενήσεται φανερόν.

ΨΗΦΙΣΜΑ.

['Επὶ ἄρχοντος Νεοκλέους, μηνὸς βοηδρομιῶνος, ἐκκλησίας συγκλήτου ὑπὸ στρατηγῶν, Εὔβουλος Μνησιθέου Κόπρειος εἶπεν, ἐπειδὴ προσήγγειλαν οἱ στρατηγοὶ ἐν τῇ ἐκκλησίᾳ ὡς ἄρα Λεωδάμαντα τὸν ναύαρχον καὶ τὰ μετ' αὐτοῦ ἀποσταλέντα σκάφη εἴκοσιν ἐπὶ τὴν τοῦ σίτου παραπομπὴν εἰς Ἑλλήσποντον ὁ παρὰ Φιλίππου στρατηγὸς Ἀμύντας καταγήοχεν εἰς Μακεδονίαν καὶ ἐν φυλακῇ ἔχει, ἐπιμεληθῆναι τοὺς πρυτάνεις καὶ τοὺς στρατηγοὺς ὅπως ἡ βουλὴ συναχθῇ καὶ αἱρεθῶσι πρέσβεις πρὸς Φίλιππον,
74 οἵτινες παραγενόμενοι διαλέξονται πρὸς αὐτὸν περὶ τοῦ ἀφεθῆναι τὸν ναύαρχον καὶ τὰ πλοῖα καὶ τοὺς στρατιώτας. καὶ εἰ μὲν δι' ἄγνοιαν ταῦτα πεποίηκεν ὁ Ἀμύντας, ὅτι οὐ μεμψιμοιρεῖ ὁ δῆμος οὐδὲν αὐτῷ· εἰ δέ τι πλημμελοῦντα παρὰ τὰ ἐπεσταλμένα λαβών, ὅτι ἐπισκεψάμενοι Ἀθηναῖοι ἐπιτιμήσουσι κατὰ τὴν τῆς ὀλιγωρίας ἀξίαν. εἰ δὲ μηδέτερον τούτων ἐστίν, ἀλλ' ἰδίᾳ ἀγνωμονοῦσιν ἢ ὁ ἀποστείλας ἢ ὁ ἀπεσταλμένος, καὶ τοῦτο λέγειν, ἵνα αἰσθανόμενος ὁ δῆμος βουλεύσηται τί δεῖ ποιεῖν.]

75 Τοῦτο μὲν τοίνυν τὸ ψήφισμα Εὔβουλος ἔγραψεν, οὐκ ἐγώ, τὸ δ' ἐφεξῆς Ἀριστοφῶν, εἶθ' Ἡγήσιππος, εἶτ' Ἀριστοφῶν πάλιν, εἶτα Φιλοκράτης, εἶτα Κηφισοφῶν, εἶτα πάντες οἱ ἄλλοι· ἐγὼ δ' οὐδὲν περὶ τούτων. λέγε.

ΨΗΦΙΣΜΑ.

['Επὶ Νεοκλέους ἄρχοντος, βοηδρομιῶνος ἔνῃ καὶ νέᾳ, βουλῆς γνώμῃ, πρυτάνεις καὶ στρατηγοὶ ἐχρημάτισαν τὰ ἐκ τῆς ἐκκλησίας ἀνενεγκόντες, ὅτι ἔδοξε τῷ δήμῳ, πρέσβεις ἑλέσθαι πρὸς Φίλιππον περὶ τῆς τῶν πλοίων ἀνακομιδῆς καὶ ἐντολὰς δοῦναι κατὰ τὰ ἐκ τῆς ἐκκλησίας ψηφίσματα. καὶ εἵλοντο τούσδε, Κηφισοφῶντα Κλέωνος Ἀναφλύστιον, Δημόκριτον

Δημοφῶντος Ἀναγυράσιον, Πολύκριτον Ἀπημάντου Κοθωκίδην. πρυτανείᾳ φυλῆς Ἱπποθωντίδος Ἀριστοφῶν Κολλυτεὺς πρόεδρος εἶπεν.]

Ὥσπερ τοίνυν ἐγὼ ταῦτα δεικνύω τὰ ψηφίσματα, 76
οὕτω καὶ σὺ δεῖξον, Αἰσχίνη, ποῖον ἐγὼ γράψας ψήφισμα αἴτιός εἰμι τοῦ πολέμου. ἀλλ' οὐκ ἂν ἔχοις· εἰ γὰρ εἶχες, οὐδὲν ἂν αὐτοῦ πρότερον νυνὶ παρέσχου. καὶ μὴν οὐδ' ὁ Φίλιππος οὐδὲν αἰτιᾶται ἐμὲ ὑπὲρ τοῦ πολέμου, ἑτέροις ἐγκαλῶν. Λέγε δ' αὐτὴν τὴν ἐπιστολὴν τὴν τοῦ Φιλίππου.

ΕΠΙΣΤΟΛΗ.

[Βασιλεὺς Μακεδόνων Φίλιππος Ἀθηναίων τῇ βουλῇ καὶ τῷ 77
δήμῳ χαίρειν. παραγενόμενοι πρὸς ἐμὲ οἱ παρ' ὑμῶν πρεσβευταί, Κηφισοφῶν καὶ Δημόκριτος καὶ Πολύκριτος, διελέγοντο περὶ τῆς τῶν πλοίων ἀφέσεως ὧν ἐναυάρχει Λεωδάμας. καθ' ὅλου μὲν οὖν ἔμοιγε φαίνεσθε ἐν μεγάλῃ εὐηθείᾳ ἔσεσθαι, εἰ οἴεσθ' ἐμὲ λανθάνειν ὅτι ἐξαπεστάλη ταῦτα τὰ πλοῖα πρόφασιν μὲν ὡς τὸν σῖτον παραπέμψοντα ἐκ τοῦ Ἑλλησπόντου εἰς Λῆμνον, βοηθήσοντα δὲ Σηλυμβριανοῖς τοῖς ὑπ' ἐμοῦ μὲν πολιορκουμένοις, οὐ συμπεριειλημμένοις δὲ ἐν ταῖς τῆς φιλίας
κοινῇ κειμέναις ἡμῖν συνθήκαις. καὶ ταῦτα συνετάχθη τῷ 78
ναυάρχῳ ἄνευ μὲν τοῦ δήμου τοῦ Ἀθηναίων, ὑπὸ δέ τινων ἀρχόντων καὶ ἑτέρων ἰδιωτῶν μὲν νῦν ὄντων, ἐκ παντὸς δὲ τρόπου βουλομένων τὸν δῆμον ἀντὶ τῆς νῦν ὑπαρχούσης πρὸς ἐμὲ φιλίας τὸν πόλεμον ἀναλαβεῖν, πολλῷ μᾶλλον φιλοτιμουμένων τοῦτο συντετελέσθαι ἢ τοῖς Σηλυμβριανοῖς βοηθῆσαι. καί ὑπολαμβάνουσιν αὐτοῖς τὸ τοιοῦτο πρόσοδον ἔσεσθαι· οὐ μέντοι μοι δοκεῖ τοῦτο χρήσιμον ὑπάρχειν οὔθ' ὑμῖν οὔτ' ἐμοί. διόπερ τά τε νῦν καταχθέντα πλοῖα πρὸς ἡμᾶς ἀφίημι ὑμῖν, καὶ τοῦ λοιποῦ, ἐὰν βούλησθε μὴ ἐπιτρέπειν τοῖς προεστηκόσιν ὑμῶν

κακοήθως πολιτεύεσθαι, ἀλλ' ἐπιτιμᾶτε, πειράσομαι κἀγὼ διαφυλάττειν τὴν εἰρήνην. εὐτυχεῖτε.]

79 Ἐνταῦθ' οὐδαμοῦ Δημοσθένην γέγραφεν, οὐδ'
αἰτίαν οὐδεμίαν κατ' ἐμοῦ. τί ποτ' οὖν τοῖς ἄλλοις
ἐγκαλῶν τῶν ἐμοὶ πεπραγμένων οὐχὶ μέμνηται; ὅτι
τῶν ἀδικημάτων ἂν ἐμέμνητο τῶν αὑτοῦ, εἴ τι περὶ
ἐμοῦ ἐγεγράφει· τούτων γὰρ εἰχόμην ἐγὼ καὶ τούτοις ἠναντιούμην. καὶ πρῶτον μὲν τὴν εἰς Πελοπόννησον πρεσβείαν ἔγραψα, ὅτε πρῶτον ἐκεῖνος εἰς
Πελοπόννησον παρεδύετο, εἶτα τὴν εἰς Εὔβοιαν,
ἡνίκ' Εὐβοίας ἥπτετο, εἶτα τὴν ἐπ' Ὠρεὸν ἔξοδον,
οὐκέτι πρεσβείαν, καὶ τὴν εἰς Ἐρέτριαν, ἐπειδὴ
τυράννους ἐκεῖνος ἐν ταύταις ταῖς πόλεσι κατέστησεν.
80 μετὰ ταῦτα δὲ τοὺς ἀποστόλους ἅπαντας ἀπέστειλα,
καθ' οὓς Χερρόνησος ἐσώθη καὶ Βυζάντιον καὶ
πάντες οἱ σύμμαχοι. ἐξ ὧν ὑμῖν μὲν τὰ κάλλιστα,
ἔπαινοι, δόξαι, τιμαί, στέφανοι, χάριτες παρὰ τῶν
εὖ πεπονθότων ὑπῆρχον· τῶν δ' ἀδικουμένων τοῖς
μὲν ὑμῖν τότε πεισθεῖσιν ἡ σωτηρία περιεγένετο,
τοῖς δ' ὀλιγωρήσασι τὸ πολλάκις ὧν ὑμεῖς προείπατε
μεμνῆσθαι, καὶ νομίζειν ὑμᾶς μὴ μόνον εὔνους ἑαυτοῖς, ἀλλὰ καὶ φρονίμους ἀνθρώπους καὶ μάντεις εἶναι·
81 πάντα γὰρ ἐκβέβηκεν ἃ προείπατε. καὶ μὴν ὅτι
πολλὰ μὲν ἂν χρήματα ἔδωκε Φιλιστίδης ὥστ' ἔχειν
Ὠρεόν, πολλὰ δὲ Κλείταρχος ὥστ' ἔχειν Ἐρέτριαν,
πολλὰ δ' αὐτὸς ὁ Φίλιππος ὥστε ταῦθ' ὑπάρχειν
ἐφ' ὑμᾶς αὐτῷ, καὶ περὶ τῶν ἄλλων μηδὲν ἐξελέγχε-

σθαι μηδ' ἃ ποιῶν ἠδίκει μηδένα ἐξετάζειν πανταχοῦ,
οὐδεὶς ἀγνοεῖ, καὶ πάντων ἥκιστα σύ· οἱ γὰρ παρὰ 82
τοῦ Κλειτάρχου καὶ τοῦ Φιλιστίδου τότε πρέσβεις
δεῦρ' ἀφικνούμενοι παρὰ σοὶ κατέλυον, Αἰσχίνη, καὶ
σὺ προὐξένεις αὐτῶν· οὓς ἡ μὲν πόλις ὡς ἐχθροὺς
καὶ οὔτε δίκαια οὔτε συμφέροντα λέγοντας ἀπήλασε,
σοὶ δ' ἦσαν φίλοι. οὐ τοίνυν ἐπράχθη τούτων
οὐδέν, ὦ βλασφημῶν περὶ ἐμοῦ καὶ λέγων ὡς σιωπῶ
μὲν λαβών, βοῶ δ' ἀναλώσας. ἀλλ' οὐ σύ γε,
ἀλλὰ βοᾷς μὲν ἔχων, παύσει δὲ οὐδέποτ', ἐὰν μή
σε οὗτοι παύσωσιν ἀτιμώσαντες τήμερον. στεφα- 83
νωσάντων τοίνυν ὑμῶν ἐμὲ ἐπὶ τούτοις τότε, καὶ
γράψαντος Ἀριστονίκου τὰς αὐτὰς συλλαβὰς
ἅσπερ οὑτοσὶ Κτησιφῶν νῦν γέγραφε, καὶ ἀναρρηθέντος ἐν τῷ θεάτρῳ τοῦ στεφάνου, καὶ δευτέρου
κηρύγματος ἤδη μοι τούτου γιγνομένου, οὔτ' ἀντεῖ-
πεν Αἰσχίνης παρὼν οὔτε τὸν εἰπόντα ἐγράψατο.
Καί μοι λέγε καὶ τοῦτο τὸ ψήφισμα λαβών.

ΨΗΦΙΣΜΑ.

[Ἐπὶ Χαιρώνδου Ἡγήμονος ἄρχοντος, γαμηλιῶνος ἕκτῃ ἀπι- 84
όντος, φυλῆς πρυτανευούσης Λεοντίδος. Ἀριστόνικος Φρεάρριος
εἶπεν, ἐπειδὴ Δημοσθένης Δημοσθένους Παιανιεὺς πολλὰς καὶ
μεγάλας χρείας παρέσχηται τῷ δήμῳ τῷ Ἀθηναίων καὶ πολλοῖς
τῶν συμμάχων καὶ πρότερον, καὶ ἐν τῷ παρόντι καιρῷ βεβοή-
θηκε διὰ τῶν ψηφισμάτων, καί τινας τῶν ἐν τῇ Εὐβοίᾳ πόλεων
ἠλευθέρωκε, καὶ διατελεῖ εὔνους ὢν τῷ δήμῳ τῷ Ἀθηναίων,
καὶ λέγει καὶ πράττει ὅ τι ἂν δύνηται ἀγαθὸν ὑπέρ τε αὐτῶν
Ἀθηναίων καὶ τῶν ἄλλων Ἑλλήνων, δεδόχθαι τῇ βουλῇ καὶ

τῷ δήμῳ τῷ Ἀθηναίων ἐπαινέσαι Δημοσθένην Δημοσθένους Παιανιέα καὶ στεφανῶσαι χρυσῷ στεφάνῳ, καὶ ἀναγορεῦσαι τὸν στέφανον ἐν τῷ θεάτρῳ Διονυσίοις, τραγῳδοῖς καινοῖς, τῆς δὲ ἀναγορεύσεως τοῦ στεφάνου ἐπιμεληθῆναι τὴν πρυτανεύουσαν φυλὴν καὶ τὸν ἀγωνοθέτην. εἶπεν Ἀριστόνικος ὁ Φρεάρριος.]

85 Ἔστιν οὖν ὅστις ὑμῶν οἶδέ τινα αἰσχύνην τῇ πόλει συμβᾶσαν διὰ τοῦτο τὸ ψήφισμα ἢ χλευασμὸν ἢ γέλωτα, ἃ νῦν οὗτος ἔφη συμβήσεσθαι, ἂν ἐγὼ στεφανῶμαι; καὶ μὴν ὅταν ᾖ νέα καὶ γνώριμα πᾶσι τὰ πράγματα, ἐάν τε καλῶς ἔχῃ, χάριτος τυγχάνει, ἐάν θ' ὡς ἑτέρως, τιμωρίας. φαίνομαι τοίνυν ἐγὼ χάριτος τετυχηκὼς τότε, καὶ οὐ μέμψεως οὐδὲ τιμωρίας.

86 Οὐκοῦν μέχρι μὲν τῶν χρόνων ἐκείνων, ἐν οἷς ταῦτ' ἐπράχθη, πάντας ἀνωμολόγημαι τοὺς χρόνους τὰ ἄριστα πράττειν τῇ πόλει, τῷ νικᾶν, ὅτ' ἐβουλεύεσθε, λέγων καὶ γράφων, τῷ καταπραχθῆναι τὰ γραφέντα, καὶ στεφάνους ἐξ αὐτῶν τῇ πόλει καὶ ἐμοὶ καὶ πᾶσιν ὑμῖν γενέσθαι, τῷ θυσίας τοῖς θεοῖς καὶ προσόδους ὡς ἀγαθῶν τούτων ὄντων ὑμᾶς πεποιῆσθαι.

87 Ἐπειδὴ τοίνυν ἐκ τῆς Εὐβοίας ὁ Φίλιππος ἐξηλάθη, τοῖς μὲν ὅπλοις ὑφ' ὑμῶν, τῇ δὲ πολιτείᾳ καὶ τοῖς ψηφίσμασι, κἂν διαρραγῶσί τινες τούτων, ὑπ' ἐμοῦ, ἕτερον κατὰ τῆς πόλεως ἐπιτειχισμὸν ἐζήτει. ὁρῶν δ' ὅτι σίτῳ πάντων ἀνθρώπων πλείστῳ χρώμεθ' ἐπεισάκτῳ, βουλόμενος τῆς σιτοπομπίας κύριος γενέσθαι, παρελθὼν ἐπὶ Θρᾴκης Βυζαντίους συμμά-

χους ὄντας αὑτῷ τὸ μὲν πρῶτον ἠξίου συμπολεμεῖν
τὸν πρὸς ὑμᾶς πόλεμον, ὡς δ' οὐκ ἤθελον οὐδ' ἐπὶ
τούτοις ἔφασαν τὴν συμμαχίαν πεποιῆσθαι, λέγον-
τες ἀληθῆ, χάρακα βαλόμενος πρὸς τῇ πόλει καὶ
μηχανήματ' ἐπιστήσας ἐπολιόρκει. τούτων δὲ γιγνο- 88
μένων ὅ τι μὲν προσῆκε ποιεῖν ὑμᾶς, οὐκέτ' ἐρωτήσω·
δῆλον γάρ ἐστιν ἅπασιν. ἀλλὰ τίς ἦν ὁ βοηθήσας
τοῖς Βυζαντίοις καὶ σώσας αὐτούς; τίς ὁ κωλύ-
σας τὸν Ἑλλήσποντον ἀλλοτριωθῆναι κατ' ἐκείνους
τοὺς χρόνους; ὑμεῖς, ὦ ἄνδρες Ἀθηναῖοι. τὸ δ'
ὑμεῖς ὅταν λέγω, τὴν πόλιν λέγω. τίς δ' ὁ τῇ πόλει
λέγων καὶ γράφων καὶ πράττων καὶ ἁπλῶς ἑαυτὸν εἰς
τὰ πράγματα ἀφειδῶς διδούς; ἐγώ. ἀλλὰ μὴν ἡλίκα 89
ταῦτα ὠφέλησεν ἅπαντας, οὐκέτ' ἐκ τοῦ λόγου δεῖ
μαθεῖν, ἀλλ' ἔργῳ πεπείρασθε· ὁ γὰρ τότε ἐνστὰς
πόλεμος ἄνευ τοῦ καλὴν δόξαν ἐνεγκεῖν ἐν πᾶσι τοῖς
κατὰ τὸν βίον ἀφθονωτέροις καὶ εὐωνοτέροις διῆγεν
ὑμᾶς τῆς νῦν εἰρήνης, ἣν οὗτοι κατὰ τῆς πατρίδος
τηροῦσιν οἱ χρηστοὶ ἐπὶ ταῖς μελλούσαις ἐλπίσιν,
ὧν διαμάρτοιεν, καὶ μετάσχοιεν ὧν ὑμεῖς οἱ τὰ βέλτιστα βουλόμενοι τοὺς θεοὺς αἰτεῖτε, μὴ μεταδοῖεν
ὑμῖν ὧν αὐτοὶ προῄρηνται. Λέγε δ' αὐτοῖς καὶ τοὺς
τῶν Βυζαντίων στεφάνους καὶ τοὺς τῶν Περινθίων,
οἷς ἐστεφάνουν ἐκ τούτων τὴν πόλιν.

ΨΗΦΙΣΜΑ ΒΥΖΑΝΤΙΩΝ.

[Ἐπὶ ἱερομνάμονος Βοσπορίχω Δαμάγητος ἐν τᾷ ἁλίᾳ ἔλεξεν, 90
ἐκ τᾶς βωλᾶς λαβὼν ῥάτραν, ἐπειδὴ ὁ δᾶμος ὁ Ἀθαναίων ἔν τε

τοῖς προγεγεναμένοις καιροῖς εὐνοέων διατελέει Βυζαντίοις καὶ τοῖς συμμάχοις καὶ συγγενέσι Περινθίοις καὶ πολλὰς καὶ μεγάλας χρείας παρέσχηται, ἔν τε τῷ παρεστακότι καιρῷ Φιλίππω τῶ Μακεδόνος ἐπιστρατεύσαντος ἐπὶ τὰν χώραν καὶ τὰν πόλιν ἐπ' ἀναστάσει Βυζαντίων καὶ Περινθίων καὶ τὰν χώραν δαίοντος καὶ δενδροκοπέοντος, βοηθήσας πλοίοις ἑκατὸν καὶ εἴκοσι καὶ σίτῳ καὶ βέλεσι καὶ ὁπλίταις ἐξείλετο ἐμὲ ἐκ τῶν μεγάλων κινδύνων καὶ ἀποκατέστασε τὰν πάτριον πολιτείαν καὶ τὼς νόμως
91 καὶ τὼς τάφως, δεδόχθαι τῷ δάμῳ τῷ Βυζαντίων καὶ Περινθίων Ἀθαναίοις δόμεν ἐπιγαμίαν, πολιτείαν, ἔγκτασιν γᾶς καὶ οἰκιᾶν, προεδρίαν ἐν τοῖς ἀγῶσι, πόθοδον ποτὶ τὰν βωλὰν καὶ τὸν δᾶμον πράτοις μετὰ τὰ ἱερά, καὶ τοῖς κατοικέειν ἐθέλουσι τὰν πόλιν ἀλειτουργήτοις ἦμεν πασᾶν τᾶν λειτουργιᾶν· στᾶσαι δὲ καὶ εἰκόνας τρεῖς ἑκκαιδεκαπάχεις ἐν τῷ Βοσπορείῳ, στεφανούμενον τὸν δᾶμον τὸν Ἀθαναίων ὑπὸ τῶ δάμω τῶ Βυζαντίων καὶ Περινθίων· ἀποστεῖλαι δὲ καὶ θεωρίας ἐς τὰς ἐν τᾷ Ἑλλάδι παναγύριας, Ἴσθμια καὶ Νέμεα καὶ Ὀλύμπια καὶ Πύθια, καὶ ἀνακαρῦξαι τὼς στεφάνως οἷς ἐστεφάνωται ὁ δᾶμος ὁ Ἀθαναίων ὑφ' ἡμῶν, ὅπως ἐπιστέωνται οἱ Ἕλλανες τάν τε Ἀθαναίων ἀρετὰν καὶ τὰν Βυζαντίων καὶ Περινθίων εὐχαριστίαν.]

92 *Λέγε καὶ τοὺς παρὰ τῶν ἐν Χερρονήσῳ στεφάνους.*

ΨΗΦΙΣΜΑ ΧΕΡΡΟΝΗΣΙΤΩΝ.

[Χερρονησιτῶν οἱ κατοικοῦντες Σηστόν, Ἐλεοῦντα, Μάδυτον, Ἀλωπεκόννησον, στεφανοῦσιν Ἀθηναίων τὴν βουλὴν καὶ τὸν δῆμον χρυσῷ στεφάνῳ ἀπὸ ταλάντων ἑξήκοντα, καὶ χάριτος βωμὸν ἱδρύονται καὶ δήμου Ἀθηναίων, ὅτι πάντων μεγίστου ἀγαθῶν παραίτιος γέγονε Χερρονησίταις, ἐξελόμενος ἐκ τῆς Φιλίππου καὶ ἀποδοὺς τὰς πατρίδας, τοὺς νόμους, τὴν ἐλευθερίαν, τὰ ἱερά. καὶ ἐν τῷ μετὰ ταῦτα αἰῶνι παντὶ οὐκ ἐλλείψει εὐχαριστῶν καὶ ποιῶν ὅ τι ἂν δύνηται ἀγαθόν. ταῦτα ἐψηφίσαντο ἐν τῷ κοινῷ βουλευτηρίῳ.]

Οὐκοῦν οὐ μόνον τὸ Χερρόνησον καὶ Βυζάντιον 93
σῶσαι, οὐδὲ τὸ κωλῦσαι τὸν Ἑλλήσποντον ὑπὸ
Φιλίππῳ γενέσθαι τότε, οὐδὲ τὸ τιμᾶσθαι τὴν πόλιν ἐκ τούτων ἡ προαίρεσις ἡ ἐμὴ καὶ ἡ πολιτεία
διεπράξατο, ἀλλὰ καὶ πᾶσιν ἔδειξεν ἀνθρώποις τήν
τε τῆς πόλεως καλοκαγαθίαν καὶ τὴν Φιλίππου
κακίαν. ὁ μέν γε φίλος καὶ σύμμαχος ὢν τοῖς Βυζαντίοις πολιορκῶν αὐτοὺς ἑωρᾶτο ὑπὸ πάντων, οὗ
τί γένοιτ' ἂν αἴσχιον ἢ μιαρώτερον; ὑμεῖς δ' οἱ καὶ 94
μεμψάμενοι πολλὰ καὶ δίκαια ἂν ἐκείνοις εἰκότως
περὶ ὧν ἠγνωμονήκεσαν εἰς ὑμᾶς ἐν τοῖς ἔμπροσθεν
χρόνοις, οὐ μόνον οὐ μνησικακοῦντες οὐδὲ προϊέμενοι
τοὺς ἀδικουμένους, ἀλλὰ καὶ σῴζοντες ἐφαίνεσθε, ἐξ
ὧν δόξαν, εὔνοιαν, τιμὴν παρὰ πάντων ἐκτᾶσθε.
καὶ μὴν ὅτι μὲν πολλοὺς ἐστεφανώκατ' ἤδη τῶν
πολιτευομένων ἅπαντες ἴσασι· δι' ὅντινα δ' ἄλλον
ἡ πόλις ἐστεφάνωται, σύμβουλον λέγω καὶ ῥήτορα,
πλὴν δι' ἐμέ, οὐδ' ἂν εἷς εἰπεῖν ἔχοι.

Ἵνα τοίνυν καὶ τὰς βλασφημίας ἃς κατὰ τῶν 95
Εὐβοέων καὶ τῶν Βυζαντίων ἐποιήσατο, εἴ τι δυσχερὲς αὐτοῖς ἐπέπρακτο πρὸς ὑμᾶς ὑπομιμνήσκων,
συκοφαντίας οὔσας ἐπιδείξω μὴ μόνον τῷ ψευδεῖς
εἶναι (τοῦτο μὲν γὰρ ὑπάρχειν ὑμᾶς εἰδότας ἡγοῦμαι), ἀλλὰ καὶ τῷ, εἰ τὰ μάλιστ' ἦσαν ἀληθεῖς.
οὕτως ὡς ἐγὼ κέχρημαι τοῖς πράγμασι συμφέρειν
χρήσασθαι, ἓν ἢ δύο βούλομαι τῶν καθ' ὑμᾶς πεπραγμένων καλῶν τῇ πόλει διεξελθεῖν, καὶ ταῦτ' ἐν

βραχέσι· καὶ γὰρ ἄνδρα ἰδίᾳ καὶ πόλιν κοινῇ πρὸς
τὰ κάλλιστα τῶν ὑπαρχόντων ἀεὶ δεῖ πειρᾶσθαι τὰ
96 λοιπὰ πράττειν. ὑμεῖς τοίνυν, ὦ ἄνδρες Ἀθηναῖοι,
Λακεδαιμονίων γῆς καὶ θαλάττης ἀρχόντων καὶ τὰ
κύκλῳ τῆς Ἀττικῆς κατεχόντων ἁρμοσταῖς καὶ
φρουραῖς, Εὔβοιαν, Τάναγραν, καὶ Βοιωτίαν ἅπα-
σαν, Μέγαρα, Αἴγιναν, Κλεωνάς, τὰς ἄλλας νήσους,
οὔτε ναῦς οὔτε τείχη τῆς πόλεως τότε κτησαμένης,
ἐξήλθετε εἰς Ἁλίαρτον καὶ πάλιν οὐ πολλαῖς ἡμέραις ὕστερον εἰς Κόρινθον, τῶν τότε Ἀθηναίων
πόλλ' ἂν ἐχόντων μνησικακῆσαι καὶ Κορινθίοις καὶ
Θηβαίοις τῶν περὶ τὸν Δεκελεικὸν πόλεμον πραχθέν-
97 των· ἀλλ' οὐκ ἐποίουν τοῦτο, οὐδ' ἐγγύς. καίτοι
τότε ταῦτα ἀμφότερα, Αἰσχίνη, οὔθ' ὑπὲρ εὐεργετῶν
ἐποίουν οὔτ' ἀκίνδυνα ἑώρων. ἀλλ' οὐ διὰ ταῦτα
προΐεντο τοὺς καταφεύγοντας ἐφ' ἑαυτούς, ἀλλ'
ὑπὲρ εὐδοξίας καὶ τιμῆς ἤθελον τοῖς δεινοῖς αὑτοὺς
διδόναι ὀρθῶς καὶ καλῶς βουλευόμενοι. πέρας μὲν
γὰρ ἅπασιν ἀνθρώποις ἐστὶ τοῦ βίου θάνατος, κἂν ἐν
οἰκίσκῳ τις αὑτὸν καθείρξας τηρῇ· δεῖ δὲ τοὺς ἀγαθοὺς ἄνδρας ἐγχειρεῖν μὲν ἅπασιν ἀεὶ τοῖς καλοῖς,
τὴν ἀγαθὴν προβαλλομένους ἐλπίδα, φέρειν δ' ὅ τι
98 ἂν ὁ θεὸς διδῷ γενναίως. ταῦτ' ἐποίουν οἱ ὑμέτεροι
πρόγονοι, ταῦθ' ὑμῶν οἱ πρεσβύτεροι, οἳ Λακεδαιμονίους οὐ φίλους ὄντας οὐδ' εὐεργέτας, ἀλλὰ πολλὰ
τὴν πόλιν ἡμῶν ἠδικηκότας καὶ μεγάλα, ἐπειδὴ
Θηβαῖοι κρατήσαντες ἐν Λεύκτροις ἀνελεῖν ἐπεχεί-

ρουν, διεκωλύσατε, οὐ φοβηθέντες τὴν τότε Θηβαίοις
ῥώμην καὶ δόξαν ὑπάρχουσαν, οὐδ' ὑπὲρ οἷα πεποιηκότων ἀνθρώπων κινδυνεύσετε διαλογισάμενοι· καὶ 99
γάρ τοι πᾶσι τοῖς Ἕλλησιν ἐδείξατε ἐκ τούτων ὅτι
κἂν ὁτιοῦν τις εἰς ὑμᾶς ἐξαμάρτῃ, τούτῳ τὴν ὀργὴν
εἰς τἄλλα ἔχετε, ἐὰν δ' ὑπὲρ σωτηρίας ἢ ἐλευθερίας
κίνδυνός τις αὐτοὺς καταλαμβάνῃ, οὔτε μνησικακή-
σετε οὔθ' ὑπολογιεῖσθε. καὶ οὐκ ἐπὶ τούτων μόνων
οὕτως ἐσχήκατε, ἀλλὰ πάλιν σφετεριζομένων Θηβαίων τὴν Εὔβοιαν οὐ περιείδετε, οὐδ' ὧν ὑπὸ Θεμίσωνος καὶ Θεοδώρου περὶ Ὠρωπὸν ἠδίκησθε ἀνεμνή-
σθητε, ἀλλ' ἐβοηθήσατε καὶ τούτοις, τῶν ἐθελοντῶν
τότε τριηράρχων πρῶτον γενομένων τῇ πόλει, ὧν
εἷς ἦν ἐγώ· ἀλλ' οὔπω περὶ τούτων. καίτοι καλὸν 100
μὲν ἐποιήσατε καὶ τὸ σῶσαι τὴν νῆσον, πολλῷ δ'
ἔτι τούτου κάλλιον τὸ καταστάντες κύριοι καὶ τῶν
σωμάτων καὶ τῶν πόλεων ἀποδοῦναι ταῦτα δικαίως
αὐτοῖς τοῖς ἐξημαρτηκόσιν εἰς ὑμᾶς, μηδὲν ὧν ἠδίκησθε ἐν οἷς ἐπιστεύθητε ὑπολογισάμενοι. μυρία
τοίνυν ἕτερα εἰπεῖν ἔχων παραλείπω, ναυμαχίας,
ἐξόδους πεζὰς, στρατείας, καὶ πάλαι γεγονυίας καὶ
νῦν ἐφ' ὑμῶν αὐτῶν, ἃς ἁπάσας ἡ πόλις τῆς τῶν
ἄλλων Ἑλλήνων ἐλευθερίας καὶ σωτηρίας πεποίηται. εἶτ' ἐγὼ τεθεωρηκὼς ἐν τοσούτοις καὶ τοιού- 101
τοις τὴν πόλιν ὑπὲρ τῶν τοῖς ἄλλοις συμφερόντων
ἐθέλουσαν ἀγωνίζεσθαι, ὑπὲρ αὐτῆς τρόπον τινὰ τῆς
βουλῆς οὔσης τί ἔμελλον κελεύσειν ἢ τί συμβουλεύ-

σειν αὐτῇ ποιεῖν; μνησικακεῖν νὴ Δία πρὸς τοὺς βουλομένους σώζεσθαι, καὶ προφάσεις ζητεῖν δι' ἃς ἅπαντα προησόμεθα. καὶ τίς οὐκ ἂν ἀπέκτεινέ με δικαίως, εἴ τι τῶν ὑπαρχόντων τῇ πόλει καλῶν λόγῳ μόνον καταισχύνειν ἐπεχείρησα; ἐπεὶ τό γε ἔργον οὐκ ἂν ἐποιήσαθ' ὑμεῖς, ἀκριβῶς οἶδ' ἐγώ· εἰ γὰρ ἐβούλεσθε, τί ἦν ἐμποδών; οὐχ ὑπῆρχον οἱ ταῦτ' ἐροῦντες οὗτοι;

102 **Β**ούλομαι τοίνυν ἐπανελθεῖν ἐφ' ἃ τούτων ἑξῆς
ἐπολιτευόμην· καὶ σκοπεῖτε ἐν τούτοις πάλιν αὖ,
τί τὸ τῇ πόλει βέλτιστον ἦν. ὁρῶν γάρ, ὦ ἄνδρες
Ἀθηναῖοι, τὸ ναυτικὸν ὑμῶν καταλυόμενον, καὶ τοὺς
μὲν πλουσίους ἀτελεῖς ἀπὸ μικρῶν ἀναλωμάτων
γιγνομένους, τοὺς δὲ μέτρια ἢ μικρὰ κεκτημένους
τῶν πολιτῶν τὰ ὄντα ἀπολλύντας, ἔτι δ' ὑστερίζουσαν ἐκ τούτων τὴν πόλιν τῶν καιρῶν, ἔθηκα νόμον
καθ' ὃν τοὺς μὲν τὰ δίκαια ποιεῖν ἠνάγκασα, τοὺς
πλουσίους, τοὺς δὲ πένητας ἔπαυσ' ἀδικουμένους,
τῇ πόλει δ' ὅπερ ἦν χρησιμώτατον, ἐν καιρῷ γίγνε-
103 σθαι τὰς παρασκευὰς ἐποίησα. καὶ γραφεὶς τὸν
ἀγῶνα τοῦτον εἰς ὑμᾶς εἰσῆλθον καὶ ἀπέφυγον, καὶ
τὸ μέρος τῶν ψήφων ὁ διώκων οὐκ ἔλαβεν. καίτοι
πόσα χρήματα τοὺς ἡγεμόνας τῶν συμμοριῶν ἢ τοὺς
δευτέρους καὶ τρίτους οἴεσθέ μοι διδόναι ὥστε μάλιστα μὲν μὴ θεῖναι τὸν νόμον τοῦτον, εἰ δὲ μή,
καταβαλόντα ἐᾶν ἐν ὑπωμοσίᾳ; τοσαῦτ', ὦ ἄνδρες
104 Ἀθηναῖοι, ὅσα ὀκνήσαιμ' ἂν πρὸς ὑμᾶς εἰπεῖν. καὶ

ταῦτ' εἰκότως ἔπραττον ἐκεῖνοι. ἦν γὰρ αὐτοῖς ἐκ
μὲν τῶν προτέρων νόμων συνεκκαίδεκα λειτουργεῖν,
αὐτοῖς μὲν μικρὰ καὶ οὐδὲν ἀναλίσκουσι, τοὺς δ'
ἀπόρους τῶν πολιτῶν ἐπιτρίβουσιν, ἐκ δὲ τοῦ ἐμοῦ
νόμου τὸ γιγνόμενον κατὰ τὴν οὐσίαν ἕκαστον τιθέναι, καὶ δυοῖν ἐφάνη τριήραρχος ὁ τῆς μιᾶς ἕκτος
καὶ δέκατος πρότερον συντελής· οὐδὲ γὰρ τριηράρχους ἔτι ὠνόμαζον ἑαυτούς, ἀλλὰ συντελεῖς. ὥστε
δὴ ταῦτα λυθῆναι καὶ μὴ τὰ δίκαια ποιεῖν ἀναγκασθῆναι, οὐκ ἔσθ' ὅ τι οὐκ ἐδίδοσαν. Καί μοι λέγε 105
πρῶτον μὲν τὸ ψήφισμα καθ' ὃ εἰσῆλθον τὴν γραφήν,
εἶτα τοὺς καταλόγους, τόν τ' ἐκ τοῦ προτέρου νόμου
καὶ τὸν κατὰ τὸν ἐμόν. λέγε.

ΨΗΦΙΣΜΑ.

[Ἐπὶ ἄρχοντος Πολυκλέους, μηνὸς βοηδρομιῶνος ἕκτῃ ἐπὶ δέκα, φυλῆς πρυτανευούσης Ἱπποθωντίδος, Δημοσθένης Δημοσθένους Παιανιεὺς εἰσήνεγκε νόμον τριηραρχικὸν ἀντὶ τοῦ προτέρου, καθ' ὃν αἱ συντέλειαι ἦσαν τῶν τριηράρχων· καὶ ἐπεχειροτόνησεν ἡ βουλὴ καὶ ὁ δῆμος· καὶ ἀπήνεγκε παρανόμων Δημοσθένει Πατροκλῆς Φλυεύς, καὶ τὸ μέρος τῶν ψήφων οὐ λαβὼν ἀπέτισε τὰς πεντακοσίας δραχμάς.]

Φέρε δὴ καὶ τὸν καλὸν κατάλογον. 106

ΚΑΤΑΛΟΓΟΣ.

[Τοὺς τριηράρχους καλεῖσθαι ἐπὶ τὴν τριήρη συνεκκαίδεκα ἐκ τῶν ἐν τοῖς λόχοις συντελειῶν, ἀπὸ εἴκοσι καὶ πέντε ἐτῶν εἰς τετταράκοντα, ἐπὶ ἴσον τῇ χορηγίᾳ χρωμένους.]

Φέρε δὴ παρὰ τοῦτον τὸν ἐκ τοῦ ἐμοῦ νόμου κατάλογον.

ΚΑΤΑΛΟΓΟΣ.

[Τοὺς τριηράρχους αἱρεῖσθαι ἐπὶ τὴν τριήρη ἀπὸ τῆς οὐσίας κατὰ τίμησιν, ἀπὸ ταλάντων δέκα· ἐὰν δὲ πλειόνων ἡ οὐσία ἀποτετιμημένη ᾖ χρημάτων, κατὰ τὸν ἀναλογισμὸν ἕως τριῶν πλοίων καὶ ὑπηρετικοῦ ἡ λειτουργία ἔστω. κατὰ τὴν αὐτὴν δὲ ἀναλογίαν ἔστω καὶ οἷς ἐλάττων οὐσία ἐστὶ τῶν δέκα ταλάντων, εἰς συντέλειαν συναγομένοις εἰς τὰ δέκα τάλαντα.]

107 Ἆρά γε μικρὰ βοηθῆσαι τοῖς πένησιν ὑμῶν δοκῶ,
ἢ μικρὰ ἀναλῶσαι ἂν τοῦ μὴ τὰ δίκαια ποιεῖν οἱ
πλούσιοι; οὐ τοίνυν μόνον τῷ μὴ καθυφεῖναι ταῦτα
σεμνύνομαι, οὐδὲ τῷ γραφεὶς ἀποφυγεῖν, ἀλλὰ καὶ
τῷ συμφέροντα θεῖναι τὸν νόμον καὶ τῷ πεῖραν ἔργῳ
δεδωκέναι. πάντα γὰρ τὸν πόλεμον τῶν ἀποστόλων
γιγνομένων κατὰ τὸν νόμον τὸν ἐμὸν οὐχ ἱκετηρίαν
ἔθηκε τριήραρχος οὐδεὶς πώποθ᾽ ὡς ἀδικούμενος παρ᾽
ὑμῖν, οὐκ ἐν Μουνυχίᾳ ἐκαθέζετο, οὐχ ὑπὸ τῶν ἀποστολέων ἐδέθη, οὐ τριήρης οὔτ᾽ ἔξω καταληφθεῖσα
ἀπώλετο τῇ πόλει, οὔτ᾽ αὐτοῦ ἀπελείφθη οὐ δυναμένη
108 ἀνάγεσθαι. καίτοι κατὰ τοὺς προτέρους νόμους
ἅπαντα ταῦτα ἐγίγνετο. τὸ δ᾽ αἴτιον, ἐν τοῖς
πένησιν ἦν τὸ λειτουργεῖν· πολλὰ δὴ τὰ ἀδύνατα
συνέβαινεν. ἐγὼ δ᾽ ἐκ τῶν ἀπόρων εἰς τοὺς εὐπό-
ρους μετήνεγκα τὰς τριηραρχίας· πάντ᾽ οὖν τὰ
δέοντα ἐγίγνετο. καὶ μὴν καὶ κατ᾽ αὐτὸ τοῦτο
ἄξιός εἰμι ἐπαίνου τυχεῖν, ὅτι πάντα τὰ τοιαῦτα

προηρούμην πολιτεύματα, ἀφ' ὧν ἅμα δόξαι καὶ
τιμαὶ καὶ δυνάμεις συνέβαινον τῇ πόλει· βάσκανον
δὲ καὶ πικρὸν καὶ κακόηθες οὐδέν ἐστι πολίτευμα
ἐμὸν, οὐδὲ ταπεινὸν, οὐδὲ τῆς πόλεως ἀνάξιον. ταὐτὸ 109
τοίνυν ἦθος ἔχων ἔν τε τοῖς κατὰ τὴν πόλιν πολιτεύμασι καὶ ἐν τοῖς Ἑλληνικοῖς φανήσομαι· οὔτε
γὰρ ἐν τῇ πόλει τὰς παρὰ τῶν πλουσίων χάριτας
μᾶλλον ἢ τὰ τῶν πολλῶν δίκαια εἱλόμην, οὔτ' ἐν
τοῖς Ἑλληνικοῖς τὰ Φιλίππου δῶρα καὶ τὴν ξενίαν
ἠγάπησα ἀντὶ τῶν κοινῇ πᾶσι τοῖς Ἕλλησι συμφερόντων.

Ἡγοῦμαι τοίνυν λοιπὸν εἶναί μοι περὶ τοῦ κη- 110
ρύγματος εἰπεῖν καὶ τῶν εὐθυνῶν· τὸ γὰρ ὡς τὰ
ἄριστά τε ἔπραττον καὶ διὰ παντὸς εὔνους εἰμὶ καὶ
πρόθυμος εὖ ποιεῖν ὑμᾶς, ἱκανῶς ἐκ τῶν εἰρημένων
δεδηλῶσθαί μοι νομίζω. καίτοι τὰ μέγιστά γε τῶν
πεπολιτευμένων καὶ πεπραγμένων ἐμαυτῷ παραλείπω, ὑπολαμβάνων πρῶτον μὲν ἐφεξῆς τοὺς περὶ
αὐτοῦ τοῦ παρανόμου λόγους ἀποδοῦναί με δεῖν,
εἶτα, κἂν μηδὲν εἴπω περὶ τῶν λοιπῶν πολιτευμάτων, ὁμοίως παρ' ὑμῶν ἑκάστῳ τὸ συνειδὸς ὑπάρχειν
μοι.

Τῶν μὲν οὖν λόγων, οὓς οὗτος ἄνω καὶ κάτω 111
διακυκῶν ἔλεγε περὶ τῶν παραγεγραμμένων νόμων,
οὔτε μὰ τοὺς θεοὺς ὑμᾶς οἶμαι μανθάνειν οὔτ' αὐτὸς
ἐδυνάμην συνεῖναι τοὺς πολλούς· ἁπλῶς δὲ τὴν
ὀρθὴν περὶ τῶν δικαίων διαλέξομαι. τοσούτου γὰρ

δέω λέγειν ὡς οὐκ εἰμὶ ὑπεύθυνος, ὃ νῦν οὗτος διέβαλλε καὶ διωρίζετο, ὥσθ' ἅπαντα τὸν βίον ὑπεύθυνος
εἶναι ὁμολογῶ ὧν ἢ διακεχείρικα ἢ πεπολίτευμαι παρ'
112 ὑμῖν. ὧν μέντοι γε ἐκ τῆς ἰδίας οὐσίας ἐπαγγειλάμενος δέδωκα τῷ δήμῳ, οὐδεμίαν ἡμέραν ὑπεύθυνος
εἶναί φημι (ἀκούεις Αἰσχίνη;) οὐδ' ἄλλον οὐδένα,
οὐδ' ἂν τῶν ἐννέα ἀρχόντων τις ὢν τύχῃ. τίς γάρ
ἐστι νόμος τοσαύτης ἀδικίας καὶ μισανθρωπίας
μεστὸς ὥστε τὸν δόντα τι τῶν ἰδίων καὶ ποιήσαντα
πρᾶγμα φιλάνθρωπον καὶ φιλόδωρον τῆς χάριτος
μὲν ἀποστερεῖν, εἰς τοὺς συκοφάντας δ' ἄγειν, καὶ
τούτους ἐπὶ τὰς εὐθύνας ὧν ἔδωκεν ἐφιστάναι; οὐδὲ
εἷς. εἰ δέ φησιν οὗτος, δειξάτω, κἀγὼ στέρξω καὶ
113 σιωπήσομαι. ἀλλ' οὐκ ἔστιν, ὦ ἄνδρες Ἀθηναῖοι,
ἀλλ' οὗτος συκοφαντῶν, ὅτι ἐπὶ τῷ θεωρικῷ τότε
ὢν ἐπέδωκα τὰ χρήματα, "ἐπῄνεσεν αὐτόν," φησίν,
"ἡ βουλὴ ὑπεύθυνον ὄντα." οὐ περὶ τούτων γε
οὐδενός, ὧν ὑπεύθυνος ἦν, ἀλλ' ἐφ' οἷς ἐπέδωκα,
ὦ συκοφάντα. ἀλλὰ καὶ τειχοποιὸς ἦσθα, φησί.
καὶ διά γε τοῦτο ὀρθῶς ἐπῃνούμην, ὅτι τἀνηλωμένα
ἐπέδωκα καὶ οὐκ ἐλογιζόμην. ὁ μὲν γὰρ λογισμὸς
εὐθυνῶν καὶ τῶν ἐξετασόντων προσδεῖται, ἡ δὲ δωρεὰ
χάριτος καὶ ἐπαίνου δικαία ἐστὶ τυγχάνειν· διόπερ
114 ταῦτ' ἔγραψεν ὁδὶ περὶ ἐμοῦ· ὅτι δ' οὕτω ταῦτα οὐ
μόνον ἐν τοῖς νόμοις, ἀλλὰ καὶ ἐν τοῖς ὑμετέροις
ἔθεσιν ὥρισται, ἐγὼ ῥᾳδίως πολλαχόθεν δείξω.
πρῶτον μὲν γὰρ Ναυσικλῆς στρατηγῶν, ἐφ' οἷς ἀπὸ

τῶν ἰδίων προεῖτο, πολλάκις ἐστεφάνωται ὑφ' ὑμῶν·
εἶθ' ὅτε τὰς ἀσπίδας Διότιμος ἔδωκε καὶ πάλιν
Χαρίδημος, ἐστεφανοῦντο· εἶθ οὑτοσὶ Νεοπτόλεμος
πολλῶν ἔργων ἐπιστάτης ὤν, ἐφ' οἷς ἐπέδωκε, τετίμηται. σχέτλιον γὰρ ἂν εἴη τοῦτό γε, εἰ τῷ τινὰ
ἀρχὴν ἄρχοντι ἢ διδόναι τῇ πόλει τὰ ἑαυτοῦ διὰ τὴν
ἀρχὴν μὴ ἐξέσται, ἢ τῶν δοθέντων ἀντὶ τοῦ κομί-
σασθαι χάριν εὐθύνας ὑφέξει. Ὅτι τοίνυν ταῦτ' 115
ἀληθῆ λέγω, λέγε τὰ ψηφίσματά μοι τὰ τούτοις
γεγενημένα αὐτὰ λαβών. λέγε.

ΨΗΦΙΣΜΑ.

[Ἄρχων Δημόνικος Φλυεύς, βοηδρομιῶνος ἕκτῃ μετ' εἰκάδα, γνώμῃ βουλῆς καὶ δήμου, Καλλίας Φρεάρριος εἶπεν ὅτι δοκεῖ τῇ βουλῇ καὶ τῷ δήμῳ στεφανῶσαι Ναυσικλέα τὸν ἐπὶ τῶν ὅπλων, ὅτι Ἀθηναίων ὁπλιτῶν δισχιλίων ὄντων ἐν Ἴμβρῳ καὶ βοηθούντων τοῖς κατοικοῦσιν Ἀθηναίων τὴν νῆσον, οὐ δυναμένου Φίλωνος τοῦ ἐπὶ τῆς διοικήσεως κεχειροτονημένου διὰ τοὺς χειμῶνας πλεῦσαι καὶ μισθοδοτῆσαι τοὺς ὁπλίτας, ἐκ τῆς ἰδίας οὐσίας ἔδωκε καὶ οὐκ εἰσέπραξε τὸν δῆμον, καὶ ἀναγορεῦσαι τὸν στέφανον Διονυσίοις τραγῳδοῖς καινοῖς.]

ΕΤΕΡΟΝ ΨΗΦΙΣΜΑ.

[Εἶπε Καλλίας Φρεάρριος, πρυτάνεων λεγόντων βουλῆς 116
γνώμῃ, ἐπειδὴ Χαρίδημος ὁ ἐπὶ τῶν ὁπλιτῶν, ἀποσταλεὶς εἰς Σαλαμῖνα, καὶ Διότιμος ὁ ἐπὶ τῶν ἱππέων, ἐν τῇ ἐπὶ τοῦ ποταμοῦ μάχῃ τῶν στρατιωτῶν τινῶν ὑπὸ τῶν πολεμίων σκυλευθέντων, ἐκ τῶν ἰδίων ἀναλωμάτων καθώπλισαν τοὺς νεανίσκους ἀσπίσιν ὀκτακοσίαις, δεδόχθαι τῇ βουλῇ καὶ τῷ δήμῳ στεφα-

νῶσαι Χαρίδημον καὶ Διότιμον χρυσῷ στεφάνῳ, καὶ ἀναγορεῦσαι Παναθηναίοις τοῖς μεγάλοις ἐν τῷ γυμνικῷ ἀγῶνι καὶ Διονυσίοις τραγῳδοῖς καινοῖς· τῆς δὲ ἀναγορεύσεως ἐπιμεληθῆναι θεσμοθέτας, πρυτάνεις, ἀγωνοθέτας.]

117 Τούτων ἕκαστος, Αἰσχίνη, τῆς μὲν ἀρχῆς ἧς ἦρχεν ὑπεύθυνος ἦν, ἐφ' οἷς δ' ἐστεφανοῦτο, οὐχ ὑπεύθυνος. οὐκοῦν οὐδ' ἐγώ· ταὐτὰ γὰρ δίκαιά ἐστί μοι περὶ τῶν αὐτῶν τοῖς ἄλλοις δήπου. ἐπέδωκα· ἐπαινοῦμαι διὰ ταῦτα, οὐκ ὢν ὧν ἐπέδωκα ὑπεύθυνος. ἦρχον· καὶ δέδωκά γε εὐθύνας ἐκείνων, οὐχ ὧν ἐπέδωκα. νὴ Δί', ἀλλ' ἀδίκως ἦρξα; εἶτα παρών, ὅτε με εἰσῆγον οἱ λογισταί, οὐ κατηγόρεις;

118 Ἵνα τοίνυν εἰδῆτε ὅτι αὐτὸς οὗτός μοι μαρτυρεῖ ἐφ' οἷς οὐχ ὑπεύθυνος ἦν ἐστεφανῶσθαι, λαβὼν ἀνάγνωθι τὸ ψήφισμα ὅλον τὸ γραφέν μοι. οἷς γὰρ οὐκ ἐγράψατο τοῦ προβουλεύματος, τούτοις ἃ διώκει συκοφαντῶν φανήσεται. λέγε.

ΨΗΦΙΣΜΑ.

[Ἐπὶ ἄρχοντος Εὐθυκλέους, πυανεψιῶνος ἐνάτῃ ἀπιόντος, φυλῆς πρυτανευούσης Οἰνηΐδος, Κτησιφῶν Λεωσθένους Ἀναφλύστιος εἶπεν, ἐπειδὴ Δημοσθένης Δημοσθένους Παιανιεὺς γενόμενος ἐπιμελητὴς τῆς τῶν τειχῶν ἐπισκευῆς καὶ προσαναλώσας εἰς τὰ ἔργα ἀπὸ τῆς ἰδίας οὐσίας τρία τάλαντα ἐπέδωκε ταῦτα τῷ δήμῳ. καὶ ἐπὶ τοῦ θεωρικοῦ κατασταθεὶς ἐπέδωκε τοῖς ἐκ πασῶν τῶν φυλῶν θεωροῖς ἑκατὸν μνᾶς εἰς θυσίας, δεδόχθαι τῇ βουλῇ καὶ τῷ δήμῳ τῷ Ἀθηναίων ἐπαινέσαι Δημοσθένην Δημοσθένους Παιανιέα ἀρετῆς ἕνεκα καὶ καλοκαγαθίας ἧς ἔχων διατελεῖ ἐν παντὶ καιρῷ εἰς τὸν δῆμον τὸν Ἀθηναίων, καὶ στεφανῶσαι χρυσῷ στεφάνῳ, καὶ ἀναγορεῦσαι τὸν στέφανον ἐν τῷ θεάτρῳ Διονυσίοις τραγῳδοῖς καινοῖς· τῆς δὲ ἀναγορεύσεως ἐπιμεληθῆναι τὸν ἀγωνοθέτην.]

Οὐκοῦν ἃ μὲν ἐπέδωκα, ταῦτ' ἐστὶν, ὧν οὐδὲν σὺ 119
γέγραψαι· ἃ δέ φησιν ἡ βουλὴ δεῖν ἀντὶ τούτων γενέσθαι μοι, ταῦτ' ἔσθ' ἃ διώκεις. τὸ λαβεῖν οὖν τὰ διδόμενα ὁμολογῶν ἔννομον εἶναι, τὸ χάριν τούτων ἀποδοῦναι παρανόμων γράφει. ὁ δὲ παμπόνηρος ἄνθρωπος καὶ θεοῖς ἐχθρὸς καὶ βάσκανος ὄντως ποῖός τις ἂν εἴη πρὸς θεῶν; οὐχ ὁ τοιοῦτος;

Καὶ μὴν περὶ τοῦ γ' ἐν τῷ θεάτρῳ κηρύττεσθαι, 120
τὸ μὲν μυριάκις μυρίους κεκηρῦχθαι παραλείπω καὶ τὸ πολλάκις αὐτὸς ἐστεφανῶσθαι πρότερον. ἀλλὰ πρὸς θεῶν οὕτω σκαιὸς εἶ καὶ ἀναίσθητος, Αἰσχίνη, ὥστ' οὐ δύνασαι λογίσασθαι ὅτι τῷ μὲν στεφανουμένῳ τὸν αὐτὸν ἔχει ζῆλον ὁ στέφανος, ὅπου ἂν ἀναρρηθῇ, τοῦ δὲ τῶν στεφανούντων ἕνεκα συμφέροντος ἐν τῷ θεάτρῳ γίγνεται τὸ κήρυγμα; οἱ γὰρ ἀκούσαντες ἅπαντες εἰς τὸ ποιεῖν εὖ τὴν πόλιν προτρέπονται, καὶ τοὺς ἀποδιδόντας τὴν χάριν μᾶλλον ἐπαινοῦσι τοῦ στεφανουμένου· διόπερ τὸν νόμον τοῦτον ἡ πόλις γέγραφεν. Λέγε δ' αὐτόν μοι τὸν νόμον λαβών.

ΝΟΜΟΣ.

["Οσους στεφανοῦσί τινες τῶν δήμων, τὰς ἀναγορεύσεις τῶν στεφάνων ποιεῖσθαι ἐν αὐτοῖς ἑκάστους τοῖς ἰδίοις δήμοις, ἐὰν μή τινας ὁ δῆμος ὁ τῶν Ἀθηναίων ἢ ἡ βουλὴ στεφανοῖ· τούτους δ' ἐξεῖναι ἐν τῷ θεάτρῳ Διονυσίοις ἀναγορεύεσθαι.]

121 Ἀκούεις, Αἰσχίνη, τοῦ νόμου λέγοντος σαφῶς,
πλὴν ἐάν τινας ὁ δῆμος ἢ ἡ βουλὴ ψηφίσηται·
τούτους δὲ ἀναγορευέτω. τί οὖν, ὦ ταλαίπωρε,
συκοφαντεῖς; τί λόγους πλάττεις; τί σαυτὸν οὐκ
ἐλλεβορίζεις ἐπὶ τούτοις; ἀλλ' οὐδ' αἰσχύνει φθόνου δίκην εἰσάγων, οὐκ ἀδικήματος οὐδενός, καὶ
νόμους τοὺς μὲν μεταποιῶν, τῶν δ' ἀφαιρῶν μέρη,
οὓς ὅλους δίκαιον ἦν ἀναγιγνώσκεσθαι τοῖς γε ὀμω-
122 μοκόσι κατὰ τοὺς νόμους ψηφιεῖσθαι; ἔπειτα
τοιαῦτα ποιῶν λέγεις ἃ δεῖ προσεῖναι τῷ δημοτικῷ,
ὥσπερ ἀνδριάντα ἐκδεδωκὼς κατὰ συγγραφήν, εἶτ'
οὐκ ἔχοντα ἃ προσῆκεν ἐκ τῆς συγγραφῆς κομιζό-
μενος, ἢ λόγῳ τοὺς δημοτικούς, ἀλλ' οὐ τοῖς πράγμασι καὶ τοῖς πολιτεύμασι γιγνωσκομένους. καὶ
βοᾷς ῥητὰ καὶ ἄρρητα ὀνομάζων, ὥσπερ ἐξ ἁμάξης,
123 ἃ σοὶ καὶ τῷ σῷ γένει πρόσεστιν, οὐκ ἐμοί. καίτοι
καὶ τοῦτο, ὦ ἄνδρες Ἀθηναῖοι. ἐγὼ λοιδορίαν
κατηγορίας τούτῳ διαφέρειν ἡγοῦμαι, τῷ τὴν μὲν
κατηγορίαν ἀδικήματ' ἔχειν, ὧν ἐν τοῖς νόμοις εἰσὶν
αἱ τιμωρίαι, τὴν δὲ λοιδορίαν βλασφημίας, ἃς κατὰ
τὴν αὑτῶν φύσιν τοῖς ἐχθροῖς περὶ ἀλλήλων συμβαί-
νει λέγειν. οἰκοδομῆσαι δὲ τοὺς προγόνους ταυτὶ
τὰ δικαστήρια ὑπείληφα οὐχ ἵνα συλλέξαντες ὑμᾶς
εἰς ταῦτα ἀπὸ τῶν ἰδίων κακῶς τὰ ἀπόρρητα λέγω-
μεν ἀλλήλους, ἀλλ' ἵνα ἐξελέγχωμεν, ἐάν τις ἠδικη-
124 κώς τι τυγχάνῃ τὴν πόλιν. ταῦτα τοίνυν εἰδὼς
Αἰσχίνης οὐδὲν ἧττον ἐμοῦ πομπεύειν ἀντὶ τοῦ

κατηγορεῖν εἵλετο. οὐ μὴν οὐδ' ἐνταῦθα ἔλαττον
ἔχων δίκαιός ἐστιν ἀπελθεῖν. ἤδη δ' ἐπὶ ταῦτα
πορεύσομαι, τοσοῦτον αὐτὸν ἐρωτήσας. πότερόν
σέ τις, Αἰσχίνη, τῆς πόλεως ἐχθρὸν ἢ ἐμὸν εἶναι
φῇ; ἐμὸν δῆλον ὅτι. εἶτα οὗ μὲν ἦν παρ' ἐμοῦ δίκην
κατὰ τοὺς νόμους ὑπὲρ τούτων λαβεῖν, εἴπερ ἠδίκουν,
ἐξέλιπες, ἐν ταῖς εὐθύναις, ἐν ταῖς γραφαῖς, ἐν ταῖς
ἄλλαις κρίσεσιν· οὗ δ' ἐγὼ μὲν ἀθῷος ἅπασι, τοῖς 125
νόμοις, τῷ χρόνῳ, τῇ προθεσμίᾳ, τῷ κεκρίσθαι περὶ
πάντων πολλάκις πρότερον, τῷ μηδεπώποτε ἐξελεγ-
χθῆναι μηδὲν ὑμᾶς ἀδικῶν, τῇ πόλει δ' ἢ πλέον ἢ
ἔλαττον ἀνάγκη τῶν γε δημοσίᾳ πεπραγμένων
μετεῖναι τῆς δόξης, ἐνταῦθα ἀπήντηκας; ὅρα μὴ
τούτων μὲν ἐχθρὸς ᾖς, ἐμὸς δὲ προσποιῇ.

Ἐπειδὴ τοίνυν ἡ μὲν εὐσεβὴς καὶ δικαία ψῆφος 126
ἅπασι δέδεικται, δεῖ δέ με, ὡς ἔοικε, καίπερ οὐ φιλο-
λοίδορον ὄντα φύσει, διὰ τὰς ὑπὸ τούτου βλασφημίας εἰρημένας ἀντὶ πολλῶν καὶ ψευδῶν αὐτὰ τἀναγκαιότατ' εἰπεῖν περὶ αὐτοῦ, καὶ δεῖξαι τίς ὢν
καὶ τίνων ῥᾳδίως οὕτως ἄρχει τοῦ κακῶς λέγειν, καὶ
λόγους τίνας διασύρει, αὐτὸς εἰρηκὼς ἃ τίς οὐκ ἂν
ὤκνησε τῶν μετρίων ἀνθρώπων φθέγξασθαι; — εἰ 127
γὰρ Αἰακὸς ἢ Ῥαδάμανθυς ἢ Μίνως ἦν κατηγορῶν,
ἀλλὰ μὴ σπερμολόγος, περίτριμμα ἀγορᾶς, ὄλεθρος
γραμματεύς, οὐκ ἂν αὐτὸν οἶμαι τοιαῦτ' εἰπεῖν οὐδ'
ἂν οὕτως ἐπαχθεῖς λόγους πορίσασθαι, ὥσπερ ἐν
τραγῳδίᾳ βοῶντα ὦ γῆ καὶ ἥλιε καὶ ἀρετὴ καὶ τὰ

τοιαῦτα, καὶ πάλιν σύνεσιν καὶ παιδείαν ἐπικαλού-
μενον, ᾗ τὰ καλὰ καὶ τὰ αἰσχρὰ διαγιγνώσκεται·
128 ταῦτα γὰρ δήπουθεν ἠκουέτ' αὐτοῦ λέγοντος. σοὶ
δὲ ἀρετῆς, ὦ κάθαρμα, ἢ τοῖς σοῖς τίς μετουσία; ἢ
καλῶν ἢ μὴ τοιούτων τίς διάγνωσις; πόθεν ἢ πῶς
ἀξιωθέντι; ποῦ δὲ παιδείας σοι θέμις μνησθῆναι, ἧς
τῶν μὲν ὡς ἀληθῶς τετυχηκότων οὐδ' ἂν εἷς εἴποι
περὶ αὑτοῦ τοιοῦτον οὐδὲν, ἀλλὰ κἂν ἑτέρου λέγοντος ἐρυθριάσειε, τοῖς δ' ἀπολειφθεῖσι μὲν ὥσπερ
σὺ, προσποιουμένοις δ' ὑπ' ἀναισθησίας τὸ τοὺς
ἀκούοντας ἀλγεῖν ποιεῖν, ὅταν λέγωσιν, οὐ τὸ δοκεῖν
τοιούτοις εἶναι περίεστιν.

129 Οὐκ ἀπορῶν δ' ὅ τι χρὴ περὶ σοῦ καὶ τῶν σῶν εἰπεῖν, ἀπορῶ τοῦ πρώτου μνησθῶ, πότερ' ὡς ὁ πατήρ
σου Τρόμης ἐδούλευε παρ' Ἐλπίᾳ τῷ πρὸς τῷ Θησείῳ
διδάσκοντι γράμματα, χοίνικας παχείας ἔχων καὶ ξύλον, ἢ ὡς ἡ μήτηρ σου τοῖς μεθημερινοῖς γάμοις ἐν τῷ
κλεισίῳ τῷ πρὸς τῷ καλαμίτῃ ἥρωϊ χρωμένη τὸν καλὸν
ἀνδριάντα καὶ τριταγωνιστὴν ἄκρον ἐξέθρεψέ σε;
ἀλλὰ πάντες ἴσασι ταῦτα, κἂν ἐγὼ μὴ λέγω. ἀλλ'
ὡς ὁ τριηραύλης Φορμίων, ὁ Δίωνος τοῦ Φρεαρρίου
δοῦλος, ἀνέστησεν αὐτὴν ἀπὸ ταύτης τῆς καλῆς ἐρ-
γασίας; ἀλλὰ νὴ τὸν Δία καὶ τοὺς θεοὺς ὀκνῶ μὴ
περὶ σοῦ τὰ προσήκοντα λέγων αὐτὸς οὐ προσή-
130 κοντας ἐμαυτῷ δόξω προῃρῆσθαι λόγους. ταῦτα
μὲν οὖν ἐάσω, ἀπ' αὐτῶν δὲ ὧν αὐτὸς βεβίωκεν
ἄρξομαι· οὐδὲ γὰρ ὧν ἔτυχεν ἦν, ἀλλ' οἷς ὁ δῆμος

καταρᾶται. ὀψὲ γάρ ποτε—, ὀψὲ λέγω; χθὲς
μὲν οὖν καὶ πρώην ἅμ' Ἀθηναῖος καὶ ῥήτωρ γέγονε,
καὶ δύο συλλαβὰς προσθεὶς τὸν μὲν πατέρα ἀντὶ
Τρόμητος ἐποίησεν Ἀτρόμητον, τὴν δὲ μητέρα σεμνῶς πάνυ Γλαυκοθέαν ὠνόμασεν, ἣν Ἔμπουσαν
ἅπαντες ἴσασι καλουμένην, ἐκ τοῦ πάντα ποιεῖν καὶ
πάσχειν δηλονότι ταύτης τῆς ἐπωνυμίας τυχοῦσαν· 131
πόθεν γὰρ ἄλλοθεν; ἀλλ' ὅμως οὕτως ἀχάριστος εἶ
καὶ πονηρὸς φύσει ὥστ' ἐλεύθερος ἐκ δούλου καὶ
πλούσιος ἐκ πτωχοῦ διὰ τουτουσὶ γεγονὼς οὐχ
ὅπως χάριν αὐτοῖς ἔχεις, ἀλλὰ μισθώσας σαυτὸν
κατὰ τουτωνὶ πολιτεύει. καὶ περὶ ὧν μὲν ἔστι τις
ἀμφισβήτησις, ὡς ἄρα ὑπὲρ τῆς πόλεως εἴρηκεν,
ἐάσω· ἃ δ' ὑπὲρ τῶν ἐχθρῶν φανερῶς ἀπεδείχθη
πράττων, ταῦτα ἀναμνήσω.

Τίς γὰρ ὑμῶν οὐκ οἶδε τὸν ἀποψηφισθέντα Ἀντι- 132
φῶντα, ὃς ἐπαγγειλάμενος Φιλίππῳ τὰ νεώρια ἐμπρή-
σειν εἰς τὴν πόλιν ἦλθεν; ὃν λαβόντος ἐμοῦ κεκρυμ-
μένον ἐν Πειραιεῖ καὶ καταστήσαντος εἰς τὴν ἐκκλησίαν βοῶν ὁ βάσκανος οὗτος καὶ κεκραγώς, ὡς ἐν
δημοκρατίᾳ δεινὰ ποιῶ τοὺς ἠτυχηκότας τῶν πολιτῶν ὑβρίζων καὶ ἐπ' οἰκίας βαδίζων ἄνευ ψηφίσματος, ἀφεθῆναι ἐποίησεν. καὶ εἰ μὴ ἡ βουλὴ ἡ ἐξ 133
Ἀρείου πάγου τὸ πρᾶγμα αἰσθομένη καὶ τὴν ὑμετέραν ἄγνοιαν ἐν οὐ δέοντι συμβεβηκυῖαν ἰδοῦσα ἐπεζήτησε τὸν ἄνθρωπον καὶ συλλαβοῦσα ἐπανήγαγεν
ὡς ὑμᾶς, ἐξήρπαστ' ἂν ὁ τοιοῦτος καὶ τὸ δίκην δοῦ-

ναι διαδὺς ἐξεπέμπ' ετ' ἂν ὑπὸ τοῦ σεμνολόγου του-
τουί· νῦν δ' ὑμεῖς στρεβλώσαντες αὐτὸν ἀπεκτεί-
134 νατε, ὡς ἔδει γε καὶ τοῦτον. τοιγαροῦν εἰδυῖα ταῦτα
ἡ βουλὴ ἡ ἐξ Ἀρείου πάγου τότε τούτῳ πεπραγμένα,
χειροτονησάντων αὐτὸν ὑμῶν σύνδικον ὑπὲρ τοῦ ἱεροῦ
τοῦ ἐν Δήλῳ ἀπὸ τῆς αὐτῆς ἀγνοίας ἧσπερ πολλὰ
προΐεσθε τῶν κοινῶν, ὡς προσείλεσθε κἀκείνην καὶ
τοῦ πράγματος κυρίαν ἐποιήσατε, τοῦτον μὲν εὐθὺς
ἀπήλασεν ὡς προδότην, Ὑπερείδῃ δὲ λέγειν προσέ-
ταξε· καὶ ταῦτα ἀπὸ τοῦ βωμοῦ φέρουσα τὴν ψῆφον
ἔπραξε, καὶ οὐδεμία ψῆφος ἠνέχθη τῷ μιαρῷ τούτῳ.

135 Καὶ ὅτι ταῦτ' ἀληθῆ λέγω, κάλει μοι τούτων τοὺς μάρτυρας.

ΜΑΡΤΥΡΕΣ.

[Μαρτυροῦσι Δημοσθένει ὑπὲρ ἁπάντων οἵδε, Καλλίας Σουνιεύς, Ζήνων Φλυεύς, Κλέων Φαληρεύς, Δημόνικος Μαραθώνιος, ὅτι τοῦ δήμου ποτὲ χειροτονήσαντος Αἰσχίνην σύνδικον ὑπὲρ τοῦ ἱεροῦ τοῦ ἐν Δήλῳ εἰς τοὺς Ἀμφικτύονας συνεδρεύσαντες ἡμεῖς ἐκρίναμεν Ὑπερείδην ἄξιον εἶναι μᾶλλον ὑπὲρ τῆς πόλεως λέγειν, καὶ ἀπεστάλη Ὑπερείδης.]

Οὐκοῦν ὅτε τούτου λέγοντος ἀπήλασεν ἡ βουλὴ καὶ προσέταξεν ἑτέρῳ, τότε καὶ προδότην εἶναι καὶ κακόνουν ὑμῖν ἀπέφηνεν.

136 Ἓν μὲν τοίνυν τοῦτο τοιοῦτο πολίτευμα τοῦ νεανίου τούτου, ὅμοιόν γε, οὐ γάρ; οἷς ἐμοῦ κατηγορεῖ· ἕτερον δὲ ἀναμιμνήσκεσθε. ὅτε γὰρ Πύθωνα Φίλιππος ἔπεμψε τὸν Βυζάντιον καὶ παρὰ τῶν

αὑτοῦ συμμάχων πάντων συνέπεμψε πρέσβεις, ὡς ἐν αἰσχύνῃ ποιήσων τὴν πόλιν καὶ δείξων ἀδικοῦσαν, τότε ἐγὼ μὲν τῷ Πύθωνι θρασυνομένῳ καὶ πολλῷ ῥέοντι καθ' ὑμῶν οὐχ ὑπεχώρησα, ἀλλ' ἀναστὰς ἀντεῖπον καὶ τὰ τῆς πόλεως δίκαια οὐχὶ προὔδωκα, ἀλλ' ἀδικοῦντα Φίλιππον ἐξήλεγξα φανερῶς οὕτως ὥστε τοὺς ἐκείνου συμμάχους αὐτοὺς ἀνισταμένους ὁμολογεῖν· οὗτος δὲ συνηγωνίζετο καὶ τἀναντία ἐμαρτύρει τῇ πατρίδι, καὶ ταῦτα ψευδῆ.

137 Καὶ οὐκ ἀπέχρη ταῦτα, ἀλλὰ πάλιν μετὰ ταῦθ' ὕστερον Ἀναξίνῳ τῷ κατασκόπῳ συνιὼν εἰς τὴν Θράσωνος οἰκίαν ἐλήφθη. καίτοι ὅστις τῷ ὑπὸ τῶν πολεμίων πεμφθέντι μόνος μόνῳ συνῄει καὶ ἐκοινολογεῖτο, οὗτος αὐτὸς ὑπῆρχε τῇ φύσει κατάσκοπος καὶ πολέμιος τῇ πατρίδι. Καὶ ὅτι ταῦτ' ἀληθῆ λέγω, κάλει μοι τούτων τοὺς μάρτυρας.

ΜΑΡΤΥΡΕΣ.

[Τελέδημος Κλέωνος, Ὑπερείδης Καλλαίσχρου, Νικόμαχος Διοφάντου μαρτυροῦσι Δημοσθένει καὶ ἐπωμόσαντο ἐπὶ τῶν στρατηγῶν εἰδέναι Αἰσχίνην Ἀτρομήτου Κοθωκίδην συνερχόμενον νυκτὸς εἰς τὴν Θράσωνος οἰκίαν καὶ κοινολογούμενον Ἀναξίνῳ, ὃς ἐκρίθη εἶναι κατάσκοπος παρὰ Φιλίππου· αὗται ἀπεδόθησαν αἱ μαρτυρίαι ἐπὶ Νικίου, ἑκατομβαιῶνος τρίτῃ ἱσταμένου.]

138 Μυρία τοίνυν ἕτερ' εἰπεῖν ἔχων περὶ αὐτοῦ παραλείπω. καὶ γὰρ οὕτω πως ἔχει. πολλὰ ἂν ἐγὼ

ἔτι τούτων ἔχοιμι δεῖξαι, ὧν οὗτος κατ' ἐκείνους τοὺς χρόνους τοῖς μὲν ἐχθροῖς ὑπηρετῶν, ἐμοὶ δ' ἐπηρεάζων εὑρέθη. ἀλλ' οὐ τίθεται ταῦτα παρ' ὑμῖν εἰς ἀκριβῆ μνήμην οὐδ' ἣν προσῆκεν ὀργήν, ἀλλὰ δεδώκατε ἔθει τινὶ φαύλῳ πολλὴν ἐξουσίαν τῷ βουλομένῳ τὸν λέγοντά τι τῶν ὑμῖν συμφερόντων ὑποσκελίζειν καὶ συκοφαντεῖν, τῆς ἐπὶ ταῖς λοιδορίαις ἡδονῆς καὶ χάριτος τὸ τῆς πόλεως συμφέρον ἀνταλλαττόμενοι· διόπερ ῥᾷόν ἐστι καὶ ἀσφαλέστερον ἀεὶ τοῖς ἐχθροῖς ὑπηρετοῦντα μισθαρνεῖν ἢ τὴν ὑπὲρ ὑμῶν ἑλόμενον τάξιν πολιτεύεσθαι.

139 Καὶ τὸ μὲν δὴ πρὸ τοῦ πολεμεῖν φανερῶς συναγωνίζεσθαι Φιλίππῳ δεινὸν μέν, ὦ γῆ καὶ θεοί, πῶς γὰρ οὔ; κατὰ τῆς πατρίδος· δότε δ', εἰ βούλεσθε, δότε αὐτῷ τοῦτο. ἀλλ' ἐπειδὴ φανερῶς ἤδη τὰ πλοῖα ἐσεσύλητο, Χερρόνησος ἐπορθεῖτο, ἐπὶ τὴν Ἀττικὴν ἐπορεύεθ' ἅνθρωπος, οὐκέτ' ἐν ἀμφισβητησίμῳ τὰ πράγματα ἦν, ἀλλ' ἐνειστήκει πόλεμος, ὅ τι μὲν πώποτ' ἔπραξεν ὑπὲρ ὑμῶν ὁ βάσκανος οὗτος ἰαμβειοφάγος, οὐκ ἂν ἔχοι δεῖξαι, οὐδ' ἔστιν οὔτε μεῖζον οὔτ' ἔλαττον ψήφισμα οὐδὲν Αἰσχίνῃ ὑπὲρ τῶν συμφερόντων τῇ πόλει. εἰ δέ φησι, νῦν δειξάτω ἐν τῷ ἐμῷ ὕδατι. ἀλλ' οὐκ ἔστιν οὐδέν. καίτοι δυοῖν αὐτὸν ἀνάγκη θάτερον, ἢ μηδὲν τοῖς πραττομένοις ὑπ' ἐμοῦ τότ' ἔχοντ' ἐγκαλεῖν μὴ γράφειν παρὰ ταῦθ' ἕτερα, ἢ τὸ τῶν ἐχθρῶν συμφέρον ζητοῦντα μὴ φέρειν εἰς μέσον τὰ τούτων ἀμείνω.

Ἆρ' οὖν οὐδ' ἔλεγεν, ὥσπερ οὐδ' ἔγραφεν, ἡνίκα 140
ἐργάσασθαί τι δέοι κακόν; οὐ μὲν οὖν ἦν εἰπεῖν ἑτέρῳ. καὶ τὰ μὲν ἄλλα καὶ φέρειν ἐδύναθ', ὡς ἔοικεν, ἡ πόλις καὶ ποιῶν οὗτος λανθάνειν· ἓν δ' ἐπεξειργάσατο, ὦ ἄνδρες Ἀθηναῖοι, τοιοῦτον ὃ πᾶσι τοῖς προτέροις ἐπέθηκε τέλος· περὶ οὗ τοὺς πολλοὺς ἀνήλωσε λόγους, τὰ τῶν Ἀμφισσέων τῶν Λοκρῶν διεξιὼν δόγματα, ὡς διαστρέψων τἀληθές. τὸ δ' οὐ τοιοῦτόν ἐστι. πόθεν; οὐδέποτ' ἐκνίψει σὺ τἀκεῖ πεπραγμένα σαυτῷ· οὐχ οὕτω πολλὰ ἐρεῖς.

Καλῶ δ' ἐναντίον ὑμῶν, ὦ ἄνδρες Ἀθηναῖοι, τοὺς 141
θεοὺς πάντας καὶ πάσας, ὅσοι τὴν χώραν ἔχουσι τὴν Ἀττικήν, καὶ τὸν Ἀπόλλω τὸν Πύθιον, ὃς πατρῷός ἐστι τῇ πόλει, καὶ ἐπεύχομαι πᾶσι τούτοις, εἰ μὲν ἀληθῆ πρὸς ὑμᾶς εἴποιμι καὶ εἶπον τότ' εὐθὺς ἐν τῷ δήμῳ, ὅτε πρῶτον εἶδον τουτονὶ τὸν μιαρὸν τούτου τοῦ πράγματος ἁπτόμενον (ἔγνων γάρ, εὐθέως ἔγνων), εὐτυχίαν μοι δοῦναι καὶ σωτηρίαν, εἰ δὲ πρὸς ἔχθραν ἢ φιλονεικίας ἰδίας ἕνεκ' αἰτίαν ἐπάγω τούτῳ ψευδῆ, πάντων τῶν ἀγαθῶν ἀνόνητόν με ποιῆσαι.

Τί οὖν ταῦτ' ἐπήραμαι καὶ διετεινάμην οὑτωσὶ 142
σφοδρῶς; ὅτι καὶ γράμματ' ἔχων ἐν τῷ δημοσίῳ κείμενα, ἐξ ὧν ταῦτ' ἐπιδείξω σαφῶς, καὶ ὑμᾶς εἰδὼς τὰ πεπραγμένα μνημονεύοντας, ἐκεῖνο φοβοῦμαι, μὴ τῶν εἰργασμένων αὐτῷ κακῶν ὑποληφθῇ οὗτος ἐλάττων· ὅπερ πρότερον συνέβη, ὅτε τοὺς ταλαιπώρους

Φωκέας ἐποίησεν ἀπολέσθαι τὰ ψευδῆ δεῦρ' ἀπαγ-
143 γείλας. τὸν γὰρ ἐν Ἀμφίσσῃ πόλεμον, δι' ὃν εἰς
Ἐλάτειαν ἦλθε Φίλιππος καὶ δι' ὃν ᾑρέθη τῶν
Ἀμφικτυόνων ἡγεμών, ὃς ἅπαντ' ἀνέτρεψε τὰ τῶν
Ἑλλήνων, οὗτός ἐστιν ὁ συγκατασκευάσας καὶ πάντων εἷς ἀνὴρ τῶν μεγίστων αἴτιος κακῶν. καὶ τότ'
εὐθὺς ἐμοῦ διαμαρτυρομένου καὶ βοῶντος ἐν τῇ
ἐκκλησίᾳ "πόλεμον εἰς τὴν Ἀττικὴν εἰσάγεις, Αἰσχίνη, πόλεμον Ἀμφικτυονικόν" οἱ μὲν ἐκ παρακλή-
σεως συγκαθήμενοι οὐκ εἴων με λέγειν, οἱ δ' ἐθαύ-
μαζον καὶ κενὴν αἰτίαν διὰ τὴν ἰδίαν ἔχθραν ἐπάγειν
144 με ὑπελάμβανον αὐτῷ. ἥτις δ' ἡ φύσις, ὦ ἄνδρες
Ἀθηναῖοι, γέγονε τούτων τῶν πραγμάτων, καὶ τίνος
ἕνεκα ταῦτα συνεσκευάσθη καὶ πῶς ἐπράχθη, νῦν
ἀκούσατε, ἐπειδὴ τότε ἐκωλύθητε· καὶ γὰρ εὖ πρᾶγμα
συντεθὲν ὄψεσθε, καὶ μεγάλα ὠφελήσεσθε πρὸς ἱστο-
ρίαν τῶν κοινῶν, καὶ ὅση δεινότης ἦν ἐν τῷ Φιλίππῳ
θεάσεσθε.

145 Οὐκ ἦν τοῦ πρὸς ὑμᾶς πολέμου πέρας οὐδ' ἀπαλ-
λαγὴ Φιλίππῳ, εἰ μὴ Θηβαίους καὶ Θετταλοὺς
ἐχθροὺς ποιήσειε τῇ πόλει. ἀλλὰ καίπερ ἀθλίως
καὶ κακῶς τῶν στρατηγῶν τῶν ὑμετέρων πολεμούντων αὐτῷ ὅμως ὑπ' αὐτοῦ τοῦ πολέμου καὶ τῶν
λῃστῶν μυρία ἔπασχε κακά. οὔτε γὰρ ἐξήγετο τῶν
ἐκ τῆς χώρας γιγνομένων οὐδὲν οὔτ' εἰσήγετο ὧν
146 ἐδεῖτ' αὐτῷ· ἦν δὲ οὔτ' ἐν τῇ θαλάττῃ τότε κρείττων
ὑμῶν οὔτ' εἰς τὴν Ἀττικὴν ἐλθεῖν δυνατὸς μήτε Θετ-

ταλῶν ἀκολουθούντων μήτε Θηβαίων διιέντων· συνέ-
βαινε δὲ αὐτῷ τῷ πολέμῳ κρατοῦντι τοὺς ὁποιουσ-
δήποθ' ὑμεῖς ἐξεπέμπετε στρατηγούς (ἐῶ γὰρ τοῦτό
γε) αὐτῇ τῇ φύσει τοῦ τόπου καὶ τῶν ὑπαρχόντων
ἑκατέροις κακοπαθεῖν. εἰ μὲν οὖν τῆς ἰδίας ἕνεκ' 147
ἔχθρας ἢ τοὺς Θετταλοὺς ἢ τοὺς Θηβαίους συμπείθοι βαδίζειν ἐφ' ὑμᾶς, οὐδένα ἡγεῖτο προσέξειν αὐτῷ
τὸν νοῦν· ἐὰν δὲ τὰς ἐκείνων κοινὰς προφάσεις λαβὼν ἡγεμὼν αἱρεθῇ, ῥᾷον ἤλπιζε τὰ μὲν παρακρού-
σεσθαι, τὰ δὲ πείσειν. τί οὖν; ἐπιχειρεῖ, θεάσασθ'
ὡς εὖ, πόλεμον ποιῆσαι τοῖς Ἀμφικτύοσι καὶ περὶ
τὴν Πυλαίαν ταραχήν· εἰς γὰρ ταῦτ' εὐθὺς αὐτοὺς
ὑπελάμβανεν αὐτοῦ δεήσεσθαι. εἰ μὲν τοίνυν τοῦτο 148
ἢ τῶν παρ' ἑαυτοῦ πεμπομένων ἱερομνημόνων ἢ τῶν
ἐκείνου συμμάχων εἰσηγοῖτό τις, ὑπόψεσθαι τὸ
πρᾶγμα ἐνόμιζε καὶ τοὺς Θηβαίους καὶ τοὺς Θετταλοὺς καὶ πάντας φυλάξεσθαι, ἂν δ' Ἀθηναῖος ᾖ
καὶ παρ' ὑμῶν τῶν ὑπεναντίων ὁ τοῦτο ποιῶν,
εὐπόρως λήσειν· ὅπερ συνέβη. πῶς οὖν ταῦτ' 149
ἐποίησεν; μισθοῦται τουτονί. οὐδενὸς δὲ προει-
δότος, οἶμαι, τὸ πρᾶγμα οὐδὲ φυλάττοντος, ὥσπερ
εἴωθε τὰ τοιαῦτα παρ' ὑμῖν γίγνεσθαι, προβληθεὶς
πυλάγορας οὗτος καὶ τριῶν ἢ τεττάρων χειροτονησάντων αὐτὸν ἀνερρήθη. ὡς δὲ τὸ τῆς πόλεως
ἀξίωμα λαβὼν ἀφίκετο εἰς τοὺς Ἀμφικτύονας,
πάντα τἆλλ' ἀφεὶς καὶ παριδὼν ἐπέραινεν ἐφ' οἷς
ἐμισθώθη, καὶ λόγους εὐπροσώπους καὶ μύθους,

ὅθεν ἡ Κιρραία χώρα καθιερώθη, συνθεὶς καὶ διε-
150 ξελθὼν ἀνθρώπους ἀπείρους λόγων καὶ τὸ μέλλον οὐ
προορωμένους, τοὺς ἱερομνήμονας, πείθει ψηφίσασθαι
περιελθεῖν τὴν χώραν ἣν οἱ μὲν Ἀμφισσεῖς σφῶν
αὐτῶν οὖσαν γεωργεῖν ἔφασαν, οὗτος δὲ τῆς ἱερᾶς
χώρας ᾐτιᾶτο εἶναι, οὐδεμίαν δίκην τῶν Λοκρῶν
ἐπαγόντων ἡμῖν, οὐδ᾽ ἃ νῦν οὗτος προφασίζεται,
λέγων οὐκ ἀληθῆ. γνώσεσθε δ᾽ ἐκεῖθεν. οὐκ ἐνῆν
ἄνευ τοῦ προσκαλέσασθαι δήπου τοῖς Λοκροῖς
δίκην κατὰ τῆς πόλεως τελέσασθαι. τίς οὖν ἐκλήτευσεν ἡμᾶς; ἐπὶ ποίας ἀρχῆς; εἰπὲ τὸν εἰδότα,
δεῖξον. ἀλλ᾽ οὐκ ἂν ἔχοις, ἀλλὰ κενῇ προφάσει
151 ταύτῃ κατεχρῶ καὶ ψευδεῖ. περιιόντων τοίνυν τὴν
χώραν τῶν Ἀμφικτυόνων κατὰ τὴν ὑφήγησιν τὴν
τούτου, προσπεσόντες οἱ Λοκροὶ μικροῦ μὲν κατηκόντισαν ἅπαντας, τινὰς δὲ καὶ συνήρπασαν τῶν
ἱερομνημόνων. ὡς δ᾽ ἅπαξ ἐκ τούτων ἐγκλήματα
καὶ πόλεμος πρὸς τοὺς Ἀμφισσεῖς ἐταράχθη, τὸ
μὲν πρῶτον ὁ Κόττυφος αὐτῶν τῶν Ἀμφικτυόνων
ἤγαγε στρατιάν, ὡς δ᾽ οἱ μὲν οὐκ ἦλθον, οἱ δ᾽
ἐλθόντες οὐδὲν ἐποίουν, εἰς τὴν ἐπιοῦσαν πυλαίαν
ἐπὶ τὸν Φίλιππον εὐθὺς ἡγεμόνα ἦγον οἱ κατεσκευ-
ασμένοι καὶ πάλαι πονηροὶ τῶν Θετταλῶν καὶ τῶν
152 ἐν ταῖς ἄλλαις πόλεσι. καὶ προφάσεις εὐλόγους
εἰλήφεσαν· ἢ γὰρ αὐτοὺς εἰσφέρειν καὶ ξένους τρέ-
φειν ἔφασαν δεῖν καὶ ζημιοῦν τοὺς μὴ ταῦτα ποιοῦντας, ἢ ἐκεῖνον αἱρεῖσθαι· τί δεῖ τὰ πολλὰ λέγειν;

ᾑρέθη γὰρ ἐκ τούτων ἡγεμών. καὶ μετὰ ταῦτ᾽ εὐθέως δύναμιν συλλέξας καὶ παρελθὼν ὡς ἐπὶ τὴν
Κιρραίαν, ἐρρῶσθαι φράσας πολλὰ Κιρραίοις καὶ
Λοκροῖς, τὴν Ἐλάτειαν καταλαμβάνει. εἰ μὲν οὖν 153
μὴ μετέγνωσαν εὐθέως, ὡς τοῦτ᾽ εἶδον, οἱ Θηβαῖοι
καὶ μεθ᾽ ἡμῶν ἐγένοντο, ὥσπερ χειμάρρους ἂν ἅπαν
τοῦτο τὸ πρᾶγμα εἰς τὴν πόλιν εἰσέπεσε· νῦν δὲ
τό γ᾽ ἐξαίφνης ἐπέσχον αὐτὸν ἐκεῖνοι, μάλιστα μέν,
ὦ ἄνδρες Ἀθηναῖοι, θεῶν τινὸς εὐνοίᾳ πρὸς ὑμᾶς,
εἶτα μέντοι καί, ὅσον καθ᾽ ἕνα ἄνδρα, καὶ δι᾽ ἐμέ.
δὸς δέ μοι τὰ δόγματα ταῦτα καὶ τοὺς χρόνους ἐν
οἷς ἕκαστα πέπρακται, ἵν᾽ εἰδῆτε ἡλίκα πράγματα
ἡ μιαρὰ κεφαλὴ ταράξασα αὕτη δίκην οὐκ ἔδωκε.
λέγε μοι τὰ δόγματα. 154

ΔΟΓΜΑ ΑΜΦΙΚΤΥΟΝΩΝ.

[Ἐπὶ ἱερέως Κλειναγόρου, ἐαρινῆς πυλαίας, ἔδοξε τοῖς πυλαγόροις καὶ τοῖς συνέδροις τῶν Ἀμφικτυόνων καὶ τῷ κοινῷ τῶν Ἀμφικτυόνων, ἐπειδὴ Ἀμφισσεῖς ἐπιβαίνουσιν ἐπὶ τὴν ἱερὰν χώραν καὶ σπείρουσι καὶ βοσκήμασι κατανέμουσιν, ἐπελθεῖν τοὺς πυλαγόρους καὶ τοὺς συνέδρους, καὶ στήλαις διαλαβεῖν τοὺς ὅρους, καὶ ἀπειπεῖν τοῖς Ἀμφισσεῦσι τοῦ λοιποῦ μὴ ἐπιβαίνειν.]

ΕΤΕΡΟΝ ΔΟΓΜΑ.

[Ἐπὶ ἱερέως Κλειναγόρου, ἐαρινῆς πυλαίας, ἔδοξε τοῖς πυ- 155
λαγόροις καὶ τοῖς συνέδροις τῶν Ἀμφικτυόνων καὶ τῷ κοινῷ
τῶν Ἀμφικτυόνων, ἐπειδὴ οἱ ἐξ Ἀμφίσσης τὴν ἱερὰν χώραν
κατανειμάμενοι γεωργοῦσι καὶ βοσκήματα νέμουσι, καὶ κωλυό-

μενοι τοῦτο ποιεῖν, ἐν τοῖς ὅπλοις παραγενόμενοι, τὸ κοινὸν τῶν Ἑλλήνων συνέδριον κεκωλύκασι μετὰ βίας, τινὰς δὲ καὶ τετραυματίκασι, τὸν στρατηγὸν τὸν ᾑρημένον τῶν Ἀμφικτυόνων Κόττυφον τὸν Ἀρκάδα πρεσβεῦσαι πρὸς Φίλιππον τὸν Μακεδόνα, καὶ ἀξιοῦν ἵνα βοηθήσῃ τῷ τε Ἀπόλλωνι καὶ τοῖς Ἀμφικτύοσιν, ὅπως μὴ περιίδῃ ὑπὸ τῶν ἀσεβῶν Ἀμφισσέων τὸν θεὸν πλημμελούμενον· καὶ διότι αὐτὸν στρατηγὸν αὐτοκράτορα αἱροῦνται οἱ Ἕλληνες οἱ μετέχοντες τοῦ συνεδρίου τῶν Ἀμφικτυόνων.]

Λέγε δὴ καὶ τοὺς χρόνους ἐν οἷς ταῦτ' ἐγίγνετο· εἰσὶ γὰρ καθ' οὓς ἐπυλαγόρησεν οὗτος. λέγε.

ΧΡΟΝΟΙ.

[Ἄρχων Μνησιθείδης, μηνὸς ἀνθεστηριῶνος ἕκτῃ ἐπὶ δέκα.]

156 Δὸς δή μοι τὴν ἐπιστολὴν ἥν, ὡς οὐχ ὑπήκουον οἱ Θηβαῖοι, πέμπει πρὸς τοὺς ἐν Πελοποννήσῳ συμμάχους ὁ Φίλιππος, ἵν' εἰδῆτε καὶ ἐκ ταύτης σαφῶς ὅτι τὴν μὲν ἀληθῆ πρόφασιν τῶν πραγμάτων, τὸ ταῦτ' ἐπὶ τὴν Ἑλλάδα καὶ τοὺς Θηβαίους καὶ ὑμᾶς πράττειν, ἀπεκρύπτετο, κοινὰ δὲ καὶ τοῖς Ἀμφικτύοσι δόξαντα ποιεῖν προσεποιεῖτο· ὁ δὲ τὰς ἀφορμὰς ταύτας καὶ τὰς προφάσεις αὐτῷ παρασχὼν οὗτος ἦν. λέγε.

ΕΠΙΣΤΟΛΗ.

157 [Βασιλεὺς Μακεδόνων Φίλιππος Πελοποννησίων τῶν ἐν τῇ συμμαχίᾳ τοῖς δημιουργοῖς καὶ τοῖς συνέδροις καὶ τοῖς ἄλλοις συμμάχοις πᾶσι χαίρειν. ἐπειδὴ Λοκροὶ οἱ καλούμενοι Ὀζό-

λαι, κατοικοῦντες ἐν Ἀμφίσσῃ, πλημμελοῦσιν εἰς τὸ ἱερὸν τοῦ Ἀπόλλωνος τοῦ ἐν Δελφοῖς καὶ τὴν ἱερὰν χώραν ἐρχόμενοι μεθ' ὅπλων λεηλατοῦσι, βούλομαι τῷ θεῷ μεθ' ὑμῶν βοηθεῖν καὶ ἀμύνασθαι τοὺς παραβαίνοντάς τι τῶν ἐν ἀνθρώποις εὐσεβῶν· ὥστε συναντᾶτε μετὰ τῶν ὅπλων εἰς τὴν Φωκίδα, ἔχοντες ἐπισιτισμὸν ἡμερῶν τετταράκοντα, τοῦ ἐνεστῶτος μηνὸς λῴου, ὡς ἡμεῖς ἄγομεν, ὡς δὲ Ἀθηναῖοι, βοηδρομιῶνος, ὡς δὲ Κορίνθιοι, πανήμου. τοῖς δὲ μὴ συναντήσασι πανδημεὶ χρησόμεθα [τοῖς δὲ συμβούλοις ἡμῖν κειμένοις] ἐπιζημίοις. εὐτυχεῖτε.]

Ὁρᾶθ' ὅτι φεύγει μὲν τὰς ἰδίας προφάσεις, εἰς 158
δὲ τὰς Ἀμφικτυονικὰς καταφεύγει. τίς οὖν ὁ ταῦτα
συμπαρασκευάσας αὐτῷ; τίς ὁ τὰς προφάσεις ταύτας ἐνδούς; τίς ὁ τῶν κακῶν τῶν γεγενημένων
μάλιστα αἴτιος; οὐχ οὗτος; μὴ τοίνυν λέγετε, ὦ
ἄνδρες Ἀθηναῖοι, περιιόντες ὡς ὑφ' ἑνὸς τοιαῦτα
πέπονθεν ἡ Ἑλλὰς ἀνθρώπου. οὐχ ὑφ' ἑνὸς, ἀλλ'
ὑπὸ πολλῶν καὶ πονηρῶν τῶν παρ' ἑκάστοις, ὦ γῆ
καὶ θεοί· ὧν εἷς οὑτοσὶ, ὃν, εἰ μηδὲν εὐλαβηθέντα 159
τἀληθὲς εἰπεῖν δέοι, οὐκ ἂν ὀκνήσαιμι ἔγωγε κοινὸν
ἀλιτήριον τῶν μετὰ ταῦτα ἀπολωλότων ἁπάντων
εἰπεῖν, ἀνθρώπων, τόπων, πόλεων· ὁ γὰρ τὸ σπέρμα
παρασχὼν, οὗτος τῶν φύντων αἴτιος. ὃν ὅπως
ποτὲ οὐκ εὐθὺς ἰδόντες ἀπεστράφητε θαυμάζω.
πλὴν πολύ τι σκότος, ὡς ἔοικεν, ἐστὶ παρ' ὑμῖν
πρὸ τῆς ἀληθείας.

Συμβέβηκε τοίνυν μοι τῶν κατὰ τῆς πατρίδος 160
τούτῳ πεπραγμένων ἁψαμένῳ εἰς ἃ τούτοις ἐναν-

τιούμενος αὐτὸς πεπολίτευμαι ἀφῖχθαι· ἃ πολλῶν
μὲν ἕνεκ' ἂν εἰκότως ἀκούσαιτέ μου, μάλιστα δ' ὅτι
αἰσχρόν ἐστιν, ὦ ἄνδρες Ἀθηναῖοι, εἰ ἐγὼ μὲν τὰ
ἔργα τῶν ὑπὲρ ὑμῶν πόνων ὑπέμεινα, ὑμεῖς δὲ μηδὲ
161 τοὺς λόγους αὐτῶν ἀνέξεσθε. ὁρῶν γὰρ ἐγὼ Θηβαίους, σχεδὸν δὲ καὶ ὑμᾶς ὑπὸ τῶν τὰ Φιλίππου
φρονούντων καὶ διεφθαρμένων παρ' ἑκατέροις, ὃ μὲν
ἦν ἀμφοτέροις φοβερὸν καὶ φυλακῆς πολλῆς δεόμε-
νον, τὸ τὸν Φίλιππον ἐᾶν αὐξάνεσθαι, παρορῶντας
καὶ οὐδὲ καθ' ἓν φυλαττομένους, εἰς ἔχθραν δὲ καὶ
τὸ προσκρούειν ἀλλήλοις ἑτοίμως ἔχοντας, ὅπως
τοῦτο μὴ γένοιτο παρατηρῶν διετέλουν, οὐκ ἀπὸ
τῆς ἐμαυτοῦ γνώμης μόνον ταῦτα συμφέρειν ὑπο-
162 λαμβάνων, ἀλλ' εἰδὼς Ἀριστοφῶντα καὶ πάλιν Εὔβουλον πάντα τὸν χρόνον βουλομένους πρᾶξαι ταύτην τὴν φιλίαν, καὶ περὶ τῶν ἄλλων πολλάκις
ἀντιλέγοντας ἑαυτοῖς τοῦθ' ὁμογνωμονοῦντας ἀεί.
οὓς σὺ ζῶντας μέν, ὦ κίναδος, κολακεύων παρηκολούθεις, τεθνεώτων δ' οὐκ αἰσθάνει κατηγορῶν· ἃ
γὰρ περὶ Θηβαίων ἐπιτιμᾷς ἐμοί, ἐκείνων πολὺ
μᾶλλον ἢ ἐμοῦ κατηγορεῖς, τῶν πρότερον ἢ ἐγὼ
163 ταύτην τὴν συμμαχίαν δοκιμασάντων. ἀλλ' ἐκεῖσε
ἐπάνειμι, ὅτι τὸν ἐν Ἀμφίσσῃ πόλεμον τούτου μὲν
ποιήσαντος, συμπεραναμένων δὲ τῶν ἄλλων τῶν
συνεργῶν αὐτῷ τὴν πρὸς Θηβαίους ἔχθραν, συνέβη
τὸν Φίλιππον ἐλθεῖν ἐφ' ἡμᾶς, οὗπερ ἕνεκα τὰς
πόλεις οὗτοι συνέκρουον, καὶ εἰ μὴ προεξανέστημεν

μικρὸν, οὐδ' ἀναλαβεῖν ἂν ἐδυνήθημεν· οὕτω μέχρι πόρρω προήγαγον οὗτοι τὴν ἔχθραν. ἐν οἷς δ' ἦτε ἤδη τὰ πρὸς ἀλλήλους, τουτωνὶ τῶν ψηφισμάτων ἀκούσαντες καὶ τῶν ἀποκρίσεων εἴσεσθε. Καί μοι λέγε ταῦτα λαβών.

ΨΗΦΙΣΜΑ.

[Ἐπὶ ἄρχοντος Ἡροπύθου, μηνὸς ἐλαφηβολιῶνος ἕκτῃ φθί- 164
νοντος, φυλῆς πρυτανευούσης Ἐρεχθηΐδος, βουλῆς καὶ στρατηγῶν γνώμῃ, ἐπειδὴ Φίλιππος ἃς μὲν κατείληφε πόλεις τῶν
ἀστυγειτόνων, τινὰς δὲ πορθεῖ, κεφαλαίῳ δὲ ἐπὶ τὴν Ἀττικὴν
παρασκευάζεται παραγίγνεσθαι, παρ' οὐδὲν ἡγούμενος τὰς ἡμετέρας συνθήκας, καὶ τοὺς ὅρκους λύειν ἐπιβάλλεται καὶ τὴν
εἰρήνην, παραβαίνων τὰς κοινὰς πίστεις, δεδόχθαι τῇ βουλῇ
καὶ τῷ δήμῳ πέμπειν πρὸς αὐτὸν πρέσβεις, οἵτινες αὐτῷ διαλέξονται καὶ παρακαλέσουσιν αὐτὸν μάλιστα μὲν τὴν πρὸς
ἡμᾶς ὁμόνοιαν διατηρεῖν καὶ τὰς συνθήκας, εἰ δὲ μή, πρὸς τὸ
βουλεύσασθαι δοῦναι χρόνον τῇ πόλει καὶ τὰς ἀνοχὰς ποιήσασθαι μέχρι τοῦ θαργηλιῶνος μηνός. ᾑρέθησαν ἐκ τῆς
βουλῆς Σῖμος Ἀναγυράσιος, Εὐθύδημος Φλυάσιος, Βουλαγόρας
Ἀλωπεκῆθεν.]

ΕΤΕΡΟΝ ΨΗΦΙΣΜΑ.

[Ἐπὶ ἄρχοντος Ἡροπύθου, μηνὸς μουνυχιῶνος ἕνῃ καὶ νέᾳ, 165
πολεμάρχου γνώμῃ, ἐπειδὴ Φίλιππος εἰς ἀλλοτριότητα Θηβαίους πρὸς ἡμᾶς ἐπιβάλλεται καταστῆσαι, παρεσκεύασται δὲ
καὶ παντὶ τῷ στρατεύματι πρὸς τοὺς ἔγγιστα τῆς Ἀττικῆς
παραγίγνεσθαι τόπους, παραβαίνων τὰς πρὸς ἡμᾶς ὑπαρχού-
σας αὐτῷ συνθήκας, δεδόχθαι τῇ βουλῇ καὶ τῷ δήμῳ πέμψαι
πρὸς αὐτὸν κήρυκα καὶ πρέσβεις, οἵτινες ἀξιώσουσι καὶ παρακαλέσουσιν αὐτὸν ποιήσασθαι τὰς ἀνοχὰς, ὅπως ἐνδεχομένως

ὁ δῆμος βουλεύσηται· καὶ γὰρ νῦν οὐ κέκρικε βοηθεῖν ἐν οὐδενὶ τῶν μετρίων. ᾑρέθησαν ἐκ τῆς βουλῆς Νέαρχος Σωσινόμου, Πολυκράτης Ἐπίφρονος, καὶ κῆρυξ Εὔνομος Ἀναφλύστιος ἐκ τοῦ δήμου.]

166 *Λέγε δὴ καὶ τὰς ἀποκρίσεις.*

ΑΠΟΚΡΙΣΙΣ ΑΘΗΝΑΙΟΙΣ.

[Βασιλεὺς Μακεδόνων Φίλιππος Ἀθηναίων τῇ βουλῇ καὶ τῷ δήμῳ χαίρειν. ἣν μὲν ἀπ' ἀρχῆς εἴχετε πρὸς ἡμᾶς αἵρεσιν, οὐκ ἀγνοῶ, καὶ τίνα σπουδὴν ποιεῖσθε προσκαλέσασθαι βουλόμενοι Θετταλοὺς καὶ Θηβαίους, ἔτι δὲ καὶ Βοιωτούς· βέλτιον δ' αὐτῶν φρονούντων καὶ μὴ βουλομένων ἐφ' ὑμῖν ποιήσασθαι τὴν ἑαυτῶν αἵρεσιν, ἀλλὰ κατὰ τὸ συμφέρον ἱσταμένων, νῦν ἐξ ὑποστροφῆς ἀποστείλαντες ὑμεῖς πρός με πρέσβεις καὶ κήρυκα συνθηκῶν μνημονεύετε καὶ τὰς ἀνοχὰς αἰτεῖσθε, κατ' οὐδὲν ὑφ' ἡμῶν πεπλημμελημένοι. ἐγὼ μέντοι ἀκούσας τῶν πρεσβευτῶν συγκατατίθεμαι τοῖς παρακαλουμένοις καὶ ἕτοιμός εἰμι ποιεῖσθαι τὰς ἀνοχάς, ἄν περ τοὺς οὐκ ὀρθῶς συμβουλεύοντας ὑμῖν παραπέμψαντες τῆς προσηκούσης ἀτιμίας ἀξιώσητε. ἔρρωσθε.]

ΑΠΟΚΡΙΣΙΣ ΘΗΒΑΙΟΙΣ.

167 [Βασιλεὺς Μακεδόνων Φίλιππος Θηβαίων τῇ βουλῇ καὶ τῷ δήμῳ χαίρειν. ἐκομισάμην τὴν παρ' ὑμῶν ἐπιστολήν, δι' ἧς μοι τὴν ὁμόνοιαν ἀνανεοῦσθε καὶ τὴν εἰρήνην ὄντως ἐμοὶ ποιεῖτε. πυνθάνομαι μέντοι διότι πᾶσαν ὑμῖν Ἀθηναῖοι προσφέρονται φιλοτιμίαν βουλόμενοι ὑμᾶς συγκαταίνους γενέσθαι τοῖς ὑπ' αὐτῶν παρακαλουμένοις. πρότερον μὲν οὖν ὑμῶν κατεγίγνωσκον ἐπὶ τῷ μέλλειν πείθεσθαι ταῖς ἐκείνων ἐλπίσι καὶ ἐπακολουθεῖν αὐτῶν τῇ προαιρέσει. νῦν δ' ἐπιγνοὺς ὑμᾶς τὰ πρὸς ἡμᾶς ἐζητηκότας ἔχειν εἰρήνην μᾶλλον ἢ ταῖς ἑτέρων ἐπα-

κολουθεῖν γνώμαις, ἥσθην καὶ μᾶλλον ὑμᾶς ἐπαινῶ κατὰ πολλά, μάλιστα δ' ἐπὶ τῷ βουλεύσασθαι περὶ τούτων ἀσφαλέστερον καὶ τὰ πρὸς ἡμᾶς ἔχειν ἐν εὐνοίᾳ· ὅπερ οὐ μικρὰν ὑμῖν οἴσειν ἐλπίζω ῥοπήν, ἐάν περ ἐπὶ ταύτης μένητε τῆς προθέσεως. ἔρρωσθε.]

Οὕτω διαθεὶς ὁ Φίλιππος τὰς πόλεις πρὸς ἀλλή- 168
λας διὰ τούτων, καὶ τούτοις ἐπαρθεὶς τοῖς ψηφίσμασι καὶ ταῖς ἀποκρίσεσιν, ἧκεν ἔχων τὴν δύναμιν
καὶ τὴν Ἐλάτειαν κατέλαβεν, ὡς οὐδ' ἂν εἴ τι γένοιτο ἔτι συμπνευσάντων ἂν ἡμῶν καὶ τῶν Θηβαίων.
ἀλλὰ μὴν τὸν τότε συμβάντα ἐν τῇ πόλει θόρυβον
ἴστε μὲν ἅπαντες· μικρὰ δ' ἀκούσατε ὅμως, αὐτὰ
τἀναγκαιότατα.

Ἑσπέρα μὲν γὰρ ἦν, ἧκε δ' ἀγγέλλων τις ὡς 169
τοὺς πρυτάνεις ὡς Ἐλάτεια κατείληπται. καὶ μετὰ
ταῦτα οἱ μὲν εὐθὺς ἐξαναστάντες μεταξὺ δειπνοῦντες
τούς τ' ἐκ τῶν σκηνῶν τῶν κατὰ τὴν ἀγορὰν ἐξεῖργον καὶ τὰ γέρρα ἐνεπίμπρασαν, οἱ δὲ τοὺς στρατηγοὺς μετεπέμποντο καὶ τὸν σαλπικτὴν ἐκάλουν·
καὶ θορύβου πλήρης ἦν ἡ πόλις. τῇ δ' ὑστεραίᾳ
ἅμα τῇ ἡμέρᾳ οἱ μὲν πρυτάνεις τὴν βουλὴν ἐκάλουν
εἰς τὸ βουλευτήριον, ὑμεῖς δ' εἰς τὴν ἐκκλησίαν
ἐπορεύεσθε, καὶ πρὶν ἐκείνην χρηματίσαι καὶ προ-
βουλεῦσαι πᾶς ὁ δῆμος ἄνω καθῆτο. καὶ μετὰ 170
ταῦτα ὡς εἰσῆλθεν ἡ βουλὴ καὶ ἀπήγγειλαν οἱ πρυτάνεις τὰ προσηγγελμένα ἑαυτοῖς καὶ τὸν ἥκοντα
παρήγαγον κἀκεῖνος εἶπεν, ἠρώτα μὲν ὁ κῆρυξ "τίς

ἀγορεύειν βούλεται;" παρῄει δ' οὐδείς. πολλάκις
δὲ τοῦ κήρυκος ἐρωτῶντος οὐδὲν μᾶλλον ἀνίστατ'
οὐδείς, ἁπάντων μὲν τῶν στρατηγῶν παρόντων,
ἁπάντων δὲ τῶν ῥητόρων, καλούσης δὲ τῆς πατρίδος
τῇ κοινῇ φωνῇ τὸν ἐροῦνθ' ὑπὲρ σωτηρίας· ἣν γὰρ
ὁ κῆρυξ κατὰ τοὺς νόμους φωνὴν ἀφίησι, ταύτην
171 κοινὴν τῆς πατρίδος δίκαιόν ἐστιν ἡγεῖσθαι. καίτοι εἰ μὲν τοὺς σωθῆναι τὴν πόλιν βουλομένους
παρελθεῖν ἔδει, πάντες ἂν ὑμεῖς καὶ οἱ ἄλλοι Ἀθηναῖοι ἀναστάντες ἐπὶ τὸ βῆμα ἐβαδίζετε· πάντες
γὰρ οἶδ' ὅτι σωθῆναι αὐτὴν ἐβούλεσθε· εἰ δὲ τοὺς
πλουσιωτάτους, οἱ τριακόσιοι· εἰ δὲ τοὺς ἀμφότερα
ταῦτα, καὶ εὔνους τῇ πόλει καὶ πλουσίους, οἱ μετὰ
172 ταῦτα τὰς μεγάλας ἐπιδόσεις ἐπιδόντες· καὶ γὰρ
εὐνοίᾳ καὶ πλούτῳ τοῦτ' ἐποίησαν· ἀλλ' ὡς ἔοικεν,
ἐκεῖνος ὁ καιρὸς καὶ ἡ ἡμέρα ἐκείνη οὐ μόνον εὔνουν
καὶ πλούσιον ἄνδρα ἐκάλει, ἀλλὰ καὶ παρηκολουθηκότα τοῖς πράγμασιν ἐξ ἀρχῆς, καὶ συλλελογισμένον ὀρθῶς τίνος ἕνεκα ταῦτ' ἔπραττεν ὁ Φίλιππος
καὶ τί βουλόμενος; ὁ γὰρ μὴ ταῦτ' εἰδὼς μηδ' ἐξη-
τακὼς πόρρωθεν ἐπιμελῶς, οὔτ' εἰ εὔνους ἦν οὔτ' εἰ
πλούσιος, οὐδὲν μᾶλλον ἔμελλεν ὅ τι χρὴ ποιεῖν
173 εἴσεσθαι οὐδ' ὑμῖν ἕξειν συμβουλεύειν. ἐφάνην
τοίνυν οὗτος ἐν ἐκείνῃ τῇ ἡμέρᾳ ἐγώ, καὶ παρελθὼν
εἶπον εἰς ὑμᾶς, ἅ μου δυοῖν ἕνεκ' ἀκούσατε προσ-
σχόντες τὸν νοῦν, ἑνὸς μέν, ἵν' εἰδῆτε ὅτι μόνος τῶν
λεγόντων καὶ πολιτευομένων ἐγὼ τὴν τῆς εὐνοίας

τάξιν ἐν τοῖς δεινοῖς οὐκ ἔλιπον, ἀλλὰ καὶ λέγων καὶ
γράφων ἐξηταζόμην τὰ δέονθ' ὑπὲρ ὑμῶν ἐν αὐτοῖς
τοῖς φοβεροῖς, ἑτέρου δέ, ὅτι μικρὸν ἀναλώσαντες
χρόνον πολλῷ πρὸς τὰ λοιπὰ τῆς πάσης πολιτείας
ἔσεσθ' ἐμπειρότεροι. εἶπον τοίνυν ὅτι "τοὺς μὲν 174
ὡς ὑπαρχόντων Θηβαίων Φιλίππῳ λίαν θορυβουμέ-
νους ἀγνοεῖν τὰ παρόντα πράγμαθ' ἡγοῦμαι· εὖ γὰρ
οἶδ' ὅτι, εἰ τοῦθ' οὕτως ἐτύγχανεν ἔχον, οὐκ ἂν αὐτὸν ἠκούομεν ἐν Ἐλατείᾳ ὄντα, ἀλλ' ἐπὶ τοῖς ἡμε-
τέροις ὁρίοις. ὅτι μέντοι ἵν' ἕτοιμα ποιήσηται τὰ
ἐν Θήβαις ἥκει, σαφῶς ἐπίσταμαι. ὡς δ' ἔχει" 175
ἔφην "ταῦτα, ἀκούσατέ μου. ἐκεῖνος ὅσους ἢ πεῖσαι χρήμασι Θηβαίων ἢ ἐξαπατῆσαι ἐνῆν, ἅπαντας
ηὐτρέπισται· τοὺς δ' ἀπ' ἀρχῆς ἀνθεστηκότας αὐτῷ
καὶ νῦν ἐναντιουμένους οὐδαμῶς πεῖσαι δύναται. τί
οὖν βούλεται, καὶ τίνος ἕνεκα τὴν Ἐλάτειαν κατεί-
ληφεν; πλησίον δύναμιν δείξας καὶ παραστήσας τὰ
ὅπλα τοὺς μὲν ἑαυτοῦ φίλους ἐπᾶραι καὶ θρασεῖς
ποιῆσαι, τοὺς δ' ἐναντιουμένους καταπλῆξαι, ἵν' ἢ
συγχωρήσωσι φοβηθέντες ἃ νῦν οὐκ ἐθέλουσιν, ἢ
βιασθῶσιν. εἰ μὲν τοίνυν προαιρησόμεθ' ἡμεῖς" 176
ἔφην "ἐν τῷ παρόντι, εἴ τι δύσκολον πέπρακται
Θηβαίοις πρὸς ἡμᾶς, τούτου μεμνῆσθαι καὶ ἀπιστεῖν αὐτοῖς ὡς ἐν τῇ τῶν ἐχθρῶν οὖσι μερίδι, πρῶτον μὲν ἃ ἂν εὔξαιτο Φίλιππος ποιήσομεν, εἶτα
φοβοῦμαι μὴ προσδεξαμένων τῶν νῦν ἀνθεστηκό-
των αὐτῷ καὶ μιᾷ γνώμῃ πάντων φιλιππισάντων

εἰς τὴν Ἀττικὴν ἔλθωσιν ἀμφότεροι. ἂν μέντοι
πεισθῆτ᾽ ἐμοὶ καὶ πρὸς τῷ σκοπεῖν ἀλλὰ μὴ φιλο-
νεικεῖν περὶ ὧν ἂν λέγω γένησθε, οἶμαι καὶ τὰ
δέοντα λέγειν δόξειν καὶ τὸν ἐφεστηκότα κίνδυνον
177 τῇ πόλει διαλύσειν. τί οὖν φημὶ δεῖν; πρῶτον μὲν
τὸν παρόντα ἐπανεῖναι φόβον, εἶτα μεταθέσθαι καὶ
φοβεῖσθαι πάντας ὑπὲρ Θηβαίων· πολὺ γὰρ τῶν
δεινῶν εἰσιν ἡμῶν ἐγγυτέρω, καὶ προτέροις αὐτοῖς
ἐστιν ὁ κίνδυνος· ἔπειτ᾽ ἐξελθόντας Ἐλευσῖνάδε
τοὺς ἐν ἡλικίᾳ καὶ τοὺς ἱππέας δεῖξαι πᾶσιν ὑμᾶς
αὐτοὺς ἐν τοῖς ὅπλοις ὄντας, ἵνα τοῖς ἐν Θήβαις
φρονοῦσι τὰ ὑμέτερα ἐξ ἴσου γένηται τὸ παρρη-
σιάζεσθαι περὶ τῶν δικαίων, εἰδόσιν ὅτι, ὥσπερ τοῖς
πωλοῦσι Φιλίππῳ τὴν πατρίδα πάρεσθ᾽ ἡ βοηθή-
σουσα δύναμις ἐν Ἐλατείᾳ, οὕτω τοῖς ὑπὲρ τῆς
ἐλευθερίας ἀγωνίζεσθαι βουλομένοις ὑπάρχεθ᾽ ὑμεῖς
178 ἕτοιμοι καὶ βοηθήσετ᾽, ἐάν τις ἐπ᾽ αὐτοὺς ἴῃ. μετὰ
ταῦτα χειροτονῆσαι κελεύω δέκα πρέσβεις, καὶ
ποιῆσαι τούτους κυρίους μετὰ τῶν στρατηγῶν καὶ
τοῦ πότε δεῖ βαδίζειν ἐκεῖσε καὶ τῆς ἐξόδου. ἐπειδὰν δ᾽ ἔλθωσιν οἱ πρέσβεις εἰς Θήβας, πῶς χρήσασθαι τῷ πράγματι παραινῶ; τούτῳ πάνυ μοι
προσέχετε τὸν νοῦν. μὴ δεῖσθαι Θηβαίων μηδὲν
(αἰσχρὸς γὰρ ὁ καιρὸς), ἀλλ᾽ ἐπαγγέλλεσθαι βοη-
θήσειν, ἂν κελεύωσιν, ὡς ἐκείνων μὲν ὄντων ἐν τοῖς
ἐσχάτοις, ἡμῶν δὲ ἄμεινον ἢ ᾽κεῖνοι τὸ μέλλον προ-
ορωμένων· ἵν᾽ ἐὰν μὲν δέξωνται ταῦτα καὶ πεισθῶ-

σιν ἡμῖν, καὶ ἃ βουλόμεθα ὦμεν διῳκημένοι καὶ μετὰ
προσχήματος ἀξίου τῆς πόλεως ταῦτα πράξωμεν,
ἂν δ' ἄρα μὴ συμβῇ κατατυχεῖν, ἐκεῖνοι μὲν αὑτοῖς
ἐγκαλῶσιν, ἄν τι νῦν ἐξαμαρτάνωσιν, ἡμῖν δὲ μηδὲν
αἰσχρὸν μηδὲ ταπεινὸν ᾖ πεπραγμένον." Ταῦτα 179
καὶ παραπλήσια τούτοις εἰπὼν κατέβην. συνεπαι-
νεσάντων δὲ πάντων καὶ οὐδενὸς εἰπόντος ἐναντίον
οὐδὲν οὐκ εἶπον μὲν ταῦτα, οὐκ ἔγραψα δὲ, οὐδ'
ἔγραψα μὲν, οὐκ ἐπρέσβευσα δὲ, οὐδ' ἐπρέσβευσα
μὲν, οὐκ ἔπεισα δὲ Θηβαίους, ἀλλ' ἀπὸ τῆς ἀρχῆς
διὰ πάντων ἄχρι τῆς τελευτῆς διεξῆλθον, καὶ ἔδωκ'
ἐμαυτὸν ὑμῖν ἁπλῶς εἰς τοὺς περιεστηκότας τῇ πόλει κινδύνους. Καί μοι φέρε τὸ ψήφισμα τὸ τότε
γενόμενον.

Καίτοι τίνα βούλει σὲ, Αἰσχίνη, καὶ τίνα ἐμαυ- 180
τὸν ἐκείνην τὴν ἡμέραν εἶναι θῶ; βούλει ἐμαυτὸν
μὲν, ὃν ἂν σὺ λοιδορούμενος καὶ διασύρων καλέσαις,
Βάτταλον, σὲ δὲ μηδ' ἥρω τὸν τυχόντα, ἀλλὰ τούτων τινὰ τῶν ἀπὸ τῆς σκηνῆς, Κρεσφόντην ἢ Κρέοντα ἢ ὃν ἐν Κολλυτῷ ποτὲ Οἰνόμαον κακῶς ὑποκρινόμενος ἐπέτριψας; τότε τοίνυν κατ' ἐκεῖνον τὸν
καιρὸν ὁ Παιανιεὺς ἐγὼ Βάτταλος Οἰνομάου τοῦ
Κοθωκίδου σοῦ πλείονος ἄξιος ὢν ἐφάνην τῇ πατρίδι. σὺ μέν γε οὐδὲν οὐδαμοῦ χρήσιμος ἦσθα·
ἐγὼ δὲ πάντα, ὅσα προσῆκε τὸν ἀγαθὸν πολίτην,
ἔπραττον. Λέγε τὸ ψήφισμά μοι.

ΨΗΦΙΣΜΑ ΔΗΜΟΣΘΕΝΟΥΣ.

181 [Ἐπὶ ἄρχοντος Ναυσικλέους, φυλῆς πρυτανευούσης Αἰαντίδος, σκιροφοριῶνος ἕκτῃ ἐπὶ δέκα, Δημοσθένης Δημοσθένους Παιανιεὺς εἶπεν, ἐπειδὴ Φίλιππος ὁ Μακεδόνων βασιλεὺς ἔν τε τῷ παρεληλυθότι χρόνῳ παραβαίνων φαίνεται τὰς γεγενημένας αὐτῷ συνθήκας πρὸς τὸν Ἀθηναίων δῆμον περὶ τῆς εἰρήνης, ὑπεριδὼν τοὺς ὅρκους καὶ τὰ παρὰ πᾶσι τοῖς Ἕλλησι νομιζόμενα εἶναι δίκαια, καὶ πόλεις παραιρεῖται οὐδὲν αὐτῷ προσηκούσας, τινὰς δὲ καὶ Ἀθηναίων οὔσας δοριαλώτους πεποίηκεν οὐδὲν προαδικηθεὶς ὑπὸ τοῦ δήμου τοῦ Ἀθηναίων, ἔν τε τῷ
182 παρόντι ἐπὶ πολὺ προάγει τῇ τε βίᾳ καὶ τῇ ὠμότητι. καὶ γὰρ Ἑλληνίδας πόλεις ἃς μὲν ἐμφρούρους ποιεῖ καὶ τὰς πολιτείας καταλύει, τινὰς δὲ καὶ ἐξανδραποδιζόμενος κατασκάπτει, εἰς ἐνίας δὲ καὶ ἀντὶ Ἑλλήνων βαρβάρους κατοικίζει ἐπὶ τὰ ἱερὰ καὶ τοὺς τάφους ἐπάγων, οὐδὲν ἀλλότριον ποιῶν οὔτε τῆς ἑαυτοῦ πατρίδος οὔτε τοῦ τρόπου, καὶ τῇ νῦν αὐτῷ παρούσῃ τύχῃ κατακόρως χρώμενος, ἐπιλελησμένος ἑαυτοῦ ὅτι ἐκ μικροῦ καὶ
183 τοῦ τυχόντος γέγονεν ἀνελπίστως μέγας. καὶ ἕως μὲν πόλεις ἑώρα παραιρούμενον αὐτὸν βαρβάρους καὶ ἰδίας, ὑπελάμβανεν ἔλαττον εἶναι ὁ δῆμος ὁ Ἀθηναίων τὸ εἰς αὐτὸν πλημμελεῖσθαι· νῦν δὲ ὁρῶν Ἑλληνίδας πόλεις τὰς μὲν ὑβριζομένας, τὰς δὲ ἀναστάτους γιγνομένας, δεινὸν ἡγεῖται εἶναι καὶ ἀνάξιον τῆς τῶν προγόνων δόξης τὸ περιορᾶν τοὺς Ἕλληνας καταδουλουμέ-
184 νους. διὸ δεδόχθαι τῇ βουλῇ καὶ τῷ δήμῳ τῷ Ἀθηναίων, εὐξαμένους καὶ θύσαντας τοῖς θεοῖς καὶ ἥρωσι τοῖς κατέχουσι τὴν πόλιν καὶ τὴν χώραν τὴν Ἀθηναίων, καὶ ἐνθυμηθέντας τῆς τῶν προγόνων ἀρετῆς, διότι περὶ πλείονος ἐποιοῦντο τὴν τῶν Ἑλλήνων ἐλευθερίαν διατηρεῖν ἢ τὴν ἰδίαν πατρίδα, διακοσίας ναῦς καθέλκειν εἰς τὴν θάλατταν καὶ τὸν ναύαρχον ἀναπλεῖν ἐντὸς Πυλῶν, καὶ τὸν στρατηγὸν καὶ τὸν ἵππαρχον τὰς πεζὰς καὶ τὰς ἱππικὰς δυνάμεις Ἐλευσῖνάδε ἐξάγειν, πέμψαι δὲ καὶ πρέσβεις πρὸς τοὺς ἄλλους Ἕλληνας, πρῶτον

δὲ πάντων πρὸς Θηβαίους διὰ τὸ ἐγγυτάτω εἶναι τὸν Φίλιπ- 185
πον τῆς ἐκείνων χώρας, παρακαλεῖν δὲ αὐτοὺς μηδὲν κατα-
πλαγέντας τὸν Φίλιππον ἀντέχεσθαι τῆς ἑαυτῶν καὶ τῆς
τῶν ἄλλων Ἑλλήνων ἐλευθερίας, καὶ ὅτι ὁ Ἀθηναίων δῆμος,
οὐδὲν μνησικακῶν εἴ τι πρότερον γέγονεν ἀλλότριον ταῖς πόλεσι πρὸς ἀλλήλας, βοηθήσει καὶ δυνάμεσι καὶ χρήμασι καὶ
βέλεσι καὶ ὅπλοις, εἰδὼς ὅτι αὐτοῖς μὲν πρὸς ἀλλήλους διαμ-
φισβητεῖν περὶ τῆς ἡγεμονίας οὖσιν Ἕλλησι καλόν, ὑπὸ δὲ
ἀλλοφύλου ἀνθρώπου ἄρχεσθαι καὶ τῆς ἡγεμονίας ἀποστερεῖσθαι ἀνάξιον εἶναι καὶ τῆς τῶν Ἑλλήνων δόξης καὶ τῆς τῶν
προγόνων ἀρετῆς. ἔτι δὲ οὐδὲ ἀλλότριον ἡγεῖται εἶναι ὁ Ἀθη- 186
ναίων δῆμος τὸν Θηβαίων δῆμον οὔτε τῇ συγγενείᾳ οὔτε τῷ
ὁμοφύλῳ. ἀναμιμνήσκεται δὲ καὶ τὰς τῶν προγόνων τῶν
ἑαυτοῦ εἰς τοὺς Θηβαίων προγόνους εὐεργεσίας· καὶ γὰρ τοὺς
Ἡρακλέους παῖδας ἀποστερουμένους ὑπὸ Πελοποννησίων τῆς
πατρῴας ἀρχῆς κατήγαγον, τοῖς ὅπλοις κρατήσαντες τοὺς ἀντι-
βαίνειν πειρωμένους τοῖς Ἡρακλέους ἐκγόνοις, καὶ τὸν Οἰδίπουν καὶ τοὺς μετ' ἐκείνου ἐκπεσόντας ὑπεδεξάμεθα, καὶ ἕτερα
πολλὰ ἡμῖν ὑπάρχει φιλάνθρωπα καὶ ἔνδοξα πρὸς Θηβαίους·
διόπερ οὐδὲ νῦν ἀποστήσεται ὁ Ἀθηναίων δῆμος τῶν Θηβαίοις 187
τε καὶ τοῖς ἄλλοις Ἕλλησι συμφερόντων. συνθέσθαι δὲ πρὸς
αὐτοὺς συμμαχίαν καὶ ἐπιγαμίαν ποιήσασθαι καὶ ὅρκους δοῦναι
καὶ λαβεῖν. πρέσβεις Δημοσθένης Δημοσθένους Παιανιεύς,
Ὑπερείδης Κλεάνδρου Σφήττιος, Μνησιθείδης Ἀντιφάνους
Φρεάρριος, Δημοκράτης Σωφίλου Φλυεύς, Κάλλαισχρος Διο-
τίμου Κοθωκίδης.]

Αὕτη τῶν περὶ Θήβας ἐγένετο πραγμάτων ἀρχὴ 188
καὶ κατάστασις πρώτη, τὰ πρὸ τούτων εἰς ἔχθραν
καὶ μῖσος καὶ ἀπιστίαν τῶν πόλεων ὑπηγμένων ὑπὸ
τούτων. τοῦτο τὸ ψήφισμα τὸν τότε τῇ πόλει
περιστάντα κίνδυνον παρελθεῖν ἐποίησεν ὥσπερ

νέφος. ἦν μὲν τοίνυν τοῦ δικαίου πολίτου τότε
δεῖξαι πᾶσιν, εἴ τι τούτων εἶχεν ἄμεινον, μὴ νῦν
189 ἐπιτιμᾶν. ὁ γὰρ σύμβουλος καὶ ὁ συκοφάντης,
οὐδὲ τῶν ἄλλων οὐδὲν ἐοικότες, ἐν τούτῳ πλεῖστον
ἀλλήλων διαφέρουσιν· ὁ μέν γε πρὸ τῶν πραγμάτων γνώμην ἀποφαίνεται, καὶ δίδωσιν ἑαυτὸν ὑπεύθυνον τοῖς πεισθεῖσι, τῇ τύχῃ, τοῖς καιροῖς, τῷ
βουλομένῳ· ὁ δὲ σιγήσας ἡνίκ' ἔδει λέγειν, ἄν τι
190 δύσκολον συμβῇ, τοῦτο βασκαίνει. ἦν μὲν οὖν,
ὅπερ εἶπον, ἐκεῖνος ὁ καιρὸς τοῦ γε φροντίζοντος
ἀνδρὸς τῆς πόλεως καὶ τῶν δικαίων λόγων· ἐγὼ δὲ
τοσαύτην ὑπερβολὴν ποιοῦμαι ὥστε, ἂν νῦν ἔχῃ τις
δεῖξαί τι βέλτιον, ἢ ὅλως εἴ τι ἄλλο ἐνῆν πλὴν ὧν
ἐγὼ προειλόμην, ἀδικεῖν ὁμολογῶ. εἰ γὰρ ἔσθ' ὅ
τι τις νῦν ἑόρακεν, ὃ συνήνεγκεν ἂν τότε πραχθέν,
τοῦτ' ἐγώ φημι δεῖν ἐμὲ μὴ λαθεῖν. εἰ δὲ μήτ' ἔστι
μήτε ἦν μήτ' ἂν εἰπεῖν ἔχοι μηδεὶς μηδέπω καὶ τήμερον, τί τὸν σύμβουλον ἐχρῆν ποιεῖν; οὐ τῶν φαινο-
191 μένων καὶ ἐνόντων τὰ κράτιστα ἑλέσθαι; τοῦτο
τοίνυν ἐποίησα ἐγώ, τοῦ κήρυκος ἐρωτῶντος, Αἰσχίνη, "τίς ἀγορεύειν βούλεται," οὐ "τίς αἰτιᾶσθαι
περὶ τῶν παρεληλυθότων," οὐδὲ "τίς ἐγγυᾶσθαι τὰ
μέλλοντ' ἔσεσθαι." σοῦ δ' ἀφώνου κατ' ἐκείνους
τοὺς χρόνους ἐν ταῖς ἐκκλησίαις καθημένου ἐγὼ
παριὼν ἔλεγον. ἐπειδὴ δ' οὐ τότε, ἀλλὰ νῦν δεῖξον.
εἰπὲ τίς ἢ λόγος, ὅντιν' ἐχρῆν εὑρεῖν, ἢ καιρὸς
συμφέρων ὑπ' ἐμοῦ παρελείφθη τῇ πόλει; τίς δὲ

συμμαχία, τίς πρᾶξις, ἐφ' ἣν μᾶλλον ἔδει με ἀγαγεῖν τουτουσί;

Ἀλλὰ μὴν τὸ μὲν παρεληλυθὸς ἀεὶ παρὰ πᾶσιν 192
ἀφεῖται, καὶ οὐδεὶς περὶ τούτου προτίθησιν οὐδαμοῦ
βουλήν· τὸ δὲ μέλλον ἢ τὸ παρὸν τὴν τοῦ συμβούλου τάξιν ἀπαιτεῖ. τότε τοίνυν τὰ μὲν ἔμελλεν, ὡς
ἐδόκει, τῶν δεινῶν, τὰ δ' ἤδη παρῆν, ἐν οἷς τὴν
προαίρεσίν μου σκόπει τῆς πολιτείας, μὴ τὰ συμβάντα συκοφάντει. τὸ μὲν γὰρ πέρας, ὡς ἂν ὁ
δαίμων βουληθῇ, πάντων γίγνεται· ἡ δὲ προαίρεσις
αὐτὴ τὴν τοῦ συμβούλου διάνοιαν δηλοῖ. μὴ δὴ τοῦτο 193
ὡς ἀδίκημα ἐμὸν θῇς, εἰ κρατῆσαι συνέβη Φιλίππῳ
τῇ μάχῃ· ἐν γὰρ τῷ θεῷ τὸ τούτου τέλος ἦν, οὐκ
ἐν ἐμοί. ἀλλ' ὡς οὐχ ἅπαντα ὅσα ἐνῆν κατ' ἀνθρώ-
πινον λογισμὸν εἱλόμην, καὶ δικαίως ταῦτα καὶ ἐπιμελῶς ἔπραξα καὶ φιλοπόνως ὑπὲρ δύναμιν, ἢ ὡς
οὐ καλὰ καὶ τῆς πόλεως ἄξια πράγματα ἐνεστησάμην καὶ ἀναγκαῖα, ταῦτά μοι δεῖξον, καὶ τότ' ἤδη
κατηγόρει μου. εἰ δ' ὁ συμβὰς σκηπτὸς μὴ μόνον 194
ἡμῶν, ἀλλὰ καὶ πάντων τῶν ἄλλων Ἑλλήνων μείζων γέγονε, τί χρὴ ποιεῖν; ὥσπερ ἂν εἴ τις ναύκληρον
πάντ' ἐπὶ σωτηρίᾳ πράξαντα, καὶ πᾶσι κατασκευάσαντα τὸ πλοῖον ἀφ' ὧν ὑπελάμβανε σωθήσεσθαι,
εἶτα χειμῶνι χρησάμενον καὶ πονησάντων αὐτῷ
τῶν σκευῶν ἢ καὶ συντριβέντων ὅλως, τῆς ναυαγίας
αἰτιῷτο. ἀλλ' οὔτ' ἐκυβέρνων τὴν ναῦν, φήσειεν
ἄν, ὥσπερ οὐδ' ἐστρατήγουν ἐγώ, οὔτε τῆς τύχης

195 κύριος ἦν, ἀλλ' ἐκείνη τῶν πάντων. ἀλλ' ἐκεῖνο
λογίζου καὶ ὅρα, εἰ μετὰ Θηβαίων ἡμῖν ἀγωνιζομέ-
νοις οὕτως εἵμαρτο πρᾶξαι, τί χρῆν προσδοκᾶν, εἰ
μηδὲ τούτους ἔσχομεν συμμάχους, ἀλλὰ Φιλίππῳ
προσέθεντο, ὑπὲρ οὗ τότ' ἐκεῖνος πάσας ἀφῆκε φωνάς; καὶ εἰ νῦν τριῶν ἡμερῶν ἀπὸ τῆς Ἀττικῆς
ὁδὸν τῆς μάχης γενομένης τοσοῦτος κίνδυνος καὶ
φόβος περιέστη τὴν πόλιν, τί ἄν, εἴ που τῆς χώρας
ταὐτὸ τοῦτο πάθος συνέβη, προσδοκῆσαι χρῆν; ἆρ'
οἶσθ' ὅτι νῦν μὲν στῆναι, συνελθεῖν, ἀναπνεῦσαι,
πολλὰ μία ἡμέρα καὶ δύο καὶ τρεῖς ἔδοσαν τῶν εἰς
σωτηρίαν τῇ πόλει, τότε δ' —, οὐκ ἄξιον εἰπεῖν, ἅ
γε μηδὲ πεῖραν ἔδωκε θεῶν τινὸς εὐνοίᾳ καὶ τῷ προβαλέσθαι τὴν πόλιν ταύτην τὴν συμμαχίαν, ἧς σὺ
κατηγορεῖς.

196 Ἔστι δὲ ταυτὶ πάντα μοι, τὰ πολλά, πρὸς ὑμᾶς,
ὦ ἄνδρες δικασταί, καὶ τοὺς περιεστηκότας ἔξωθεν
καὶ ἀκροωμένους, ἐπεὶ πρός γε τοῦτον τὸν κατάπτυστον βραχὺς καὶ σαφὴς ἐξήρκει λόγος. εἰ μὲν
γὰρ ἦν σοὶ πρόδηλα τὰ μέλλοντα, Αἰσχίνη, μόνῳ
τῶν ἄλλων, ὅτ' ἐβουλεύεθ' ἡ πόλις περὶ τούτων,
τότ' ἔδει προλέγειν· εἰ δὲ μὴ προῄδεις, τῆς αὐτῆς
ἀγνοίας ὑπεύθυνος εἶ τοῖς ἄλλοις, ὥστε τί μᾶλλον
197 ἐμοῦ σὺ ταῦτα κατηγορεῖς ἢ ἐγὼ σοῦ; τοσοῦτον
γὰρ ἀμείνων ἐγὼ σοῦ πολίτης γέγονα εἰς αὐτὰ ταῦθ'
ἃ λέγω (καὶ οὔπω περὶ τῶν ἄλλων διαλέγομαι)
ὅσον ἐγὼ μὲν ἔδωκα ἐμαυτὸν εἰς τὰ πᾶσι δοκοῦντα

συμφέρειν, οὐδένα κίνδυνον ὀκνήσας ἴδιον οὐδ' ὑπο-
λογισάμενος, σὺ δὲ οὔθ' ἕτερα εἶπες βελτίω τούτων
(οὐ γὰρ ἂν τούτοις ἐχρῶντο), οὔτ' εἰς ταῦτα χρήσιμον οὐδὲν σαυτὸν παρέσχες, ὅπερ δ' ἂν ὁ φαυλότατος καὶ δυσμενέστατος ἄνθρωπος τῇ πόλει, τοῦτο
πεποιηκὼς ἐπὶ τοῖς συμβᾶσιν ἐξήτασαι, καὶ ἅμα
Ἀρίστρατος ἐν Νάξῳ καὶ Ἀριστόλεως ἐν Θάσῳ, οἱ
καθάπαξ ἐχθροὶ τῆς πόλεως, τοὺς Ἀθηναίων κρίνουσι φίλους καὶ Ἀθήνησιν Αἰσχίνης Δημοσθένους
κατηγορεῖ. καίτοι ὅτῳ τὰ τῶν Ἑλλήνων ἀτυχή- 198
ματα ἐνευδοκιμεῖν ἀπέκειτο, ἀπολωλέναι μᾶλλον
οὗτός ἐστι δίκαιος ἢ κατηγορεῖν ἑτέρου· καὶ ὅτῳ
συνενηνόχασιν οἱ αὐτοὶ καιροὶ καὶ τοῖς τῆς πόλεως
ἐχθροῖς, οὐκ ἔνι τοῦτον εὔνουν εἶναι τῇ πατρίδι.
δηλοῖς δὲ καὶ ἐξ ὧν ζῇς καὶ ποιεῖς καὶ πολιτεύει
καὶ πάλιν οὐ πολιτεύει. πράττεταί τι τῶν ὑμῖν
δοκούντων συμφέρειν, ἄφωνος Αἰσχίνης. ἀντέ-
κρουσέ τι καὶ γέγονεν οἷον οὐκ ἔδει, πάρεστιν
Αἰσχίνης· ὥσπερ τὰ ῥήγματα καὶ τὰ σπάσματα,
ὅταν τι κακὸν τὸ σῶμα λάβῃ, τότε κινεῖται.

Ἐπειδὴ δὲ πολὺς τοῖς συμβεβηκόσιν ἔγκειται, βού- 199
λομαί τι καὶ παράδοξον εἰπεῖν. καί μου πρὸς Διὸς
καὶ θεῶν μηδεὶς τὴν ὑπερβολὴν θαυμάσῃ, ἀλλὰ μετ'
εὐνοίας ὃ λέγω θεωρησάτω. εἰ γὰρ ἦν ἅπασι πρόδηλα τὰ μέλλοντα γενήσεσθαι, καὶ προῄδεσαν πάντες,
καὶ σὺ προὔλεγες, Αἰσχίνη, καὶ διεμαρτύρου βοῶν
καὶ κεκραγώς, ὃς οὐδ' ἐφθέγξω, οὐδ' οὕτως ἀποστατέον

τῇ πόλει τούτων ἦν, εἴπερ δόξης ἢ προγόνων ἢ τοῦ
200 μέλλοντος αἰῶνος εἶχε λόγον. νῦν μέν γε ἀποτυχεῖν δοκεῖ τῶν πραγμάτων, ὃ πᾶσι κοινόν ἐστιν
ἀνθρώποις, ὅταν τῷ θεῷ ταῦτα δοκῇ· τότε δ' ἀξιοῦσα προεστάναι τῶν ἄλλων, εἶτ' ἀποστᾶσα τούτου, Φιλίππῳ προδεδωκέναι πάντας ἂν ἔσχεν αἰτίαν.
εἰ γὰρ ταῦτα προεῖτο ἀκονιτί, περὶ ὧν οὐδένα κίνδυνον ὅντιν' οὐχ ὑπέμειναν οἱ πρόγονοι, τίς οὐχὶ κατέ-
201 πτυσεν ἂν σοῦ; μὴ γὰρ τῆς πόλεώς γε, μηδ' ἐμοῦ.
τίσι δ' ὀφθαλμοῖς πρὸς Διὸς ἑωρῶμεν ἂν τοὺς εἰς
τὴν πόλιν ἀνθρώπους ἀφικνουμένους, εἰ τὰ μὲν
πράγματ' εἰς ὅπερ νυνὶ περιέστη, ἡγεμὼν δὲ καὶ
κύριος ᾑρέθη Φίλιππος ἁπάντων, τὸν δ' ὑπὲρ τοῦ
μὴ γενέσθαι ταῦτ' ἀγῶνα ἕτεροι χωρὶς ἡμῶν ἦσαν
πεποιημένοι, καὶ ταῦτα μηδεπώποτε τῆς πόλεως ἐν
τοῖς ἔμπροσθε χρόνοις ἀσφάλειαν ἄδοξον μᾶλλον ἢ
202 τὸν ὑπὲρ τῶν καλῶν κίνδυνον ᾑρημένης. τίς γὰρ
οὐκ οἶδεν Ἑλλήνων, τίς δὲ βαρβάρων, ὅτι καὶ παρὰ
Θηβαίων καὶ παρὰ τῶν ἔτι τούτων πρότερον ἰσχυ-
ρῶν γενομένων Λακεδαιμονίων καὶ παρὰ τοῦ Περσῶν βασιλέως μετὰ πολλῆς χάριτος τοῦτ' ἂν ἀσμένως ἐδόθη τῇ πόλει, ὅ τι βούλεται λαβούσῃ καὶ τὰ
ἑαυτῆς ἐχούσῃ τὸ κελευόμενον ποιεῖν καὶ ἐᾶν ἕτερον
203 τῶν Ἑλλήνων προεστάναι. ἀλλ' οὐκ ἦν ταῦθ', ὡς
ἔοικε, τοῖς τότ' Ἀθηναίοις πάτρια οὐδ' ἀνεκτὰ οὐδ'
ἔμφυτα, οὐδ' ἐδυνήθη πώποτε τὴν πόλιν οὐδεὶς ἐκ
παντὸς τοῦ χρόνου πεῖσαι τοῖς ἰσχύουσι μέν, μὴ

δίκαια δὲ πράττουσι προσθεμένην ἀσφαλῶς δουλεύ-
ειν, ἀλλ' ἀγωνιζομένη περὶ πρωτείων καὶ τιμῆς καὶ
δόξης κινδυνεύουσα πάντα τὸν αἰῶνα διατετέλεκε.
καὶ ταῦθ' οὕτω σεμνὰ καὶ προσήκοντα τοῖς ὑμετέ- 204
ροις ἤθεσιν ὑμεῖς ὑπολαμβάνετ' εἶναι ὥστε καὶ τῶν
προγόνων τοὺς ταῦτα πράξαντας μάλιστ' ἐπαινεῖτε,
εἰκότως. τίς γὰρ οὐκ ἂν ἀγάσαιτο τῶν ἀνδρῶν
ἐκείνων τῆς ἀρετῆς, οἳ καὶ τὴν χώραν καὶ τὴν πόλιν
ἐκλιπεῖν ὑπέμειναν εἰς τὰς τριήρεις ἐμβάντες ὑπὲρ
τοῦ μὴ τὸ κελευόμενον ποιῆσαι, τὸν μὲν ταῦτα συμ-
βουλεύσαντα Θεμιστοκλέα στρατηγὸν ἑλόμενοι, τὸν
δ' ὑπακούειν ἀποφηνάμενον τοῖς ἐπιταττομένοις
Κυρσίλον καταλιθώσαντες, οὐ μόνον αὐτὸν, ἀλλὰ
καὶ αἱ γυναῖκες αἱ ὑμέτεραι τὴν γυναῖκ' αὐτοῦ. οὐ 205
γὰρ ἐζήτουν οἱ τότ' Ἀθηναῖοι οὔτε ῥήτορα οὔτε
στρατηγὸν δι' ὅτου δουλεύσουσιν εὐτυχῶς, ἀλλ' οὐδὲ
ζῆν ἠξίουν, εἰ μὴ μετ' ἐλευθερίας ἐξέσται τοῦτο
ποιεῖν. ἡγεῖτο γὰρ αὐτῶν ἕκαστος οὐχὶ τῷ πατρὶ
καὶ τῇ μητρὶ μόνον γεγενῆσθαι, ἀλλὰ καὶ τῇ πατρίδι. διαφέρει δὲ τί; ὅτι ὁ μὲν τοῖς γονεῦσι μόνον
γεγενῆσθαι νομίζων τὸν τῆς εἱμαρμένης καὶ τὸν
αὐτόματον θάνατον περιμένει, ὁ δὲ καὶ τῇ πατρίδι
ὑπὲρ τοῦ μὴ ταύτην ἐπιδεῖν δουλεύουσαν ἀποθνή-
σκειν ἐθελήσει, καὶ φοβερωτέρας ἡγήσεται τὰς
ὕβρεις καὶ τὰς ἀτιμίας, ἃς ἐν δουλευούσῃ τῇ πόλει
φέρειν ἀνάγκη, τοῦ θανάτου.

Εἰ μὲν τοίνυν τοῦτ' ἐπεχείρουν λέγειν, ὡς ἐγὼ 206

προήγαγον ὑμᾶς ἄξια τῶν προγόνων φρονεῖν, οὐκ ἔσθ' ὅστις οὐκ ἂν εἰκότως ἐπιτιμήσειέ μοι. νῦν δ' ἐγὼ μὲν ὑμετέρας τὰς τοιαύτας προαιρέσεις ἀποφαίνω, καὶ δείκνυμι ὅτι καὶ πρὸ ἐμοῦ τοῦτ' εἶχε τὸ φρόνημα ἡ πόλις, τῆς μέντοι διακονίας τῆς ἐφ' ἑκάστοις τῶν πε-
207 πραγμένων καὶ ἐμαυτῷ μετεῖναί φημι, οὗτος δὲ τῶν ὅλων κατηγορῶν; καὶ κελεύων ὑμᾶς ἐμοὶ πικρῶς ἔχειν ὡς φόβων καὶ κινδύνων αἰτίῳ τῇ πόλει, τῆς μὲν εἰς τὸ παρὸν τιμῆς ἐμὲ ἀποστερῆσαι γλίχεται, τὰ δ' εἰς ἅπαντα τὸν λοιπὸν χρόνον ἐγκώμια ὑμῶν ἀφαιρεῖται. εἰ γὰρ ὡς οὐ τὰ βέλτιστα ἐμοῦ πολιτευσαμένου τουδὶ καταψηφιεῖσθε, ἡμαρτηκέναι δόξετε, οὐ τῇ τῆς τύχης ἀγνωμοσύνῃ τὰ συμβάντα παθεῖν.
208 ἀλλ' οὐκ ἔστιν, οὐκ ἔστιν ὅπως ἡμάρτετε, ἄνδρες Ἀθηναῖοι, τὸν ὑπὲρ τῆς ἁπάντων ἐλευθερίας καὶ σωτηρίας κίνδυνον ἀράμενοι, μὰ τοὺς Μαραθῶνι προκινδυνεύσαντας τῶν προγόνων καὶ τοὺς ἐν Πλαταιαῖς παραταξαμένους καὶ τοὺς ἐν Σαλαμῖνι ναυμαχήσαντας καὶ τοὺς ἐπ' Ἀρτεμισίῳ καὶ πολλοὺς ἑτέρους τοὺς ἐν τοῖς δημοσίοις μνήμασι κειμένους ἀγαθοὺς ἄνδρας, οὓς ἅπαντας ὁμοίως ἡ πόλις τῆς αὐτῆς ἀξιώσασα τιμῆς ἔθαψεν, Αἰσχίνη, οὐχὶ τοὺς κατορθώσαντας αὐτῶν οὐδὲ τοὺς κρατήσαντας μόνους. δικαίως. ὃ μὲν γὰρ ἦν ἀνδρῶν ἀγαθῶν ἔργον, ἅπασι πέπρακται· τῇ τύχῃ δ', ἣν ὁ δαίμων
209 ἔνειμεν ἑκάστοις, ταύτῃ κέχρηνται. ἔπειτ', ὦ κατάρατε καὶ γραμματοκύφων, σὺ μὲν τῆς παρὰ τουτωνὶ

τιμῆς καὶ φιλανθρωπίας ἔμ᾽ ἀποστερῆσαι βουλόμενος τρόπαια καὶ μάχας καὶ παλαιὰ ἔργα ἔλεγες, ὧν
τίνος προσεδεῖτο ὁ παρὼν ἀγὼν ουτοσί; ἐμὲ δέ, ὦ
τριταγωνιστά, τὸν περὶ τῶν πρωτείων σύμβουλον
τῇ πόλει παριόντα τὸ τίνος φρόνημα λαβόντ᾽ ἀνα-
βαίνειν ἐπὶ τὸ βῆμ᾽ ἔδει; τὸ τοῦ τούτων ἀνάξια 210
ἐροῦντος; δικαίως μέντ᾽ ἂν ἀπέθανον. ἐπεὶ οὐδ᾽ ὑμᾶς,
ὦ ἄνδρες Ἀθηναῖοι, ἀπὸ τῆς αὐτῆς διανοίας δεῖ τάς
τε ἰδίας δίκας καὶ τὰς δημοσίας κρίνειν, ἀλλὰ τὰ
μὲν τοῦ καθ᾽ ἡμέραν βίου συμβόλαια ἐπὶ τῶν ἰδίων
νόμων καὶ ἔργων σκοποῦντας, τὰς δὲ κοινὰς προαιρέσεις εἰς τὰ τῶν προγόνων ἀξιώματα ἀποβλέποντας. καὶ παραλαμβάνειν γε ἅμα τῇ βακτηρίᾳ καὶ
τῷ συμβόλῳ τὸ φρόνημα τὸ τῆς πόλεως νομίζειν
ἕκαστον ὑμῶν δεῖ, ὅταν τὰ δημόσια εἰσίητε κρινοῦν-
τες, εἴπερ ἄξια ἐκείνων πράττειν οἴεσθε χρῆναι.

Ἀλλὰ γὰρ ἐμπεσὼν εἰς τὰ πεπραγμένα τοῖς 211
προγόνοις ὑμῶν ἔστιν ἃ τῶν ψηφισμάτων παρέβην
καὶ τῶν πραχθέντων. ἐπανελθεῖν οὖν, ὁπόθεν εἰς
ταῦτ᾽ ἐξέβην, βούλομαι.

Ὡς γὰρ ἀφικόμεθ᾽ εἰς τὰς Θήβας, κατελαμβάνο-
μεν Φιλίππου καὶ Θετταλῶν καὶ τῶν ἄλλων συμμάχων παρόντας πρέσβεις, καὶ τοὺς μὲν ἡμετέρους
φίλους ἐν φόβῳ, τοὺς δ᾽ ἐκείνου θρασεῖς. ὅτι δ᾽
οὐ νῦν ταῦτα λέγω τοῦ συμφέροντος ἕνεκα ἐμαυτῷ
λέγε μοι τὴν ἐπιστολὴν ἣν τότ᾽ ἐπέμψαμεν εὐθὺς
οἱ πρέσβεις. καίτοι τοσαύτῃ γ᾽ ὑπερβολῇ συκο- 212

φαντίας οὗτος κέχρηται ὥστ', εἰ μέν τι τῶν δεόντων ἐπράχθη, τὸν καιρὸν, οὐκ ἐμέ φησιν αἴτιον γεγενῆσθαι, τῶν δ' ὡς ἑτέρως συμβάντων ἁπάντων ἐμὲ καὶ τὴν ἐμὴν τύχην αἰτίαν εἶναι. καὶ ὡς ἔοικεν, ὁ σύμβουλος καὶ ῥήτωρ ἐγὼ τῶν μὲν ἐκ λόγου καὶ τοῦ βουλεύσασθαι πραχθέντων οὐδενὸς αὐτῷ συναίτιος εἶναι δοκῶ, τῶν δ' ἐν τοῖς ὅπλοις καὶ κατὰ τὴν στρατηγίαν ἀτυχηθέντων μόνος αἴτιος εἶναι. πῶς ἂν ὠμότερος συκοφάντης γένοιτ' ἢ καταρατότερος; λέγε τὴν ἐπιστολήν.

ΕΠΙΣΤΟΛΗ.

213 Ἐπειδὴ τοίνυν ἐποιήσαντο τὴν ἐκκλησίαν, προσῆγον ἐκείνους προτέρους διὰ τὸ τὴν τῶν συμμάχων τάξιν ἐκείνους ἔχειν. καὶ παρελθόντες ἐδημηγόρουν πολλὰ μὲν Φίλιππον ἐγκωμιάζοντες, πολλὰ δ' ὑμῶν κατηγοροῦντες, πάνθ' ὅσα πώποτ' ἐναντία ἐπράξατε Θηβαίοις ἀναμιμνήσκοντες. τὸ δ' οὖν κεφάλαιον, ἠξίουν ὧν μὲν εὖ πεπόνθεσαν ὑπὸ Φιλίππου χάριν αὐτοὺς ἀποδοῦναι, ὧν δ' ὑφ' ὑμῶν ἠδίκηντο δίκην λαβεῖν, ὁποτέρως βούλονται, ἢ διέντας αὐτοὺς ἐφ' ὑμᾶς ἢ συνεμβαλόντας εἰς τὴν Ἀττικὴν, καὶ ἐδείκνυσαν, ὡς ᾤοντο, ἐκ μὲν ὧν αὐτοὶ συνεβούλευον τὰ ἐκ τῆς Ἀττικῆς βοσκήματα καὶ ἀνδράποδα καὶ τἄλλ' ἀγαθὰ εἰς τὴν Βοιωτίαν ἥξοντα, ἐκ δὲ ὧν ἡμᾶς ἐρεῖν ἔφασαν τὰ ἐν τῇ Βοιωτίᾳ διαρπασθησόμενα ὑπὸ τοῦ πολέμου. καὶ ἄλλα πολλὰ πρὸς τούτοις, εἰς

ταὐτὰ δὲ πάντα συντείνοντ' ἔλεγον. ἃ δ' ἡμεῖς 214
πρὸς ταῦτα ἀντείπομεν, τὰ μὲν καθ' ἕκαστα ἐγὼ μὲν ἀντὶ παντὸς ἂν τιμησαίμην εἰπεῖν τοῦ βίου, ὑμᾶς δὲ δέδοικα, μὴ παρεληλυθότων τῶν καιρῶν, ὥσπερ ἂν εἰ κατακλυσμὸν γεγενῆσθαι τῶν πραγμάτων ἡγούμενοι, μάταιον ὄχλον τοὺς περὶ τούτων λόγους νομίσητε· ὅ τι δ' οὖν ἐπείσαμεν ἡμεῖς καὶ ἃ ἡμῖν ἀπεκρίναντο, ἀκούσατε. Λέγε ταυτὶ λαβών.

ΑΠΟΚΡΙΣΙΣ ΘΗΒΑΙΩΝ.

Μετὰ ταῦτα τοίνυν ἐκάλουν ὑμᾶς καὶ μετεπέμ- 215
ποντο. ἐξῆτε, ἐβοηθεῖτε, ἵνα τἀν μέσῳ παραλείπω, οὕτως οἰκείως ὑμᾶς ἐδέχοντο ὥστ' ἔξω τῶν ὁπλιτῶν καὶ τῶν ἱππέων ὄντων εἰς τὰς οἰκίας καὶ τὸ ἄστυ δέχεσθαι τὴν στρατιὰν ἐπὶ παῖδας καὶ γυναῖκας καὶ τὰ τιμιώτατα. καίτοι τρία ἐν ἐκείνῃ τῇ ἡμέρᾳ πᾶσιν ἀνθρώποις ἔδειξαν ἐγκώμια Θηβαῖοι καθ' ὑμῶν τὰ κάλλιστα, ἓν μὲν ἀνδρείας, ἕτερον δὲ δικαιοσύνης, τρίτον δὲ σωφροσύνης. καὶ γὰρ τὸν ἀγῶνα μεθ' ὑμῶν μᾶλλον ἢ πρὸς ὑμᾶς ἑλόμενοι ποιήσασθαι καὶ ἀμείνους εἶναι καὶ δικαιότερ' ἀξιοῦν ὑμᾶς ἔκριναν Φιλίππου· καὶ τὰ παρ' αὐτοῖς καὶ παρὰ πᾶσι δ' ἐν πλείστῃ φυλακῇ, παῖδας καὶ γυναῖκας, ἐφ' ὑμῖν ποιήσαντες σωφροσύνης πίστιν περὶ ὑμῶν ἔχοντες
ἔδειξαν. ἐν οἷς πᾶσιν, ἄνδρες Ἀθηναῖοι, κατά γ' 216
ὑμᾶς ὀρθῶς ἐφάνησαν ἐγνωκότες. οὔτε γὰρ εἰς τὴν πόλιν εἰσελθόντος τοῦ στρατοπέδου οὐδεὶς οὐδὲν

οὐδὲ ἀδίκως ὑμῖν ἐνεκάλεσεν· οὕτω σώφρονας παρέσχετε ὑμᾶς αὐτούς· δίς τε συμπαραταξάμενοι τὰς πρώτας μάχας, τήν τ' ἐπὶ τοῦ ποταμοῦ καὶ τὴν χειμερινὴν, οὐκ ἀμέμπτους μόνον ὑμᾶς αὐτοὺς, ἀλλὰ καὶ θαυμαστοὺς ἐδείξατε τῷ κόσμῳ, ταῖς παρασκευαῖς, τῇ προθυμίᾳ. ἐφ' οἷς παρὰ μὲν τῶν ἄλλων ὑμῖν ἐγίγνοντο ἔπαινοι, παρὰ δ' ὑμῶν θυσίαι καὶ
217 πομπαὶ τοῖς θεοῖς. καὶ ἔγωγε ἡδέως ἂν ἐροίμην Αἰσχίνην, ὅτε ταῦτ' ἐπράττετο καὶ ζήλου καὶ χαρᾶς καὶ ἐπαίνων ἡ πόλις ἦν μεστὴ, πότερον συνέθυε καὶ συνευφραίνετο τοῖς πολλοῖς, ἢ λυπούμενος καὶ στένων καὶ δυσμεναίνων τοῖς κοινοῖς ἀγαθοῖς οἴκοι καθῆτο. εἰ μὲν γὰρ παρῆν καὶ μετὰ τῶν ἄλλων ἐξητάζετο, πῶς οὐ δεινὰ ποιεῖ, μᾶλλον δ' οὐδ' ὅσια, εἰ ὧν ὡς ἀρίστων αὐτὸς τοὺς θεοὺς ἐποιήσατο μάρτυρας, ταῦθ' ὡς οὐκ ἄριστα νῦν ὑμᾶς ἀξιοῖ ψηφίσασθαι τοὺς ὀμωμοκότας τοὺς θεούς; εἰ δὲ μὴ παρῆν, πῶς οὐκ ἀπολωλέναι πολλάκις ἐστὶ δίκαιος, εἰ ἐφ' οἷς ἔχαιρον οἱ ἄλλοι, ταῦτα ἐλυπεῖτο ὁρῶν; Λέγε δὴ καὶ ταῦτα τὰ ψηφίσματά μοι.

ΨΗΦΙΣΜΑΤΑ ΘΥΣΙΩΝ.

218 Οὐκοῦν ἡμεῖς μὲν ἐν θυσίαις ἦμεν τότε, Θηβαῖοι δ' ἐν τῷ δι' ἡμᾶς σεσῶσθαι νομίζειν, καὶ περιειστήκει τοῖς βοηθείας δεήσεσθαι δοκοῦσιν ἀφ' ὧν ἔπραττον οὗτοι, αὐτοὺς βοηθεῖν ἑτέροις ἐξ ὧν ἐπείσθητ' ἐμοί. ἀλλὰ μὴν οἵας τότ' ἠφίει φωνὰς ὁ Φίλιππος

καὶ ἐν οἵαις ἦν ταραχαῖς ἐπὶ τούτοις, ἐκ τῶν ἐπιστο-
λῶν τῶν ἐκείνου μαθήσεσθε ὧν εἰς Πελοπόννησον
ἔπεμπεν. καί μοι λέγε ταύτας λαβών, ἵν' εἰδῆτε ἡ
ἐμὴ συνέχεια καὶ πλάνοι καὶ ταλαιπωρίαι καὶ τὰ
πολλὰ ψηφίσματα, ἃ νῦν οὗτος διέσυρε, τί ἀπειργάσατο.

Καίτοι πολλοὶ παρ' ὑμῖν, ἄνδρες Ἀθηναῖοι, γεγό- 219
νασι ῥήτορες ἔνδοξοι καὶ μεγάλοι πρὸ ἐμοῦ, Καλλίστρατος ἐκεῖνος, Ἀριστοφῶν, Κέφαλος, Θρασύβουλος, ἕτεροι μυρίοι· ἀλλ' ὅμως οὐδεὶς πώποτε
τούτων διὰ παντὸς ἔδωκεν ἑαυτὸν εἰς οὐδὲν τῇ πόλει,
ἀλλ' ὁ μὲν γράφων οὐκ ἂν ἐπρέσβευσεν, ὁ δὲ πρεσ-
βεύων οὐκ ἂν ἔγραψεν. ὑπέλειπε γὰρ αὑτῶν ἕκαστος
ἑαυτῷ ἅμα μὲν ῥᾳστώνην, ἅμα δ', εἴ τι γένοιτ', ἀναφοράν. τί οὖν; εἴποι τις ἄν, σὺ τοσοῦτον ὑπερῆρας 220
τοὺς ἄλλους ῥώμῃ καὶ τόλμῃ ὥστε πάντα ποιεῖν αὐτός;
οὐ ταῦτα λέγω, ἀλλ' οὕτως ἐπεπείσμην μέγαν εἶναι
τὸν κατειληφότα κίνδυνον τὴν πόλιν ὥστ' οὐκ ἐδόκει
μοι χώραν οὐδὲ πρόνοιαν οὐδεμίαν τῆς ἰδίας ἀσφαλείας
διδόναι, ἀλλ' ἀγαπητὸν εἶναι, εἰ μηδὲν παραλιπών
τις ἃ δεῖ πράξειεν. ἐπεπείσμην δ' ὑπὲρ ἐμαυτοῦ, 221
τυχὸν μὲν ἀναισθητῶν, ὅμως δ' ἐπεπείσμην, μήτε
γράφοντ' ἂν ἐμοῦ γράψαι βέλτιον μηδένα, μήτε
πράττοντα πρᾶξαι, μήτε πρεσβεύοντα πρεσβεῦσαι
προθυμότερον μηδὲ δικαιότερον. διὰ ταῦτα ἐν πᾶσιν ἐμαυτὸν ἔταττον. Λέγε τὰς ἐπιστολὰς τὰς τοῦ
Φιλίππου.

ΕΠΙΣΤΟΛΑΙ.

222 *Εἰς ταῦτα κατέστησε Φίλιππον ἡ ἐμὴ πολιτεία, Αἰσχίνη· ταύτην τὴν φωνὴν ἐκεῖνος ἀφῆκε, πολλοὺς καὶ θρασεῖς τὰ πρὸ τούτων τῇ πόλει ἐπαιρόμενος λόγους. ἀνθ' ὧν δικαίως ἐστεφανούμην ὑπὸ τουτωνὶ, καὶ σὺ παρὼν οὐκ ἀντέλεγες, ὁ δὲ γραψάμενος Διώνδας τὸ μέρος τῶν ψήφων οὐκ ἔλαβεν. Καί μοι λέγε ταῦτα τὰ ψηφίσματα τὰ τότε μὲν ἀποπεφευγότα, ὑπὸ τούτου δ' οὐδὲ γραφέντα.*

ΨΗΦΙΣΜΑΤΑ.

223 *Ταυτὶ τὰ ψηφίσματ', ὦ ἄνδρες Ἀθηναῖοι, τὰς αὐτὰς συλλαβὰς καὶ ταὐτὰ ῥήματ' ἔχει ἅπερ πρότερον μὲν Ἀριστόνικος, νῦν δὲ Κτησιφῶν γέγραφεν οὑτοσί. καὶ ταῦτ' Αἰσχίνης οὔτ' ἐδίωξεν αὐτὸς οὔτε τῷ γραψαμένῳ συγκατηγόρησεν. καίτοι τότε τὸν Δημομέλην τὸν ταῦτα γράφοντα καὶ τὸν Ὑπερείδην, εἴπερ ἀληθῆ μου νῦν κατηγορεῖ, μᾶλλον ἂν εἰκότως*
224 *ἢ τόνδ' ἐδίωκεν. διὰ τί; ὅτι τῷδε μὲν ἔστ' ἀνενεγκεῖν ἐπ' ἐκείνους καὶ τὰς τῶν δικαστηρίων γνώσεις καὶ τὸ τοῦτον αὐτὸν ἐκείνων μὴ κατηγορηκέναι ταὐτὰ γραψάντων ἅπερ οὗτος νυνὶ, καὶ τὸ τοὺς νόμους μηκέτ' ἐᾶν περὶ τῶν οὕτω πραχθέντων κατηγορεῖν. καὶ πολλὰ ἕτερα· τότε δ' αὐτὸ τὸ πρᾶγμ' ἂν ἐκρίνετο ἐφ' αὑτοῦ, πρίν τι τούτων προλαβεῖν.*
225 *ἀλλ' οὐκ ἦν, οἶμαι, τότε, ὃ νυνὶ ποιεῖ, ἐκ παλαιῶν*

χρόνων καὶ ψηφισμάτων πολλῶν ἐκλέξαντα ἃ μήτε
προῄδει μηδεὶς μήτ' ἂν ᾠήθη τήμερον ῥηθῆναι διαβάλλειν, καὶ μετενεγκόντα τοὺς χρόνους καὶ προφάσεις ἀντὶ τῶν ἀληθῶν ψευδεῖς μεταθέντα τοῖς
πεπραγμένοις δοκεῖν τι λέγειν. οὐκ ἦν τότε ταῦτα, 226
ἀλλ' ἐπὶ τῆς ἀληθείας, ἐγγὺς τῶν ἔργων, ἔτι μεμνη-
μένων ὑμῶν καὶ μόνον οὐκ ἐν ταῖς χερσὶν ἕκαστα
ἐχόντων, πάντες ἐγίγνοντ' ἂν οἱ λόγοι. διόπερ τοὺς
παρ' αὐτὰ τὰ πράγματ' ἐλέγχους φυγὼν νῦν ἥκει,
ῥητόρων ἀγῶνα νομίζων, ὥς γ' ἐμοὶ δοκεῖ, καὶ οὐχὶ
τῶν πεπολιτευμένων ἐξέτασιν ποιήσειν ὑμᾶς, καὶ
λόγου κρίσιν, οὐχὶ τοῦ τῇ πόλει συμφέροντος
ἔσεσθαι.

Εἶτα σοφίζεται, καὶ φησὶ προσήκειν, ἧς μὲν 227
οἴκοθεν ἥκετ' ἔχοντες δόξης περὶ ἡμῶν ἀμελῆσαι,
ὥσπερ δ', ὅταν οἰόμενοι περιεῖναι χρήματά τῳ λογίζησθε, ἂν καθαραὶ ὦσιν αἱ ψῆφοι καὶ μηδὲν περιῇ,
συγχωρεῖτε, οὕτω καὶ νῦν τοῖς ἐκ τοῦ λόγου φαινομέ-
νοις προσθέσθαι. θεάσασθε τοίνυν ὡς σαθρόν, ὡς
ἔοικεν, ἔστι φύσει πᾶν ὅ τι ἂν μὴ δικαίως ᾖ πεπραγμένον. ἐκ γὰρ αὐτοῦ τοῦ σοφοῦ τούτου παραδείγ- 228
ματος ὡμολόγηκε νῦν γ' ἡμᾶς ὑπάρχειν ἐγνωσμένους
ἐμὲ μὲν λέγειν ὑπὲρ τῆς πατρίδος, αὐτὸν δ' ὑπὲρ
Φιλίππου· οὐ γὰρ ἂν μεταπείθειν ὑμᾶς ἐζήτει μὴ
τοιαύτης οὔσης τῆς ὑπαρχούσης ὑπολήψεως περὶ
ἑκατέρου. καὶ μὴν ὅτι γε οὐ δίκαια λέγει μεταθέ- 229
σθαι ταύτην τὴν δόξαν ἀξιῶν, ἐγὼ διδάξω ῥᾳδίως, οὐ

τιθεὶς ψήφους (οὐ γάρ ἐστιν ὁ τῶν πραγμάτων
οὗτος λογισμός), ἀλλ' ἀναμιμνήσκων ἕκαστα ἐν
βραχέσι, λογισταῖς ἅμα καὶ μάρτυσι τοῖς ἀκούου-
230 σιν ὑμῖν χρώμενος. ἡ γὰρ ἐμὴ πολιτεία, ἧς οὗτος
κατηγορεῖ, ἀντὶ μὲν τοῦ Θηβαίους μετὰ Φιλίππου
συνεμβαλεῖν εἰς τὴν χώραν, ὃ πάντες ᾤοντο, μεθ'
ἡμῶν παραταξαμένους ἐκεῖνον κωλύειν ἐποίησεν,
ἀντὶ δὲ τοῦ ἐν τῇ Ἀττικῇ τὸν πόλεμον εἶναι ἑπτα-
κόσια στάδια ἀπὸ τῆς πόλεως ἐπὶ τοῖς Βοιωτῶν
ὁρίοις γενέσθαι, ἀντὶ δὲ τοῦ τοὺς λῃστὰς ἡμᾶς φέρειν καὶ ἄγειν ἐκ τῆς Εὐβοίας ἐν εἰρήνῃ τὴν Ἀττικὴν ἐκ θαλάττης εἶναι πάντα τὸν πόλεμον, ἀντὶ δὲ
τοῦ τὸν Ἑλλήσποντον ἔχειν Φίλιππον, λαβόντα
Βυζάντιον, συμπολεμεῖν τοὺς Βυζαντίους μεθ' ἡμῶν
231 πρὸς ἐκεῖνον. ἆρά σοι ψήφοις ὅμοιος ὁ τῶν ἔργων
λογισμὸς φαίνεται; ἢ δεῖν ἀντανελεῖν ταῦτα, ἀλλ'
οὐχ ὅπως τὸν ἅπαντα χρόνον μνημονευθήσεται σκέ-
ψασθαι; καὶ οὐκέτι προστίθημι ὅτι τῆς μὲν ὠμό-
τητος, ἣν ἐν οἷς καθάπαξ τινῶν κύριος κατέστη
Φίλιππος ἔστιν ἰδεῖν, ἑτέροις πειραθῆναι συνέβη,
τῆς δὲ φιλανθρωπίας, ἣν τὰ λοιπὰ τῶν πραγμάτων
ἐκεῖνος περιβαλλόμενος ἐπλάττετο, ὑμεῖς καλῶς ποιοῦντες τοὺς καρποὺς κεκόμισθε. ἀλλ' ἐῶ ταῦτα.
232 Καὶ μὴν οὐδὲ τοῦτ' εἰπεῖν ὀκνήσω, ὅτι ὁ τὸν
ῥήτορα βουλόμενος δικαίως ἐξετάζειν καὶ μὴ συκοφαντεῖν, οὐκ ἂν οἷα σὺ νῦν ἔλεγες, τοιαῦτα κατηγόρει, παραδείγματα πλάττων καὶ ῥήματα καὶ σχή-

ματα μιμούμενος (πάνυ γὰρ παρὰ τοῦτο, οὐχ ὁρᾷς;
γέγονε τὰ τῶν Ἑλλήνων, εἰ τουτὶ τὸ ῥῆμα, ἀλλὰ
μὴ τουτὶ διελέχθην ἐγώ, ἢ δευρὶ τὴν χεῖρα, ἀλλὰ
μὴ δευρὶ παρήνεγκα), ἀλλ' ἐπ' αὐτῶν τῶν ἔργων 233
ἂν ἐσκόπει τίνας εἶχεν ἀφορμὰς ἡ πόλις καὶ τίνας
δυνάμεις, ὅτ' εἰς τὰ πράγματ' εἰσῄειν, καὶ τίνας
συνήγαγον αὐτῇ μετὰ ταῦτ' ἐπιστὰς ἐγώ, καὶ πῶς
εἶχε τὰ τῶν ἐναντίων. εἶτ' εἰ μὲν ἐλάττους ἐποίησα
τὰς δυνάμεις, παρ' ἐμοὶ τἀδίκημ' ἂν ἐδείκνυεν ὄν, εἰ
δὲ πολλῷ μείζους, οὐκ ἂν ἐσυκοφάντει. ἐπειδὴ δὲ
σὺ τοῦτο πέφευγας, ἐγὼ ποιήσω· καὶ σκοπεῖτε εἰ
δικαίως χρήσομαι τῷ λόγῳ.

Δύναμιν μὲν τοίνυν εἶχεν ἡ πόλις τοὺς νησιώτας, 234
οὐχ ἅπαντας, ἀλλὰ τοὺς ἀσθενεστάτους· οὔτε γὰρ
Χίος οὔτε Ῥόδος οὔτε Κέρκυρα μεθ' ἡμῶν ἦν·
χρημάτων δὲ σύνταξιν εἰς πέντε καὶ τετταράκοντα
τάλαντα, καὶ ταῦτ' ἦν προεξειλεγμένα· ὁπλίτην δ'
ἢ ἱππέα πλὴν τῶν οἰκείων οὐδένα. ὃ δὲ πάντων
καὶ φοβερώτατον καὶ μάλισθ' ὑπὲρ τῶν ἐχθρῶν,
οὗτοι παρεσκευάκεισαν τοὺς περιχώρους πάντας
ἔχθρας ἢ φιλίας ἐγγυτέρω, Μεγαρέας, Θηβαίους,
Εὐβοέας. τὰ μὲν τῆς πόλεως οὕτως ὑπῆρχεν ἔχοντα, 235
καὶ οὐδεὶς ἂν ἔχοι παρὰ ταῦτ' εἰπεῖν ἄλλο οὐδέν·
τὰ δὲ τοῦ Φιλίππου, πρὸς ὃν ἦν ἡμῖν ὁ ἀγών,
σκέψασθε πῶς. πρῶτον μὲν ἦρχε τῶν ἀκολουθούντων αὐτὸς αὐτοκράτωρ ὤν, ὃ τῶν εἰς τὸν πόλεμον μέγιστόν ἐστιν ἁπάντων· εἶθ' οὗτοι τὰ ὅπλα

εἶχον ἐν ταῖς χερσὶν ἀεί· ἔπειτα χρημάτων ηὐπόρει,
καὶ ἔπραττεν ἃ δόξειεν αὐτῷ, οὐ προλέγων ἐν τοῖς
ψηφίσμασιν, οὐδ' ἐν τῷ φανερῷ βουλευόμενος,
[οὐδ' ὑπὸ τῶν συκοφαντούντων κρινόμενος,] οὐδὲ
γραφὰς φεύγων παρανόμων, οὐδ' ὑπεύθυνος ὢν
οὐδενί, ἀλλ' ἁπλῶς αὐτὸς δεσπότης, ἡγεμών, κύριος
236 πάντων. ἐγὼ δ' ὁ πρὸς τοῦτον ἀντιτεταγμένος
(καὶ γὰρ τοῦτ' ἐξετάσαι δίκαιον) τίνος κύριος ἦν;
οὐδενός· αὐτὸ γὰρ τὸ δημηγορεῖν πρῶτον, οὗ μόνου
μετεῖχον ἐγώ, ἐξ ἴσου προὐτίθεθ' ὑμεῖς τοῖς παρ'
ἐκείνου μισθαρνοῦσι καὶ ἐμοί, καὶ ὅσα οὗτοι περι-
γένοιντο ἐμοῦ (πολλὰ δ' ἐγίγνετο ταῦτα, δι' ἣν
ἕκαστον τύχοι πρόφασιν), ταῦθ' ὑπὲρ τῶν ἐχθρῶν
237 ἀπῆτε βεβουλευμένοι. ἀλλ' ὅμως ἐκ τοιούτων ἐλατ-
τωμάτων ἐγὼ συμμάχους μὲν ὑμῖν ἐποίησα Εὐβοέας,
Ἀχαιούς, Κορινθίους, Θηβαίους, Μεγαρέας, Λευκα-
δίους, Κερκυραίους, ἀφ' ὧν μύριοι μὲν καὶ πεντακισ-
χίλιοι ξένοι, δισχίλιοι δ' ἱππεῖς ἄνευ τῶν πολιτικῶν
δυνάμεων συνήχθησαν· χρημάτων δὲ ὅσων ἐδυνήθην
238 ἐγὼ πλείστην συντέλειαν ἐποίησα. εἰ δὲ λέγεις ἢ τὰ
πρὸς Θηβαίους δίκαια, Αἰσχίνη, ἢ τὰ πρὸς Βυζαντίους ἢ τὰ πρὸς Εὐβοέας, ἢ περὶ τῶν ἴσων νυνὶ
διαλέγει, πρῶτον μὲν ἀγνοεῖς ὅτι καὶ πρότερον τῶν
ὑπὲρ τῶν Ἑλλήνων ἐκείνων ἀγωνισαμένων τριήρων,
τριακοσίων οὐσῶν τῶν πασῶν, τὰς διακοσίας ἡ πόλις παρέσχετο, καὶ οὐκ ἐλαττοῦσθαι νομίζουσα οὐδὲ
κρίνουσα τοὺς ταῦτα συμβουλεύσαντας οὐδὲ ἀγα-

νακτοῦσα ἐπὶ τούτοις ἑωρᾶτο (αἰσχρὸν γάρ), ἀλλὰ
τοῖς θεοῖς ἔχουσα χάριν, εἰ κοινοῦ κινδύνου τοῖς
Ἕλλησι περιστάντος αὐτὴ διπλάσια τῶν ἄλλων
εἰς τὴν ἁπάντων σωτηρίαν παρέσχετο. εἶτα κενὰς 239
χαρίζει χάριτας τουτοισὶ συκοφαντῶν ἐμέ. τί γὰρ
νῦν λέγεις οἷα ἐχρῆν πράττειν, ἀλλ᾽ οὐ τότ᾽ ὢν ἐν
τῇ πόλει καὶ παρὼν ταῦτ᾽ ἔγραφες, εἴπερ ἐνεδέχετο
παρὰ τοὺς παρόντας καιρούς, ἐν οἷς οὐχ ὅσα ἐβουλόμεθα, ἀλλ᾽ ὅσα δοίη τὰ πράγματ᾽ ἔδει δέχεσθαι·
ὁ γὰρ ἀντωνούμενος καὶ ταχὺ τοὺς παρ᾽ ἡμῶν ἀπε-
λαυνομένους προσδεξόμενος καὶ χρήματα προσθή-
σων ὑπῆρχεν ἕτοιμος.

Ἀλλ᾽ εἰ νῦν ἐπὶ τοῖς πεπραγμένοις κατηγορίας 240
ἔχω, τί ἂν οἴεσθε, εἰ τότ᾽ ἐμοῦ περὶ τούτων ἀκριβολογουμένου, ἀπῆλθον αἱ πόλεις καὶ προσέθεντο
Φιλίππῳ, καὶ ἅμα Εὐβοίας καὶ Θηβῶν καὶ Βυζαντίου κύριος κατέστη, τί ποιεῖν ἂν ἢ τί λέγειν τοὺς
ἀσεβεῖς ἀνθρώπους τουτουσί; οὐχ ὡς ἐξεδόθησαν;
οὐχ ὡς ἀπηλάθησαν βουλόμενοι μεθ᾽ ἡμῶν εἶναι; 241
εἶτα τοῦ μὲν Ἑλλησπόντου διὰ Βυζαντίων ἐγκρατὴς καθέστηκε, καὶ τῆς σιτοπομπίας τῆς τῶν Ἑλλήνων κύριος, πόλεμος δ᾽ ὅμορος καὶ βαρὺς εἰς τὴν
Ἀττικὴν διὰ Θηβαίων κεκόμισται, ἄπλους δ᾽ ἡ θά-
λαττα ὑπὸ τῶν ἐκ τῆς Εὐβοίας ὁρμωμένων λῃστῶν
γέγονεν; οὐκ ἂν ταῦτ᾽ ἔλεγον, καὶ πολλά γε πρὸς
τούτοις ἕτερα; πονηρόν, ὦ ἄνδρες Ἀθηναῖοι, πονη- 242
ρὸν ὁ συκοφάντης ἀεὶ καὶ πανταχόθεν βάσκανον

καὶ φιλαίτιον· τοῦτο δὲ καὶ φύσει κίναδος τἀνθρώ-
πιόν ἐστιν, οὐδὲν ἐξ ἀρχῆς ὑγιὲς πεποιηκὸς οὐδ'
ἐλεύθερον, αὐτοτραγικὸς πίθηκος, ἀρουραῖος Οἰνό-
μαος, παράσημος ῥήτωρ. τί γὰρ ἡ σὴ δεινότης εἰς
ὄνησιν ἥκει τῇ πατρίδι; νῦν ἡμῖν λέγεις περὶ τῶν
243 παρεληλυθότων; ὥσπερ ἂν εἴ τις ἰατρὸς ἀσθενοῦσι
μὲν τοῖς κάμνουσιν εἰσιὼν μὴ λέγοι μηδὲ δεικνύοι
δι' ὧν ἀποφεύξονται τὴν νόσον, ἐπειδὴ δὲ τελευτή-
σειέ τις αὐτῶν καὶ τὰ νομιζόμεν' αὐτῷ φέροιτο, ἀκο-
λουθῶν ἐπὶ τὸ μνῆμα διεξίοι "εἰ τὸ καὶ τὸ ἐποίησεν
ἄνθρωπος οὑτοσί, οὐκ ἂν ἀπέθανεν." ἐμβρόντητε,
εἶτα νῦν λέγεις;

244 Οὐ τοίνυν οὐδὲ τὴν ἧτταν, εἰ ταύτῃ γαυριᾷς ἐφ'
ᾗ στένειν σε, ὦ κατάρατε, προσῆκεν, ἐν οὐδενὶ τῶν
παρ' ἐμοὶ γεγονυῖαν εὑρήσετε τῇ πόλει. οὑτωσὶ δὲ
λογίζεσθε. οὐδαμοῦ πώποθ', ὅποι πρεσβευτὴς
ἐπέμφθην ὑφ' ὑμῶν ἐγὼ, ἡττηθεὶς ἀπῆλθον τῶν
παρὰ Φιλίππου πρέσβεων, οὐκ ἐκ Θετταλίας, οὐκ
ἐξ Ἀμβρακίας, οὐκ ἐξ Ἰλλυριῶν, οὐ παρὰ τῶν Θρᾳκῶν βασιλέων, οὐκ ἐκ Βυζαντίου, οὐκ ἄλλοθεν οὐδα-
μόθεν, οὐ τὰ τελευταῖα ἐκ Θηβῶν, ἀλλ' ἐν οἷς κρα-
τηθεῖεν οἱ πρέσβεις αὐτοῦ τῷ λόγῳ, ταῦτα τοῖς
245 ὅπλοις ἐπιὼν κατεστρέφετο. ταῦτ' οὖν ἀπαιτεῖς
παρ' ἐμοῦ, καὶ οὐκ αἰσχύνει τὸν αὐτὸν εἴς τε μαλακίαν σκώπτων καὶ τῆς Φιλίππου δυνάμεως ἀξιῶν
ἕνα ὄντα κρείττω γενέσθαι; καὶ ταῦτα τοῖς λόγοις;
τίνος γὰρ ἄλλου κύριος ἦν ἐγώ; οὐ γὰρ τῆς γε

ἑκάστου ψυχῆς, οὐδὲ τῆς τύχης τῶν παραταξαμέ-
νων, οὐδὲ τῆς στρατηγίας, ἧς ἔμ' ἀπαιτεῖς εὐθύνας·
οὕτω σκαιὸς εἶ. ἀλλὰ μὴν ὧν γ' ἂν ὁ ῥήτωρ ὑπεύθυ- 246
νος εἴη, πᾶσαν ἐξέτασιν λάμβανε· οὐ παραιτοῦμαι.
τίνα οὖν ἐστι ταῦτα; ἰδεῖν τὰ πράγματα ἀρχόμενα
καὶ προαισθέσθαι καὶ προειπεῖν τοῖς ἄλλοις. ταῦτα
πέπρακταί μοι. καὶ ἔτι τὰς ἑκασταχοῦ βραδυτῆτας,
ὄκνους, ἀγνοίας, φιλονεικίας, ἃ πολιτικὰ ταῖς πόλεσι
πρόσεστιν ἁπάσαις καὶ ἀναγκαῖα ἁμαρτήματα, ταῦθ'
ὡς εἰς ἐλάχιστα συστεῖλαι, καὶ τοὐναντίον εἰς ὁμόνοιαν καὶ φιλίαν καὶ τοῦ τὰ δέοντα ποιεῖν ὁρμὴν
προτρέψαι. καὶ ταῦτά μοι πάντα πεποίηται, καὶ
οὐδεὶς μήποθ' εὕρῃ τὸ κατ' ἐμὲ οὐδὲν ἐλλειφθέν.
εἰ τοίνυν τις ἔροιτο ὁντινοῦν τίσι τὰ πλεῖστα Φίλιπ- 247
πος ὧν κατέπραξε διῳκήσατο, πάντες ἂν εἴποιεν τῷ
στρατοπέδῳ καὶ τῷ διδόναι καὶ διαφθείρειν τοὺς ἐπὶ
τῶν πραγμάτων. οὐκοῦν τῶν μὲν δυνάμεων οὔτε κύριος οὔθ' ἡγεμὼν ἦν ἐγώ, ὥστε οὐδ' ὁ λόγος τῶν κατὰ
ταῦτα πραχθέντων πρὸς ἐμέ. καὶ μὴν τῷ διαφθαρῆναι χρήμασιν ἢ μὴ κεκράτηκα Φιλίππου· ὥσπερ γὰρ
ὁ ὠνούμενος νενίκηκε τὸν λαβόντα, ἐὰν πρίηται, οὕτως
ὁ μὴ λαβὼν μηδὲ διαφθαρεὶς νενίκηκε τὸν ὠνούμενον.
ὥστε ἀήττητος ἡ πόλις τὸ κατ' ἐμέ.

Ἃ μὲν τοίνυν ἐγὼ παρεσχόμην εἰς τὸ δικαίως 248
τοιαῦτα γράφειν τουτονὶ περὶ ἐμοῦ, πρὸς πολλοῖς
ἑτέροις ταῦτα καὶ παραπλήσια τούτοις ἐστίν· ἃ δ'
οἱ πάντες ὑμεῖς, ταῦτ' ἤδη λέξω. μετὰ γὰρ τὴν

μάχην εὐθὺς ὁ δῆμος, εἰδὼς καὶ ἑορακὼς πάντα ὅσα ἔπραττον ἐγώ, ἐν αὐτοῖς τοῖς δεινοῖς καὶ φοβεροῖς ἐμβεβηκώς, ἡνίκ' οὐδ' ἀγνωμονῆσαί τι θαυμαστὸν ἦν τοὺς πολλοὺς πρὸς ἐμέ, πρῶτον μὲν περὶ σωτηρίας τῆς πόλεως τὰς ἐμὰς γνώμας ἐχειροτόνει, καὶ πάνθ' ὅσα τῆς φυλακῆς ἕνεκα ἐπράττετο, ἡ διάταξις τῶν φυλάκων, αἱ τάφροι, τὰ εἰς τὰ τείχη χρήματα, διὰ τῶν ἐμῶν ψηφισμάτων ἐγίγνετο· ἔπειθ' αἱρούμενος σιτώνην ἐκ πάντων ἐμὲ ἐχειροτόνησεν ὁ δῆμος.

249 καὶ μετὰ ταῦτα συστάντων οἷς ἦν ἐπιμελὲς κακῶς ἐμὲ ποιεῖν, καὶ γραφάς, εὐθύνας, εἰσαγγελίας, πάντα ταῦτ' ἐπαγόντων μοι, οὐ δι' ἑαυτῶν τό γε πρῶτον, ἀλλὰ δι' ὧν μάλισθ' ὑπελάμβανον ἀγνοήσεσθαι (ἴστε γὰρ δήπου καὶ μέμνησθε ὅτι τοὺς πρώτους χρόνους κατὰ τὴν ἡμέραν ἑκάστην ἐκρινόμην ἐγώ, καὶ οὔτ' ἀπόνοια Σωσικλέους οὔτε συκοφαντία Φιλοκράτους οὔτε Διώνδου καὶ Μελάντου μανία οὔτ' ἄλλ' οὐδὲν ἀπείρατον ἦν τούτοις κατ' ἐμοῦ), ἐν τοίνυν τούτοις πᾶσι μάλιστα μὲν διὰ τοὺς θεούς, δεύτερον δὲ δι' ὑμᾶς καὶ τοὺς ἄλλους Ἀθηναίους ἐσωζόμην. δικαίως· τοῦτο γὰρ καὶ ἀληθές ἐστι καὶ ὑπὲρ τῶν ὀμωμοκότων καὶ γνόντων τὰ εὔορκα δικαστῶν.

250 οὐκοῦν ἐν μὲν οἷς εἰσηγγελλόμην, ὅτ' ἀπεψηφίζεσθέ μου καὶ τὸ μέρος τῶν ψήφων τοῖς διώκουσιν οὐ μετεδίδοτε, τότ' ἐψηφίζεσθε τὰ ἄριστά με πράττειν· ἐν οἷς δὲ τὰς γραφὰς ἀπέφευγον, ἔννομα καὶ γράφειν καὶ λέγειν ἀπεδεικνύμην· ἐν οἷς δὲ τὰς εὐθύνας

ἐπεσημαίνεσθε, δικαίως καὶ ἀδωροδοκήτως πάντα πεπρᾶχθαί μοι προσωμολογεῖτε. τούτων οὖν οὕτως ἐχόντων τί προσῆκεν ἢ τί δίκαιον ἦν τοῖς ὑπ' ἐμοῦ πεπραγμένοις θέσθαι τὸν Κτησιφῶντα ὄνομα, οὐχ ὃ τὸν δῆμον ἑώρα τιθέμενον, οὐχ ὃ τοὺς ὀμωμοκότας δικαστὰς, οὐχ ὃ τὴν ἀλήθειαν παρὰ πᾶσι βεβαιοῦσαν;

Ναὶ, φησὶν, ἀλλὰ τὸ τοῦ Κεφάλου καλὸν, τὸ 251
μηδεμίαν γραφὴν φυγεῖν. καὶ νὴ Δί' εὔδαιμόν γε. ἀλλὰ τί μᾶλλον ὁ πολλάκις μὲν φυγὼν, μηδεπώποτε δ' ἐξελεγχθεὶς ἀδικῶν ἐν ἐγκλήματι γίγνοιτ' ἂν διὰ τοῦτο δικαίως; καίτοι πρός γε τοῦτον, ἄνδρες Ἀθηναῖοι, καὶ τὸ τοῦ Κεφάλου καλὸν εἰπεῖν ἔστι μοι. οὐδεμίαν γὰρ πώποτ' ἐγράψατό με οὐδ' ἐδίωξε γραφὴν, ὥστε ὑπὸ σοῦ γε ὡμολόγημαι μηδὲν εἶναι τοῦ Κεφάλου χείρων πολίτης.

Πανταχόθεν μὲν τοίνυν ἄν τις ἴδοι τὴν ἀγνωμο- 252
σύνην αὐτοῦ καὶ τὴν βασκανίαν, οὐχ ἥκιστα δ' ἀφ' ὧν περὶ τῆς τύχης διελέχθη. ἐγὼ δ' ὅλως μὲν, ὅστις ἄνθρωπος ὢν ἀνθρώπῳ τύχην προφέρει, ἀνόητον ἡγοῦμαι· ἣν γὰρ ὁ βέλτιστα πράττειν νομίζων καὶ ἀρίστην ἔχειν οἰόμενος οὐκ οἶδεν εἰ μενεῖ τοιαύτη μέχρι τῆς ἑσπέρας, πῶς χρὴ περὶ ταύτης λέγειν ἢ πῶς ὀνειδίζειν ἑτέρῳ; ἐπειδὴ δ' οὗτος πρὸς πολλοῖς ἄλλοις καὶ περὶ τούτων ὑπερηφάνως χρῆται τῷ λόγῳ, σκέψασθ', ὦ ἄνδρες Ἀθηναῖοι, καὶ θεωρήσατε ὅσῳ καὶ ἀληθέστερον καὶ ἀνθρωπινώτερον ἐγὼ

253 περὶ τῆς τύχης τούτου διαλεχθήσομαι. ἐγὼ τὴν
μὲν τῆς πόλεως τύχην ἀγαθὴν ἡγοῦμαι, καὶ ταῦθ'
ὁρῶ καὶ τὸν Δία τὸν Δωδωναῖον ἡμῖν μαντευόμενον,
τὴν μέντοι τῶν πάντων ἀνθρώπων, ἣ νῦν ἐπέχει,
χαλεπὴν καὶ δεινήν· τίς γὰρ Ἑλλήνων ἢ τίς βαρβάρων οὐ πολλῶν κακῶν ἐν τῷ παρόντι πεπείραται;
254 τὸ μὲν τοίνυν προελέσθαι τὰ κάλλιστα καὶ τὸ τῶν
οἰηθέντων Ἑλλήνων, εἰ πρόοιντο ἡμᾶς, ἐν εὐδαιμονίᾳ
διάξειν, τούτων αὐτῶν ἄμεινον πράττειν τῆς ἀγαθῆς
τύχης τῆς πόλεως εἶναι τίθημι· τὸ δὲ προσκροῦσαι καὶ μὴ πάνθ' ὡς ἐβουλόμεθ' ἡμῖν συμβῆναι
τῆς τῶν ἄλλων ἀνθρώπων τύχης τὸ ἐπιβάλλον ἐφ'
255 ἡμᾶς μέρος μετειληφέναι νομίζω τὴν πόλιν. τὴν δ'
ἰδίαν τύχην τὴν ἐμὴν καὶ τὴν ἑνὸς ἡμῶν ἑκάστου ἐν
τοῖς ἰδίοις ἐξετάζειν δίκαιον εἶναι νομίζω. ἐγὼ μὲν
οὖν οὑτωσὶ περὶ τῆς τύχης ἀξιῶ, ὀρθῶς καὶ δικαίως,
ὡς ἐμαυτῷ δοκῶ, νομίζω δὲ καὶ ὑμῖν· ὁ δὲ τὴν ἰδίαν
τύχην τὴν ἐμὴν τῆς κοινῆς τῆς πόλεως κυριωτέραν
εἶναί φησι, τὴν μικρὰν καὶ φαύλην τῆς ἀγαθῆς καὶ
μεγάλης. καὶ πῶς ἔνι τοῦτο γενέσθαι;
256 Καὶ μὴν εἴ γε τὴν ἐμὴν τύχην πάντως ἐξετάζειν,
Αἰσχίνη, προαιρεῖ, πρὸς τὴν σεαυτοῦ σκόπει, κἂν
εὕρῃς τὴν ἐμὴν βελτίω τῆς σῆς, παῦσαι λοιδορούμενος αὐτῇ. σκόπει τοίνυν εὐθὺς ἐξ ἀρχῆς. καί μου
πρὸς Διὸς μηδεμίαν ψυχρότητα καταγνῷ μηδείς.
ἐγὼ γὰρ οὔτ' εἴ τις πενίαν προπηλακίζει, νοῦν ἔχειν
ἡγοῦμαι, οὔτ' εἴ τις ἐν ἀφθόνοις τραφεὶς ἐπὶ τούτῳ

σεμνύνεται· ἀλλ᾽ ὑπὸ τῆς τουτουὶ τοῦ χαλεποῦ βλασφημίας καὶ συκοφαντίας εἰς τοιούτους λόγους ἐμπίπτειν ἀναγκάζομαι, οἷς ἐκ τῶν ἐνόντων ὡς ἂν δύνωμαι μετριώτατα χρήσομαι.

Ἐμοὶ μὲν τοίνυν ὑπῆρξεν, Αἰσχίνη, παιδὶ μὲν 257
ὄντι φοιτᾶν εἰς τὰ προσήκοντα διδασκαλεῖα, καὶ ἔχειν ὅσα χρὴ τὸν μηδὲν αἰσχρὸν ποιήσοντα δι᾽ ἔνδειαν, ἐξελθόντι δὲ ἐκ παίδων ἀκόλουθα τούτοις πράττειν, χορηγεῖν, τριηραρχεῖν, εἰσφέρειν, μηδεμιᾶς φιλοτιμίας μήτε ἰδίας μήτε δημοσίας ἀπολείπεσθαι, ἀλλὰ καὶ τῇ πόλει καὶ τοῖς φίλοις χρήσιμον εἶναι, ἐπειδὴ δὲ πρὸς τὰ κοινὰ προσελθεῖν ἔδοξέ μοι, τοιαῦτα πολιτεύματα ἑλέσθαι ὥστε καὶ ὑπὸ τῆς πατρίδος καὶ ὑπ᾽ ἄλλων Ἑλλήνων πολλῶν πολλάκις ἐστεφανῶσθαι, καὶ μηδὲ τοὺς ἐχθροὺς ὑμᾶς, ὡς οὐ καλά γ᾽ ἦν ἃ προειλόμην, ἐπιχειρεῖν λέγειν.
ἐγὼ μὲν δὴ τοιαύτῃ συμβεβίωκα τύχῃ, καὶ πόλλ᾽ 258
ἂν ἔχων ἕτερ᾽ εἰπεῖν περὶ αὐτῆς παραλείπω, φυλαττόμενος τὸ λυπῆσαί τινα ἐν οἷς σεμνύνομαι. σὺ δ᾽ ὁ σεμνὸς ἀνὴρ καὶ διαπτύων τοὺς ἄλλους σκόπει πρὸς ταύτην ποίᾳ τινὶ κέχρησαι τύχῃ, δι᾽ ἣν παῖς μὲν ὢν μετὰ πολλῆς ἐνδείας ἐτράφης, ἅμα τῷ πατρὶ πρὸς τῷ διδασκαλείῳ προσεδρεύων, τὸ μέλαν τρίβων καὶ τὰ βάθρα σπογγίζων καὶ τὸ παιδαγωγεῖον κορῶν, οἰκέτου τάξιν, οὐκ ἐλευθέρου παιδὸς ἔχων,
ἀνὴρ δὲ γενόμενος τῇ μητρὶ τελούσῃ τὰς βίβλους 259
ἀνεγίγνωσκες καὶ τἆλλα συνεσκευωροῦ, τὴν μὲν

νύκτα νεβρίζων καὶ κρατηρίζων καὶ καθαίρων τοὺς
τελουμένους καὶ ἀπομάττων τῷ πηλῷ καὶ τοῖς πιτύ-
ροις καὶ ἀνιστὰς ἀπὸ τοῦ καθαρμοῦ κελεύων λέγειν
"ἔφυγον κακὸν, εὗρον ἄμεινον," ἐπὶ τῷ μηδένα πώποτε τηλικοῦτ' ὀλολύξαι σεμνυνόμενος (καὶ ἔγωγε
νομίζω· μὴ γὰρ οἴεσθ' αὐτὸν φθέγγεσθαι μὲν οὕτω
260 μέγα, ὀλολύζειν δ' οὐχ ὑπέρλαμπρον), ἐν δὲ ταῖς
ἡμέραις τοὺς καλοὺς θιάσους ἄγων διὰ τῶν ὁδῶν,
τοὺς ἐστεφανωμένους τῷ μαράθῳ καὶ τῇ λεύκῃ, τοὺς
ὄφεις τοὺς παρείας θλίβων καὶ ὑπὲρ τῆς κεφαλῆς αἰω-
ρῶν, καὶ βοῶν εὐοῖ σαβοῖ, καὶ ἐπορχούμενος ὑῆς ἄττης
ἄττης ὑῆς, ἔξαρχος καὶ προηγεμὼν καὶ κιστοφόρος καὶ
λικνοφόρος καὶ τοιαῦτα ὑπὸ τῶν γρᾳδίων προσαγορευό-
μενος, μισθὸν λαμβάνων τούτων ἔνθρυπτα καὶ στρεπ-
τοὺς καὶ νεήλατα, ἐφ' οἷς τίς οὐκ ἂν ὡς ἀληθῶς αὑτὸν
261 εὐδαιμονίσειε καὶ τὴν αὑτοῦ τύχην; ἐπειδὴ δ' εἰς
τοὺς δημότας ἐνεγράφης ὁπωσδήποτε ἐῶ γὰρ τοῦτό
γε, ἐπειδὴ δ' οὖν ἐνεγράφης, εὐθέως τὸ κάλλιστον
ἐξελέξω τῶν ἔργων, γραμματεύειν καὶ ὑπηρετεῖν
τοῖς ἀρχιδίοις. ὡς δ' ἀπηλλάγης ποτὲ καὶ τούτου,
πάνθ' ἃ τῶν ἄλλων κατηγορεῖς αὐτὸς ποιήσας, οὐ
κατῄσχυνας μὰ Δί' οὐδὲν τῶν προϋπηργμένων τῷ
262 μετὰ ταῦτα βίῳ, ἀλλὰ μισθώσας σαυτὸν τοῖς βαρυ-
στόνοις ἐπικαλουμένοις ἐκείνοις ὑποκριταῖς, Σιμύλῳ
καὶ Σωκράτει, ἐτριταγωνίστεις, σῦκα καὶ βότρυς καὶ
ἐλάας συλλέγων ὥσπερ ὀπωρώνης ἐκ τῶν ἀλλοτρίων
χωρίων, πλείω λαμβάνων ἀπὸ τούτων τραύματα ἢ τῶν

ἀγώνων, οὓς ὑμεῖς περὶ τῆς ψυχῆς ἠγωνίζεσθε· ἦν γὰρ
ἄσπονδος καὶ ἀκήρυκτος ὑμῖν πρὸς τοὺς θεατὰς πόλεμος, ὑφ’ ὧν πολλὰ τραύματ’ εἰληφὼς εἰκότως τοὺς
ἀπείρους τῶν τοιούτων κινδύνων ὡς δειλοὺς σκώπ-
τεις. ἀλλὰ γὰρ παρεὶς ὧν τὴν πενίαν αἰτιάσαιτ’ 263
ἄν τις, πρὸς αὐτὰ τά τοῦ τρόπου σου βαδιοῦμαι κατη-
γορήματα. τοιαύτην γὰρ εἵλου πολιτείαν, ἐπειδή
ποτε καὶ τοῦτ’ ἐπῆλθέ σοι ποιῆσαι, δι’ ἣν εὐτυχού-
σης μὲν τῆς πατρίδος λαγὼ βίον ἔζης δεδιὼς καὶ τρέ-
μων καὶ ἀεὶ πληγήσεσθαι προσδοκῶν ἐφ’ οἷς σαυτῷ
συνῄδεις ἀδικοῦντι, ἐν οἷς δ’ ἠτύχησαν οἱ ἄλλοι, θρασὺς
ὢν ὑφ’ ἁπάντων ὦψαι. καίτοι ὅστις χιλίων πολιτῶν 264
ἀποθανόντων ἐθάρρησε, τί οὗτος παθεῖν ὑπὸ τῶν ζώντων δίκαιός ἐστιν; πολλὰ τοίνυν ἕτερ’ εἰπεῖν ἔχων
περὶ αὐτοῦ παραλείψω· οὐ γὰρ ὅσ’ ἂν δείξαιμι προσ-
όντ’ αἰσχρὰ τούτῳ καὶ ὀνείδη, πάντ’ οἶμαι δεῖν εὐχερῶς
λέγειν, ἀλλ’ ὅσα μηδὲν αἰσχρόν ἐστιν εἰπεῖν ἐμοί.

Ἐξέτασον τοίνυν παρ’ ἄλληλα τὰ σοὶ κἀμοὶ βε- 265
βιωμένα, πράως, μὴ πικρῶς, Αἰσχίνη· εἶτ’ ἐρώτησον τουτουσὶ τὴν ποτέρου τύχην ἂν ἕλοιθ’ ἕκαστος
αὐτῶν. ἐδίδασκες γράμματα, ἐγὼ δ’ ἐφοίτων. ἐτέλεις, ἐγὼ δ’ ἐτελούμην. ἐχόρευες, ἐγὼ δ’ ἐχορή-
γουν. ἐγραμμάτευες, ἐγὼ δ’ ἠκκλησίαζον. ἐτριταγωνίστεις, ἐγὼ δ’ ἐθεώρουν. ἐξέπιπτες, ἐγὼ δ’
ἐσύριττον. ὑπὲρ τῶν ἐχθρῶν πεπολίτευσαι πάντα,
ἐγὼ δ’ ὑπὲρ τῆς πατρίδος. ἐῶ τἆλλα, ἀλλὰ νυνὶ 266
τήμερον ἐγὼ μὲν ὑπὲρ τοῦ στεφανωθῆναι δοκιμάζο-

μαι, τὸ δὲ μηδ' ὁτιοῦν ἀδικεῖν ἀνωμολόγημαι, σοὶ δὲ συκοφάντῃ μὲν εἶναι δοκεῖν ὑπάρχει, κινδυνεύεις δὲ εἴτε δεῖ σ' ἔτι τοῦτο ποιεῖν, εἴτ' ἤδη πεπαῦσθαι μὴ μεταλαβόντα τὸ μέρος τῶν ψήφων. ἀγαθῇ γ', οὐχ ὁρᾷς; τύχῃ συμβεβιωκὼς τῆς ἐμῆς ὡς φαύλης κατηγορεῖς.

267 Φέρε δὴ καὶ τὰς τῶν λειτουργιῶν μαρτυρίας, ὧν λελειτούργηκα, ὑμῖν ἀναγνῶ. παρ' ἃς παρανάγνωθι καὶ σύ μοι τὰς ῥήσεις ἃς ἐλυμαίνου,

ἥκω νεκρῶν κευθμῶνα καὶ σκότου πύλας

καὶ

κακαγγελεῖν μὲν ἴσθι μὴ θέλοντά με,

καὶ κακὸν κακῶς σε μάλιστα μὲν οἱ θεοί, ἔπειτα οὗτοι πάντες ἀπολέσειαν, πονηρὸν ὄντα καὶ πολίτην καὶ τριταγωνιστήν.

Λέγε τὰς μαρτυρίας.

ΜΑΡΤΥΡΙΑΙ.

268 Ἐν μὲν τοίνυν τοῖς πρὸς τὴν πόλιν τοιοῦτος· ἐν δὲ τοῖς ἰδίοις εἰ μὴ πάντες ἴστε ὅτι κοινὸς καὶ φιλάνθρωπος καὶ τοῖς δεομένοις ἐπαρκῶν, σιωπῶ καὶ οὐδὲν ἂν εἴποιμι οὐδὲ παρασχοίμην περὶ τούτων οὐδεμίαν μαρτυρίαν, οὔτ' εἴ τινας ἐκ τῶν πολεμίων ἐλυσάμην, οὔτ' εἴ τισι θυγατέρας συνεξέδωκα, οὔτε τῶν τοιούτων
269 οὐδέν. καὶ γὰρ οὕτω πως ὑπείληφα. ἐγὼ νομίζω τὸν μὲν εὖ παθόντα δεῖν μεμνῆσθαι πάντα τὸν χρό-

νον, τὸν δὲ ποιήσαντα εὐθὺς ἐπιλελῆσθαι, εἰ δεῖ τὸν μὲν χρηστοῦ, τὸν δὲ μὴ μικροψύχου ποιεῖν ἔργον ἀνθρώπου. τὸ δὲ τὰς ἰδίας εὐεργεσίας ὑπομιμνήσκειν καὶ λέγειν μικροῦ δεῖν ὅμοιόν ἐστι τῷ ὀνειδίζειν. οὐ δὴ ποιήσω τοιοῦτον οὐδὲν, οὐδὲ προαχθήσομαι, ἀλλ' ὅπως ποθ' ὑπείλημμαι περὶ τούτων, ἀρκεῖ μοι.

Βούλομαι δὲ τῶν ἰδίων ἀπαλλαγεὶς ἔτι μικρὰ 270
πρὸς ὑμᾶς εἰπεῖν περὶ τῶν κοινῶν. εἰ μὲν γὰρ
ἔχεις, Αἰσχίνη, τῶν ὑπὸ τοῦτον τὸν ἥλιον εἰπεῖν
ἀνθρώπων ὅστις ἀθῷος τῆς Φιλίππου πρότερον καὶ
νῦν τῆς Ἀλεξάνδρου δυναστείας γέγονεν, ἢ τῶν
Ἑλλήνων ἢ τῶν βαρβάρων, ἔστω, συγχωρῶ σοι
τὴν ἐμὴν εἴτε τύχην εἴτε δυστυχίαν ὀνομάζειν βούλει πάντων αἰτίαν γεγενῆσθαι. εἰ δὲ καὶ τῶν 271
μηδεπώποτ' ἰδόντων ἐμὲ μηδὲ φωνὴν ἀκηκοότων
ἐμοῦ πολλοὶ πολλὰ καὶ δεινὰ πεπόνθασι, μὴ μόνον
κατ' ἄνδρα, ἀλλὰ καὶ πόλεις ὅλαι καὶ ἔθνη, πόσῳ
δικαιότερον καὶ ἀληθέστερον τὴν ἁπάντων, ὡς ἔοικεν,
ἀνθρώπων τύχην κοινὴν καὶ φοράν τινα πραγμάτων
χαλεπὴν καὶ οὐχ οἵαν ἔδει τούτων αἰτίαν ἡγεῖσθαι;
σὺ τοίνυν ταῦτ' ἀφεὶς ἐμὲ τὸν παρὰ τουτοισὶ πεπο- 272
λιτευμένον αἰτιᾷ, καὶ ταῦτ' εἰδὼς ὅτι, καὶ εἰ μὴ τὸ
ὅλον, μέρος γ' ἐπιβάλλει τῆς βλασφημίας ἅπασι,
καὶ μάλιστα σοί. εἰ μὲν γὰρ ἐγὼ κατ' ἐμαυτὸν
αὐτοκράτωρ ὢν περὶ τῶν πραγμάτων ἐβουλευόμην,
ἦν ἂν τοῖς ἄλλοις ῥήτορσιν ὑμῖν ἐμὲ αἰτιᾶσθαι· εἰ 273

δὲ παρῆτε μὲν ἐν ταῖς ἐκκλησίαις ἁπάσαις, ἀεὶ δ'
ἐν κοινῷ τὸ συμφέρον ἡ πόλις προὐτίθει σκοπεῖν,
πᾶσι δὲ ταῦτ' ἐδόκει τότ' ἄριστ' εἶναι, καὶ μάλιστα
σοὶ (οὐ γὰρ ἐπ' εὐνοίᾳ γ' ἐμοὶ παρεχώρεις ἐλπίδων
καὶ ζήλου καὶ τιμῶν, ἃ πάντα προσῆν τοῖς τότε
πραττομένοις ὑπ' ἐμοῦ, ἀλλὰ τῆς ἀληθείας ἡττώμε-
νος δηλονότι καὶ τῷ μηδὲν ἔχειν εἰπεῖν βέλτιον),
πῶς οὐκ ἀδικεῖς καὶ δεινὰ ποιεῖς τούτοις νῦν ἐγκα-
274 λῶν ὧν τότ' οὐκ εἶχες λέγειν βελτίω; παρὰ μὲν
τοίνυν τοῖς ἄλλοις ἔγωγ' ὁρῶ πᾶσιν ἀνθρώποις διωρισμένα καὶ τεταγμένα πως τὰ τοιαῦτα. ἀδικεῖ τις
ἑκών, ὀργὴν καὶ τιμωρίαν κατὰ τούτου. ἐξήμαρτέ
τις ἄκων, συγγνώμην ἀντὶ τῆς τιμωρίας τούτῳ.
οὔτ' ἀδικῶν τις οὔτ' ἐξαμαρτάνων, εἰς τὰ πᾶσι
δοκοῦντα συμφέρειν ἑαυτὸν δοὺς οὐ κατώρθωσε μεθ'
ἁπάντων; οὐκ ὀνειδίζειν οὐδὲ λοιδορεῖσθαι τῷ τοι-
275 ούτῳ δίκαιον, ἀλλὰ συνάχθεσθαι. φανήσεται ταῦτα
πάντα οὕτως οὐ μόνον ἐν τοῖς νομίμοις, ἀλλὰ καὶ ἡ
φύσις αὐτὴ τοῖς ἀγράφοις νόμοις καὶ τοῖς ἀνθρωπίνοις ἔθεσι διώρικεν. Αἰσχίνης τοίνυν τοσοῦτον
ὑπερβέβληκεν ἅπαντας ἀνθρώπους ὠμότητι καὶ
συκοφαντίᾳ ὥστε καὶ ὧν αὐτὸς ὡς ἀτυχημάτων
ἐμέμνητο, καὶ ταῦτ' ἐμοῦ κατηγορεῖ.

276 Καὶ πρὸς τοῖς ἄλλοις, ὥσπερ αὐτὸς ἁπλῶς καὶ
μετ' εὐνοίας πάντας εἰρηκὼς τοὺς λόγους, φυλάττειν
ἐμὲ καὶ τηρεῖν ἐκέλευεν, ὅπως μὴ παρακρούσομαι
μηδ' ἐξαπατήσω, δεινὸν καὶ γόητα καὶ σοφιστὴν

καὶ τὰ τοιαῦτ᾽ ὀνομάζων, ὡς ἐὰν πρότερός τις εἴπῃ
τὰ προσόνθ᾽ ἑαυτῷ περὶ ἄλλου, καὶ δὴ ταῦθ᾽ οὕτως
ἔχοντα, καὶ οὐκέτι τοὺς ἀκούοντας σκεψομένους τίς
ποτ᾽ αὐτός ἐστιν ὁ ταῦτα λέγων. ἐγὼ δ᾽ οἶδ᾽ ὅτι
γιγνώσκετε τοῦτον ἅπαντες, καὶ πολὺ τούτῳ μᾶλλον
ἢ ἐμοὶ νομίζετε ταῦτα προσεῖναι. κἀκεῖνο εὖ οἶδ᾽ 277
ὅτι τὴν ἐμὴν δεινότητα—ἔστω γάρ. καίτοι ἔγωγ᾽
ὁρῶ τῆς τῶν λεγόντων δυνάμεως τοὺς ἀκούοντας τὸ
πλεῖστον κυρίους· ὡς γὰρ ἂν ὑμεῖς ἀποδέξησθε καὶ
πρὸς ἕκαστον ἔχητ᾽ εὐνοίας, οὕτως ὁ λέγων ἔδοξε
φρονεῖν. εἰ δ᾽ οὖν ἐστι καὶ παρ᾽ ἐμοί τις ἐμπειρία
τοιαύτη, ταύτην μὲν εὑρήσετε πάντες ἐν τοῖς κοινοῖς
ἐξεταζομένην ὑπὲρ ὑμῶν ἀεὶ καὶ οὐδαμοῦ καθ᾽ ὑμῶν
οὐδ᾽ ἰδίᾳ, τὴν δὲ τούτου τοὐναντίον οὐ μόνον τῷ λέγειν
ὑπὲρ τῶν ἐχθρῶν, ἀλλὰ καὶ εἴ τις ἐλύπησέ τι τοῦτον ἢ προσέκρουσέ που, κατὰ τούτων. οὐ γὰρ
αὐτῇ δικαίως, οὐδ᾽ ἐφ᾽ ἃ συμφέρει τῇ πόλει, χρῆται.
οὔτε γὰρ τὴν ὀργὴν οὔτε τὴν ἔχθραν οὔτ᾽ ἄλλο 278
οὐδὲν τῶν τοιούτων τὸν καλὸν κἀγαθὸν πολίτην δεῖ
τοὺς ὑπὲρ τῶν κοινῶν εἰσεληλυθότας δικαστὰς
ἀξιοῦν αὑτῷ βεβαιοῦν, οὐδ᾽ ὑπὲρ τούτων εἰς ὑμᾶς
εἰσιέναι, ἀλλὰ μάλιστα μὲν μὴ ἔχειν ταῦτ᾽ ἐν τῇ
φύσει, εἰ δ᾽ ἄρ᾽ ἀνάγκη, πρᾴως καὶ μετρίως διακεί-
μεν᾽ ἔχειν. ἐν τίσιν οὖν σφοδρὸν εἶναι τὸν πολιτευόμενον καὶ τὸν ῥήτορα δεῖ; ἐν οἷς τῶν ὅλων τι
κινδυνεύεται τῇ πόλει, καὶ ἐν οἷς πρὸς τοὺς ἐναν-
τίους ἐστὶ τῷ δήμῳ, ἐν τούτοις· ταῦτα γὰρ γενναίου

279 καὶ ἀγαθοῦ πολίτου. μηδενὸς δὲ ἀδικήματος πώποτε δημοσίου, προσθήσω δὲ μηδ' ἰδίου, δίκην
ἀξιώσαντα λαβεῖν παρ' ἐμοῦ μήθ' ὑπὲρ τῆς πόλεως
μήθ' ὑπὲρ αὑτοῦ, στεφάνου καὶ ἐπαίνου κατηγορίαν
ἥκειν συνεσκευασμένον, καὶ τοσουτουσὶ λόγους ἀνη-
λωκέναι ἰδίας ἔχθρας καὶ φθόνου καὶ μικροψυχίας
ἐστὶ σημεῖον, οὐδενὸς χρηστοῦ. τὸ δὲ δὴ καὶ
τοὺς πρὸς ἐμὲ αὐτὸν ἀγῶνας ἐάσαντα νῦν ἐπὶ
280 τόνδ' ἥκειν καὶ πᾶσαν ἔχει κακίαν. καί μοι δοκεῖς
ἐκ τούτων, Αἰσχίνη, λόγων ἐπίδειξίν τινα καὶ φωνασκίας βουλόμενος ποιήσασθαι τοῦτον προελέσθαι
τὸν ἀγῶνα, οὐκ ἀδικήματος οὐδενὸς λαβεῖν τιμωρίαν.
ἔστι δ' οὐχ ὁ λόγος τοῦ ῥήτορος, Αἰσχίνη, τίμιον,
οὐδ' ὁ τόνος τῆς φωνῆς, ἀλλὰ τὸ ταὐτὰ προαιρεῖ-
σθαι τοῖς πολλοῖς καὶ τὸ τοὺς αὐτοὺς μισεῖν καὶ
281 φιλεῖν οὕσπερ ἂν ἡ πατρίς. ὁ γὰρ οὕτως ἔχων τὴν
ψυχήν, οὗτος ἐπ' εὐνοίᾳ πάντ' ἐρεῖ· ὁ δ' ἀφ' ὧν ἡ
πόλις προορᾶταί τινα κίνδυνον ἑαυτῇ, τούτους θερα-
πεύων οὐκ ἐπὶ τῆς αὐτῆς ὁρμεῖ τοῖς πολλοῖς, οὔκουν
οὐδὲ τῆς ἀσφαλείας τὴν αὐτὴν ἔχει προσδοκίαν.
ἀλλ', ὁρᾷς; ἐγώ· ταὐτὰ γὰρ συμφέρονθ' εἱλόμην
τουτοισί, καὶ οὐδὲν ἐξαίρετον οὐδ' ἴδιον πεποίημαι.
282 ἆρ' οὖν οὐδὲ σύ; καὶ πῶς; ὃς εὐθέως μετὰ τὴν
μάχην πρεσβευτὴς ἐπορεύου πρὸς Φίλιππον, ὃς ἦν
τῶν ἐν ἐκείνοις τοῖς χρόνοις συμφορῶν αἴτιος τῇ
πατρίδι, καὶ ταῦτ' ἀρνούμενος πάντα τὸν ἔμπροσθε
χρόνον ταύτην τὴν χρείαν, ὡς πάντες ἴσασιν. καί-

τοι τίς ὁ τὴν πόλιν ἐξαπατῶν; οὐχ ὁ μὴ λέγων ἃ
φρονεῖ; τῷ δ' ὁ κῆρυξ καταρᾶται δικαίως; οὐ τῷ
τοιούτῳ; τί δὲ μεῖζον ἔχοι τις ἂν εἰπεῖν ἀδίκημα
κατ' ἀνδρὸς ῥήτορος ἢ εἰ μὴ ταὐτὰ φρονεῖ καὶ λέγει;
σὺ τοίνυν οὗτος εὑρέθης. εἶτα σὺ φθέγγει καὶ βλέ- 283
πειν εἰς τὰ τουτωνὶ πρόσωπα τολμᾷς; πότερ' οὐχ
ἡγεῖ γιγνώσκειν αὐτοὺς ὅστις εἶ; ἢ τοσοῦτον ὕπνον
καὶ λήθην ἅπαντας ἔχειν ὥστ' οὐ μεμνῆσθαι τοὺς
λόγους οὓς ἐδημηγόρεις ἐν τῷ πολέμῳ, καταρώμενος
καὶ διομνύμενος μηδὲν εἶναι σοὶ καὶ Φιλίππῳ πρᾶγμα, ἀλλ' ἐμὲ τὴν αἰτίαν σοι ταύτην ἐπάγειν τῆς
ἰδίας ἕνεκ' ἔχθρας, οὐκ οὖσαν ἀληθῆ. ὡς δ' ἀπηγ- 284
γέλθη τάχισθ' ἡ μάχη, οὐδὲν τούτων φροντίσας
εὐθέως ὡμολόγεις καὶ προσεποιοῦ φιλίαν, καὶ ξενίαν
εἶναί σοι πρὸς αὐτόν, τῇ μισθαρνίᾳ ταῦτα μετατιθέ-
μενος τὰ ὀνόματα· ἐκ ποίας γὰρ ἴσης ἢ δικαίας
προφάσεως Αἰσχίνῃ τῷ Γλαυκοθέας τῆς τυμπανιστρίας ξένος ἢ φίλος ἢ γνώριμος ἦν Φίλιππος; ἐγὼ
μὲν οὐχ ὁρῶ, ἀλλ' ἐμισθώθης ἐπὶ τῷ τὰ τουτωνὶ
συμφέροντα διαφθείρειν. ἀλλ' ὅμως οὕτω φανερῶς
αὐτὸς εἰλημμένος προδότης καὶ κατὰ σαυτοῦ μηνυ-
τὴς ἐπὶ τοῖς συμβᾶσι γεγονὼς ἐμοὶ λοιδορεῖ καὶ
ὀνειδίζεις ταῦτα, ὧν πάντας μᾶλλον αἰτίους εὑρήσεις.

Πολλὰ καὶ καλὰ καὶ μεγάλα ἡ πόλις, Αἰσχίνη, 285
καὶ προείλετο καὶ κατώρθωσε δι' ἐμοῦ, ὧν οὐκ ἠμνη-
μόνησεν. σημεῖον δέ· χειροτονῶν γὰρ ὁ δῆμος τὸν
ἐροῦντ' ἐπὶ τοῖς τετελευτηκόσι παρ' αὐτὰ τὰ συμ-

βάντα οὐ σὲ ἐχειροτόνησε προβληθέντα, καίπερ
εὔφωνον ὄντα, οὐδὲ Δημάδην, ἄρτι πεποιηκότα τὴν
εἰρήνην, οὐδ᾽ Ἡγήμονα, οὐδ᾽ ἄλλον ὑμῶν οὐδένα,
ἀλλ᾽ ἐμέ. καὶ παρελθόντος σοῦ καὶ Πυθοκλέους
ὠμῶς καὶ ἀναιδῶς, ὦ Ζεῦ καὶ θεοί, καὶ κατηγορούν-
των ἐμοῦ ταὐτὰ ἃ καὶ σὺ νυνί, καὶ λοιδορουμένων, ἔτ᾽
286 ἄμεινον ἐχειροτόνησεν ἐμέ. τὸ δ᾽ αἴτιον οὐκ ἀγνοεῖς
μέν, ὅμως δὲ φράσω σοι κἀγώ. ἀμφότερ᾽ ᾔδεσαν
οὗτοι, τήν τ᾽ ἐμὴν εὔνοιαν καὶ προθυμίαν, μεθ᾽ ἧς
τὰ πράγματ᾽ ἔπραττον, καὶ τὴν ὑμετέραν ἀδικίαν·
ἃ γὰρ εὐθενούντων τῶν πραγμάτων ἠρνεῖσθε διομνύ-
μενοι, ταῦτ᾽ ἐν οἷς ἔπταισεν ἡ πόλις ὡμολογήσατε.
τοὺς οὖν ἐπὶ τοῖς κοινοῖς ἀτυχήμασιν ὧν ἐφρόνουν
λαβόντας ἄδειαν ἐχθροὺς μὲν πάλαι, φανεροὺς δὲ τόθ᾽
287 ἡγήσαντο αὐτοῖς γεγενῆσθαι· εἶτα καὶ προσήκειν
ὑπολαμβάνοντες τὸν ἐροῦντ᾽ ἐπὶ τοῖς τετελευτηκόσι
καὶ τὴν ἐκείνων ἀρετὴν κοσμήσοντα μήθ᾽ ὁμωρόφιον
μήθ᾽ ὁμόσπονδον γεγενημένον εἶναι τοῖς πρὸς ἐκείνους παραταξαμένοις, μηδ᾽ ἐκεῖ μὲν κωμάζειν καὶ
παιανίζειν ἐπὶ ταῖς τῶν Ἑλλήνων συμφοραῖς μετὰ
τῶν αὐτοχείρων τοῦ φόνου, δεῦρο δ᾽ ἐλθόντα τιμᾶσθαι, μηδὲ τῇ φωνῇ δακρύειν ὑποκρινόμενον τὴν
ἐκείνων τύχην, ἀλλὰ τῇ ψυχῇ συναλγεῖν. τοῦτο
δ᾽ ἑώρων παρ᾽ ἑαυτοῖς καὶ παρ᾽ ἐμοί, παρὰ δ᾽ ὑμῖν
οὔ. διὰ ταῦτ᾽ ἔμ᾽ ἐχειροτόνησαν καὶ οὐχ ὑμᾶς.
288 καὶ οὐχ ὁ μὲν δῆμος οὕτως, οἱ δὲ τῶν τετελευτηκότων πατέρες καὶ ἀδελφοὶ οἱ ὑπὸ τοῦ δήμου τόθ᾽

αἱρεθέντες ἐπὶ τὰς ταφὰς ἄλλως πως, ἀλλὰ δέον ποιεῖν αὐτοὺς τὸ περίδειπνον ὡς παρ' οἰκειοτάτῳ τῶν τετελευτηκότων, ὥσπερ τἄλλ' εἴωθε γίγνεσθαι, τοῦτ' ἐποίησαν παρ' ἐμοί. εἰκότως· γένει μὲν γὰρ ἕκαστος ἑκάστῳ μᾶλλον οἰκεῖος ἦν ἐμοῦ, κοινῇ δὲ πᾶσιν οὐδεὶς ἐγγυτέρω· ᾧ γὰρ ἐκείνους σωθῆναι καὶ κατορθῶσαι μάλιστα διέφερεν, οὗτος καὶ παθόντων ἃ μήποτ' ὤφελον τῆς ὑπὲρ ἁπάντων λύπης πλεῖστον μετεῖχεν.

Λέγε δ' αὐτῷ τουτὶ τὸ ἐπίγραμμα, ὃ δημοσίᾳ 289
προείλετο ἡ πόλις αὐτοῖς ἐπιγράψαι, ἵν' εἰδῇς, Αἰσχίνη, καὶ ἐν αὐτῷ τούτῳ σαυτὸν ἀγνώμονα καὶ συκοφάντην ὄντα καὶ μιαρόν. Λέγε.

ΕΠΙΓΡΑΜΜΑ.

Οἵδε πάτρας ἕνεκα σφετέρας εἰς δῆριν ἔθεντο
ὅπλα, καὶ ἀντιπάλων ὕβριν ἀπεσκέδασαν.
μαρνάμενοι δ' ἀρετῆς καὶ δείματος οὐκ ἐσάωσαν
ψυχάς, ἀλλ' Ἀΐδην κοινὸν ἔθεντο βραβῆ,
οὕνεκεν Ἑλλήνων, ὡς μὴ ζυγὸν αὐχένι θέντες
δουλοσύνης στυγερὰν ἀμφὶς ἔχωσιν ὕβριν.
γαῖα δὲ πατρὶς ἔχει κόλποις τῶν πλεῖστα καμόντων
σώματ', ἐπεὶ θνητοῖς ἐκ Διὸς ἥδε κρίσις·
μηδὲν ἁμαρτεῖν ἐστι θεοῦ καὶ πάντα κατορθοῦν,
ἐν βιοτῇ μοῖραν δ' οὔ τι φυγεῖν ἔπορεν.

Ἀκούεις, Αἰσχίνη, καὶ ἐν αὐτῷ τούτῳ μηδὲν ἁμαρ- 290
τεῖν ἐστι θεοῦ καὶ πάντα κατορθοῦν; οὐ τῷ συμβούλῳ τὴν τοῦ κατορθοῦν τοὺς ἀγωνιζομένους ἀνέθηκε

δύναμιν, ἀλλὰ τοῖς θεοῖς. τί οὖν, ὦ κατάρατ', ἐμοὶ
περὶ τούτων λοιδορεῖ, καὶ λέγεις ἃ σοὶ καὶ τοῖς σοῖς
οἱ θεοὶ τρέψειαν εἰς κεφαλήν;

291 Πολλὰ τοίνυν, ὦ ἄνδρες Ἀθηναῖοι, καὶ ἄλλα
κατηγορηκότος αὐτοῦ καὶ κατεψευσμένου, μάλιστ'
ἐθαύμασα πάντων, ὅτι τῶν συμβεβηκότων τότε
τῇ πόλει μνησθεὶς οὐχ ὡς ἂν εὔνους καὶ δίκαιος
πολίτης ἔσχε τὴν γνώμην, οὐδ' ἐδάκρυσεν, οὐδ'
ἔπαθε τοιοῦτον οὐδὲν τῇ ψυχῇ, ἀλλ' ἐπάρας τὴν φωνὴν καὶ γεγηθὼς καὶ λαρυγγίζων ᾤετο μὲν ἐμοῦ κατηγορεῖν δηλονότι, δεῖγμα δ' ἐξέφερε καθ' ἑαυτοῦ ὅτι
τοῖς γεγενημένοις ἀνιαροῖς οὐδὲν ὁμοίως ἔσχε τοῖς
292 ἄλλοις. καίτοι τὸν τῶν νόμων καὶ τῆς πολιτείας
φάσκοντα φροντίζειν, ὥσπερ οὗτος νυνὶ, καὶ εἰ μηδὲν
ἄλλο, τοῦτό γ' ἔχειν δεῖ, ταὐτὰ λυπεῖσθαι καὶ ταὐτὰ
χαίρειν τοῖς πολλοῖς, καὶ μὴ τῇ προαιρέσει τῶν
κοινῶν ἐν τῷ τῶν ἐναντίων μέρει τετάχθαι· ὃ σὺ νυνὶ
πεποιηκὼς εἶ φανερὸς, ἐμὲ πάντων αἴτιον καὶ δι' ἐμὲ εἰς
πράγματα φάσκων ἐμπεσεῖν τὴν πόλιν, οὐκ ἀπὸ τῆς
ἐμῆς πολιτείας οὐδὲ προαιρέσεως ἀρξαμένων ὑμῶν
293 τοῖς Ἕλλησι βοηθεῖν, ἐπεὶ ἔμοιγ' εἰ τοῦτο δοθείη
παρ' ὑμῶν, δι' ἐμὲ ὑμᾶς ἠναντιῶσθαι τῇ κατὰ τῶν
Ἑλλήνων ἀρχῇ πραττομένῃ, μείζων ἂν δοθείη δωρεὰ
συμπασῶν ὧν τοῖς ἄλλοις δεδώκατε. ἀλλ' οὔτ' ἂν
ἐγὼ ταῦτα φήσαιμι (ἀδικοίην γὰρ ἂν ὑμᾶς), οὔτ'
ἂν ὑμεῖς εὖ οἶδ' ὅτι συγχωρήσαιτε· οὗτός τ' εἰ
δίκαια ἐποίει, οὐκ ἂν ἕνεκα τῆς πρὸς ἐμὲ ἔχθρας τὰ

μέγιστα τῶν ὑμετέρων καλῶν ἔβλαπτε καὶ διέβαλλεν.

Ἀλλὰ τί ταῦτ' ἐπιτιμῶ, πολλῷ σχετλιώτερα 294
ἄλλα κατηγορηκότος αὐτοῦ καὶ κατεψευσμένου; ὃς γὰρ ἐμοῦ φιλιππισμόν, ὦ γῆ καὶ θεοί, κατηγορεῖ, τί οὗτος οὐκ ἂν εἴποι; καίτοι νὴ τὸν Ἡρακλέα καὶ πάντας θεούς, εἴ γ' ἐπ' ἀληθείας δέοι σκοπεῖσθαι, τὸ καταψεύδεσθαι καὶ δι' ἔχθραν τι λέγειν ἀνελόντας ἐκ μέσου, τίνες ὡς ἀληθῶς εἰσὶν οἷς ἂν εἰκότως καὶ δικαίως τὴν τῶν γεγενημένων αἰτίαν ἐπὶ τὴν κεφαλὴν ἀναθεῖεν ἅπαντες, τοὺς ὁμοίους τούτῳ παρ' ἑκάστῃ τῶν πόλεων εὕροιτ' ἄν, οὐ τοὺς ἐμοί· οἵ, 295
ὅτ' ἦν ἀσθενῆ τὰ Φιλίππου πράγματα καὶ κομιδῇ μικρά, πολλάκις προλεγόντων ἡμῶν καὶ παρακαλούντων καὶ διδασκόντων τὰ βέλτιστα, τῆς ἰδίας ἕνεκ' αἰσχροκερδίας τὰ κοινῇ συμφέροντα προΐεντο, τοὺς ὑπάρχοντας ἕκαστοι πολίτας ἐξαπατῶντες καὶ διαφθείροντες, ἕως δούλους ἐποίησαν, Θετταλοὺς Δάοχος, Κινέας, Θρασυδαῖος, Ἀρκάδας Κερκιδᾶς, Ἱερώνυμος, Εὐκαμπίδας, Ἀργείους Μύρτις, Τελέδαμος, Μνασέας, Ἠλείους Εὐξίθεος, Κλεότιμος, Ἀρίσταιχμος, Μεσσηνίους οἱ Φιλιάδου τοῦ θεοῖς ἐχθροῦ παῖδες Νέων καὶ Θρασύλοχος, Σικυωνίους Ἀρίστρατος, Ἐπιχάρης, Κορινθίους Δείναρχος, Δημάρατος, Μεγαρέας Πτοιόδωρος, Ἕλιξος, Περίλαος, Θηβαίους Τιμόλας, Θεογείτων, Ἀνεμοίτας, Εὐβοέας Ἵππαρχος, Κλείταρχος, Σωσίστρατος. ἐπιλείψει με λέ- 296

γοντα ἡ ἡμέρα τὰ τῶν προδοτῶν ὀνόματα. οὗτοι πάντες εἰσίν, ἄνδρες Ἀθηναῖοι, τῶν αὐτῶν βουλευμάτων ἐν ταῖς αὐτῶν πατρίσιν ὧνπερ οὗτοι παρ' ὑμῖν, ἄνθρωποι μιαροὶ καὶ κόλακες καὶ ἀλάστορες, ἠκρωτηριασμένοι τὰς ἑαυτῶν ἕκαστοι πατρίδας, τὴν ἐλευθερίαν προπεπωκότες πρότερον μὲν Φιλίππῳ, νῦν δὲ Ἀλεξάνδρῳ, τῇ γαστρὶ μετροῦντες καὶ τοῖς αἰσχίστοις τὴν εὐδαιμονίαν, τὴν δ' ἐλευθερίαν καὶ τὸ μηδένα ἔχειν δεσπότην αὐτῶν, ἃ τοῖς προτέροις Ἕλλησιν ὅροι τῶν ἀγαθῶν ἦσαν καὶ κανόνες, ἀνατετροφότες.

297 Ταύτης τοίνυν τῆς οὕτως αἰσχρᾶς καὶ περιβοήτου συστάσεως καὶ κακίας, μᾶλλον δ', ὦ ἄνδρες Ἀθηναῖοι, προδοσίας, εἰ δεῖ μὴ ληρεῖν, τῆς τῶν Ἑλλήνων ἐλευθερίας, ἥ τε πόλις παρὰ πᾶσιν ἀνθρώποις ἀναίτιος γέγονεν ἐκ τῶν ἐμῶν πολιτευμάτων καὶ ἐγὼ παρ' ὑμῖν. εἶτά μ' ἐρωτᾷς ἀντὶ ποίας ἀρετῆς ἀξιῶ τιμᾶσθαι; ἐγὼ δή σοι λέγω ὅτι τῶν πολιτευομένων παρὰ τοῖς Ἕλλησι διαφθαρέντων ἁπάντων, ἀρξαμένων ἀπὸ σοῦ, πρότερον μὲν ὑπὸ Φιλίππου,
298 νῦν δ' ὑπ' Ἀλεξάνδρου, ἐμὲ οὔτε καιρὸς οὔτε φιλανθρωπία λόγων οὔτ' ἐπαγγελιῶν μέγεθος οὔτ' ἐλπὶς οὔτε φόβος οὔτ' ἄλλο οὐδὲν ἐπῆρεν οὐδὲ προηγάγετο ὧν ἔκρινα δικαίων καὶ συμφερόντων τῇ πατρίδι οὐδὲν προδοῦναι, οὐδ', ὅσα συμβεβούλευκα πώποτε τουτοισί, ὁμοίως ὑμῖν ὡσπερανεὶ τρυτάνη ῥέπων ἐπὶ τὸ λῆμμα συμβεβούλευκα, ἀλλ' ἀπ' ὀρθῆς καὶ δικαίας

καὶ ἀδιαφθόρου τῆς ψυχῆς, καὶ μεγίστων δὴ πραγμάτων τῶν κατ᾽ ἐμαυτὸν ἀνθρώπων προστὰς πάντα
ταῦτα ὑγιῶς καὶ δικαίως πεπολίτευμαι. διὰ ταῦτ᾽
ἀξιῶ τιμᾶσθαι. τὸν δὲ τειχισμὸν τοῦτον, ὃν σύ 299
μου διέσυρες, καὶ τὴν ταφρείαν ἄξια μὲν χάριτος
καὶ ἐπαίνου κρίνω, πῶς γὰρ οὔ; πόρρω μέντοι που
τῶν ἐμαυτῷ πεπολιτευμένων τίθεμαι. οὐ λίθοις
ἐτείχισα τὴν πόλιν οὐδὲ πλίνθοις ἐγώ, οὐδ᾽ ἐπὶ τούτοις μέγιστον τῶν ἐμαυτοῦ φρονῶ· ἀλλ᾽ ἐὰν τὸν
ἐμὸν τειχισμὸν βούλῃ δικαίως σκοπεῖν, εὑρήσεις
ὅπλα καὶ πόλεις καὶ τόπους καὶ λιμένας καὶ ναῦς
καὶ ἵππους καὶ πολλοὺς τοὺς ὑπὲρ τούτων ἀμυνουμένους. ταῦτα προυβαλόμην ἐγὼ πρὸ τῆς Ἀττι- 300
κῆς, ὅσον ἦν ἀνθρωπίνῳ λογισμῷ δυνατόν, καὶ τούτοις ἐτείχισα τὴν χώραν, οὐχὶ τὸν κύκλον τοῦ
Πειραιῶς οὐδὲ τοῦ ἄστεως. οὐδέ γ᾽ ἡττήθην ἐγὼ
τοῖς λογισμοῖς Φιλίππου, πολλοῦ γε καὶ δεῖ, οὐδὲ
ταῖς παρασκευαῖς, ἀλλ᾽ οἱ τῶν συμμάχων στρατηγοὶ καὶ αἱ δυνάμεις τῇ τύχῃ. τίνες αἱ τούτων ἀποδείξεις; ἐναργεῖς καὶ φανεραί. σκοπεῖτε δέ.

Τί χρῆν τὸν εὔνουν πολίτην ποιεῖν, τί τὸν μετὰ 301
πάσης προνοίας καὶ προθυμίας καὶ δικαιοσύνης ὑπὲρ
τῆς πατρίδος πολιτευόμενον; οὐκ ἐκ μὲν θαλάττης
τὴν Εὔβοιαν προβαλέσθαι πρὸ τῆς Ἀττικῆς, ἐκ δὲ
τῆς μεσογείας τὴν Βοιωτίαν, ἐκ δὲ τῶν πρὸς Πελοπόννησον τόπων τοὺς ὁμόρους ταύτῃ; οὐ τὴν σιτοπομπίαν, ὅπως παρὰ πᾶσαν φιλίαν ἄχρι τοῦ

302 Πειραιῶς κομισθήσεται, προϊδέσθαι; καὶ τὰ μὲν
σῶσαι τῶν ὑπαρχόντων ἐκπέμποντα βοηθείας καὶ
λέγοντα καὶ γράφοντα τοιαῦτα, τὴν Προκόννησον,
τὴν Χερρόνησον, τὴν Τένεδον, τὰ δ' ὅπως οἰκεῖα καὶ
σύμμαχ' ὑπάρξει πρᾶξαι, τὸ Βυζάντιον, τὴν Ἄβυ-
δον, τὴν Εὔβοιαν; καὶ τῶν μὲν τοῖς ἐχθροῖς ὑπαρχουσῶν δυνάμεων τὰς μεγίστας ἀφελεῖν, ὧν δ'
303 ἐνέλειπε τῇ πόλει, ταῦτα προσθεῖναι; ταῦτα τοίνυν
ἅπαντα πέπρακται τοῖς ἐμοῖς ψηφίσμασι καὶ τοῖς
ἐμοῖς πολιτεύμασιν, ἃ καὶ βεβουλευμένα, ὦ ἄνδρες
Ἀθηναῖοι, ἐὰν ἄνευ φθόνου τις βούληται σκοπεῖν,
ὀρθῶς εὑρήσει καὶ πεπραγμένα πάσῃ δικαιοσύνῃ, καὶ
τὸν ἑκάστου καιρὸν οὐ παρεθέντα οὐδ' ἀγνοηθέντα
οὐδὲ προεθέντα ὑπ' ἐμοῦ, καὶ ὅσα εἰς ἑνὸς ἀνδρὸς δύναμιν καὶ λογισμὸν ἧκεν, οὐδὲν ἐλλειφθέν. εἰ δὲ ἢ
δαίμονός τινος ἢ τύχης ἰσχὺς ἢ στρατηγῶν φαυλότης
ἢ τῶν προδιδόντων τὰς πόλεις ὑμῶν κακία ἢ πάντα
ταῦτα ἅμα ἐλυμαίνετο τοῖς ὅλοις, ἕως ἀνέτρεψαν, τί
304 Δημοσθένης ἀδικεῖ; εἰ δ' οἷος ἐγὼ παρ' ὑμῖν κατὰ
τὴν ἐμαυτοῦ τάξιν, εἷς ἐν ἑκάστῃ τῶν Ἑλληνίδων
πόλεων ἀνὴρ ἐγένετο, μᾶλλον δ' εἰ ἕνα ἄνδρα μόνον
Θετταλία καὶ ἕνα ἄνδρα Ἀρκαδία ταὐτὰ φρονοῦντα
ἔσχεν ἐμοί, οὐδεὶς οὔτε τῶν ἔξω Πυλῶν Ἑλλήνων
οὔτε τῶν εἴσω τοῖς παροῦσι κακοῖς ἐκέχρητ' ἄν,
ἀλλὰ πάντες ἂν ὄντες ἐλεύθεροι καὶ αὐτόνομοι μετὰ
πάσης ἀδείας ἀσφαλῶς ἐν εὐδαιμονίᾳ τὰς ἑαυτῶν
ᾤκουν πατρίδας, τῶν τοσούτων καὶ τοιούτων ἀγαθῶν

ὑμῖν καὶ τοῖς ἄλλοις Ἀθηναίοις ἔχοντες χάριν δι'
ἐμέ. ἵνα δ' εἰδῆτε ὅτι πολλῷ τοῖς λόγοις ἐλάττοσι 305
χρῶμαι τῶν ἔργων, εὐλαβούμενος τὸν φθόνον, λέγε
μοι ταυτὶ καὶ ἀνάγνωθι λαβὼν τὸν ἀριθμὸν τῶν
βοηθειῶν κατὰ τὰ ἐμὰ ψηφίσματα.

ἈΡΙΘΜΟΣ ΒΟΗΘΕΙΩΝ.

Ταῦτα καὶ τοιαῦτα πράττειν, Αἰσχίνη, τὸν καλὸν 306
κἀγαθὸν πολίτην δεῖ, ὧν κατορθουμένων μὲν μεγίστοις ἀναμφισβητήτως ὑπῆρχεν εἶναι, καὶ τὸ
δικαίως προσῆν, ὡς ἑτέρως δὲ συμβάντων τὸ γοῦν
εὐδοκιμεῖν περίεστι καὶ τὸ μηδένα μέμφεσθαι τὴν
πόλιν μηδὲ τὴν προαίρεσιν αὐτῆς, ἀλλὰ τὴν τύχην
κακίζειν τὴν οὕτω τὰ πράγματα κρίνασαν, οὐ μὰ 307
Δί' οὐκ ἀποστάντα τῶν συμφερόντων τῇ πόλει,
μισθώσαντα δ' αὑτὸν τοῖς ἐναντίοις, τοὺς ὑπὲρ τῶν
ἐχθρῶν καιροὺς ἀντὶ τῶν τῆς πατρίδος θεραπεύειν,
οὐδὲ τὸν μὲν πράγματ' ἄξια τῆς πόλεως ὑποστάντα
λέγειν καὶ γράφειν καὶ μένειν ἐπὶ τούτων προελό-
μενον βασκαίνειν, ἂν δέ τις ἰδίᾳ τι λυπήσῃ, τοῦτο
μεμνῆσθαι καὶ τηρεῖν, οὐδέ γ' ἡσυχίαν ἄγειν ἄδικον
καὶ ὕπουλον, ὃ σὺ ποιεῖς πολλάκις. ἔστι γάρ, 308
ἔστιν ἡσυχία δικαία καὶ συμφέρουσα τῇ πόλει, ἣν
οἱ πολλοὶ τῶν πολιτῶν ὑμεῖς ἁπλῶς ἄγετε. ἀλλ'
οὐ ταύτην οὗτος ἄγει τὴν ἡσυχίαν, πολλοῦ γε καὶ
δεῖ, ἀλλ' ἀποστὰς ὅταν αὐτῷ δόξῃ τῆς πολιτείας
(πολλάκις δὲ δοκεῖ) φυλάττει πηνίκ' ἔσεσθε μεστοὶ

τοῦ συνεχῶς λέγοντος ἢ παρὰ τῆς τύχης τι συμβέβηκεν ἐναντίωμα ἢ ἄλλο τι δύσκολον γέγονε (πολλὰ
309 δὲ τἀνθρώπινα)· εἶτ' ἐπὶ τούτῳ τῷ καιρῷ ῥήτωρ
ἐξαίφνης ἐκ τῆς ἡσυχίας ὥσπερ πνεῦμ' ἐφάνη, καὶ
πεφωνασκηκὼς καὶ συνειλοχὼς ῥήματα καὶ λόγους
συνείρει τούτους σαφῶς καὶ ἀπνευστί, ὄνησιν μὲν
οὐδεμίαν φέροντας οὐδ' ἀγαθοῦ κτῆσιν οὐδενός, συμ-
φορὰν δὲ τῷ τυχόντι τῶν πολιτῶν καὶ κοινὴν αἰσχύνην. καίτοι ταύτης τῆς μελέτης καὶ τῆς ἐπιμελείας,
Αἰσχίνη, εἴπερ ἐκ ψυχῆς δικαίας ἐγίγνετο καὶ τὰ
τῆς πατρίδος συμφέροντα προῃρημένης, τοὺς καρποὺς ἔδει γενναίους καὶ καλοὺς καὶ πᾶσιν ὠφελίμους
εἶναι, συμμαχίας πόλεων, πόρους χρημάτων, ἐμπορίου κατασκευήν, νόμων συμφερόντων θέσεις, τοῖς
310 ἀποδειχθεῖσιν ἐχθροῖς ἐναντιώματα. τούτων γὰρ
ἁπάντων ἦν ἐν τοῖς ἄνω χρόνοις ἐξέτασις, καὶ ἔδωκεν ὁ παρελθὼν χρόνος πολλὰς ἀποδείξεις ἀνδρὶ
καλῷ τε κἀγαθῷ, ἐν οἷς οὐδαμοῦ σὺ φανήσει γεγο-
νώς, οὐ πρῶτος, οὐ δεύτερος, οὐ τρίτος, οὐ τέταρτος,
οὐ πέμπτος, οὐχ ἕκτος, οὐχ ὁποστοσοῦν, οὔκουν ἐπί
311 γ' οἷς ἡ πατρὶς ηὐξάνετο. τίς γὰρ συμμαχία σοῦ
πράξαντος γέγονε τῇ πόλει; τίς δὲ βοήθεια ἢ κτῆ-
σις εὐνοίας ἢ δόξης; τίς δὲ πρεσβεία, τίς διακονία
δι' ἣν πόλις ἐντιμοτέρα; τί τῶν οἰκείων ἢ τῶν
Ἑλληνικῶν καὶ ξενικῶν, οἷς ἐπέστης, ἐπηνώρθωται;
ποῖαι τριήρεις; ποῖα βέλη; ποῖοι νεώσοικοι; τίς
ἐπισκευὴ τειχῶν; ποῖον ἱππικόν; τί τῶν ἁπάντων

σὺ χρήσιμος εἶ; τίς ἢ τοῖς εὐπόροις ἢ τοῖς ἀπόροις
πολιτικὴ καὶ κοινὴ βοήθεια χρημάτων; οὐδεμία.
ἀλλ', ὦ τᾶν, εἰ μηδὲν τούτων, εὔνοιά γε καὶ προθυ- 312
μία· ποῦ; πότε; ὅστις, ὦ πάντων ἀδικώτατε, οὐδ'
ὅτε ἅπαντες, ὅσοι πώποτ' ἐφθέγξαντ' ἐπὶ τοῦ βήματος, εἰς σωτηρίαν ἐπεδίδοσαν, καὶ τὸ τελευταῖον
Ἀριστόνικος τὸ συνειλεγμένον εἰς τὴν ἐπιτιμίαν
ἀργύριον, οὐδὲ τότε οὔτε παρῆλθες οὔτ' ἐπέδωκας
οὐδὲν, οὐκ ἀπορῶν, πῶς γάρ; ὅς γε κεκληρονόμηκας
μὲν τῶν Φίλωνος τοῦ κηδεστοῦ χρημάτων πλειόνων
ἢ πεντεταλάντων, διτάλαντον δ' εἶχες ἔρανον δωρεὰν
παρὰ τῶν ἡγεμόνων τῶν συμμοριῶν ἐφ' οἷς ἐλυμήνω
τὸν τριηραρχικὸν νόμον. ἀλλ' ἵνα μὴ λόγον ἐκ 313
λόγου λέγων τοῦ παρόντος ἐμαυτὸν ἐκκρούσω, παραλείψω ταῦτα. ἀλλ' ὅτι γ' οὐχὶ δι' ἔνδειαν οὐκ ἐπέδωκας, ἐκ τούτων δῆλον, ἀλλὰ φυλάττων τὸ μηδὲν
ἐναντίον γενέσθαι παρὰ σοῦ τούτοις οἷς ἅπαντα
πολιτεύει. ἐν τίσιν οὖν σὺ νεανίας καὶ πηνίκα
λαμπρός; ἡνίκ' ἂν κατὰ τουτωνὶ δέῃ, ἐν τούτοις
λαμπροφωνότατος, μνημονικώτατος, ὑποκριτὴς ἄρι-
στος, τραγικὸς Θεοκρίνης.

Εἶτα τῶν πρότερον γεγενημένων ἀγαθῶν ἀνδρῶν 314
μέμνησαι. καὶ καλῶς ποιεῖς. οὐ μέντοι δίκαιόν
ἐστιν, ὦ ἄνδρες Ἀθηναῖοι, τὴν πρὸς τοὺς τετελευτη-
κότας εὔνοιαν ὑπάρχουσαν προλαβόντα παρ' ὑμῶν
πρὸς ἐκείνους ἐξετάζειν καὶ παραβάλλειν ἐμὲ τὸν
νῦν ζῶντα μεθ' ὑμῶν. τίς γὰρ οὐκ οἶδε τῶν πάν- 315

των ὅτι τοῖς μὲν ζῶσι πᾶσιν ὕπεστί τις ἢ πλείων ἢ
ἐλάττων φθόνος, τοὺς τεθνεῶτας δὲ οὐδὲ τῶν ἐχθρῶν
οὐδεὶς ἔτι μισεῖ; οὕτως οὖν ἐχόντων τούτων τῇ
φύσει, πρὸς τοὺς πρὸ ἐμαυτοῦ νῦν ἐγὼ κρίνωμαι καὶ
θεωρῶμαι; μηδαμῶς· οὔτε γὰρ δίκαιον οὔτ' ἴσον,
Αἰσχίνη, ἀλλὰ πρὸς σὲ καὶ ἄλλον εἴ τινα βούλει
316 τῶν ταὐτά σοι προῃρημένων καὶ ζώντων. κἀκεῖνο
σκόπει. πότερον κάλλιον καὶ ἄμεινον τῇ πόλει διὰ
τὰς τῶν πρότερον εὐεργεσίας, οὔσας ὑπερμεγέθεις,
οὐ μὲν οὖν εἴποι τις ἂν ἡλίκας, τὰς ἐπὶ τὸν παρόντα
βίον γιγνομένας εἰς ἀχαριστίαν καὶ προπηλακισμὸν
ἄγειν, ἢ πᾶσιν, ὅσοι τι μετ' εὐνοίας πράττουσι, τῆς
317 παρὰ τούτων τιμῆς καὶ φιλανθρωπίας μετεῖναι; καὶ
μὴν εἰ καὶ τοῦτ' ἄρα δεῖ με εἰπεῖν, ἡ μὲν ἐμὴ πολιτεία καὶ προαίρεσις, ἄν τις ὀρθῶς σκοπῇ, ταῖς τῶν
τότ' ἐπαινουμένων ἀνδρῶν ὁμοία καὶ ταὐτὰ βουλο-
μένη φανήσεται, ἡ δὲ σὴ ταῖς τῶν τοὺς τοιούτους
τότε συκοφαντούντων· δῆλον γὰρ ὅτι καὶ κατ' ἐκείνους ἦσάν τινες, οἳ διέσυρον μὲν τοὺς ὄντας τότε,
τοὺς δὲ πρότερον γεγενημένους ἐπῄνουν, βάσκανον
318 πρᾶγμα καὶ ταὐτὸ ποιοῦντες σοί· εἶτα λέγεις ὡς
οὐδὲν ὅμοιός εἰμι ἐκείνοις ἐγώ; σὺ δ' ὅμοιος, Αἰσχίνη; ὁ δ' ἀδελφὸς ὁ σός; ἄλλος δέ τις τῶν νῦν
ῥητόρων; ἐγὼ μὲν γὰρ οὐδένα φημί. ἀλλὰ πρὸς
τοὺς ζῶντας, ὦ χρηστέ, ἵνα μηδὲν ἄλλ' εἴπω, τὸν
ζῶντα ἐξέταζε καὶ τοὺς καθ' αὑτόν, ὥσπερ τἄλλα
πάντα, τοὺς ποιητάς, τοὺς χορούς, τοὺς ἀγωνιστάς.

ὁ Φιλάμμων οὐχ ὅτι Γλαύκου τοῦ Καρυστίου καί 319
τινων ἑτέρων πρότερον γεγενημένων ἀθλητῶν ἀσθε-
νέστερος ἦν, ἀστεφάνωτος ἐκ τῆς Ὀλυμπίας ἀπῄει,
ἀλλ᾽ ὅτι τῶν εἰσελθόντων πρὸς αὐτὸν ἄριστα ἐμά-
χετο, ἐστεφανοῦτο καὶ νικῶν ἀνηγορεύετο. καὶ σὺ
πρὸς τοὺς νῦν ὅρα με ῥήτορας, πρὸς σαυτόν, πρὸς
ὅντινα βούλει τῶν ἁπάντων· οὐδένα ἐξίσταμαι. ὧν, 320
ὅτε μὲν τῇ πόλει τὰ βέλτιστα ἑλέσθαι παρῆν, ἐφα-
μίλλου τῆς εἰς τὴν πατρίδα εὐνοίας ἐν κοινῷ πᾶσι
κειμένης, ἐγὼ κράτιστα λέγων ἐφαινόμην, καὶ τοῖς
ἐμοῖς καὶ ψηφίσμασι καὶ νόμοις καὶ πρεσβείαις
ἅπαντα διῳκεῖτο, ὑμῶν δὲ οὐδεὶς ἦν οὐδαμοῦ, πλὴν
εἰ τούτοις ἐπηρεάσαι τι δέοι· ἐπειδὴ δὲ ἃ μήποτ᾽
ὤφελε συνέβη, καὶ οὐκέτι συμβούλων, ἀλλὰ τῶν
τοῖς ἐπιταττομένοις ὑπηρετούντων καὶ τῶν κατὰ τῆς
πατρίδος μισθαρνεῖν ἑτοίμων καὶ τῶν κολακεύειν
ἕτερον βουλομένων ἐξέτασις ἦν, τηνικαῦτα σὺ καὶ
τούτων ἕκαστος ἐν τάξει καὶ μέγας καὶ λαμπρὸς
ἱπποτρόφος, ἐγὼ δ᾽ ἀσθενής, ὁμολογῶ, ἀλλ᾽ εὔνους
μᾶλλον ὑμῶν τουτοισί. δύο δ᾽, ὦ ἄνδρες Ἀθηναῖοι, 321
τὸν φύσει μέτριον πολίτην ἔχειν δεῖ (οὕτω γάρ μοι
περὶ ἐμαυτοῦ λέγοντι ἀνεπιφθονώτατον εἰπεῖν), ἐν
μὲν ταῖς ἐξουσίαις τὴν τοῦ γενναίου καὶ τοῦ πρωτείου τῇ πόλει προαίρεσιν διαφυλάττειν, ἐν παντὶ
δὲ καιρῷ καὶ πράξει τὴν εὔνοιαν· τούτου γὰρ ἡ φύσις κυρία, τοῦ δύνασθαι δὲ καὶ ἰσχύειν ἕτερα. ταύτην τοίνυν παρ᾽ ἐμοὶ μεμενηκυῖαν εὑρήσετε ἁπλῶς.

322 ὁρᾶτε δέ. οὐκ ἐξαιτούμενος, οὐκ Ἀμφικτυονικὰς
δίκας ἐπαγόντων, οὐκ ἀπειλούντων, οὐκ ἐπαγγελλομένων, οὐχὶ τοὺς καταράτους τούτους ὥσπερ θηρία
μοι προσβαλλόντων, οὐδαμῶς ἐγὼ προδέδωκα τὴν
εἰς ὑμᾶς εὔνοιαν. τὸ γὰρ ἐξ ἀρχῆς εὐθὺς ὀρθὴν καὶ
δικαίαν τὴν ὁδὸν τῆς πολιτείας εἱλόμην, τὰς τιμάς,
τὰς δυναστείας, τὰς εὐδοξίας τὰς τῆς πατρίδος θερα-
323 πεύειν, ταύτας αὔξειν, μετὰ τούτων εἶναι. οὐκ ἐπὶ
μὲν τοῖς ἑτέρων εὐτυχήμασι φαιδρὸς ἐγὼ καὶ γεγηθὼς κατὰ τὴν ἀγορὰν περιέρχομαι, τὴν δεξιὰν προ-
τείνων καὶ εὐαγγελιζόμενος τούτοις οὓς ἂν ἐκεῖσε
ἀπαγγέλλειν οἴωμαι, τῶν δὲ τῆς πόλεως ἀγαθῶν
πεφρικὼς ἀκούω καὶ στένων καὶ κύπτων εἰς τὴν
γῆν, ὥσπερ οἱ δυσσεβεῖς οὗτοι, οἳ τὴν μὲν πόλιν
διασύρουσιν, ὥσπερ οὐχ αὑτοὺς διασύροντες, ὅταν
τοῦτο ποιῶσιν, ἔξω δὲ βλέπουσι, καὶ ἐν οἷς ἀτυχη-
σάντων τῶν Ἑλλήνων ηὐτύχησεν ἕτερος, ταῦτ'
ἐπαινοῦσι καὶ ὅπως τὸν ἅπαντα χρόνον μενεῖ φασὶ
δεῖν τηρεῖν.

324 Μὴ δῆτ', ὦ πάντες θεοί, μηδεὶς τοῦθ' ὑμῶν ἐπι-
νεύσειεν, ἀλλὰ μάλιστα μὲν καὶ τούτοις βελτίω τινὰ
νοῦν καὶ φρένας ἐνθείητε, εἰ δ' ἄρ' ἔχουσιν ἀνιάτως,
τούτους μὲν αὐτοὺς καθ' ἑαυτοὺς ἐξώλεις καὶ προώλεις ἐν γῇ καὶ θαλάττῃ ποιήσατε, ἡμῖν δὲ τοῖς λοι-
ποῖς τὴν ταχίστην ἀπαλλαγὴν τῶν ἐπηρτημένων
φόβων δότε καὶ σωτηρίαν ἀσφαλῆ.

NOTES.

NOTES.

§§ **1, 2.** Exordium: a solemn prayer reiterated shortly after (8). MAY HEAVEN INSPIRE THE ASSEMBLY TO GIVE ME SUCH A TRIAL AS MY MERITS DESERVE AND IMPARTIAL JUSTICE DICTATES.

1. Page 1, line 1. **πρῶτον μέν.** "To commence a speech with prayer," says Dissen, "was unusual in the Greek law courts. One instance is found in Lycurgus (*c. Leocr.* 136)" [*εὔχομαι γὰρ τῇ Ἀθηνᾷ καὶ τοῖς ἄλλοις θεοῖς...ἐμὲ μὲν ἄξιον κατήγορον ποιῆσαι.*] "The Romans rather affected the practice: Servius (on Vergil. *Æn.* xi. 301), Majores nullam orationem nisi invocatis numinibus inchoabant. Cf. Ciceron. *Div. in Cæcil.* 13": also *pro L. Murenâ* 1, and *pro C. Cornelio* (fragm.). In this instance, the solemn appeal to heaven is occasioned by the unjust demand of Æschines that Demosthenes should be required, in his speech, to follow the order of the indictment and the prosecution. — 2. **ὅσην εὔνοιαν, κ. τ. λ.,** *that the same good-will which I ever bear to the state and all of yourselves may subsist for me on your part in the present trial.* The *εὔνοια* of Demosthenes had been specified in Ctesiphon's decree as a ground for giving him the crown. *κηρύττεταί τις ἐν τῷ θεάτρῳ ὅτι στεφανοῦται ἀρετῆς ἕνεκα καὶ ἀνδραγαθίας καὶ εὐνοίας,* Æsch. *c. Ctes.* 89, 2. In connection with *διατελῶ ἔχων* the word *ὑπάρξαι* is very appropriate: his *constant* patriotism, he assumes, will have accumulated for him a *fund* of popularity on which he may draw at this crisis. The emphatic *τουτονί* adds emphasis to the expression of this idea. — 4. *εἰς* = *for,* or *in respect to.* — 5. **ἔπειτα** belongs to the class of adverbs which are in themselves antithetic: hence the *μέν* after *πρῶτον* does not require to be followed by *δέ* or any similar particle. — **ὅπερ, κ. τ. λ.,** *that which is most in the interest of yourselves and your character for piety and honor.* For *ὅπερ* we find *ὅ τι μέλλει συνοίσειν* in the parallel passage, inf. 8. With this sense of εὐσέβεια cf. Soph. *El.* 968, εὐσέβειαν ἐκ πατρὸς κάτω θανόντος οἴσει. Here εὐσέβεια refers to their oath in particular, δόξα to equity in general. For δόξα in 8 the orator substitutes εὐδοξία as more explicit. — 6. **παραστῆσαι,** *to inspire.* παραστήσαντα ἐλπίδας, p. 448, l. 9. οὐ γὰρ ἡ πληγὴ παρέστησε τὴν ὀργὴν ἀλλ' ἡ ἀτιμία, p. 537, l. 22. Whiston translates it, *to put into your hearts.* — 7. **μὴ τὸν ἀντίδικον,** *not to take my opponent for your adviser respecting the manner in which you ought to hear me.* Æschin. p. 82 (fin.), ἀξιώσατε τὸν Δημοσθένην τὸν αὐτὸν τρόπον ἀπολογεῖσθαι ὅνπερ κἀγὼ κατηγόρηκα, *i. e.* let him reply to the charge of special illegality before he defends his general character. — 8. **ὑμᾶς ἐμοῦ.** Observe the juxtaposition and the emphasis, suggesting the absurdity as well as the injustice of such dictation: how *you* ought to hear *me.* — **2.** 9. **τὸν ὅρκον.** A clause in the oath of the Heliastæ was ἀκροάσομαι τοῦ τε κατηγόρου καὶ τοῦ ἀπολογουμένου ὁμοίως ἀμφοῖν, p. 747, l. 9. With ὅρκον repeat σύμβουλον ποιήσασθαι = *to consult.* — 11. **ἀκροάσασθαι.** Bekker from Σ. The common reading was ἀκροᾶσθαι. The present infinitive would refer to the universal principle, the aorist to its particular application in any given case. — 12. **οὐ μόνον.** The μόνον must be understood as repeated after the following οὐδέ, ... *not merely to have formed no prejudice, not merely to show your good-will in equal measure to both sides.* Another instance of this very common ellipsis is in 93. — 14. **τῇ τάξει, κ. τ. λ.,** *to allow each of the opposing orators so to deal with his defence and its arrangement as he has desired and predetermined to do.* The force of these perfects represents the speaker as *having chosen* his line of defence *fully* and on principle before the trial begins, after which he cannot lightly abandon it. There is no need to take τῇ τάξει καὶ τῇ ἀπολογίᾳ as a hendiadys.

3, 4. AESCHINES, IN THIS TRIAL, HAS TWO SPECIAL ADVANTAGES OVER ME: (1) HE HAS NO CHARACTER TO LOSE; (2) THE SIDE OF THE CASE HE SPEAKS FOR IS THE MOST ENTERTAINING AND INTERESTING.

3. 17. **Πολλὰ μὲν, κ. τ. λ.,** *now while I have many disadvantages... there are two which are especially great.* In this favorite Attic construction δέ introduces the principal sentence, μέν the subordinate: frequently, as in the present example, they form the apodosis and protasis of a strictly concessive sentence. The καί is emphatic; *non copulat sed intendit* (Stallbaum on *Protag.* 315 D); a use especially marked in the phrases καὶ μάλα, καὶ πάνυ, and the like. — 18. **ἀγῶνα.** This word denotes the Grecian games, primarily the vast assembly that was wont to witness them, and then the contest and struggle for the prize. Its use by the Attic orators to express a *trial* in the courts is highly significant. The Athenian dicasteries at this time had become, as it were, the *games* or *spectacles* of the age, in which the orators were the athletes, and the people found their favorite *amusement* in being present as spectators. And to this contest and spectacle — *τουτονὶ τὸν ἀγῶνα* — a greater concourse had come together from all Greece than had ever before been known to be present on any such occasion. See Æsch. c. Ctes. 56, and Cic. de Opt. Gen. Orat. 7. — Page 2, line 1. **οὐ περὶ τῶν ἴσων,** *not for an equal stake;* that is, I have far *more* at stake than he has. — 3. **ἑλεῖν,** *to win his cause;* like our own phrase, *to get a verdict.* *ἑλεῖν* in this sense is used of the prosecutor only, and usually in conjunction with *γραφή*. *γραφὰς πολλὰς καὶ μεγάλας διώξας εἷλεν οὐδεμίαν*, Antiph. p. 115, l. 24. *γραφή* as distinguished from *εἰσαγγελία* is an indictment directed against criminal documents or orations, *εἰσαγγελία* against criminal conduct; inf. 249. Both words are descriptive of *public* accusations, never of *private*, for *γραφὴ ἰδία* (c. *Mid.* p. 529) implies that, in injuring the *individual* prosecutor, the accused has injured the *state;* because, at the time of the attack, the prosecutor was a State officer, or the like. *δίκη* as a general term for all varieties of actions would include *public* prosecutions, although, as a legal term, its special meaning is a *private* suit. — 4. **ἐμοὶ μέν.** The aposiopesis is due to euphemism; it would be ominous (*δυσχερές*) to allude to an adverse verdict. He implies: I have position and reputation at stake; Æschines possesses neither, and therefore has nothing to lose; hence he accuses me, *ἐκ περιουσίας, at a monstrous advantage.* Reiske holds that this latter phrase includes the idea, *in sheer wantonness*, or, *by way of pastime.* Whiston renders it, *from a superabundant stock;* adding, for explanation, "hence his loss will be comparatively small, as he has not much to lose." And he quotes Brougham as rendering: "he brings his charge an unprovoked volunteer, ex abundanti." The former, in his edition, places a dash after the clause: *οὐ βούλομαι...τοῦ λόγου*, as well as before it, thus making it parenthetical, and *οὗτος δ'* antithetic to *ἐμοὶ μέν.* — 6. **ἕτερον δέ,** *and the other* (sc. disadvantage), *the natural instinct of all mankind to enjoy the hearing of invectives.* — 4. 10. **πᾶσιν...ἐνοχλεῖ,** *offends everybody.* *ὅ τι ἂν μὴ καθ' ἡμέραν ἐνοχλῇ παροράτε*, p. 398, l. 7. The verb *ἐνοχλεῖν* is usually transitive. *οὐχὶ τῶν ἐνοχλούντων ὑμᾶς*; p. 622, l. 12; but Lysias constructs it as a neuter, c. *Andoc.*

p. 107, *ἐν γοῦν ἐπίστανται μὴ ἐνοχλεῖν τοῖς ἠδικημένοις*, and so does Demosthenes, p. 341, l. 3, *ἐνοχλοῦντας καὶ προσιόντας ὑμῖν*. *ὡς ἔπος εἰπεῖν* qualifies the otherwise too unqualified *πᾶσιν*: *everybody, so to speak.* C. 671; Cu. 564; G. 268; H. 772.* — 11. **κἂν μέν,** *and if, in precaution against this, I abstain from stating what I have done...I shall be thought incapable of clearing myself from the charges, or showing my claims for honorable distinction.* His dilemma is this: either he must praise himself, and so disgust the court, or else hold his peace, and so make a tacit admission that Æschines is in the right. *δεικνύναι*, to *exhibit* rather than *prove*. — 14. **ἁ...πεπολίτευμαι,** *my conduct and policy.* A fondness for such pairs of words closely related in signification is characteristic of our orator's style. Cf. *βεβούληται καὶ προήρηται*, 2, *λοιδοριῶν καὶ κατηγοριῶν*, 3, *et passim*. — 16. **ὡς μετριώτατα.** This usual ellipsis of *δυνατόν ἐστι*, or the like, resembles our own idiom, "as best may be"; *quam modestissime.* C. 553; Cu. 631, a; H. 664. — 17. **ὅ τι δ' ἄν.** *But, whatever the case itself constrains me to, of that he who set such a trial on foot deserves to incur the blame;* i. e. self-defence justifies self-laudation. Reiske cites Quintil. *Inst. Or.* xi. 1, 22, Neque hoc dico non aliquando de rebus a se gestis oratori esse dicendum, sicut eidem Demostheni pro Ctesiphonte, quod tamen ita emendavit ut necessitatem id faciendi ostenderet, invidiamque omnem in eum regeret qui hoc se coegisset. Plutarch, *Mor.* 541 E, calls it *λαμπρὰν τῷ Δημοσθένει παρρησίαν*.

5–7. MY STAKE IN THIS CASE IS QUITE AS HEAVY AS CTESIPHON'S. I IMPLORE YOU NOT TO BE PREJUDICED BY THE SPEECH FOR THE PROSECUTION, BUT TO BEAR IN MIND YOUR OATH AS JURORS.

5. 21. **ἐμοί τε καὶ Κτησιφῶντι.** *τε* is wanting in Σ, probably by accidental omission. In this clause he declares the close connection of Ctesiphon with himself as regards the trial, in the next the *ἐμοί* stands emphatically alone. Translate, *and deserves on my own part an earnestness by no means inferior.* The datives are ethical. C. 462; Cu. 433; G. 184, 3; H. 596. — 23. **πάντων** = *anything whatever* (*cuiusvis*). So in the common phrase, *παντός ἐστιν* (*cuivis contingit*), "it is in the power of anybody (and everybody)." *τὸ μὲν ὀργισθῆναι παντὸς καὶ ῥᾳδιον.* Aristot. *N. E.* 11, 9. — 25. **τῆς παρ' ὑμῶν εὐνοίας.** This replies to the taunt of Æschines on p. 84, *σὺ δ' οὔτε περὶ τῆς οὐσίας οὔτε περὶ τοῦ σώματος οὔτε περὶ τῆς ἐπιτιμίας ἀγωνίζῃ· ἀλλὰ περὶ τίνος ἐστιν αὐτῷ ἡ*

* The references are to the grammars of Crosby, Rev. Ed. 1871; Curtius, Harper's Ed. 1872; Goodwin; and Hadley.

σπουδή; περὶ χρυσῶν στεφάνων καὶ κηρυγμάτων ἐν τῷ θεάτρῳ. — 6. P. 3, l. 3. **δικαίως.** This adverb and the four following words belong clearly to ἀκοῦσαι. *I beg and implore you, while I am making my defence upon the charges, to hear me with justice as the laws direct.* — **ἐξ ἀρχῆς.** *Originally,* not as the earliest lawgiver, but as the most influential. Hence τιθεὶς, which is strictly of one despotic lawgiver, whereas τιθέμενος is of a republic or community. — 4. **εὔνους ὑμῖν.** So Ar. *Nub.* 1190, Σόλων ὁ παλαιὸς ἦν φιλόδημος τὴν φύσιν. Translate, *being well disposed towards you, and a friend to the people.* — **οὐ μόνον, κ. τ. λ.** *Thought it essential should be rendered valid, not merely by the fact of recording them, but also by the fact of you, the jurors, having taken an oath.* To appreciate the force of the tenses δικάζοντας and ὀμωμοκέναι we must recollect that a body of 6,000 was chosen annually by lot from the whole of the commons; out of these again, the Archons selected by lot the jury for each particular case, and they took the oath every time prior to trying a cause. — 7. 6. **οὐκ ἀπιστῶν.** *Not because he distrusted you.* C. 674; Cu. 581; G. 277, 2; H. 789, c. — 7. **αἰτίας καὶ διαβολάς.** αἰτία, according to Demosthenes, means an accusation relying on the bare word of the accuser. ὅταν τις ψιλῷ χρησάμενος λόγῳ μὴ παράσχηται πίστιν ὧν λέγει, p. 600, l. 4. Hence we find it conjoined with διαβολαί here and with λοιδορία (*l. c.*). Observe the orator's fondness for *pairs* of kindred words. Cf. note, 4. — 8. **ὁ διώκων,** *the prosecutor,* i. e. the accuser in his official capacity; the Scotch "pursuer"; opposed to ὁ φεύγων, *the defendant.* This difference between διώκειν and κατηγορεῖν is strongly marked in 9, εἰ μὲν οὖν περὶ ὧν ἐδίωκε μόνον κατηγόρησεν. — 9. **ἰσχύει** = *is strong;* that is, has the advantage. — **παρελθεῖν.** Originally, *to outstrip and pass by* in a race; hence, metaphorically, *to defeat, circumvent, get the better of.* τὰ ἔργα τοὺς λόγους παρέρχεται, p. 132, 7. — 11. **διαφυλάττων.** The compound δια-, of persistence and continuance, as in διασώζειν, διαζῆν, κ. τ. λ. — **τὰ δίκαια, κ. τ. λ.** *Shall likewise* (καὶ) *admit with favor the just pleas of him who speaks at a later period, and having first devoted himself as a fair and impartial hearer to both sides, thus and thus only* (οὕτω) (i. e. only *after having* heard both sides) *let him form his decision on the whole case.* Hence the Aorist παρασχών. C. 674, d; Cu. 496; H. 717.

8. With so serious a struggle before me I reiterate my prayer to heaven.

16. **ὡς ἔοικε.** To be taken closely with παντός. Actually the

prosecution did not assail Demosthenes' life on all points, but obviously its intention was to do so. Compare note, ὡς ἔπος εἰπεῖν, 4. — 17. **λόγον διδόναι.** *To give an account.* So λ. αἰτεῖν, λαμβάνειν, not to be confounded with the other usage, "to give a man opportunity of speaking." — 18. **πάλιν.** See the notes on the parallel passage in 1. The exordium of this oration is longer and more impassioned than is usual with Demosthenes. The success of his defence depended entirely on his being permitted to choose his own order of arrangement, and to place in the foreground of his argument his public policy, in which he was sure of the sympathy of the Athenian dicastery. Having secured this point in his introduction, he had in fact swept away the chief reliance and support of his antagonist, and could now meet him, as it were, in the open field, on the main question, where he had nothing to fear. His renewed and impassioned appeal to the gods for an impartial hearing was further justified, not to say necessitated, by his adversary's representation of him as an ill-starred and accursed enemy of the gods.

9. AS ÆSCHINES HAS TRAVELLED OUT OF THE INDICTMENT, I SHALL DO THE SAME.

26. **Εἰ κατηγόρησεν...ἂν ἀπελογούμην.** *If he had* (at the time when he spoke) *accused me, I should have been now defending myself.* The speech of Æschines is a thing of the past, that of Demosthenes is going on in the present. Hence we have the aorist in the protasis, the imperfect in the apodosis. Many grammars give an erroneous rule about the meaning of this imperfect indicative with ἄν, according to which rule they would render ἀπελογούμην ἄν, "I should defend myself," as if there was some prospect of his doing so. But that would require in Greek the optative in lieu of the indicative. There can clearly be but a shade of difference between the imperfect indicative and the aorist of the same mood, whenever they appear in exactly the same construction. Whichever of the two be combined with ἄν in the apodosis of a conditional sentence, the very nature of the tense excludes all consideration of *future* prospects *now.* Such prospects *were* once *future* in a time gone by, if a certain condition had been then fulfilled; but they are so no longer. The imperfect under these circumstances implies a little more than the aorist: it implies that the action of the verb is to be viewed as a matter of duration and continuity. C. 615; Cu. 537, sqq.; G. 222; H. 742. — 27. **προβουλεύματος.** At the time when Æschines brought

his action, the bill of Ctesiphon had received the sanction of the βουλή, and was then offered to the δῆμος, that their votes might be taken upon it. Strictly speaking, the bill could not be called a ψήφισμα until it received their sanction. See Smith's Dic. of Antiq. Art. Βουλή. — P. 4, l. 2. **ἀνήλωκε**, *has lavished*, a word descriptive of reckless rather than of reasonable expenditure. Some discussion has arisen about the augment, as used in Attic, of the past tenses of ἀναλίσκω (see Lobeck's *Ajax*, 1049). But there seems to be little doubt about the true reading here. — 5. **ἵνα μηδεὶς, κ. τ. λ.**, *that none of you may give me a more prejudiced hearing of the rights which concern this indictment, because he has been carried away by the pleadings extraneous to the case.* This is the usual translation, and according to this we must understand by the phrase ἀλλότριον ἀκούειν *to hear with a judgment not one's own*, i. e. already imbued with the views of another. Cf. γναθμοῖσι γελοίων ἀλλοτρίοισι, Homer *Odyss*. xvii. 452, of laughing with an expression not one's own, i. e. forced. The comparative adverb only adds the sense of *more than the average*, or *more than he would do if let alone.* ἠγμένος, *carried with violence*, a common meaning of ἄγω, as especially in the phrase φέρειν καὶ ἄγειν. The construction of ἀκούειν with a double genitive (1) of the person, (2) of the thing, as here, is somewhat unusual though quite grammatical. The genitive of the person could be regarded as limiting the genitive of the thing = *my just arguments touching the indictment.* Compare τὰ τοῦ λέγοντος ὑστέρου δίκαια, 7.

10, 11. TO HIS SLANDERS ON MY PRIVATE CHARACTER I REPLY FOR THE PRESENT BY APPEALING TO YOUR PERSONAL KNOWLEDGE OF ME. I SHALL DEAL WITH HIS IMPUTATIONS ON MY PUBLIC CHARACTER FIRST.

10. 8. **λοιδορούμενος**, *all his abusive slander.* The active and middle voices of λοιδορεῖν are used with very slight difference of meaning: strictly the active = to abuse the man; the middle = to get the man abused, or abuse him for one's own purposes. So πλάττειν and πλάττεσθαι. Cf. ἐπλάττετο in this same section. — 10. **εἰ μὲν ἴστε**, *if you know me to be* [supply ὄντα] *such a man as the prosecutor just now* [imperfect tense] *accused me of being* — [and you must know me thoroughly well] *for I have lived nowhere else than among yourselves — do not so much as tolerate the sound of my voice, not even if I have with extreme ability conducted all my public administration; but rise from your seats and condemn me at once.* φωνή is very appropriate here, φωνεῖν meaning "to speak *aloud.*" Ἄναξ δ' ὁ πρέσβυς τόδ' εἶπε φωνῶν. Æsch. *Ag.* 205. Demosthenes says, "Refuse not merely to hear my arguments, but even the sound of my voice." There were three methods of silencing an orator: συρίττειν = to hiss him down; ἐκρίπτειν = to hustle him off the Bema; or lastly, as here, to rise from their seats, drop in their votes in condemnation of Ctesiphon, and so abruptly terminate the trial. — 14. **εἰ δὲ πολλῷ.** *But if you have conceived and are well aware that I myself — ay, and my family too — are far superior to the prosecutor, and of a superior descent, and as good (to say nothing beyond the mark) as any average individuals.* The object of γιγνώσκετε was to have been ἐμέ alone, καὶ τοὺς ἐμούς is added as an after-thought, but too late to alter the singular βελτίω. It is common, however, in such constructions, for the predicate to agree with the nearer or the more prominent subject, especially if the predicate precedes. C. 497; G. 138, N. 2, b; H. 511, h. The word μετρίων is always of the *juste milieu:* here of fair respectability in character and position. παρέχειν ἑαυτὸν μέτριον (Æschin. p. 1, l. 3). Self-laudation, as *burdensome* to the hearer, is well described by ἐπαχθές. πόλυς ἦν τοῖς ἐπαίνοις καὶ ἐπαχθής. Æschin. p. 33, l. 29. — **11.** 21. **κακοήθης... εὐήθες ᾠήθης.** Here is a triple paronomasia. εὐήθες is used sarcastically and in a bad sense, as we sometimes use *good-natured* and *well-meaning* to denote weakness. Jacobs imitates the Greek in German by the words, *argmüthig...gutmüthig*; and we might translate them imperfectly thus: *ill-natured as you are, you entertained the good-natured notion.* Paronomasia is not frequent in Demosthenes, but is sometimes used with great ingenuity and force. Thus he plays on the name of Eubulus: εἰ κακῶς ἐμὲ βούλει ποιεῖν, Εὔβουλε. — 25. **τετύφωμαι.** *I am not so blind,* literally, *so obscured with mist* (τῦφος). Harpocration, however, derives τυφοῦσθαι from τυφώς, and explains it *to be storm-struck.* Demosthenes combines it with μαίνεσθαι (p. 409, l. 11), and with ληρεῖν (p. 116, l. 6): he contrasts it with ἀπιστεῖν (p. 682, l. 6). The prevailing idea of the verb is therefore *blind folly.* — 26. **ὑπὲρ τῶν πεπολιτευμένων.** The difference in meaning between ὑπέρ and περί is slight in the Attic orators. The sense of *concerning* is common to both, the sense of *defending* is limited to ὑπέρ. Probably this latter sense may have risen from the fact of the hero in the field of battle standing *over* his prostrate friend to protect him from the enemy's assault. — 27. **πομπείας.** Language fit only for a Dionysiac procession (Harpocr.). A specimen will be found in Aristoph. *Ranae,* 416 sqq.

Translate: *ribaldry which has been so profusely indulged in.* — P. 5, l. 1. **ἂν βουλομένοις ᾖ**, *if it be the wish of* the assembly; otherwise it is not worth while. On this Dative of Relation, see Madvig, *Gr. S.* § 38. d.; C. 459, N.; Cu. 435; G. 184, N. 6; H. 601, a.

12–16. IN PROSECUTING CTESIPHON, ÆSCHINES HAS LAID THE GRAVEST CHARGES AGAINST MYSELF; BUT, THOUGH HE HAS DONE SO WITH THE UTMOST MALICE, YET HE HAS NOT AFFORDED THE STATE AN OPPORTUNITY TO VISIT ME WITH JUST PUNISHMENT. THAT COULD ONLY HAVE BEEN ACCOMPLISHED BY A FAIR TRIAL IN WHICH I SHOULD MYSELF HAVE BEEN THE DEFENDANT. ÆSCHINES OUGHT TO HAVE BROUGHT ACTIONS AGAINST ME, IN A LEGAL FORM, AT THE VERY TIME OF EACH ALLEGED OFFENCE. IF THESE OFFENCES OF MINE WERE GRAVE ENOUGH TO SUPPLY MATERIALS FOR THE PRESENT CHARGE AGAINST CTESIPHON, *a fortiori* I OUGHT MYSELF TO HAVE BEEN INDICTED FOR COMMITTING THEM.

An immense amount of valuable criticism has been expended on this passage. After carefully weighing the whole of it, I extract the above as the best solution. But none of the editors state distinctly what appears to me the gist of the argument. Æschines, the orator contends, is grossly in the wrong, *for two reasons,* (1) because his accusation is malicious, (2) because it is futile for purposes of justice. His accusation is (1) malicious, for he puts me into a position where I cannot come forward to plead in my own defence. His accusation is (2) futile, for he never indicted me when I was committing the offences, and the time for legal punishment has long gone by. Terrible as the crimes may be with which I am charged, the state can do nothing now to inflict an adequate penalty. Most of the editors seem to consider the whole passage, 12, 13, as obscure and involved in point of language. But there is no just reason for so pronouncing. Only to understand the construction of the sentences the reader must bear in mind their exact sequence and mutual relation. τὰ μὲν κατηγορημένα stands in antithesis to the concessive sentence introduced by τοῦ δὲ παρόντος. The protasis of this concessive sentence is headed by ἐχθροῦ μέν, the apodosis of it by τῶν μέντοι κατηγοριῶν. To the protasis refer the words which follow from οὐ γάρ to Ἀθηναῖοι: to the apodosis refer the words from ἀλλ' ἐφ' οἷς to γραφόμενον. He is wrong, says the orator, both ways, for he ought not to have done what he has done, *but* he ought to have done what he has left undone. ἀλλά is clearly the natural particle to link these two clauses together.

12. *Now the accusations he has brought are many and serious; and for some of them the laws assign heavy — ay, the extreme — penalties; but although the very principle of the present trial implies at once an enemy's malice and violence and abuse and insult and everything else of the kind, yet for the charges and accusations which have been laid (if indeed they were true) it is not in the power of the state to inflict an adequate penalty, or in fact anything like it.* — P. 5, l. 5. **προαίρεσις** = the deliberate moral choice by which the prosecutor selected his process of action; its intense maliciousness appeared (1) in the virulence of the accusations against Demosthenes; (2) in the indirect mode of attack which was designed to exclude Demosthenes himself from a personal hearing. — 6. **αὐτῇ.** This reading appears the best, although *αὕτη* is found in Σ and some other MSS. — 8. **μέντοι.** The particle *μέντοι* is always adversative, and in antithesis to *μέν* is far stronger than *δέ*, indeed almost as strong as ἀλλά. — 13. *For he must not deprive one of access to the commons and a fair hearing; still less must he do so in a style of malice and envy: no, indeed, gentlemen of Athens, it is neither proper nor constitutional nor just: but* [here supply *ἔδει* from the *δεῖ* preceding] *his duty was in whatever cases he saw me injuring the state (especially supposing them to be so monstrous as he was just now ranting about and reciting), to take advantage of the legal penalties at the very moment when the said offences were committed; if he saw me commit what deserved impeachment, impeaching me, and bringing me in that manner to trial before your court; or if he saw me proposing unconstitutional measures, indicting me for unconstitutional conduct. For it is not possible, I presume, that he should prosecute Ctesiphon now on my account, and yet have foreborne to prosecute myself, had he thought he could secure a conviction.* — 11. **προσελθεῖν τῷ δήμῳ** simply means, in connection with the context, to be placed in the official position of defendant. In λόγου *τυχεῖν*, *to get a speaking*, we have a suggestive contrast with our own idiom, *to get a hearing*. At the beginning of Æschin. *de F. L.* we find this phrase immediately followed by *ἀπολογίας τυχών*. — 12. **τάξει.** More strictly, *position*, but a word of such various uses must be rendered according to its collocation. *ἐν ἐχθροῦ τάξει* (p. 481, l. 21), in the *quality* of. *τὴν τοῦ συμβούλου τάξιν* (p. 292, l. 14), the *province* or *part* of. In *ἐτραγῴδει* there is not only a general allusion to the pompous declamation of the theatre, but a tacit reference to the former profession of Æschines as an actor. The more frequent taunt is *τριταγωνιστεῖν*, as in this speech, p. 314, l. 12, etc., *διεξιέναι*, in the sense of *reciting*, is an apt combination.

Æschin. p. 75, l. 35. — 17. **παρ' αὐτά.** The time of accusation being exactly parallel to the time when the offences were committed. *παρὰ καιρούς* (p. 470, l. 12), *παρὰ χορηγίαν* (p. 514, l. 8), etc. — 18. **εἰσαγγελία** may be rendered by our word *impeachment*, but strictly means a public prosecution for some offence which legislation has omitted to notice, and for which, in consequence, no penalty is specified. — 20. **παράνομα** consisted in proposing a *ψήφισμα*, which would violate either the letter or spirit of any existing law. We have no exact equivalent for it, but *unconstitutional* is nearer the meaning than *illegal.* A fuller explanation of these and other judicial words may be found in Smith's Dictionary of Antiquities. — **14.** 23. **καὶ μήν**, *and really:* often wrongly translated moreover. *μήν* is the strongest asseverative particle, like the colloquial use of *I declare* in English. In the formula *ἦ μήν* this sense is particularly prominent; also in Greek Tragedy, where a new character enters and is introduced by the chorus. In questions and negatives *μήν* is hardly translatable, but adds the strongest possible emphasis to the word which immediately precedes it. — 25. **εἰσὶ νόμοι.** Here we must observe, as Dissen suggests, the contrast between the *ἀγῶνες ἀτίμητοι* and the *ἀγῶνες τιμητοί*: in the former case the laws themselves directed the nature and degree of punishment to be inflicted on the guilty; in the latter it was at the discretion of the jury to assign whatever penalty they thought proper; *τιμωρίαι*, *penalties* appointed by law, refer to the *ἀτίμητοι; ἀγῶνες καὶ κρίσεις* refer to the *τιμητοί*; and the phrase *τἀπιτίμια*, *punishments,* applies equally to a verdict affecting purse or person under either form of trial. — P. 6, l. 2. **τοῖς πρὸς ἐμέ** = *the provisions applicable to my case.* — **ὡμολογεῖτο ἄν.** *Would have been consistent with.* A similar use of the active voice, *ὁμολογεῖν*, is found in Antiph. *de Chor.* p. 145. *τοῖς λόγοις τοὺς μάρτυρας ὁμολογοῦντας καὶ τοῖς μάρτυσιν τὰ ἔργα.* — **15.** 4. **τοὺς παρ' αὐτὰ...ἐλέγχους.** *The inquiries at the time of the deeds themselves.* *ἐλέγχους* is to be taken in emphatic contrast with *αἰτίας καὶ σκώμματα καὶ λοιδορίας;* also *παρ' αὐτὰ τὰ πράγματα* with *τοσούτους ὕστερον χρόνοις.* *Avoiding the inquiries proper at the time,* he has brought together heaps of *accusations and scoffings and revilings* long *afterwards.* — 7. **ὑποκρίνεται.** *He is playing his part.* Vid. sup. 13, **ἐτραγῴδει.** Not very far from our own idea of *hypocrisy:* his conduct is underhand and dishonest; he plays the part of Ctesiphon's accuser, being really mine. — **κρίνει τουτονί.** *Brings my client here to trial.* *κρίνω* in its most technical sense, of the prosecutor entailin κρίσις on the defendant. So *c. Mid.* p. 581, l. 13, etc. — 9. **προΐστα-ται.** *He makes the prominent feature of the trial.* A rare use of προϊ-στάναι. To *put in front* is, of course, the literal meaning, but the classical writers generally use it of *putting in front,* as a screen, or a champion. — **ἀπηντηκώς.** *Having never faced me on this ground.* ἀπαντᾶν of encountering an adversary point blank, and ἐπὶ of the ground selected for the combat. Dissen cites the c. *Mid.* p. 563, ἐπὶ ταῦτα δὲ ἀπήντων ὡς ἥλωκεν ἤδη. — 10. **τὴν ἑτέρου...φαίνεται.** *He is clearly seen to be seeking to take away the civil rights of another.* ἐπιτιμία is the opposite of ἀτιμία in its civil sense. See Dict. of Antiq. If Ctesiphon were cast in the suit he would have a fine inflicted upon him, and until this fine were paid he would be a public debtor and consequently ἄτιμος. Æschines had laid the damages at the enormous sum of fifty talents. — **16.** 15. **ἐξετασμόν.** According to some grammarians this is not a pure Attic form. Certainly ἐξέτασις is the usual word, and ἐξετασμός does not occur elsewhere except in Plutarch. But Dissen marks the true distinction : ἐξετασμὸν ποιεῖσθαι, *disceptare,* de litigantibus, at ποιεῖν ἐξέτασιν judicum est, cf. 226 : τῶν πεπολιτευμένων εξέτασιν ποιήσειν ὑμᾶς. — 17. **ἑτέρῳ ὅτῳ.** Either by attraction for ἕτερον ὅτῳ, or else an indirect question : *to seek what other person we can do a mischief to.* The former is the usual interpretation.

17. I DENOUNCE THE WHOLE ACCUSATION AS FALSE ; BUT I SHALL ALSO EXPOSE ITS FALSEHOOD IN DETAIL. I MUST THEREFORE REMIND YOU OF THE HISTORICAL CIRCUMSTANCES.

20. **ἐπ' ἀληθείας οὐδεμιᾶς.** *Nor with any truth whatever.* The sense of ἐπί is (1) superposition : and hence (2) intimate connection. When the accusative follows ἐπί, *moving towards* that connection is implied ; when the dative, *resting in* that connection ; when the genitive, *being in* that connection *and yet separate.* This complex notion is due to the fact, that separation is one essential force belonging to the genitive case. So a ship is ἐπ' ἀγκύρας, connected with an anchor but separated from it by the cable : a rider is ἐφ' ἵππου, for there is no material union between the man and his horse. Yet in this last, and in many other instances, the dative might be put for the genitive with only a slight distinction of meaning. The distinction may be stated thus. When two objects are heterogeneous, capable of being joined together but incapable of coalescing, then, if the writer wishes to *impress* on the reader the idea of their *close union,* he puts the dative

after ἐπί, if he does not wish to impress that idea but yet to state their connection, he puts the genitive. ἐπὶ γῆς is *on* (and *above*) the surface of the earth; it is opposed to ὑπὸ γῆς (Soph. *O. T.* 416): but ἐπὶ τῇ χώρᾳ is *in* the country. With nouns representing the abstract (e. g. ἀληθείας) the genitive is peculiarly appropriate. — 21. **καθ' ἕν.** To be taken adverbially. There is a valuable note on this use of κατά in Buttmann's *Midias* (Index, s. v.). He points out that such expressions are generally adverbial, but observes that κατά, in many cases, coalesces entirely with the accusative which follows it, so as to be treated as a noun for purposes of construction. ὁ μὲν ἀθρόους πείθει ὁ δὲ καθ' ἕνα, Plat. *Alc.* I. 22; ἀντέσχομεν πρός τε σύμπαντας καὶ καθ' ἑκάστους, Thucyd. II. 64. Cf. Herod. II. 93. — 24. **Φιλοκράτους.** A politician of some prominence at the close of the Olynthian war. His name recurs again and again in the rival speeches of the orator and Æschines, each of them disclaiming complicity with him and imputing such complicity to the other; ὁ σὸς, Αἰσχίνη, κοινωνὸς, οὐχ ὁ ἐμός (*inf.* 21). Philocrates, in the year 348, proposed that Philip should be allowed to send envoys to Athens, and to treat of peace. For this a charge of παράνομα was laid against him, and, as he was too ill to speak for himself, Demosthenes addressed the assembly in his defence. In the year 347 Philocrates proposed to send envoys to Philip for a peace negotiation, and named Demosthenes as one of them. See *Introduction*, II. In 346, on the famous 18th of Elaphebolion (*inf.* **κοινοῦ συνεδρίου**, 22), it was Philocrates who advocated peace and alliance with Macedon. This policy proving a disgrace to Athens, Hyperides impeached him shortly after, and he fled into exile sooner than face a trial. They condemned him in his absence. It is clear that he was bribed by Philip and made an ostentatious display of the money so acquired. — 26. **κατ' ἐκείνους.** *Throughout the course of that period:* κατά, always of motion along (or guidance by) a definite line, moral or material. The accusative which follows κατά describes the whole of that line's direction, the genitive denotes its starting or finishing point. When this genitive marks the finishing point, hostility is usually implied. — 27. **πρός.** *With an eye to the subsisting crisis:* πρός, as distinguished from κατά, is suggestive of a mark or goal, rather than of the line which leads to it. πρός followed by the accusative = acting with that goal or mark in view; by the dative = having reached the goal and remaining there; by the genitive (case of separation, as before) = being at the goal and taking action from it.

18–24. LET ME RECALL TO YOUR MINDS THE HISTORY OF THE YEARS 357 TO 346; THE DISSENSIONS OF GREECE, AND PHILIP'S ADVANTAGES THEREIN. PEACE WAS CONCLUDED THROUGH THE TREACHERY OF ÆSCHINES AND HIS PARTY. I, AT LEAST, HAD NOTHING TO DO WITH IT. IF IT WAS *my* DOING, WHY DID THEY NOT DENOUNCE ME AT THE TIME?

18. P. 7, l. 1. **τοῦ Φωκικοῦ.** *Introduction*, II. — **συστάντος.** *Having been set in operation.* *συνίσταναι* is to *organize* either for good or evil. The orator wishes to impute external agency, originating in Macedon or at Athens, as the prime cause of the Phocian outbreak. — 2. **ἐπολιτευόμην.** *Had not yet engaged in politics:* lit. *was not yet, at that time, administering the government.* The definite *οὔπω* gives to the imperfect the force of a pluperfect. This use of *πολιτεύεσθαι* is suggestive: the ideal *citizen* was to take an active part in *administration.* — **τότε.** His earliest public speeches were *adv. Leptin.* and *c. Androt.* spoken in 355, that is, two years *after* the beginning of the Phocian war. His earliest political speech, *de Symmoriis*, was in 354. — 4. **σωθῆναι.** *To hold their own.* We could not wish them victory, their cause being a wrong one, but only a safe issue under compromise. — **οὐ δίκαια.** *Anything but right:* the common figure meiosis; so immediately below, *οὐκ ἀλόγως*, *οὐ μετρίως*, and *passim.* — **ποιοῦντας.** i. e. in the whole of their policy. Dindorf refers this remark to their plunder of the Delphic treasury in particular. But if the orator had meant to imply such a special instance of wrong-doing, he would surely have written *ποιήσαντας.* — 5. **ἐφησθῆναι.** Like *ἐπιχαίρειν*, always of *malicious* joy. This tone of Athenian feeling towards Thebes is illustrated throughout the *adv. Leptin.* Observe the force of *ἂν* = *you would have been delighted at.* On the participial construction in Greek where other languages would employ a substantival sentence cf. C. 677; Cu. 592; H. 800; Madv. *Gk. S.* 174 b. — 7. **Λεύκτροις.** The Sacred or Phocian war commenced fourteen years after the date of this battle, and five years after the date of Mantinea. *ἐκέχρηντο* refers to the period between Leuctra and Mantinea, during which the Thebans retained their supremacy in Greece, and made their four consecutive invasions of the Peloponnesus. *οἷς* dative by attraction. *ἐν* is the regular preposition to denote the place of a battle. — 8. **διειστήκει.** *Was eternally divided.* They *had become completely* divided, and hence were perpetually in that state. — 9. **οἱ μισοῦντες.** These, as Pausanias informs us (4. 28), were the Mes-

senians with the Argives and Arcadians, who all looked to Athens for aid and alliance. — 10. **οἱ πρότερον.** At the close of the Peloponnesian war the Lacedæmonians established a council of oligarchs in every Greek city where the step was practicable, the said council (δεκαρχία) consisting of ten members (ἁρμοσταί) chosen from among such of the inhabitants as favored the supremacy of Lacedæmon. Their tyranny in the several states appears to have been unlimited. Xen. *Hellenic.* III., 5. 13. ; Isocr. *Panath.*, p. 239. They were all put down immediately after the Lacedæmonian defeat at Leuctra. — 12. **ἄκριτος.** *Promiscuous*, i. e. involving infinite complications and combinations. The various meanings of ἄκριτος all trace back to the primary derivation, *that which cannot be separately distinguished.* Whiston refers, by way of illustration, to the Homeric usage of this word in μῦθοι ἄκριτοι, *endless words*, and ἄχεα ἄκριτα, *interminable sorrows.* — **19.** 14. **οὐ...ἀφανῆ.** *Anything but hard to perceive.* Another instance of meiosis. — **προδόταις.** The alleged traitors in each state are specified by name in 295. Some of them, as Bremi observes, were probably conciliated by Philip's courtesy, and their own antagonism to the democracy; not by pecuniary bribes. — 14 - 16. **τοῖς παρ' ἑκάστοις...ἐτάραττεν.** *By lavishing money on the traitors in the several states, he was embroiling them all and stirring them up against each other.* The imperfects suggest the sustained and gradual progress of Philip's intrigues. For αὐτούς some MSS. read ἀλλήλους, probably a correction. The reflexive pronoun, in all the best authors, is occasionally used as a synonyme of the reciprocal. ἑκάστοις and πάντας are in emphatic antithesis. — 16. **ἐν οἷς ἡμάρτανον.** *By the mistakes and misjudgments of others he was making his own preparations, and fostering his growth to the ruin of all.* ἐν of cause or means, the ground on which he took his stand, and the depot from which he drew his materials. ἄλλοι, those who were not treacherous but merely ill-advised, distinct from προδόταις. **κατά,** of hostility, is like our colloquial phrase to come *down upon.* See 17, note **κατ' ἐκείνους,** end. — 18. **τῷ μήκει τοῦ πολέμου.** The war lasted nine years. — 19. **νῦν δ' ἀτυχεῖς.** An obvious allusion to the destruction of Thebes by Alexander, five years before this speech was delivered. — 20. **καταφεύγειν.** The Theban alliance with Athens did not really take place till Philip seized Elatea, nearly nineteen years after the time the orator refers to. ὡς = *as*, or *since.* **φανεροὶ.. ἀναγκασθησόμενοι** personal for impersonal construction = *it was manifest to all that they would soon be compelled.*

C. 573, c; Cu. 571; G. 280; H. 771. — 23. **ἐπηγγείλατο.** *Made proffers of.* ἐπαγγέλλεσθαι denotes publicity with a view to some definite effect or cause. Hence it includes the meanings "to command," "to denounce," "to promise," "to make a profession." — 20. 23. **τί οὖν.** *What then co-operated with him to catch you in a state of almost wilful deception?* ὀλίγου δεῖν qualifies ἑκόντας only: the force of the imperfect participle (ἐξαπατωμένους) reminds them that their state of deception had been chronic. As regards the construction of ὀλίγου δεῖν, the ὀλίγου is the natural genitive following a verb of privation, and δεῖν is a substantival infinitive used adverbially in the accusative case (like ἀρχήν, τέλος, προῖκα, κ. τ. λ.): this accusative is closely akin to the accusative of Relation. C. 665; H. 575, a. — 25. **ἡ τῶν ἄλλων.** The article agrees with a feminine nominative implied in εἴτε...εἰπεῖν. *The cowardice, ought I to call it, or the ignorance.* So ἡ ὑμετέρα, εἴτε χρὴ φιλανθρωπίαν λέγειν, εἴθ' ὅτι δήποτε, c. *Aristoc.* p. 671 (fin.). — 27. **πόλεμον** refers to the whole period between the capture of Amphipolis by Philip in the year 358 and the peace which was concluded in 346. The expenses of the war are estimated by Æschines at 1500 talents (*de F. L.*, p. 37). — P. 8, l. 2. **σώμασιν.** *Troops:* soldiers regarded as so many "head." Our own use of "person" is somewhat analogous. Whiston aptly cites τὰ ἐλεύθερα σώματα ἀφῆκε Λύσανδρος. Xen. *Hell.* II., 1, 20. — 5. **ὑπηκούσατε.** *Lent an ear:* "acquiescence" is meant, not "subjection." συγχωρηθεῖσα, afterwards, implies a concession involving sacrifices. — 8. **ἐν αὐτῇ.** From the year 346 to 338. See *Introduction*, II. — **πραγμάτων.** *Troubles:* the constant Attic euphemism, especially when speaking of litigation. — 10. **ὑπὲρ τῆς ἀληθείας,** *for the sake of the truth,* not because they concern me at all, as he proceeds to argue. **ἀκριβολογοῦμαι καὶ διεξέρχομαι** = *I am stating accurately and rehearsing at length.* — 21. 11. **τὰ μάλιστα.** *Ever so much:* another adverbial accusative: = granting the condition to be fulfilled at its maximum. The addition of τὰ μάλιστα invariably converts a conditional sentence into a concessive. — 13. **δήπου.** *I presume,* as που is *I think.* δή always signifies in truth, and its compounds retain that essential meaning whether seriously or ironically. So δῆθεν (always ironical), forsooth, ὅτε δή, when actually, i. e. the moment when, ἐπειδή, since in fact, etc. — 14. **'Αριστόδημος.** A famous tragic actor highly esteemed by Philip, and intrusted by the state with a sort of roving commission to inquire Philip's probable policy, when visiting Macedonia on a professional tour. Æschin. *de F. L.*, p. 49. Dem. *de F. L.*, pp. 344, 371, 442. Cf. Cic. *de Repub.* IV., 11. — **ὁ δ' ἐκδεξάμενος καὶ γράψας,** *the person who seconded him and drew up the resolution.* μετὰ τούτου. With Æschines, cf. οὗτος above, 20. — 16. **'Αγνούσιος.** Hagnus was the name of the deme to which Philocrates (17, note) belonged. It was originally written with a smooth breathing, as if derived from the plant ἄγνος (ἄγονος), the *agnus castus.* See Vömel, *Prolegom.*, 144; Smith's Dic. of Antiq. and Dic. of Geog. — 17. **οὐχ ὁ ἐμός.** Up to the close of 347 the orator seems to have been at least on good terms with Philocrates, though their policy was not at any time identical. Philocrates was always proposing and advocating peace negotiations in Philip's interest. Demosthenes, whenever he assented to these negotiations, did so under a sense of stern political necessity; for instance, when it became imperative to rescue the prisoners on the capture of Olynthus. After the beginning of 346 the policy of Philocrates was yet more decidedly opposite to that of the orator. The statement of Æschines (*de F. L.*, p. 30, *c. Ctes.*, p. 64) that the two were acting in concert is totally inconsistent with historical facts on record. — 19. **Εὔβουλος.** Of the deme Anaphlystus, the orator and demagogue who supported Midias against Demosthenes. Not to be confounded with the comic poet, whose deme was the Cettian. — —**Κηφισοφῶν.** Named in the psephisma 29 as one of the ambassadors sent to Philip. "Cephisophon supported Æschines in the accusation against Ctesiphon." WHISTON. — **ἐγὼ δ' οὐδὲν οὐδαμοῦ.** It has been the fashion to stigmatize this statement as a deliberate falsehood on the orator's part; but, I think, most unjustly. He is referring *only to the peace of the year* 346; at least, his language commits him to nothing further; and in all the discussions of that period we cannot find, from historical records, that the orator ever declared himself in favor of *the peace proposed by Philocrates.* He expressly denies having done so (*de F. L.*, pp. 345, 346). The only evidence that he did is the assertion of Æschines (*c. Ctesiph.*, p. 64) that Demosthenes delivered an oration in support of Philocrates on the day of the second assembly. Little credit need be attached to this in any case; but Æschines himself (*de F. L.*, p. 36) quotes a ψήφισμα to prove that, on that second day of the assembly, *no speaking was allowed* and nothing transacted but voting. See Grote. — 22. 20, 21. **τούτων...δεικνυμένων;** *Although these things are so, and shown to be so by the truth itself.* ἐπί = on the basis of. — 22. **ἄρα.** *As it seems:* the lightest of inferential particles implying a sequence and connection, but only a slight one, whether temporal or logical. It frequently, as here, suggests irony = *forsooth.* — 23. **αἴτιος.** *The guilty cause.* There are two heads of the accusation: (1) making peace, (2) making peace for Athens independently. *καί* = *also.* On the nominative case see Madv. *Gr. S.* 161; C. 667; Cu. 570; G. 136, N. 2; H. 775. — 24. **κοίνου συνεδρίου.** A *general synod* met at Athens, formed of representatives from each of the confederate states. The orator touches here on the much-vexed question, reproduced again and again in the speeches of himself and Æschines, as to the policy they advocated respectively, on the 18th and 19th of Elaphebolion (approximately the end of March), in the year 346. Immediately after the fall of Olynthus, in the spring of 347, Athens had sent envoys to all the eligible Grecian states, urging them to join in their own negotiations with Philip, and to take the result, whether peace or war. In the spring of 346 the general synod were sitting to receive the report of these envoys. What actually passed at the sitting has not been put on record, but we can deduce from the conflicting orations: (1) that some of the envoys had returned, but many were still absent; (2) that the synod passed a resolution recommending that two *ἐκκλησίαι* be convened *immediately on the return of all the envoys,* and that the subject of peace be then and there debated. This recommendation of the confederate Synod was accepted, but only in part. The two assemblies (already mentioned) were held on the 18th and 19th of Elaphebolion, and the question of peace was fully discussed. *But this was done without waiting for the return of the absent envoys.* — 25. **εἶτ' ὦ—τί.** *Then you—by what name could one rightly call you;* that is, what name can I find that is bad enough for you. — 26. **ἔστιν,** *when and where was it that* YOU, *being present and seeing me robbing the state of so important a negotiation and alliance as you were just now rehearsing, expressed indignation or came forward and made known and explained what you now charge me with.* *πρᾶξις καὶ συμμαχία* is on no account to be taken as a hendiadys; the former word generalizes what the latter specifies, and *πρᾶξις* simply means *negotiation.* The emphasis on *σύ* must be carefully preserved. The *παρα-* in *παρέρχεσθαι* is suggestive: in all the ancient assemblies the speakers were required to address the meeting from a raised platform or pulpit; in passing to it from their seat they would move *before* or *alongside of* their audience. — 23. P. 9, l. 3, 4. **εἰ...ἐπεπράκειν ἐγὼ Φιλίππῳ,** *if* I *had sold to* PHILIP *the preventing,* etc., that is, *if I had been bought (bribed) by Philip to prevent*, etc. Observe the emphatic juxtaposition of ἐγώ and Φιλίππῳ. — 5. **λοιπὸν ἦν.** *You had still the opportunity.* This throws an emphasis on the pluperfect ἐπεπράκειν. — 6. **τοίνυν.** *Well then.* The particle is much stronger than ἄρα, and almost as strong as οὖν. Both οὖν and τοίνυν are distinctly transitional, as well as being illative. It resembles *now then* in colloquial English. As regards etymology, οὖν=ἐόν, epic neut. part. of εἰμί, in the acc. abs. (*quæ quum ita sint*). — 8. **εἰκότως.** *And naturally so.* To render the force of this favorite adverb a separate sentence is indispensable. — 9. **τότε.** "Demosthenes intimates that envoys had been sent *previously*, viz., just after the fall of Olynthus, to invite the other Greeks to form a confederacy against Philip. He denies that any such embassy was sent out *while* 'the peace' was negotiating, and in this he seems to speak the truth." Grote, XI., 508 (Eng. ed.). Whiston; cf. 22, note κοινοῦ συνεδρίου. — 10. **ἐξεληλεγμένοι.** *Thoroughly tested*, and proved unwilling to unite with Athens against Philip. ἐξ-, in composition, of intensity. The perf. passive of ἐλέγχω has always the double reduplication. — 24. 14. **αὐτοί.** *Yourselves.* αὐτός and its cases, when used emphatically, are placed in a prominent part of the sentence (e. g. the beginning), or else have καί prefixed as an intensive. The force of ἅμα is better expressed with αὐτοί, *while at the same time you yourselves.* — 15. **Εὐρυβάτου.** On the rather uncertain authority of Ephorus (the historian of Cumæ) we are told that Eurybatus was a citizen of Ephesus, who received money from Crœsus to raise troops for his war with the Persians, and then deserted to the camp of Cyrus. The same name appears to have been borne by one of the Cercopes (fire-diviners). See Lobeck, *Aglaoph.* 2, p. 1306. In either case the Scholiasts are safe in taking the person mentioned as a type of γοής, κλέπτης, πανοῦργος. Cf. Æsch. c. *Ctesiph.*, p. 71. — 17. **τί γὰρ καὶ βουλόμενοι.** *For with what intent after all?* — 18. **τούτῳ τῷ καιρῷ.** I understand the orator to mean, by *this crisis*, the date of those two meetings on the recommendation of the Synod. The mission of the envoys having, by then, been proved a complete failure, Athens might be said to have abandoned her task of soliciting the Grecian states with her embassies. Why, asks the orator, should she have resumed it, and for what end should she have asked the states to co-operate? For peace? Nay, but the other states were enjoying that; Athens alone had need of it. For war? Nay, but all idea or possibility of war was over, and peace was the only question. In this instance, as in the *ἐγὼ δ' οὐδὲν οὐδαμοῦ* (21, note, s. v.), the orator could justify his statement as virtually true, if not literally. — 21. **ἐξ ἀρχῆς.** The *original* peace of the year 346 is distinguished by this epithet from the peace which followed Chæronea. — **οὐδ' αἴτιος.** *Nor in any way responsible.* *οὔτε...οὔτε* are co-ordinate, while *οὐδέ* is subordinate and emphatic. C. 701, c; Cu. 625, Obs.; H. 858, b. — **ἡγεμών.** All that the orator denies is the fact of his taking a prominent part in the peace proposals of Philocrates (*c. Ctesiph.*, p. 62, 63); he does not say that he opposed peace in the abstract, but only that he neither originated nor supported the peace which was actually made. When the public assembly had agreed to accept it, he did his utmost to make the best of a bad bargain, but that by no means committed him to having approved the measure.

25-28. COMPARE MY POLITICAL CONDUCT WITH THAT OF MY ACCUSERS, AT THE TIME WHEN THE CITY HAD DECIDED ON PEACE. WHEN THE OATHS HAD BEEN TAKEN BY US AND OUR ALLIES, I PROPOSED A DECREE TO ACCELERATE THE DEPARTURE OF OUR OWN DELEGATES, WHO WERE TO ADMINISTER THE OATHS TO PHILIP. ÆSCHINES IGNORES *this* DECREE, AND ASSAILS ME ABOUT ANOTHER WHICH WAS MERELY TRIVIAL, REFERRING TO THE RECEPTION OF THE MACEDONIAN DELEGATES AT ATHENS.

25. 24. **ἐποιήσατο** = made *on her own part;* the middle *ποιεῖσθαι* having here a fuller sense than it usually has in connection with *εἰρήνην.* On Philip's part, as the context shows us, peace was not yet concluded. — 25. **σκέψασθε.** In the imperative mood the sole force of the aorist, as contrasted with the present, is to indicate a single and complete act instead of a protracted and continuous process. In the subjunctive, optative, and infinitive moods the aorist sometimes exhibits this same difference from the present; at other times it retains its natural force as a preterite. — P. 10, l. 2. **ἔγραψα βουλεύων.** *Moved a resolution, being a member of the Council.* On the 25th of Elaphebolion the oaths of peace and alliance were administered, to Athens and all her allies, by Antipater, as Philip's delegate. It was now essential for Athens herself to send delegates *with all speed,* and administer the same oath to Philip. Yet for 7 days nothing was done; on the 8th day (Munychion the 3d) a resolution, that delegates should start at once, was proposed by Demosthenes, as he alleges here. Æschines admits it was proposed that day, but does not mention by whom (*de F. L.*, p. 40, l. 28 sq.). According to Demosthenes

(*de F. L.*, p. 390) the delegates on leaving Athens went and stopped at Oreus in Eubœa, and wasted many days there before they started for Macedonia. They were fifty days altogether before they achieved the interview with Philip at Pella. This explains the sequel, οὗτοι... ἠθέλησαν. — 4. **τούς ὅρκους ἀπολαμβάνειν,** to receive the oaths *in return* (ἀπό). — 26. 6. **ἐδύνατο.** *Id quo valebat? Of what avail were this?* (Vömel.) — 8. **τῶν ὅρκων.** The oaths on the Athenian part *and* the oaths on the Macedonian. The genitive dependent on any word of interval (like μεταξύ) specifies the two extreme points between which the interval lies; or one such extreme point, the mention of the other being unnecessary because implied by the context. Cf. the parallel passage *de F. L.*, p. 393, 181, τὸν μεταξὺ χρόνον τοῦ τοὺς ὅρκους ἀπολαβεῖν, where one extremity alone is named, the obtaining Philip's attestation. — 11. **ἐξελύσασθε.** The active voice is more usual in the sense of *breaking up*. ἐξελύσατε is the reading of Σ here. But the middle voice gives the better additional sense, *on your own part and in your own armaments.* — 13. **ἐπραγματεύετο.** *Was making this his chief concern.* The verb is always of laborious and systematic effort, never transitive, though frequently constructed with a cognate accusative. — 14. **τῆς πόλεως.** Possessive genitive depending on ὅσα. The state might be said to *possess* these places in Thrace, as the Thracians were their allies [Bremi]. The optative προλάβοι (*præoccuparet*) is due to the *oratio obliqua*. — 27. 16. **προορώμενος.** An historic present, as is also γράφω which follows. Hence followed by the final clause ἵνα γίγνοιντο, although ἐν οἷς ἂν ᾖ would strictly belong to the present time; but this is an instance of the common Greek idiom which sacrifices grammar for the sake of vivid and graphic delineation in the subordinate clause. — 21. **διέσυρε.** *Was pulling to pieces.* διασύρειν (always metaphorical) denotes sarcastic ridicule. Cf. Æschin. *c. Ctesiph.*, p. 65, l. 37, οὗτος ἐστιν ὁ πρῶτος ἐξευρὼν Σέρριον τεῖχος καὶ Μυρτίσκην καὶ Ἐργίσκην...χώρια ὧν οὐδὲ τὰ ὀνόματα ᾔδειμεν πρότερον, where the perversion of the names is of course intentional. — 22. **Σέρρειον.** Herod. VII., 59, Livy XXXI., 16. Myrtenus is only found in this passage. Ergiske in *De Halon.*, p. 85. They were all, apparently, places on the sea-coast of Thrace, and hence important to Philip as opening the way for his acquisitions in that quarter. The article seems to be prefixed to these names here because Æschines had spoken contemptuously of them. Cf. Phil. III., 16, where Σέρρειον occurs without the article. — 22. **οὕτω** = under these circumstances and no others. 7, end. Madvig., 175 a. — 24. **ἐπικαίρους.** Cf. ὧν τὸ μὲν ἐπικαιρότατον χώριον πρὸς τὰ ἐπὶ Θρᾴκης ἐπιχρῆσθαι. Thucyd., I., 68. — 25. **χρημάτων.** Dissen refers this to the gold mines of Crenides, afterwards called Philippi, from which Philip, when he got possession of them, managed to obtain more than a thousand talents annually. — **πολλῶν μὲν...πολλῶν δέ,** *an abundant supply both of money and of men.* — 26. **ἐκ τούτων,** *from these,* as source and means. — **28.** P. 11, l. 1. **εἰ.** We should rather expect this object-sentence to be introduced by ὅτι, but the use of εἰ, instead, is common after verbs expressing disapprobation. *But that I, being on the Council, thought proper to introduce the embassadors,* sc. into the theatre, as was customary at Athens, *this is a matter he taunts me about.* — 3. **ἐχρῆν.** *Ought to have:* strictly imperfect: it was right to do it, but it was not done. — 4. **μή.** To be taken closely with προσάγειν, γράψαι preceding = *ought I to have moved not to introduce.* This is obvious from the μὴ κατανεῖμαι of the next clause. — 5. **διαλεχθῶσιν.** On the subjunctive after the historic tenses, see Madv., 131 b, and note on 27, **προορώμενος.** C. 653; Cu. 531 b; G. 216, 2; H. 740. — **ἀρχιτέκτονα.** The person who hired the theatre from the state, kept it in order and repair, and took the profits of the admission payments: analogous to our "lessee." He was also called θεατρώνης and θεατροπώλης. — **θέαν κατανεῖμαι,** *to assign them seats,* literally (like λόγον διδόναι, 13), *to allow them a seeing:* θέαν καταλαμβάνειν is the correlative expression. c. *Mid.* 572. — 6. **τοῖν δυοῖν** = the unreserved places, literally, *in the two oboli seats.* The price is put for the locus. Two obols was the payment demanded from everybody except those who received, by privilege, reserved seats (προεδρία). The poorer citizens were often presented, from the Theoric fund, with the money to pay for admission (*Philip.*, 4, p. 141). Some editors understand ἐν of the means, i. e. *by payment of;* but less aptly. — 9. **λέγε,** i. q. ἀναγίγνωσκε. The latter is more strictly correct, but the former equally common. λαβὲ τὸ βίβλιον καὶ λέγε, Plat. *Theætet.*, 143 c. λέγειν suggests the *vocal* element of reading, ἀναγιγνώσκειν suggests the *intellectual.* The latter strictly means to *re*-know, know *up*, or know thoroughly, which can only be by *reading* a *written* document. The orator is here addressing the secretary (γραμματεύς) of the Archons.

29. ΨΗΦΙΣΜΑ. Clearly not a genuine document. And the same may be said of all the documents, of which thirty-four are appealed

to and twenty-seven given at length, in this oration. The question is too voluminous by far for discussion in the present work, but the points of interest will be briefly noticed in their places. For further information, see Böckh (*Comm. de Archontibus Pseudonymis, apud Acta Academiæ Borussicæ,* 1827), Droysen (*Museum Rhenanum,* Vol. II., 1845). An attempted defence of these documents as genuine will be found in Böhneck (*Quæst.,* Vol. I., p. 321 sq.) and Vömel (*Museum Rhenanum,* 1842, p. 535). In a paper on "The Chronology of some of the Events mentioned in Demosthenes on the Crown," read by Professor W. W. Goodwin of Harvard University before the American Philological Association, at its meeting in New Haven, in 1872, the authority of these documents is discussed. The Professor says that, if these documents are taken as authority, it is absolutely impossible to make any consistent chronology of the events which preceded the battle of Chæronea, and it will strike every one who examines the subject that not a single name of an Archon, and not a single date given in the documents, can be shown to be correct. See Transactions of the Am. Phil. Assoc., 1871 and 1872. See, also, a concise *resumé* of the arguments, on both sides, in Professor Champlin's "Appendix on the Documents," in his edition of the "Oration on the Crown." — **Μνησιφίλου.** The real name of the Archon in 347 B. C. was Themistocles. — **ἑκατομβαιῶνος.** The meeting was held on Munychion the 3d, not on Hecatombæon the 30th. For the names of the Attic months, and the manner of numbering the days of the month, see Lid. and Sc. Lex., and Smith's Dic. of Antiqq., Greek Calendar. From the same sources, the student should also acquaint himself with the constitution of the *βουλή*, and the presidency (*πρυτανεία*) of the *ἐκκλησία*. — **δεδόχθαι.** The usual elliptic infinitive in public proclamations, [*ὁ δεῖνα*] *εἶπεν* being understood. The reading *δεδόχθω* is found, but is obviously a mere correction. — **καὶ τῷ δήμῳ.** This is incorrect. Referring to the same decree in the *de F. L.*, 389, the orator says *γράφω ψήφισμα βουλεύων, τὴν βουλὴν ποιήσαντος τοῦ δήμου κυρίαν.* That is, the *δῆμος* had given absolute power to the *βουλὴ* to pass *ψηφίσματα* for the time on their own authority. The *δῆμος*, therefore, had nothing to do with this *ψήφισμα*. Æschines, *de F. L.*, p. 40, calls it distinctly *τὸ βουλῆς ψήφισμα.* — **ἐν τῇ πρώτῃ ἐκκλησίᾳ.** Peace was agreed to on Elaphebolion the 19th, which was the day of the *second* assembly, not the *first*. *τὴν ὑστεραίαν ἐν ᾗ τὴν εἰρήνην ἔδει κυροῦσθαι.* *de F. L.*, p. 345. — **ὑπερβολὴν** never means *delay* in classical Greek. In Σ a correction, ἀναβολήν, has been inserted by a later hand. — **καὶ δοῦναι.** But the oath of Athens and their allies had already been received by Antipater. The envoys were solely commissioned to administer the oath to Philip. *Sup.* 27. — **πρέσβεις.** The ambassadors were *ten* in number, and a list of them will be found in the Argument to the *de F. L.* None of the names in this ψήφισμα appears there excepting that of Æschines.

30. In spite of my decree the envoys threw away their opportunities, being bribed to do so by Philip.

13. **φροντίσαντες** has for its object the contents of the concessive clause ταῦτα...ζητοῦντος, *whereas I had moved this psephisma and was seeking the interest of the state, and not that of Philip, these worthy ambassadors caring little about it.* — P. 12, l. 1. **τρεῖς μῆνας.** They were absent from Athens 26 days of Munychion, all Thargelion, and 13 days of Skirophorion. But this included their journey to Macedon and back, so that ὅλους is rather a stretch of imagination. — 3. **ἡμερῶν.** The rationale of this genitive of time (*within*) may be stated thus. As the genitive plural, dependent on a word of *interval*, specifies the two extreme points between which the interval lies, so the genitive can stand adverbially to represent two extremes with an interval between them. Note **ὅρκων,** 26. Compare C. 433; G. 179; Cu. 426; H. 591. — 6. **ἡμῶν.** Demosthenes himself was one of the embassy, but no doubt he may mean by ἡμῶν that the embassy represented the nation at large. παρόντων is imperfect. — **ἤ.** *Or else.* Madv., 186, r. 1. — 7. **διημαρτήκει.** The pluperfect with ἄν is naturally stronger than the imperfect in the same construction, and the δι- still further intensifies the word = *forever and utterly.* — 8. **ἂν εἶχε.** Philip was holding the places still; if he had lost them again the orator would have said ἂν ἔσχε. Note, 9, **ἂν ἀπελογούμην.**

31–37. Another act of villany followed. Bribed by Philip, they made you the report which led to his seizure of Thermopylæ and destruction of the Phocians. I only allude to this extraneous matter because Æschines has done the like in his accusation. Remember the particulars of that historical crisis.

31. 11. **δωροδόκημα.** *Piece of venality.* The concrete put for the abstract. — 13. **πολεμεῖν καὶ διαφέρεσθαι.** *I am at war and enmity;* active hostility is implied by πολεμεῖν, passive by διαφέρεσθαι. A somewhat different view is taken by Kennedy, who holds this to be an anti-climax, and translates "war and variance." See his note on the passage. — 14. **ἐφεξῆς.** *Deinceps, in immediate succession,* like the links of a chain, which would be said ἔχεσθαι ἀλλήλων. — **32.** 17. **διὰ τούτους οὐχὶ πεισθέντας.** In consequence of *these men not having obeyed at all.* — 18. **παρ' αὐτῶν,** i. e. those envoys who were venal: this third person contrasts well with the first person in ἀπίωμεν, the orator including himself by the latter as he excludes himself by the former. Σ, however, reads ἀπίωσιν. — 20. **ποιήσαιτο.** In historic consecution introduced by the historic present ὠνεῖται. *Sup.*, 27, **προορώμενος.** — 21. **μέλλει.** The present tense is the direct form of quotation instead of the indirect, *when we had reported that he intends* (root μεν = *minds, means*) *and is preparing.* — 23. **ὥσπερ πρότερον,** i. e. in the year 353 (Whiston says, "about May, 352"; Grote, "about midsummer, 352"), when Philip wanted to effect a junction with the Thebans against the Phocians, by forcing his way through Thermopylæ, which the Phocians were then endeavoring to hold. An Athenian force was despatched with unusual expedition, under Nausicles, and placed Thermopylæ beyond the possibility of Philip's attack. The orator is constantly alluding to this. *Phil.*, I., p. 44; *de F. L.*, p. 444, etc. — 24. **ἀλλ' ἅμα.** *But that, at one and the same moment, you might be listening to us, and he be within Pylæ, and you have nothing left you to do.* It is not, I think, correct to understand ἔχειν here of *ability* = *and you be able to do nothing;* the sense would be much the same of course, but the graphic force of μηδὲν ἔχειν would be lost. — **33.** 27. **καί.** Strongly concessive = *even though.* — P. 13, l. 2. **τὰ πράγματα.** *His affairs should slip from his grasp.* A poetical use of ἐκφεύγω· τὸ δὲ ζητούμενον | ἁλωτόν· ἐκφεύγει δὲ τἀμελούμενον, Soph. *O. R.*, 110. — 3. **μισθοῦται.** On the difference between ὥστε with the indicative and the infinitive see Madv. 166 a; C. 671; Cu. 565; H. 770, 771. If the effect introduced by ὥστε can be viewed as future to the present time, or as future to a certain standing-point in the past to which the speaker transfers himself, the infinitive is then the natural mood. And the orator could so have written it here without altering the sense of the passage. — **34.** 6. **ἀξιῶ δέ.** *I require and entreat you.* In contrast with δεῖσθαι, ἀξιοῦν signifies to *ask as a right.* ἠξίουν καὶ παρεκελεύοντο ἐπεξελθεῖν, p. 515; ἠξίου δὲ καὶ πρὸς ἐμὲ αὐτῷ δι' ἐκείνου γίγνεσθαι τὰς διαλύσεις, p. 553. — 10. **ἕτερον.** Here in the sense of ἀλλότριον, *foreign,* i. e. *irrelevant,* a very rare use. ἕτερος ὁ λόγος οὗτος, οὐ πρὸς ἐμέ, p. 240. Cf. the parallel passage in 9, where *τἄλλα* is somewhat similarly put.—**ἅμα,** sc. *τοῖς ἐν τῇ γραφῇ, into the bargain.*—**αἰτίαις,** 57, **αἰτίας καὶ διαβολάς.**—11. **τούτου κεχρημένου** expresses a reason=*inasmuch as he has made use of.*—**35.** 13. **παρά.** An elegant substitute for the more obvious *ὑπό*. *On the part of.* Conversely *ὑπό* is substituted for *παρά*. *πληγὰς ὑπ' αὐτοῦ λαβών*, p. 514 (fin.).—14. **ὡς οὐ δεῖ.** Direct quotation again instead of indirect. Here, besides being more vigorous, it has the advantage of professedly quoting the speech of Æschines *verbatim.*—18. **ἥκει** preserves both its forces in this passage, a virtual perfect and an actual present: *he has been coming.* An instance of the adverbial accusative occurs immediately after in *τοὐναντίον.*—19. **τὰ ῥήματα.** "*For ties of union,*" *quoth he, in his very imposing phraseology,* "*are cemented, not by words but by identity of interests.*"—22. **ἀναλγησίας.** *Brutality* or *stupidity.* *μὴ τλῇς ἄθαπτον ὧδ' ἀναλγήτως βαλεῖν*, Soph., *Aj.* 1333. Insensibility to pain taken as a type of all want of feeling. The epithet is notorious as applied to the Thebans. Cf. *οἱ ἀναίσθητοι Θηβαῖοι*, p. 61, p. 240. *ἀρχαῖον ὄνειδος Βοιωτίαν ὗν*, Pind. *Ol.* VI., 90.—23. **βαρύτητος.** *Oppressiveness.* A rare sense of the word, almost without example. We find *ἀηδίας καὶ βαρύτητας* (Isocr. p. 239), and *ἀηδίᾳ καὶ ἀναισθησίᾳ* (Dem. p. 564), which would rather lead us to expect that *βαρύτης* should mean *vexatiousness.* That the word, however, is of more serious import we gather from *οἱ τότε μὲν βαρεῖς Θηβαῖοι*, 19, and *πόλεμος ὅμορος καὶ βαρύς*, 241. Whiston renders it *overbearing insolence.*—**36.** 25. **ὑποῦσαν.** *Underlying.* They were not at open war, but the state of ill feeling was chronic, 18, note **ἐφησθῆναι.** There are various readings, *οὖσαν* Cod. *ε*, *ὑπάρχουσαν* Aug. Vind., etc. (Vömel).—26. **οὐκ εἰς μακράν** is a meiosis, stronger in meaning than *εὐθύς.* This proleptic use of *εἰς* is noticed in Madv. *Gr. S.* 79 a.—27. **κατασκαφῆναι.** The fortifications were destroyed and the towns broken up into villages. Abæ was the only exception, either because it contained an oracle of Apollo, or because it had not been a party to plundering the Delphic treasury. Pausanias, X., 3. 2. Grote.—P. 14, l. 1. **ἀγαγόντας.** This participle and the next introduce causal sentences, Madv. *Gr. S.*, 176 b.—2. **σκευαγωγεῖν.** *Brought in your effects from the country.* 'Η *ξυγκομιδὴ ἐκ τῶν ἀγρῶν ἐς τὸ ἄστυ*, Thucyd. II., 52. *καὶ παῖδας καὶ γυναῖκας ἐκ τῶν ἀγρῶν κατακομίζειν ἐψηφίζεσθε καὶ τὰ φρούρια ἐπισκευάζειν*, Dem., *de F. L.*, p. 379 (fin.). *διὰ τὴν σὴν ἀνανδρίαν καὶ ἅμα φθόνον ἐσκευαγώγησαν ἐκ τῶν ἀγρῶν οἱ Ἀθηναῖοι*, Æschin. *de F. L.*, p. 46. In such migrations to the shelter of fortified walls, the rural population would naturally bring with them as many of their chattels as possible. *σκεύη* describes everything in the way of furniture excepting fixtures. They also brought their live stock. — 3. **χρυσίον,** which strictly means *gold plate,* is used by Æschines repeatedly of *gold given as a bribe,* pp. 78, 88, etc., where he is speaking of the bribes offered by Persia, *τὸ βασιλικὸν χρυσίον,* p. 75. Possibly the use of his adversary's favorite word is meant by the orator to be a special taunt. — 4. **ἀπέχθειαν.** *Our city got all the ill-will on the part of Thebes and Thessaly, and Philip all the gratitude connected with what had been done.* We should rather have expected *πρὸς* to be followed by a genitive here; as it is written, we must understand that Athens had to take up an attitude of *defence against* them. A similar use of *πρός* will be found in p. 368, *ὑμῖν μὲν τὴν ἔχθραν τὴν πρὸς Θηβαίους μείζω, Φιλίππῳ δὲ τὴν χάριν πεποίηκεν.* — **37. ΨΗΦΙΣΜΑ.** The inscription (**Μνησιφίλου**) and the date of this document (**δεκατῇ ἀπιόντος**) condemn it at once as spurious. The contents, however, are fairly consistent with allusions the orator makes himself, *de F. L.,* 379 (cited 36, **σκευαγωγεῖν**). He there alludes to the *φρούρια* being put in repair; here there is reference to their being garrisoned also. He there dwells on the migration of the inhabitants, here there is mention of the moving of their furniture. Yet Whiston and Newman take the opposite view, and consider the purport of this decree to conflict with the passage in the *de F. L.* — **Μνησιφίλου.** Sup. 29. — **συγκλήτου.** The *special* assembly, as distinct from the regular (*κυρία*), was *convened* by special officers; sometimes by the generals only, sometimes by a joint order of the generals and the Prytanes. If *καί* is rightly excluded by Dindorf, the latter would be intended here; if, with Bremi and Vömel, we retain *καί,* the sense becomes *by order of the generals, Prytanes, and Council.* — **δεκατῇ ἀπιόντος.** *The 30th.* Vid. CALENDAR in Dict. of Antiq. But, as Dissen observes, the month Mæmacterion B. C. 346, would, according to Meton's cycle, contain 29 days only. — **παρευρέσει.** The word is a *ἅπαξ λεγόμενον*: the Greek of the period would substitute *προφάσει*: Herodotus certainly uses *παρευρίσκειν,* as Mr. Newman remarks; but Herodotus uses it in quite a different sense, not *to make a pretext of,* but *to detect in.* *ἐσ οὗ ἀποθάνωσι, ἤ σφι παρευρεθῇ τι ἄδικον,* III., 31. — **κοιταῖον.** Greek of a later age, used twice by Polybius and once by Plutarch. The Greek of the period would substitute *κοιμᾶσθαι.* *ἀπόκοιτος* is classical, Æschin., p. 45, l. 2: but *ἀποκοιτεῖν* (inf.) and ἀφημερεύειν are both ἅπαξ λεγόμενα. The great number of unclassical words in these documents is alone sufficient to condemn them as spurious. — **ἀποτεταγμένοι.** *Detached for the outlying garrisons,* as distinct from those who were τεταγμένοι in the city itself.

38. **ἀδύνατον.** *Insuperable difficulty* = legitimate excuse. Cf. p. 262, l. 23. — **ὁ ἐπὶ τῶν ὅπλων.** *Commanding the heavy infantry* = ἐπὶ τῶν ὁπλιτῶν, (148); (ἐπὶ τῶν ἱππέων (*ib.*)). We might possibly take ὁ ἐπὶ τῶν ὅπλων, as *president of the armory department.* This officer is never mentioned excepting here and in 147; we have no description of his duties, nor can we be certain that such an office existed. It would be, however, a natural arrangement for each of the ten generals to take his special department and be designated in accordance therewith. — **ὁ ἐπὶ τῆς διοικήσεως.** The *general of the administration,* who performed various civil services more or less connected with the army. See under Στρατηγός in Dict. of Antiq. — **Ἐλευσῖνα.** This and the other four are among the φρούρια already alluded to. **ἐπί** = *with,* literally *on* the ground of. Observe the emphatic position of μισθωτός.

39-41. Read Philip's letter of that date. Mark how he defies the power of Athens, and thereby seduces to his cause the Thebans and the Thessalians. Æschines worked with him heart and soul for that ruin of Thebes which he now affects to deplore. He, forsooth, has got his reward in the shape of Theban land: I have mine in the menaces of Alexander, which actually imperilled my life.

39. P. 15. ΕΠΙΣΤΟΛΗ. It is generally agreed that this document is spurious. Vömel alone defends it as genuine. A discussion of its merits is given by Böhneck (*Qu.*, Vol. I., p. 418). — **χαίρειν.** *Greeting.* Cf. δεδόχθαι, 29, note. — **ὑφ' ἑαυτούς.** Whiston pronounces this expression to be "strange and not ordinary Greek." It is, however, perfectly classical. τάδε πάντα πειράσασθαι ὑπὸ σφᾶς ποιεῖσθαι, Thuc., IV., 61. ἑαυτῶν is not unfrequently used of the 1st and 2d persons. — **προσετίθετο.** Dissen strangely considers this as a euphemism for forcible subjection. But ἑκουσίως implies distinctly a *voluntary association,* contrasted with τὰ μὴ ὑπακούοντα...κατεσκάψαμεν. Cf. 195, ἀλλὰ Φιλίππῳ προσέθεντο. — **εἰσαγηοχότας.** Buttmann has a valuable article on this and similar forms (*Lexil.* s. v., ἀνήνοθεν, p. 139). — **κατὰ κράτος.** *By force.* This is inconsistent, as Dissen remarks, with the passage in the *de F. L.*, p. 360, τὸ μηδεμίαν τῶν

πόλεων τῶν ἐν Φωκεῦσιν ἁλῶναι πολιορκίᾳ μηδ' ἐκ προσβολῆς κατὰ κράτος, ἀλλ' ἐκ τοῦ σπείσασθαι πάντας ἄρδην ἀπολέσθαι, μέγιστόν ἐστι σημεῖον τοῦ διὰ τούτους πεισθέντας αὐτοὺς ὡς ὑπὸ Φιλίππου σωθήσονται ταῦτα παθεῖν. Jacobs, however, insinuates that the orator thus perverted the facts to exaggerate the guilt of Æschines. — **τοῖς ὅλοις.** *Absolutely.* So *τοῖς ὅλοις ἡττᾶσθαι ἐνόμιζον,* p. 127 (*fin.*). Yet Newman, indorsed by Whiston, calls the phrase a "striking peculiarity." *τὰ ὅλα,* in the sense of *one's all,* is, on the contrary, extremely common, and the adverbial usage here is derived immediately from it. Whiston renders it, *in short.* — **οὐδὲν μέτριον.** *Anything but what is fair.* A meiosis rather than a euphemism. Dissen, however, maintains the latter. — **ὁμοίως.** *All the same.* A sense nearly approaching that of the contracted *ὁμῶς.* So 110, *ὁμοίως τὸ συνειδὸς ὑπάρχειν μοι.* — **ἀντιπαρεξάγοντες.** Imperfect of desire = *inclined to* take the field, contrasted with the aorist *συνθέμενοι* of what they had *actually* done. They had not gone to war, it is true, but it is equally true that they were thinking about it. — **συμπεριειλημμένων.** *de F. L.*, p. 444, *τὴν μὲν τοίνυν εἰρήνην ταύταις ταῖς ἐλπίσι καὶ ταῖς ἐπαγωγαῖς εὕροντο παρ' ὑμῶν ἄνευ Φωκέων.* The Phocians were not mentioned in the treaty of peace, and thus their exclusion from its benefits was virtual though not special. — **προτερήσετε.** *You will get no advantage save that of being aggressors in wrong.* Whiston again considers the Greek "remarkable and unusual." Certainly *προτερεῖν* (in this sense) is common in Aristotle, and must have been quite accordant with Macedonian usage. And *ἔξω*, meaning *except*, is found in Herod., VII., 29; Thucyd., V., 97, etc., etc. — **40.** 2. **τοὺς συμμάχους.** *τοὺς Θηβαίους καὶ Θετταλούς.* — 3. **ἐγώ** stands well in emphasis at the beginning of this sentence. Cf. *ἐμοὶ μέν* below. The ordinary reading was *ταῦτα ἐγώ.* Dindorf restored *ἐγὼ ταῦτα* from Σ. — 8. **ᾤχετο λαβών.** Lit. went off with, i. e. *carried off along with him* a very frequent combination. *ἅπαντας ὑμᾶς λαβὼν ᾤχετο,* p. 347. *τὴν ἱερὰν...ᾤχετ' ἔχων τριήρη,* he carried off the sacred trireme, Phil., I., 34. — **εἰς τό.** The state of feeling into which he hurried them is introduced by *εἰς*, as if it were a material locus. *By these means he carried them away with him* (*transported them,* as it were,) *into an utter blindness and insensibility to the consequences.* Or *εἰς* may denote the *extent* to which he transported them out of themselves, *he carried them away with him to such an extent that they foresaw none of the consequences.* — 9. **προορᾶν** of the future, contrasted with *αἰσθάνεσθαι* of the present. The force of the aorist ἐᾶσαι is striking. Their blindness was chronic and continuous; their surrender into his hands was single and complete at that moment. — 10. **ὑφ' ἑαυτῷ** is stronger than ὑφ' ἑαυτούς (39) in the ratio of a case of *station* to a case of *motion*. The latter describes the *process* of subjugation, the former the *state* of actual subjection. — **41.** 13. **συναγωνιστής.** The element -αγων- in this and in συνηγωνίσατο (20) suggests the *energy* and *activity* of his support; far stronger than συνεργός. Inf. 61. — 15. **διεξιών.** *Reciting.* An allusion, as before (13, **ἐτραγῴδει**), to his histrionic profession. — **καὶ τούτων...αὐτὸς ὢν αἴτιος,** *when he is himself the author both of these calamities* (sc. of the Thebans) *and those of the Phocians.* — P. 16, l. 1. **δῆλον.** The natural prefix to a sentence of irony. — 3. **κτήματα.** Dissen cites the *de F. L.*, 368, ἀλλ' ἐν τῇ τῶν ἀπολωλότων συμμάχων χώρᾳ κτήματα καὶ γεωργία παμπληθεῖς, Φιλοκράτει μὲν τάλαντον ἔχουσαι πρόσοδον, τούτῳ δ', Αἰσχίνῃ, τριάκοντα μνᾶς. — **ἔχων** = *although you hold.* — 5. **ἐξητούμην.** *Was demanded as a victim.* Alexander had requested the surrender of ten Athenian orators (Arrian says, eight) immediately after the destruction of Thebes. Plutarch, *Vita Demosth.*, 23, *Vita Phocion.*, 17; Diodorus, 17, 15.

42. I RETURN TO THE SUBJECT.

7. **Ἀλλὰ γάρ.** An elliptic construction = ἀλλὰ [μηκέτι ταῦτα εἴπω, ἐγὼ] γάρ. A similar insertion is always implied wherever we find the phrase. *However* gives an adequate translation. — **ἐμπέπτωκα.** 256. εἰς τοιούτους λόγους ἐμπίπτειν ἀναγκάζομαι. The use of the verb in this connection is rare. But we have also ἐμπίπτειν εἰς λοιδορίαν, p. 73, l. 17. — **αὐτίκα.** Hermogenes, citing this passage, adds μάλα ὕστερον and omits μᾶλλον. The word αὐτίκα not unfrequently implies a *future* immediate sequence, νῦν μὲν οὖν ὡς οἰόμεθα τὴν εὐδαίμονα πλάττομεν... αὐτίκα δὲ τὴν ἐναντίαν σκεψόμεθα, Plat., *Rep.*, 420 C. — 9. **ἀποδείξεις.** *Demonstrative proofs*, opposed to εἰκότα and πιθανολογία, Plat., *Theætet.*, 163 A; Aristot., *Eth. N.*, I., 1 (3), παραπλήσιον γὰρ φαίνεται μαθηματικοῦ τε πιθανολογοῦντος ἀποδέχεσθαι καὶ ῥητορικὸν ἀποδείξεις ἀπαιτεῖν.

42–49. OBSERVE THE SEQUEL AFTER THE FALL OF THE PHOCIANS. THEBES AND THESSALY WERE DEVOTED TO PHILIP. THE REST OF GREECE SUSPECTED HIM, BUT KEPT THE PEACE. PHILIP'S MILITARY MOVEMENTS THEN WERE THE STEPPING-STONE TO HIS FINAL CONQUEST. I WARNED THE CITIES OF THIS, BUT IN VAIN. INDOLENT OR VENAL, THEY REFUSED TO RISE. THE RESULT HAS BEEN RUIN TO THEM, RUIN TO THE STATESMEN WHOM PHILIP CORRUPTED, AND

OF WHOM HE NOW HAS EXPRESSED HIS CONTEMPT, THE ENDS FOR WHICH HE HIRED THEM BEING OBTAINED. YOU, ÆSCHINES, ARE TRULY AN EXCEPTION; YOU REMAIN IN SECURITY AND PAY. AND WHY? BECAUSE THE END FOR WHICH PHILIP HIRED YOU WAS THWARTED THROUGHOUT BY MY OWN STEADFAST OPPOSITION.

42. 11. **ὑπό.** Of the agent, contrasting well with διά of his instruments. — 13. **οὐδὲν ἀληθές.** φενακίσας ὑμᾶς, 41; λόγοι τότε ῥηθέντες, κ. τ. λ., 35. — **43.** 15. **κατάπτυστοι.** Dissen refers this to the general detestation felt by the Greeks for the Thessalians. They are spoken of as ἄπιστοι, διπλοῖ, and branded for ἀταξία, ἀκολασία. Cf. Athen., VI., p. 260; Plat., *Crit.*, 53 D. They wished for the total destruction of Phocis (Æschin., *F. L.*, pp. 46, 47). — 16. **Θηβαῖοι.** Their attachment to Philip is accounted for by the orator *de F. L.*, p. 385, πρῶτον μὲν τοίνυν εἰρήνη γέγονεν αὐτοῖς πονοῦσι καὶ ταλαιπωρουμένοις ἤδη τῷ πολέμῳ καὶ ἡττωμένοις, εἶτα νῦν ἐχθρῶν Φωκέων ἄρδην ὄλεθρος καὶ ὅλων τῶν τειχῶν καὶ τῶν πόλεων ἀναίρεσις, κ. τ. λ. — 17. **πάντα.** *All in all.* Whiston cites Thucyd., VIII., 95: Εὔβοια γὰρ αὐτοῖς πάντα ἦν. — 18. **φωνήν.** 10, μηδὲ φωνὴν ἀνάσχησθε, note. — **ἤκουον.** Imperfect of desire = *would not.* The imperfect optative, βούλοιτο, which follows, is due to the historic consecution, and gives to εἰ the same distributive force which ἐάν possesses in a primary consecution. — 19. **ὑφορώμενοι.** Always metaphorical = *suspicantes.* ὑποβλέπω is sometimes literal. *Though viewing with suspicion what had been done, and feeling aggrieved at it.* WHISTON. — 21. **καί,** *also.* This sense is marked by the δέ which follows ἄλλοι. Cf. καὶ παραλείπω δὲ πολλά, c. *Mid.* — 24. **ἐκ πολλοῦ.** *For a long time past:* i. e. his movements had been virtually hostile to their safety in all his Illyrian campaign. Ἐκ indicates the date at which the danger first began, the period *since which* events are happening. — **πολεμούμενοι.** *Beset by war.* He means, of course, unconsciously to themselves. A strong antithesis to ἦγον εἰρήνην. To explain the paradox he gives the fuller details comprised in the next sentence. On the concessive construction of καί with a participle see Madv., *Gk. S.*, 175, e = *even though.* — **44.** 24. **ὅτε.** Of the period, 346 to 340 B. C., we have no records, as Grote remarks, to "form a consecutive history"; we can only gather an outline of facts from the speeches of the orator and Æschines. The term περιιών is very appropriate to Philip's incessant and rapid movements, and the wide area over which he directed operations. His invasion, here named, of the Illyrians appears to have been directly after he had settled his position in Thessaly, and garrisoned the town of Pheræ: i. e. in the year 344 or 343. The invasion, here named, of the Triballi is nowhere else alluded to. It must have been prior to the declaration of war in the year 340, and therefore cannot be the campaign which is mentioned by Justin (IX., 2. 3), the date of which was 339. As to Philip's *gradually subjugating some of the Greeks themselves,* that remark has reference less to the force of his arms than to the intrigues of statesmen in his pay and interest. His actual military operations directed against any Grecian states at this particular crisis were (1) the support of Messene and Argos against Sparta, (2) the support of the oligarchic revolutionists at Elis and in Eubœa, and (3) the occupation of the Thracian Chersonese which menaced the Greek cities of the Bosphorus and Hellespont. This last prospect and his actual possession of Thrace and Thessaly would realize the *δυνάμεις πολλὰς καὶ μεγάλας* here alluded to. — 26. **δυνάμεις.** *Copias. Resources.* The supplies of money and troops which the regions he thus annexed to his empire would contain and place at his disposal. — 27. **τῶν πόλεων.** Always of the independent Grecian states, when no specification is added beyond that of the article. — P. 17, l. 1. **ἐξουσίᾳ.** *The facility offered by the peace,* which enabled them to communicate *personally* with Philip, and accept his overtures of corruption. *ἐπί, in reliance upon, ἐκεῖσε,* to Philip. — 2. **τότε.** *Then,* i. e. throughout all that period and under all those circumstances. This is indicated by the imperfect tenses. — 4. **ἕτερος.** i. q. *ἀλλότριος, sup.* 34, note **ἕτερον.** — 45. 4. **Ἐγὼ μὲν...διεμαρτυρόμην,** *for I, for my part, was continually forewarning and protesting.* — 6. **ὅποι,** i. e. to Peloponnesus, Ambracia, Leucas, Corcyra, the Illyrians, Thessaly, Thrace, Byzantium, Thebes, *inf.,* p. 308, 244. — **ἐνόσουν.** *Were mad.* *κλύω σ᾽ ἐγὼ μεμηνότ᾽ οὐ μικρὰν νόσον,* Æsch., *P.,* v. 974. Others translate *were morally diseased, demoralized.* *Θετταλοὶ νοσοῦσι καὶ στασιάζουσι,* p. 22, l. 7. *προσάγεσθαι ἀεὶ τὸ νοσοῦν τῆς πόλεως,* Æschin., p. 51 (fin.). — 7. **πολιτεύεσθαι.** *Engaged in politics and action.* *πράττειν* is limited in sense to those who are actually *serving:* *πολιτεύεσθαι* includes the idea of *deliberative* statesmanship also. — 9. **πολλῶν.** The article *τῶν* preceding *ἰδιωτῶν* has to be repeated here. *Private* (i. e. *unofficial*) *persons and the commons in general, οὐ μόνον περὶ τῶν ἰδιωτῶν ἀλλὰ καὶ περὶ τῶν ῥητόρων,* Æschin., p. 2, l. 2. *ἄν τε δεινοὶ λάχωσιν ἄν τε ἰδιῶται,* Dem., p. 50, l. 6. — 6. **τῶν μὲν...πράττειν** = *the politicians and those engaged in public affairs* on the one hand. —

8. **τῶν δὲ...πολλῶν** = *the private citizens and the commons on the other.* — **τὰ μὲν...τὰ δέ** = *partly...partly.* C. 518, d; Cu. 369; G. 143; H. 525. — 10. **δελεαζομένων.** *Caught with the bait of present ease and comfort.* Reluctant to forego their luxurious state of nonchalance and exemption from trouble. The force of δελεαζομένοις is fully illustrated by Isocrates, p. 166 (*init.*), ὅμοια πάσχοντας τοῖς δελεαζομένοις τῶν ζώων, καὶ κατ' ἀρχὰς μὲν ἀπολαύοντας ὧν ἂν λάβωσιν, ὀλίγῳ δ' ὕστερον ἐν τοῖς μεγίστοις κακοῖς ὄντας. — 11. **πλὴν οὐκ.** An obvious ellipsis of πανταχόσε precedes. The construction of οὐκ is a pleonasm as in μᾶλλον ἢ οὔ, Thucyd, III., 36. If you say πανταχόσε ἥξει πλὴν ἐφ' ἑαυτούς, you deny of ἐφ' ἑαυτούς, what you affirm of πανταχόσε. Hence the redundant οὐ makes its entrance. See Buttm., *Mid.*, Exc. xi., πανταχόσε πλέουσα πλὴν οὐκ εἰς Ἀθήνας, Dem., p. 1290, l. 4. Translate *anywhere but to.* It is strange that Dobree should have proposed the omission of πλήν, which would certainly destroy the particular point of the sentence. — 14. **ὅταν βούλωνται.** *Arbitrio suo.* Cf. Aristot., *Rhet.*, I., 7, ὅταν γὰρ βούλωνται ὑπάρχει μᾶλλον ἢ τοῦ βεβαίου [χρῆσις]. — **46.** 15. **ῥᾳθυμίας.** *Indifference.* This word applies more expressly to the *feelings*, ῥᾳστώνη to the consequent and consistent *behavior.* — 16. **προεστηκόσι.** *Leaders,* including the idea of protectors and champions. — 18. **πεπρακόσιν αἰσθέσθαι.** In the simple sentence the words would have run ᾔσθοντο ἑαυτοὺς πεπρακότες: this is varied by the sentence beginning with συμβέβηκε, and then the participle has inevitably to fall into concord with αὐτοῖς. αἰσθέσθαι is subject of συμβέβηκε. The influence of τοῖς extends to οἰομένοις: *and to the leading men and those who supposed they were selling everything but themselves, to discover* (see and feel) *that they had sold themselves first.* — **ξένων.** *Plighted friends,* i. e. pledged to reciprocal hospitalities. German *Gastfreund:* ἃ is neuter to agree with ὀνόματα implied in ὠνομάζοντο. — 20. **ἀκούουσιν.** *Audiunt.* They hear the appellation in connection with themselves, i. e. bear the name of. The usage is too common both in Gk. and Lat. to need illustration here. It has only to be observed that ἀκούειν in this construction has the same case before it as after it. C. 575; Cu. 392; H. 540. — **47.** 23. **ὧν.** By attraction for τούτων ἅ: not a partitive genitive. — 25. **οὐδὲν γὰρ ἄν.** An ellipsis of ἄλλως. The construction is very common, Aristot., *Rhet.*, I., 3 contains a good instance, ὅτι δ' ἀδικεῖ οὐδέποτε ἂν ὁμολογήσειεν, οὐδὲ γὰρ ἂν ἔδει δίκης. Translate here: *For else nothing would have been a more blessed creature than a traitor.* The neuter marks contempt. Madv.,

Gk. S., I., b. 3. — 26. **πόθεν;** The favorite ironical question: stronger in the orator's lips than the strongest negative. *Impossible! Ridiculous!* — 27. **ἐγκρατής.** *Has planted himself in full possession of his object*, καταστῇ suggests the security of his position, ἐγκρατής the completeness of his conquest. For πεπρακέναι, *sup.* 46, he now substitutes its synonyme, ἀποδόσθαι. — P. 18, l. 1. **καί** = *also: he is master also of those who gave them over* (sold them) *to him.* This clause is the apodosis, as is shown by the mood of the verbs καταστῇ and ἐστί. The editor of the English edition made the apodosis begin with τὴν δέ. But δέ is connective = *and.* Whiston makes the same mistake. — 2. **τότε δή.** *From that instant.* On the emphasis conveyed by δή, *vid. sup.* note **δήπου,** 21. The ethics, politics, and rhetoric of these sections are alike remarkable, and have been often remarked by commentators. — **48.** 5. **καιρὸς ἀεί.** ἀεὶ γὰρ ἡβᾷ τοῖς γέρουσιν εὖ μάθειν, Æsch., *Ag.*, 590. Though the time of action be gone by irretrievably, the lesson can be pointed at any time with advantage. — 6. **Λασθένης** betrayed Olynthus to Philip, and was afterwards put to death by him *de F. L.*, p. 426, 451; *De Cherson.*, p. 99. So the editor of the English edition. But it seems to be a mistaken inference from the language of Demosthenes. An anecdote related by Plutarch shows that Lasthenes was resident at the court of Philip at a subsequent time. Timolaus occurs again below, p. 324, in the list of traitors. Simus and Eudicus were of the great Aleuad family in Thessaly. For the persons and places here named, see Smith's Dictionaries. — 8. **ἀπώλεσε.** Chæronea was the date of Theban ruin. Thessalian subjection dated from the occupation of Pheræ in 344, 343. The repetition of μέχρι τούτου is emphatic and highly artistic. The rhetoric is as perfect as the political lesson is sound. — **εἶτα.** *So then*, inferential; or, *since then*, temporal. The former seems the more vigorous translation, but the latter is more probable. *Since then the whole land is become full of traitors driven from city to city and insulted, — nay, what misery is there which they do not suffer?* WHISTON. **τί κακὸν οὐχί;** by a simple periphrasis for ἅπαντα κακά. Cf. Æsch., *Ag.*, 543, τί δ' οὐ στένοντες, οὐ λάχοντες, ἤματος μέρος; — 11. **ἡ οἰκουμένη.** According to Reiske, *terra a Græcis habitata.* He cites also p. 85, l. 17. But it may be doubted whether Demosthenes intended so extreme a limitation: certainly Herodotus does so in IV., 110, but that one instance is hardly conclusive. οἰκουμένη is doubtless used in a popular and rhetorical sense. — 12. **τί δ';** An ellipsis of πέπον-

θεν derived from *πασχόντων.* — **'Απίστρατος.** Of this *τύραννος*, and the history of Sicyon at the period, no record is preserved except the present and that on p. 324. — 13. **Περίλαος** attempted to betray Megara to Philip, at some period between the years 344 and 342. The attempt was frustrated by Phocion (Plutarch, *Vita Phoc.*, c. 16). — 14. **ἀπερριμμένοι.** *Outcasts.* *ἀπωστὸς γῆς ἀπορριφθήσομαι*, Soph., *Aj.*, 1019. — **49.** 18. **περιποιεῖ.** *Secures you an affluence of material for bribery:* i. e. preserves an independent constitution, by offering to betray which you may earn your pay from Macedon. — **ἐφ' ὅτῳ δωροδοκήσετε** = *for which you shall receive bribes.* — **τουτωνί.** *My audience,* i. e. the commons of the city, to whom he is actually addressing his present speech in the *ἐκκλησία*: hence the pronoun. The conservative party would naturally include the two elements he mentions, *τοὺς ἀνθισταμένους*, the leading politicians who advocated resistance to Philip, *τοὺς πολλούς*, who supported that course by their votes and numerical influence. — 21. **ἀπολώλειτε.** On the force of the pluperfect with *ἄν sup.* note **ἂν διημαρτήκει**, 30.

50-52. BUT I PAUSE AND CRAVE PARDON FOR MY TEDIUM. MY OPPONENT'S LANGUAGE, AND THE YOUTH OF SOME OF MY HEARERS, MADE MY PROLIXITY INDISPENSABLE. HE SAYS I TAUNTED HIM WITH "BEING ALEXANDER'S FRIEND." I SUPPOSE HE MEANS "BEING ALEXANDER'S HIRELING."

50. 24. **ἑωλοκρασίαν.** *The stale mess*, as Whiston aptly translates it. See his note on the passage. *ἡ κατάχυσις τῶν ζωμῶν τῶν ἑώλων δείπνων ἐπὶ τοὺς κοιμωμένους τῶν συμπινόντων*, Bekk., *Anecd.*, p. 258. *πολλὴν τὴν ἑωλοκρασίαν κατασκεδάσας τῶν φιλοσόφων*, Lucian., *Symp.*, c. 3. In Plutarch we find *ἑωλοκρασία τις ὕβρεως.* The application is obvious here. Æschines has raked up his own stale and offensive pieces of treachery and tries to transfer them to my head. — 26. **νεωτέρους.** Too young to recollect the end and sequel of the Sacred War. The minimum age for a Dikast was thirty. Those of his audience who did not now exceed that age would have been no more than fourteen at the time referred to. —27. **παρηνώχλησθε.** *Somewhat annoyed,* i. e. by the tedium of my repetitions (4, *ἐνοχλεῖ*), when you knew the facts without my telling you. The force of *ἐνοχλεῖν* is modified by the *παρα-*. — P. 19, l. 1. **καὶ ὑμεῖς.** *Even you,* the younger, for whose exclusive benefit I was speaking, but to whom perhaps my opponent's venality is just as notorious as it is to your seniors. Whiston says *you too* (as well as myself)? — **51.** 2. **καίτοι.** *And yet,* notorious a it is, he tries to disguise it under specious names, and therefore I am bound to reiterate my warnings. — 3. **ξενίαν.** *Plighted friendship,* **ξένων,** 46, ὁ τὴν ξενίαν ἐμοὶ προφέρων τὴν Ἀλεξάνδρου, Æschin., p. 63. — **που λέγων** = *somewhere in his speech.* — 8. **θεριστάς.** *Reapers,* as the type of hired laborers in general, ἰδόντες ὅτι θερίζειν ὥρα, τῇ ὑστεραίᾳ ἄγοντες τοὺς θεριστάς. Aristot., *Hist. Anim.*, VI., 30. The word is rare in the classical authors. — **52.** 14. **μισθωτός.** The orator designedly mispronounced this word, says Ulpian, that the audience, vociferously correcting his bad accent, might seem to give the answer he wanted to his question. This is obviously nonsense. Either the passage was only written and never spoken, so that the interrogation is a mere rhetorical artifice (see Long, Ciceron., *Verr.*, II., 4, 3); or else, and far more probably, the orator would take care to be surrounded by a faithful knot of his own supporters who would duly shout "μισθωτός" when appealed to. "We may be sure he knew his audience well." WHISTON.

53. I WILL NOW REPLY TO THE INDICTMENT ITSELF AND JUSTIFY THE BILL OF THE COUNCIL.

19. **προβεβουλευμένων,** sc. γεγραμμένων ἐν τῷ προβουλεύματι. So προεβούλευσεν ἡ βουλὴ ἐξιέναι, p. 567, l. 3. — 21. **μοι.** Dativus ethicus; the common formula of courtesy: *please.*

54. ΓΡΑΦΗ. Clearly spurious. Chærondas was Archon in 337 (vid. Clinton), the very year when Demosthenes was appointed Commissioner for the Walls. But the orator only received this appointment on Skirophorion the 3d (middle of May). Æschin., p. 57, l. 35. According to the present document Æschines indicted him *two months before,* viz., on Elaphebolion the 6th (middle of March) in the same year. ἱσταμένου, see Lexicon, and Calendar in Dict. of Antiq. — **ἀπήνεγκε.** *Brought a charge.* A most improbable wording of the charge as Dindorf rightly argues. But see Schömann (p. 607). A γραφὴ παρανόμων in any case appertained to the jurisdiction of the Thesmothetes, not of the Archon Eponymus. — **Ἀναφλυστίου.** Anaphlystus was a deme of the tribe Antiochis. It was situated on the west coast of Attica, a little to the north of Sunium. It is mentioned by Herodotus, IV., 99. — **στεφάνῳ.** Crowns, as a mark of honor, were originally limited to athletic contests. It was only in the period of Grecian decadence that grants of this description came into frequent usage. We see from this speech, and that of Æschines, that they were presented for even the most trivial public service, such as expedition in equipping a trireme, or effective management of any small department. — P. 20. **Διονυσίοις.** *At the Dionysiac festivals*, a time when Athens would be crowded with company. — **καινοῖς.** In theory, the tragedies performed at the great Dionysia were supposed to be new for the occasion. Practically, however, it seems to have been sufficient that the dresses, decorations, etc., should be new. The plays of Sophocles were often represented more than once. *De F. L.*, p. 418 ; Aul. Gell., *Noct. Att.*, VII., 5. We have the phrase *τραγῳδῶν ἀγωνιζομένων καινῶν* (Æschin., p. 58) and below 55, *τραγῳδῶν τῇ καινῇ*. — **ἀρετῆς.** *Merit* in general, of which *εὐνοίας* and *ἀνδραγαθίας* are mentioned as the particular details. — **55. ψευδῆ.** This states correctly the *first* count of the indictment, viz., that Ctesiphon had proposed to include in the public archives a document false in substance. — **ὑπεύθυνον.** *Waiting for an audit.* This is the *second* count in the charge ; viz., that Demosthenes, on that occasion, was ineligible for receiving a crown, as being a member of two Commissions, neither of which had as yet been audited. All public officers, except the Dikasts, were bound to render an account of their office within 30 days of its termination, the *λογισταί*, and their assessors the *εὔθυνοι*, being the court which held them responsible. *στεφανοῦν* depends on *ἐόντων*. — **τειχοποιός.** See Æschin., pp. 35 - 57. This office was the most important branch of the whole department *ἐπίσταται δημοσίων ἔργων*. It was probably annual in tenure. — **θεωρικῷ.** A special fund reserved for the expenses of public solemnities and entertainments, the money was derived in part as a *λειτουργία* from private citizens, but mainly from the public treasury. Athens was notorious for its sumptuous expenditure on such events as the festivals, sacrifices, embassies to great gymnastic contests, theatricals, etc., etc. From the Theorica, *διανομαί* (largesses) were also occasionally made to the people. The surplus of the fund was originally ordered to be given to other state expenses. But according to the law of Eubulus (Demosth., pp. 1346 - 1348) this became illegal. That law was not repealed until 339 B. C. — **μὴ ἀναγορεύειν.** The construction is here changed as if *κελευόντων* had preceded. WHISTON. — **καινῇ**, *sc. εἰσόδῳ*, *sup. καινοῖς*. — **ἐκκλησίᾳ.** The crown was to be conferred at an actual sitting of the public assembly to increase the formal solemnity of the compliment. — **τίμημα.** *Damages.* An indictment for *παράνομα* was one of the *ἀγῶνες τιμητοί*, *sup.* 14, **ἀγῶνες καὶ κρίσεις.** — **κλητῆρες.** When a summons was being served (*κλῆσις*), witnesses of the citation were required by the law to be present. The prosecutor usually took two (p. 1251, l. 5), and their names were naturally appended at the foot of the bill of indictment. — **Ῥαμνούσιος.** Rhamnus was on the east coast of Attica, six or seven miles to the north of Marathon. Pliny mentions it (IV., 7) as still existing in his time. It was famous for its statue of Nemesis. *Rhamnusia Dea*, Catull., LXVI., 71; Ovid., *Met.*, III., 406, *Trist.*, V., 8, 9.

56-59. SUCH ARE THE POINTS OF THE INDICTMENT. I WILL TAKE THEM IN THE SAME ORDER AS HE DOES. HIS FIRST AND PRINCIPAL OBJECT OF ATTACK IS MY OWN POLITICAL CAREER. ALLOW ME, THEREFORE, TO DWELL UPON THE HISTORY OF THAT PARTICULAR PERIOD. HEREAFTER I SHALL FULLY JUSTIFY CTESIPHON RESPECTING THE OFFENCES SPECIALLY CHARGED.

56. P. 20, l. 2. **αὐτῶν.** *These very points* which he attacks in Ctesiphon's decree. The juxtaposition of *δικαίως* and *ἀπολογήσομαι* has suggested a misconception of *δικαίως* in 6. There, however, *δικαίως* refers to the conduct of the court and not of the orator. — 5. **τάξιν.** Instead of following the order of the prosecutor in his *speech* as he (Æschines) demanded (contra Ctes., 206), the orator, with good reason, follows the order of the *charges* in the indictment. This is not, therefore, as alleged in the note of Holmes, inconsistent with the remonstrance in the first section, but rather in strict accordance with it. — **57.** 7. **πράττοντα.** From this word to *ἀγαθόν* an actual citation of the Psephisma is implied. The *τοῦ* before *γράψαι* substantives *ἐπαινεῖν* likewise. Both genitives depend on *κρίσιν.* — 10. **κρίσιν.** *On the written statement that I* [act as a patriot], *and the praise bestowed for such conduct, your judgment, I think, must be formed from my political proceedings.* A similar use of *ἐν* has been already noticed, 19, *ἐν οἷς ἡμάρτανον.* — 13. **εἴτε καί.** This *καί* between *εἴτε* and the second alternative has a special force noticed by Dissen. It always implies that the speaker himself decidedly prefers the first alternative. So p. 193, *εἴτ' ὀρθῶς ἐγὼ λογίζομαι εἴτε καὶ μή*: Plato., *Theæt.*, 65, *καὶ ἐκ τούτων ἐπισκέψει εἴτε ταὐτὸν εἴτε καὶ ἄλλο ἐπιστήμη καὶ αἴσθησις.* So immediately below in 58. — **58.** 14. **στεφανοῦν,** as Kennedy rightly says, depends on *κελεῦσαι* in the next sentence. We may render the passage: *his directing that they should crown me and proclaim the crown in the theatre, without having written the extra* (*πρός-*) *clause, "as soon as ever he has passed his audit."* *ὁ δὲ ῥήτωρ γέγραφε τὸν ὑπεύθυνον στεφανοῦν μὴ προσθεὶς 'ἐπειδὰν δῷ λόγον καὶ εὐθύνας.'* Æschin., p. 58. — P. 21,

l. 1. **κοινωνεῖν.** *Has to do with.* The *μέν* which follows is answered by the *μέντοι* immediately after *ἔτι*. — 4. **ἐν τούτοις,** *amongst the citizens.* — **εἴτε καὶ μή,** *or it may be not,* implying that he was worthy of it. WHISTON. — 5. **δεικτέον εἶναι.** Madv. *Gk. S.*, 84, b.; C. 682; Cu. 596; G. 281; H. 804. — 7. **ἁπλῶς.** The antithesis of *τεχνικῶς* on p. 222, second hypothesis. *Without artifice.* — **59.** 9. **ἀπαρτᾶν.** *Divorce my speech from the indictment,* i. e. wander into other topics. The verb is rarely used, and certainly its first meaning is to *suspend from*, but also from its etymology it would bear the translation [*bind and*] *drag away.* *οὐδὲ διδόντων τῶν καιρῶν Ἀμφίπολιν δέξασθαι δύναισθ' ἄν, ἀπηρτημένοι καὶ ταῖς παρασκευαῖς καὶ ταῖς γνώμαις.* *Phil.*, I., p. 43. "Being fettered and kept away both by the state of your armament, etc." Lord Brougham, as cited by Whiston, here happily remarks: "The extreme importance to Demosthenes's case of the skilful movement, so to speak, by which he availed himself of Æschines's error and at once entered on the subject of his whole administration, — thus escaping the immediate charge to which he had no answer, and overwhelming his adversary by a triumphant defence on ground of his own choosing, — requires that he should again and again defend this movement, which he here does very carefully." — 12. **γεγραμμένος.** Perfect middle of *γράφεσθαι*. The prosecutor *causes* the defendant's name and offences *to be inscribed* on the charge sheet. Hence the voice, in this usage. *For he who prosecutes in the psephisma the statement that I speak and act for your best interests, and who has impeached this as not true, he it is that has made,* etc. *ψηφίσματος* is limiting genitive with *τὸ λέγειν...με*. — 15. **εἶτα καί.** *In the next place when there were many lines of public life open to my choice.* WHISTON. — 16. **Ἑλληνικάς.** So on p. 263, l. 3, he distinguished between *τὰ κατὰ τὴν πόλιν πολιτεύματα* and *τὰ Ἑλληνικά*, Home policy and Foreign.

60–65. I BEGIN THE HISTORY FROM THE DATE OF MY OWN CAREER. GREECE WAS THEN TEEMING WITH TRAITORS WHO PLAYED INTO PHILIP'S HANDS. FOR THE POLICY PURSUED BY ATHENS I AM RESPONSIBLE. I NOW ASK THE QUESTION, WHICH PARTY WAS IT RIGHT FOR OUR STATE TO JOIN, THE CAUSE OF PHILIP OR THE CAUSE OF GREEK INDEPENDENCE? AND LOOKING AT THE FATAL SEQUEL, WHO CAN DOUBT THAT ATHENS CHOSE CORRECTLY?

60. 19. **πρὸ τοῦ.** *Sup.* 18, and note **τότε,** *ib.* — 20. **προὔλαβε.** He alludes to the capture of Amphipolis in the year 358, of Pydna in

357, and Potidæa in 356. — 21. **ἃ διεκωλύθη.** Philip had several *successes*, not enumerated here, in the period immediately following the orator's entry on public life, e. g. the conquests in Thrace, 27; but the only object in dwelling on this stage of history is to mention all of Philip's *checks and failures*, so far as they could be attributed to the orator's line of policy. — 22. **ἐπέστην.** *Took my place in this sphere*, literally = stepped into this post of duty and continued to stand there. On this pregnant force of ἐπί, see Madvig, *Gk. S.*, 79 a. — 23. **ὑφέξω.** *Render*, in submission to an inquiry. Stronger than διδόναι, 8. — **ὑπειπών.** *Having first premised thus much.* ὑπο- here of the foundation and substratum for his subsequent argument. τοσοῦτον with a force of limitation. — 25. **ὑπῆρξε.** *Possessed to begin with*, the same sense of ὑπο-. — **61.** 26. **φοράν.** *A harvest*, or *crop*, analogous to our use of *yield*. Diodorus copies the expression (XVI., 4), φορά τις προδοτῶν ὑπῆρξε. So also, φορὰ ῥητόρων πονηρῶν, Æschin., p. 87. Cf. 271, and note there. — 27. **θεοῖς ἐχθρῶν.** *God-detested.* The phrase is used almost as if it were a single word (*sup.*, p. 241, l. 12, and p. 611, l. 15), otherwise the abrupt introduction of the dative would be rather inelegant. — P. 22, l. 3. **καὶ πρότερον** = *even before.* — 4. **ἔτι χεῖρον διέθηκε,** *he brought into a still worse state of mind* (disposition). — 6. **διέστησεν.** *Split them up into many factions, the interest of all being one and the same.* διιστάναι, *sup.*, 18, **διειστήκει.** The participial clause is best preserved in its original form for translation, being antithetic but not strongly concessive. — 7. **κωλύειν.** In the position of a genitive case, in apposition to τοῦ συμφέροντος, and explanatory of it. — **62.** 9. **συνισταμένου.** *Gathering.* The passive voice. **συστάντος,** 18. **ἐν οἷς ἡμάρτανον,** 19. — 11. **προσῆκον.** *Proper.* This auxiliary use of ἦν constitutes the strongest form of the imperfect tense, Madvig, 180 d. — **πράττειν καὶ ποιεῖν,** *to achieve and effect.* So πράξει καὶ ποιήσει, p. 327, l. 28. The distinction of the meanings is scarcely perceptible, but ποιεῖν has a sense of *creation*, which πράττειν does not share, πράττειν a sense of *achievement*, which is not common to ποιεῖν. Whiston renders, *what course of conduct and action.* — 13. **πολιτείας.** Partitive, depending on ἐνταῦθα. The present tense and the emphasis on ἐγώ must be carefully preserved in translating. *The man who set himself in that department of the administration am I.* — **63.** 15. **ἀφεῖσαν.** *To have sunk her spirit and dignity, and in the position of Thessalians and Dolopians, to have aided Philip in acquiring the supremacy of the Greeks.* τάξει *sup.*, 13, note s. v. The strong feeling against the Thessalians we have seen already in 43. Dissen remarks that both they and the Dolopians had fought with the Persians against the Greeks. Herod., VII., 132, 185. The Dolopians, a remnant of the Pelasgic stock, were in scattered localities between Epirus and the foot of Pindus. — 20. **κωλύσει.** The strict construction would require the optative, but the future indicative is more vivid, and grammar is sacrificed accordingly. — 21. **περιιδεῖν.** *To allow without interference, to overlook.* This verb admits various constructions, being followed either by a participle, or by an infinitive, or by an adjective with ellipsis of the participle, or by an accusative of the person with ellipsis of the infinitive. — **64.** 21. **ἀλλά.** *Nay but.* There is no transition implied. He only repeats in stronger terms the contents of the previous sentence. — 22. **ἔγωγε.** *I for my part should like to ask the severest critic of what has been done, which sort of party he would best have liked to have our city belong to.* — 24. **συναιτίας.** *Conjointly to blame for*, not *accomplice*, which would be *μεταίτιος*. Cf. Æsch., *Eumen.*, 199. — 25. **ἧς ἄν.** This *ἄν*, and the one which follows immediately, give no sense of distribution to the relative, but qualify the optatives only. *Sup.*, 16. *ἧς* is genitive of property, with *γενέσθαι* understood. — 27. **περιεορακυίας.** The perfect of *ὁράω* and its compounds has no double augment in pure Attic, although the imperfect has. Many editions here erroneously substitute *ω* for the *ο*. Cf. Lexicon. — P. 23, l. 1. **πλεονεξίας.** This taunt is unjust. Arcadia and Messenia sought for protection against the tyrannical power of Lacedæmon, and Philip alone could give them the assistance they required. Their conduct was in no way venal, as the word *πλεονεξία* would imply. — **65.** 3. **ἀπηλλάχασιν.** *Have come off.* In this intransitive force *ἀπαλλάσσειν* always requires to be supported by an adverb. — 7. **ἦν ἄν** is preceded by *ὅμως*, in most editions, and *οὐκ* is inserted before *ἐναντιωθέντων*. The latter alteration is very suggestive of a copyist's taste and discretion. And the manuscript evidence is wholly against the *οὐκ*. The sense of the text as above is excellent. He says, if Philip had done no harm, but only good, there would have rested [in spite of much which had justified the opposition — still] a certain amount of blame upon those who had opposed his policy. The insertion of *ὅμως* will not affect the general sense, but that of *οὐκ* would destroy it. Reiske earnestly defends the *οὐκ*, but no other editor has done so. — 9. **ἀξίωμα.** *Dignity* or *authority* as distinct from actual *power*. *Philip.*, 3, p. 28; Æschin., *F. L.*, 42. — **ἡγεμονίαν.**

Leading position in reference to smaller states, who looked up to them as their actual superiors and chiefs. The Thessalians had several such dependents forming a Hegemony. Müller, *Dor.*, II., p. 65. — **ἐλευθερίαν.** *Pugna ad Chæroneam interiit, ut constat, Græciæ libertas.* (Dissen.) — 10. **πολιτείας.** *Constitutions*, i. e. democratic constitutions, *τύραννοι* being appointed by Philip to supersede the existing *πολιτεῖαι*, in the various cities where the step was possible. **ὅσων** is genitive after *περιέλεσθαι* understood.

66–78. To resume: what was the city to do when it saw the encroachments of Philip? What was I, your political adviser, to do, when I felt so deeply for the honor of Athens, and saw so clearly the character of her aggressor? I pass over his remoter encroachments; but when he came so near to ourselves and broke all faith and treaties, were we then to do nothing? It was he, not we, who broke the peace. I produce our decrees and his letter to prove it. And as to my share in the proceedings, I was not the proposer of either of these decrees; nor can you, Æschines, bring forward a single decree subversive of the peace which has my name to indorse it.

66. 14. **ἀρχὴν καὶ τυραννίδα.** *A dominion and sovereignty.* The words, as used here, are nearly synonymous both with each other and also with *δυναστεία*, *empire*, in 67. Strictly *ἀρχή* is of any official ruler (or body of rulers) as the *head* of affairs; the term applies to any form of government, including even a republic: *τυραννίς* applies to the rule of a single despot only; but *δυναστεία* might also describe a combination of oligarchs. Cf. *τὴν δυναστείαν ἥν τινες τῶν ἐν τῇ βουλῇ ἑαυτοῖς κατασκευάζουσιν.*, p. 1467, l. 16. — 16. **σύμβουλον.** *Your adviser:* the technical description of an orator when acting as a politician. *τὸν περὶ τῶν πρωτείων σύμβουλον*, inf., p. 297 (fin.). So Aristotle (*Rhet.*, I., 1) divides oratory into the three heads, *συμβουλευτικόν* (deliberative), *δικανικόν* (forensic), and *ἐπιδεικτικόν* (declamatory). — 17. **ἐμέ.** *Myself I mean:* emphatic and in apposition to *σύμβουλον*. The difference which he attributes to his own political measures as compared with those of his contemporaries, he rests on these two personal grounds: (1) that he had realized better than others the nature of Athenian ambition; (2) that he had also realized better the career and the aims of Philip. — 18. **συνῄδειν μέν** is antithetic and preliminary to *ἑώρων δέ*, *while on the one hand I knew…*

on the other I saw. Both verbs are followed by the accusative with the participle. — 19. **ἀνέβην.** *Ascended the Bema:* ascended it, he means, for the first time; here the phrase, of course, is merely the technical description of taking a part in public business. We have the more vigorous expression *ἀναπηδᾶν ἐπὶ τὸ βῆμα* in p. 78, l. 29. — 20. **πρωτείων.** *Primacy.* So in the singular; *τὴν τοῦ πρωτείου προαίρεσιν τῇ πόλει διαφυλάττειν,* p. 331, l. 24. *τὸ πρωτεῖον εἶχε,* p. 151, l. 8. — 21. **χρήματα κ. τ. λ.** *Money and men,* so *sup.*, p. 231 (*fin.*). Leland's rendering, *blood and treasure,* is decidedly beyond the mark. — 67. 25. **ὀφθαλμόν.** The date of this is probably 354 B. C. "His ita gestis Philippus iam non contentus submovere bella, ultro etiam quietos lacessit. Quum Methonam urbem oppugnaret, in prætereuntem de muris sagitta iacta dextrum oculum regis effodit." Justin, VII., 6. 13. Methone on the Thermaic gulf is there alluded to, not the Thracian Methone. But see Grote, who dates the event at a somewhat later period than Justin. Cf. also Diodor., XVI., 31 and 34; Polyæn., IV., 15. — 26. **ἐκκεκομμένον.** Constructed frequently thus, with an accusative of respect. Cf. *εἶθ' ἐξεκόπην πρότερον τὸν ὀφθαλμὸν λίθῳ,* Aristoph., *Nub.*, 24. *ἐκκοπεὶς ὁ δειλαῖος ἀμφοτέρους τοὺς ὀφθαλμούς,* Æsch., p. 24, l. 31. The verb in the active voice is connected with *ὀφθαλμόν,* in a well-known passage, p. 744, l. 20, *ἐάν τις ἕνα ἔχοντος ὀφθαλμὸν ἐκκόψῃ ἄμφω ἀντεκκόψαι παρέχειν.* — **κλεῖν.** The Scholiast says this happened in the expedition of Philip against the Illyrians, 344 B. C. Plutarch alludes to the wound (*Mor.* 177 F). The form *κλεῖν* for the more normal *κλεῖδα* is a subject of copious comments in the Lexica. Cf. *Etym. M.*, p. 318, l. 25; Schol. Hom. *Il.*, E., 146. [Dissen and Schäfer.] — **τὴν χεῖρα, τὸ σκέλος.** This, according to the Scholiast, was on his return from the Scythians and Triballi, in 340 B. C. So also Justin, IX., 3 (but speaking only of a wound in the thigh): "In femore vulneratus est Philippus." Plutarch alludes to Philip's lameness. *Quæst. Sympos.*, IX., 4. 1. — 27. **μέρος.** *Sacrificing any and every part that Fortune might like to filch from his body, so that he might live with the relics thereof surrounded by honor and glory.* As to the antecedent *μέρος* being drawn into the relative clause, the construction is very common: *πᾶν δ', τι πάσχων τις πάθος ἄνοιαν ἴσχει νόσον προσρητέον.* Plat., *Tim.*, 86. See Madvig, *G. S.*, 101 a. b, etc.; C. 553; G. 154; H. 809. The emphasis of *πᾶν* is thus increased, as Whiston rightly notices, citing Dissen. The verb *παραιρεῖσθαι* is rather of robbery than mere deprivation. Cf.

πόλεις παρῄρηται οὐδὲν αὐτῷ προσηκούσας, p. 289, l. 5. P. 24, l. 2. τῷ λοιπῷ = all that was left; as in 69, λοιπόν = the only thing remaining. — **68.** 4. **ἀδόξῳ.** Pella was insignificant in the eyes of Greece until it was invested with Philip's renown. Cf. in the *De Halonneso*, p. 78, τὸν ἐκ Πέλλης ὁρμώμενον. — 5. **τοσαύτην...ἐγγενέσθαι,** *that it became the man who was brought up in Pella to have reached such an elevation of mind*, literally, that such an elevation of mind should have been generated in him. — 9. **θεωρήμασι** includes everything under the observation of the eye or mind, — not to be limited to the theatrical *dramas* (as Kennedy), nor to *spectacles* (as Drake). Whiston's paraphrase is far better: *everything that meets your ears and eyes;* but even that is inadequate. We may render perhaps *in every expression and every contemplation.* — 11. **αὐτεπαγγέλτους.** Somewhat redundant in connection with ἐθελοντάς. We can combine the two by paraphrase; *of your own free-will and accord.* Better with Whiston, *by your own offer, and of your own free-will.* αὕτη (δύναμις) πάρεστιν αὐτεπάγγελτος ἄνευ κινδύνων καὶ δαπάνης διδοῦσα ἑαυτήν. Thucyd., I., 33. For ἐθελοντάς cf. Lys., p. 181, l. 36, and p. 182, l. 9. — **παραχωρῆσαι.** *Concedere.* Cf. οὐ γὰρ ἐπ' εὐνοίᾳ γ' ἐμοὶ παρεχώρεις ἐλπίδων καὶ ζήλου καὶ τιμῶν, p. 317, l. 9. παραχωρῶ σοὶ τοῦ βήματος. Æsch., p. 77. — **69.** 16. **ἔγραφον,** *was the mover of your resolutions, and the adviser of your counsels.* WHISTON. — **καὶ ἐγώ.** *I myself.* Another example of the intensive καί. *Sup.*, 3 **πολλὰ μέν.** — 18. **πάντα.** *Dismissing all the rest*, dismissing all of Philip's remoter conquests from our present consideration. Amphipolis, Pydna, and Potidæa ("always enumerated in this order." GROTE) were captured by Philip in three successive years, commencing with 358; the island of Halonnesus probably in the year 345. The inhabitants of the adjoining island, Peparethus, attacked Halonnesus in 342 B. C., and ejected the Macedonian garrison. Philip then attacked and devastated Peparethus. See Winiewski, *Comment.*, p. 128, etc.; and Vömel's dissertation on the *De Halonneso.* — **70.** 20. **Σέρρειον.** Cf. *sup.*, 27. — **Δορίσκον.** Also in Thrace, captured by Philip with other Thracian towns in 345. — 22. **οὐδ'...οἶδα.** *I do not so much as know whether they occurred or not.* In the same sense as πάντα τἄλλα ἀφείς. On εἰ as the usual particle to introduce a simple dependent question, see Madvig, *G. S.*, 199, b. 2. — 23. **ἔχθραν,** i. e. enmity with Philip. — 24. **Εὐβούλου** of Anaphlystus. *Sup.*, 21 (*fin.*). Ruhnken, *Or. Gr.*, p. 65 sq.; Böckh (*Econ. Ath.*), p. 242. According to others his deme was Probalisia, but this correction is not adequately supported. He was the constant advocate of peace-policy, and so far acted in concert with Phocion. A stronger connection afterwards subsisted between Eubulus and Æschines as leaders of the Macedonian party. —**'Αριστοφῶντος** of Azenia probably, Æsch., p. 81, l. 39. Demosthenes calls him *δεινὸς λέγειν*, *adv. Leptin.*, p. 501. There were two other persons of the same name who belonged to this period: Aristophon of Colyttus, *c. Mid.*, p. 584, and Aristophon the Archon Eponymus of the year 330, when this oration was delivered. See Clinton (*Fast. Hell.*, II., p. 147), and Böhnecke (*Quæst.*, I., 659). Eubulus and Aristophon were both dead at this time. WHISTON. — **Διοπείθους.** The commander of the Athenian forces in Thrace, 343 B. C. While Philip was engaged against the Thracians in the north, Diopeithes attacked the sea-coast of Thrace, and captured two of the cities. Philip, unable to crush him by force of arms, tried, but without success, to induce the Athenians to recall him. See the speech *De Chersoneso*. — 25. **ἐμῶν,** i. e. the decrees were *their* proposal, not *mine*. — **ὄντων** = *although they were*. —**71.** 26. **οὐδέ** = *not even*. — 27. **Εὔβοιαν.** Philip's intrigues in Eubœa commenced probably about 349 B. C., when he promoted the hostilities between the Eubœans and the Athenians, but the peace of 346 then suspended his operations. He resumed them in 343 towards the close of the year as we gather from *c. Philipp.*, 2, compared with the *de F. L.* Cf. *De Chers.*, p. 98, l. 23 sq. — P. 25, l. 1. **σφετεριζόμενος.** *Annexing;* more exactly, *appropriating*. — **ἐπιτείχισμα.** *A base of hostile operations*, p. 133, l. 22. *τυραννίδα ἀπαντικρὺ τῆς Ἀττικῆς ἐπετείχισεν ὑμῖν ἐν τῇ Εὐβοίᾳ.* We have the form *ἐπιτειχισμός*, 87. Thuc., I., 142, etc. — 2. **Μεγάροις.** Philip attacked the city (probably in 343 B. C.) at the invitation of Pterilaus, Ptœodorus, and Helixus, pp. 368, 435. Phocion, however, rescued Megara then, and it did not fall into Philip's hands until after Chæronea. Hence the word, *ἐπιχειρῶν*. — 3. **Ὠρεόν.** Oreus, Eretria, and Porthmus were the three cities of Eubœa which afforded the most convenient bases of hostility against the Athenians. Philistides was the leader of the Macedonian party at Oreus, Cleitarchus at Eretria. The date of Philip's success was probably 342 B. C. Cf. pp. 98, 99, 104, and again 112, 115, 125. — 5. **Ἑλλήσποντον.** Philip's fleet had possession of the Hellespont in the year 342–1. He commenced the siege of Perinthus in 340, but, after three months' unsuccessful blockade, he withdrew a part of his forces to make an attack on Byzantium. The combined fleet under Phocion succeeded in protecting the city. Plutarch., *Demosth.*, 17, *Phocion*, 14. — 7. **ἃς μὲν...ἃς δέ.** For τὰς μέν, and τὰς δέ, the regular inflections of the old demonstrative τός, as we find ὅς in Homer, and καὶ ὅς in prose. WHISTON. — 8. **κατάγων.** *Bringing home.* ἐλθεῖν μὲν εἰς γῆν ἔσθ' ὅτῳ μετῇ πάτρας· | φεύγων δ' ἀνὴρ ἥκει τε καὶ κατέρχεται. Aristoph., *Ran.*, 1163, 5. — **ἠδίκει.** The imperfects here describe the acts of Philip as a continuous and protracted course of outrage. — 11. **ἢ μή,** *sc.* φανῆναι. The orator might have written ἢ οὔ (*sc.* ἐχρῆν); but the construction he has chosen is the more vigorous of the two. The difference may be stated thus in paraphrase: ἢ μή = ought he to have abstained from coming forward? and ἢ οὔ = was it not his duty to come forward? cf. C. 686, c. g.; Cu. 615, 617; G. 283, 3, Note; H. 536, 537. — 72. 12. **Μυσῶν λείαν.** The notorious proverb describing *a helpless victim.* The state of Mysia, as exposed to pirates and brigands in the absence of its monarch Telephus, is said by the Scholiast to have given rise to the phrase. Harpocr., *s. v.* Μυσῶν. The proverb is quoted by Aristotle, *Rhet.*, I., 12. Telephus belongs to the mythical period of the Trojan war. Paus., X., 28, etc. Euripides made him the hero of a tragedy as we see from the amusing passage, Arist., *Ach.*, 430, etc. — **καλουμένην** = *so called,* or, *as the phrase is.* οὖσαν is complementary to ὀφθῆναι and denotes state emphatically = *to be seen in the state of the Mysian booty, as the phrase is.* — 13. **ζώντων καὶ ὄντων.** The same combination, p. 935, l. 16 (quoted by Reiske): Τιμοδήμῳ καὶ νῦν ἔτι ζῶντι καὶ ὄντι. A very weak conjecture has been made of ὁρώντων in lieu of ὄντων. — **περιείργασμαι.** P. 154, l. 20, σοὶ δὲ κίνδυνος εἰ μηδὲν τῶν ἄλλων πλέον περιεργάσει, ἀλλὰ τοὐναντίον σοὶ μὲν ἐξ ὧν ἐργάζει καὶ περιεργάζει... The sense of περιεργάζεσθαι is to exceed the proper limits of operation, hence *to over-do it, to over-meddle.* Kennedy uses the latter word in translating the passage cited. Whiston renders, *superfluous has been my labor in speaking on these subjects.* A good example of περιεργάζεσθαι will be found in Herodotus's well-known story about the Samian exiles, III., 46; also in the charge against Socrates, Plat. Apol., 19, c. — 20. **προλέγων.** So again *inf.*, p. 306, l. 1, and Antipho., p. 126, l. 17, προλεγόντων (cautioning) αὐτῷ τῶν ἄλλων ἰατρῶν. — 21. **προΐεσθαι.** *Sup.*, 67. — 73. 22. **καὶ μήν.** *And, as to the peace, I protest* (μήν) *it was he who broke it* (*when he seized those ships*), *it was not the city.* See 139. "At the same time" (340 B. C.) "it appears that he now let loose his cruisers against the

Athenian merchantmen, many of whom he captured and appropriated. These captures, together with the incursions on the Chersonese, served as last additional provocations, working up the minds of the Athenians to a positive declaration of war." GROTE. — 25. **τίς.** *Who is to blame for what.* Here and elsewhere *τίς*, as an interrogative, approximates somewhat to the relative *ὅστις*. Strictly, however, there is always a difference, which we have to ignore in translating, as it can only be conveyed by paraphrase; e. g. here *φανερὸν* = *We shall see the answer to the question, Who,* etc.? Again, p. 962, l. 20, *οὐ γὰρ ὁρῶ καιρὸν ἐν τίνι μᾶλλον ἂν τις βοηθήσειεν αὐτῷ.* "The opportunity which answers the question 'In what crisis, etc.?'" Pind., *Nem.*, VII., 56, *οὐκ ἔχω εἰπεῖν | τίνι τοῦτο Μοῖρα τέλος ἔμπεδον | ὤρεξε.* "I cannot solve the question 'To whom, etc.?'" Many other instances might be cited. — P. 26. **ΨΗΦΙΣΜΑ.** Another spurious document, defended however by Vömel, and in part by Böhnecke. There is no historical mention elsewhere of the capture of these ships by Amyntas and their subsequent restitution. Other indications of spuriousness will be noticed in their place. — **Νεοκλέους.** No Archon Eponymus at this period is recorded as bearing the name. Theophrastus was the Eponymus of 340 B. C. — **μηνός.** The mention of the day of the month is omitted. — **συγκλήτου.** This required to be summoned by the Prytanes as well as by the Strategi. — **Κόπρειος.** Of the deme Coprus, which was in the tribe Hippothoontis. But it is clearly the famous Eubulus of whom he is speaking, and we know his deme to have been Anaphlystus. *Sup.*, 70. The only various readings are *Κύπριος* and *Κυθήριος.* — **ναύαρχον.** Whiston appears to think that a genuine document would have had *στρατηγὸν* here. The word *ναύαρχος*, however, is used by Thucyd., VIII., 16, 20, and by Xen., *Hellen.*, V., 1. 5. — **καταγήοχεν.** Cf. 39, **εἰσαγηοχότας.** *κατάγειν τὰ πλοῖα* (of piracy). Lys., p. 150, l. 11. — 74. **μεμψιμοιρεῖ,** as Whiston rightly says, is a word belonging only to the Greek of a later period. Luci., *Jup. Trag.*, c. 40; Polyb., IV., 60. 9. In any case it would be most unlikely to be used in a formal and solemn document. Before *ὅτι οὐ μ.* we have to supply *φήσουσιν* from *διαλέξονται.* The construction is awkward and unusual. — **πλημμελοῦντα.** Another awkward ellipsis. We supply with Wolf, [*τὸν ναύαρχον Λεωδάμαντα*] *λαβών.* — **ὀλιγωρίας.** Here *neglect of duty.* The classical use is simply *neglect* and *contempt* in general. — **ἀξίαν.** So *ζημίαν κατὰ τὴν ἀξίαν εἴληφε*, p. 155, l. 13. — **ἰδίᾳ.** *Wilfully,* Kennedy interprets. Others *solely.* A more exact translation would be *on their own account,* i. e. without provocation or justification.—**ἀγνωμονοῦσιν,** *are committing trespass* (Kennedy). This is quite classical. Xen., *Hell.*, I., 7. 33.—**ἀποστείλας.** *Either the man who gave or the man who has received the commission,* i. e. either Philip or Amyntas.—**λέγειν** depends on εἶπεν at the beginning of the psephisma = *that they* (the ambassadors) *state this also.* A few *codices* prefix γράψαι, others substitute it for λέγειν.—75. 2. **Ἡγήσιππος,** p. 129, l. 18, Æschin., c, *Ctes.*, 118. A strong partisan of the Anti-Macedonian side at Athens. Envoy to Philip 344 B. C. See pp. 81, 84, 85, *F. L.*, 364. Supposed author of the *De Halonneso.*—**Ἀριστοφῶν,** 70.—3. **Φιλοκράτης,** 17.—**Κηφισοφῶν.** Sup., 21, in connection with Eubulus. One of the envoys to Philip on the peace question, and the friend of Æschines.—4. **πάντες οἱ ἄλλοι.** He ceases to enumerate the individual names and comprehends the rest of the proposers in one formula; clearly he refers to a large number of psephisms which he is turning over as he speaks.—**ΨΗΦΙΣΜΑ.** Also spurious. As being merely βουλῆς γνώμη (*by vote of the Boule*) it should have been entitled προβούλευμα. But this misnomer is only consistent with its other deficiencies.—**Νεοκλέους.** *Sup.*, 73.—**ἀνενεγκόντες,** *having reported.* A rare Attic use of the word at this period. Thucyd. (V., 28) has ἀνήνεγκαν τοὺς λόγους ἔς τε τὰς ἀρχὰς καὶ τὸν δῆμον. The word χρηματίζειν is technically accurate for *transacting business* (*in the ecclesia*). Πρὶν ἐκείνην (βουλὴν) χρηματίσαι καὶ προβουλεῦσαι. 169 (*fin.*). Here it means, *introduced* for the consideration of the boule.—**ἀνακομιδῆς** = *restoration.*—**ἄφεσις,** *release,* is used to express the same thing in the preceding psephisma and the following letter of Philip.—P. 27. **Ἀριστοφῶν Κολλυτεύς** see 70. The name is also spelt Κολυττεύς. The deme referred to was in the tribe Ægeis; whereas the tribe Hippothoontis is cited as πρυτανεύουσα. But still a member of the tribe Ægeis might have been a πρόεδρος at this time. He might, that is, have been one of the nine πρόεδροι from the nine φυλαί who were out of πρυτανεία. So Böhnecke argues. It is singular that even Kennedy should accept this and the preceding document as genuine. For πρυτανεία and πρόεδρος see Lexicon and Dict. of Antiq.—76. 4. **ἂν ἔχοις.** This, as referring distinctly to the future, contrasts well with the conditional sentence of past time which immediately follows: εἰ γάρ...παρέσχου, *if you had been able all the while* (imperfect)...*you would now have brought it forward* (aorist). *Sup*, 9.—77. **ΕΠΙΣΤΟΛΗ.** This document is clearly spurious, though accepted by Kennedy, and defended, as usual, by Vömel and Böhnecke. The siege of Selymbria by Philip, which is here alluded to, is nowhere else so much as mentioned in any historical record. Yet the sieges of Byzantium and Perinthus, which belong to the same period, are constantly referred to by Demosthenes, Philochorus, Diodorus, and Justin. See Grote. — **χαίρειν** depends on γράφει or some similar word, which is omitted here as in classical and sacred epistles generally. — **πρεσβευταί.** The form πρέσβεις is, no doubt, more usual to express *envoys* in the plural, as Newman observes. Whiston, however, cites Deinarchus c. *Demosth.*, 22 : τῶν πρεσβευτῶν ὡς τοῦτον ἐλθόντων. A more interesting passage is in [Andocidis] c. *Alcibiad.*, p. 28 (*fin.*) : πρεσβευτὰς οὖν πάντας ὑμᾶς ἡμεῖς οἱ πρέσβεις ποιοῦμεν· ὁ γὰρ τὴν χεῖρα μέλλων αἴρειν οὗτος ὁ πρεσβεύων ἐστίν, ὁπότερ' ἂν αὐτῷ δοκῇ, καὶ τὴν εἰρήνην καὶ τὸν πόλεμον ποιεῖν. We may infer from this that πρέσβεις was the technical name for envoys, but πρεσβευταί the more forcible expression implying plenipotentiaries. — **Λεωδάμας.** A correction suggested by Reiske and adopted by Dindorf, as consistent with 73. The *codices* have Λαομέδων. — **καθ' ὅλου,** *absolutely.* On εὐηθείᾳ cf. 11. — **Λῆμνον.** Lemnos still belonged to Athens, according to the peace of Antalcidas, as did also Imbros and Scyros. Æschin., p. 37 ; Xen., *Hist. Gr.*, V., 1. 31. — **βοηθήσοντα δέ.** Supply ὡς ἀληθῶς, in contrast to πρόφασιν μέν which precedes. — 78. **συνετάχθη.** The verb συντάσσειν is usually of military operations *to arrange, drill,* or *discipline,* — its extension here to mean *these orders were given,* is post-classical, although Hesychius, cited by Schäfer, gives Συντάξει = παραγγελεῖ. — **ἰδιωτῶν μέν.** The letter, if genuine, might have been expected to exclude Demosthenes (76) in some specific manner ; but this description *out of office* would apply at that time to him as much as to any one. — **φιλοτιμουμένων.** *Ambitious,* somewhat ironically put. Cf. φιλοτιμίας, 66. — **συντετελέσθαι.** Perfectum significanter positum de re quam isti quam primum ratam videre velint (DISSEN). Rather of the *full* and *complete* accomplishment of that purpose which they desire. And so in the very instance Dissen quotes, p. 91 : περὶ τούτων δ' οἶμαι τὴν ταχίστην συμφέρειν καὶ βεβουλεῦσθαι καὶ πάρεσκευάσθαι. — **πρόσοδον,** *a source of revenue.* τὰς συμμάχων συμφορὰς προσόδους τοῖς πρέσβεσι. *F. L.*, 159.

79-84. PHILIP HIMSELF HAS MADE NO MENTION OF MY NAME. INDEED, HAD HE DONE SO, HE WOULD ONLY HAVE REVEALED HIS OWN DISGRACEFUL CONDUCT AND MY PATRIOTIC RESISTANCE.

I THWARTED HIM BY PROPOSING THE EMBASSIES TO EUBŒA AND TO THE PELOPONNESUS, BY PROPOSING THE MILITARY MOVEMENTS WHICH SAVED THE CHERSONESUS AS WELL AS EUBŒA. THIS BROUGHT YOU THE GREATEST GLORY AND STRENGTHENED YOUR POSITION WITH YOUR ALLIES. BUT A FORTUNE IN MONEY MIGHT HAVE BEEN MADE BY A MAN WHO WOULD HAVE PLAYED INTO PHILIP'S HAND ABOUT EUBŒA, AS ÆSCHINES SAYS THAT I DID: ÆSCHINES, WHO ENTERTAINED IN HIS HOUSE THE ENVOYS OF THESE EUBŒAN TYRANTS! I WHO RECEIVED A CROWN OF HONOR, UNQUESTIONED BY ÆSCHINES, FOR OVERTHROWING THEIR POLICY!

79. P. 28, l. 1. **οὐδαμοῦ.** The spurious document mentions, it is true, no special names whatever except those of the ambassadors; yet nothing can be more pointed than *ἰδιωτῶν* as referring to Demosthenes. Had this been the genuine document the orator would never have brought it forward. Again it nowhere specifies *τοῖς ἄλλοις* whom Philip is described as *ἐγκαλῶν* here. — 5. **εἰχόμην.** *I clave:* that is, with the tenacity of a determined foe = *laid hold of, grappled with,* as rendered by Whiston. The emphatic position of the words and the form of the imperfect tense should be noted, *for with these I was continually grappling and these I was constantly opposing.* — 7. **πρεσβείαν.** Dated about 344. *c. Philipp.* 3, p. 109. Demosthenes himself was one of the legates as well as the proposer of the psephism. — **ὅτε πρῶτον.** On the state of Greece at this time, cf. *Philipp.* 3, p. 115. — 8. **παρεδύετο,** *was trying to steal into.* He did not actually invade the Peloponnese till after Chæronea. *ἡ γοῦν παρανομία αὕτη ῥᾳδίως λανθάνει παραδυομένη.* Plato, *Rep.*, 424 D. — **τὴν ἐς Εὔβοιαν.** B. C. 342. — 10. **οὐκέτι.** The psephism on this occasion was to authorize the despatch of a military force to Eubœa, a step beyond the mere commissioning of envoys. The date was 341 – 340. Phocion commanded, and his efforts were successful. Diod., XVI. 74. — **Ἐρετρίαν.** This is the same expedition which first liberated Oreus and then Eretria. Cf. Æschin. *c. Ctes.*, pp. 67, 68, for the other side of the question. — 11. **τυράννους.** 71. — **80.** 12. **ἀποστόλους,** *naval expeditions.* Dissen considers that the revision of the trierarchic laws (105 sq.) is partly alluded to here, as well as the actual despatch of the fleet. — **ἀπέστειλα.** Of course, as Schäfer remarks, *ἔγραψα ἀποστεῖλαι* is what the orator means, p. 262, l. 15: *τῶν ἀποστόλων γιγνομένων κατὰ τὸν νόμον τὸν ἐμόν.* — 13. **Χερρόνησος.** 73, note **καὶ μήν.** — 14. **πάντες οἱ σύμμαχοι.** He alludes to Proconnesus and Tenedos and the like, p. 326.

— 17. **ὑμῖν** depends on πεισθεῖσιν: *those who took your advice,* as opposed to *those who neglected it.* **τῶν ἀδικουμένων** is genitive of the whole after the partitives τοῖς μέν...τοῖς δέ· περιεγένετο is to be repeated with τὸ...μεμνῆσθαι καὶ νομίζειν. — **81.** 24. **ὑπάρχειν,** *to have these substantial materials for your injury,* ὑπάρξαι 1 note. — 25. **ἐξελέγχεσθαι.** The verb ἐξελέγχειν means to investigate and *expose;* ἐξετάζειν (*inf.*) to *question* merely. — P. 29, l. 1. **πανταχοῦ,** *anywhere:* cf. the use of πάντων, 5, note. — **82.** 5. **κατέλυον.** This very technical use of καταλύειν is easily traced: the verb signifies 1. to unloose (sc. the sandals), 2. to rest, 3. to *lodge.* παρ' ἐμοὶ γὰρ Γοργίας καταλύει Plat., *Gorg.*, 447 B. The expression is common in Plato, but rare in the orators, who employ the word more commonly of dissolution, destruction, or termination. — 6. **προὐξένεις,** *were their public host.* The office of πρόξενος was analogous to that of our own consul, and the consul is called πρόξενος in modern Greek. For full particulars see Dict. Ant. Hospitium. — **αὐτῶν.** The genitive follows προξενεῖν always in its literal sense: it is a possessive genitive (= εἶναι πρόξενον αὐτῶν) the visitor having a claim on the plighted friend of his native city: p. 194, l. 18; p. 1237, l. 17. In the secondary sense, to *address,* to *recommend,* προξενεῖν is followed by the dative: p. 969, l. 18; p. 1250, l. 20. — 8. **ἦσαν.** We have to supply οἵ for the subject out of οὓς before ἡ πόλις. — **οὐ τοίνυν ἐπράχθη,** *accordingly none of these things was effected,* which Philip and his partisans designed. Whiston. — 9. **σιωπῶ μέν.** *That I hold my tongue when I have got a fee, and raise my voice when I have spent it.* Æschin., p. 85, l. 8: σὺ δ' οἶμαι λαβὼν μὲν σεσίγηκας, ἀναλώσας δὲ κέκραγας, i. e. you accept a bribe to induce you to be silent, but when the money is gone you break your silence and your word together. — 12. **ἀτιμώσαντες,** by disfranchising you. See Böckh (*Econ. Ath.*, I. 409). If Æschines failed to obtain the fifth part of the votes he would be liable to disfranchisement. This was called ἐπωβελίαν ὀφλεῖν. Cf. p. 834, l. 25; p. 1251, l. 2, etc. The object of such penalties was to prevent prosecutions on insufficient grounds. — **οὗτοι,** sc. the judges. — **83.** 13. **τούτοις,** i. e. my successful resistance on this occasion to Cleitarchus and Philistides. — **συλλαβάς,** *the same identical words:* literally, *syllables.* δύο συλλαβὰς προσθείς, p. 270, l. 22. πάντα τὸν νόμον μέχρι τῆς ὑστάτης συλλαβῆς, p. 734, l. 23. This Aristonicus is incidentally mentioned with honor by Demosthenes (below, 312) as having contributed for the salvation of the state after the disastrous battle at Chæronea a sum of money which had been collected by his friends as the means of recovering the ἐπιτιμία which he had lost. — 16. **ἐν τῷ θεάτρῳ.** These words are very important, I think, for the true interpretation of δευτέρου κηρύγματος which follows. We know from Æschines (*c. Ctes.*, p. 58) the exact terms of the law which directed these proclamations. If the crown was conferred by the βουλή, the locus of proclamation was to be the βουλευτήριον; if by the δῆμος, the locus of proclamation was to be the Pnyx at the time of an ἐκκλησία; these, according to the cited law, were the only two places in which the said proclamations could legally be made: μηδαμοῦ ἄλλοθι *l. c.* Æschines is careful to insist upon this, as, of course, one point in his accusation depended entirely upon it. He then anticipates his opponent's reply, saying that Demosthenes will quote another law, τὸν Διονυσιακὸν νόμον, which permitted an exception to the law already cited. According to this Dionysiac law, it was quite legitimate for such proclamations to be made, not merely in the two places specified, but also *in the theatre* itself, if only a special vote should have first been passed by the δῆμος to sanction the exceptional proceeding: νόμον δεδωκότα ἐξουσίαν ποιεῖσθαι τὴν ἀνάρρησιν τοῦ στεφάνου τραγῳδοῖς ἐν τῷ θεάτρῳ ἐὰν ψηφίσηται ὁ δῆμος. This exception, according to Æschines, only applied to a crown conferred by a foreign city on an Athenian. But the orator contradicts him in 120. Of course as a locus of proclamation the theatre had the advantage of considerably greater publicity, being open to all at Athens, citizens and strangers alike, whereas the βουλευτήριον and the ἐκκλησία would only admit the presence each of their respective members. The addition therefore of ἐν τῷ θεάτρῳ enhanced the notoriety of such a donation; it also enhanced the compliment, as it implied that the services of the στεφανούμενος were cosmopolitan instead of merely Athenian. We can well understand that whereas the grants of crowns were common enough at this time at Athens, it was not quite so common to receive the grant of a crown which would be proclaimed *in the theatre.* It would only be done in the event of special and peculiar circumstances, deserving special and peculiar honor. Demosthenes says, below, 120, μυρίους μυριάκις κεκηρῦχθαι, but this is an obvious hyperbole: he only means that the exception to the law had very constantly been taken advantage of (but in each case, no doubt, on some plea of exceptional reasons). Had it been the normal practice thus to proclaim the crowns, that particular point of the indictment, which Æschines urges so strongly, would have been a simple absurdity. — 16. **δευτέρου.**

And whereas the present is now the second proclamation IN THE THEATRE *which is coming off in my honor.* We may paraphrase thus: Whereas this proposal of Ctesiphon's that my crown should be proclaimed (*in the theatre*) is not the *first* honor (of the *same exceptional* kind) which I have already received, but the *second.* With *κηρύγματος* we supply *ἐν τῷ θεάτρῳ*, carrying on the idea of the words from where they occur immediately before. As to *τούτου*, the pronoun itself can hardly refer to any proclamation but that proposed by Ctesiphon; any other would probably be *ἐκείνου*. But the tense of *γιγνομένου* is what most forcibly points to the same conclusion; it is an instance of the present with the force of a future, when the speaker feels certain that the future event is to come off almost directly. The orator speaks in fact with the confidence of a winning cause: he is so assured of Ctesiphon's acquittal that he looks on his own crown and its proclamation as things that are actually in the present. (On this use of the tense see Madvig, 110, a. 3.) Had he referred to his previous crowning which was proposed by Aristonicus, he would infallibly have written *γενομένου* here. The interpretation may rest entirely on this change of tense as contrasted with the aorists *γράψαντος* and *ἀναρρηθέντος*. As regards the number of occasions on which it was proposed to crown the orator, we have his own assertion *τὸ πολλάκις αὐτὸς ἐστεφανῶσθαι πρότερον*, 120. Historically we can trace but four occasions: (1) on his own proposal, in 346, when he returned from the first embassy to Philip; (2) on the proposal of Aristonicus, in 340; (3) on the proposal of Demomeles and Hyperides, in 338, *vid.* 223; (4) on this proposal of Ctesiphon. I believe occasion (2) was the first when the crowning was to be proclaimed *in the theatre;* and occasion (4) was the second (*δευτέρου τούτου*) *of the same exceptional kind.* We arrive at this result by a simple process of exhaustion: *τούτου* cannot refer to (1) or (3), because the present context mentions neither of them: and it cannot refer to (2) because of the tense of *γιγνομένου* as has been explained above. Reiske and Schäfer, though referring *τούτου* to Ctesiphon's proposal, do not, I think, appreciate the point of *ἐν τῷ θεάτρῳ*: at least they pass it in silence. Böhnecke refers *τούτου* to the proposal of Aristonicus. And Whiston apparently inclines to that view himself. Indeed, Reiske is partly converted by Böhnecke's showing the probable fact that Aristonicus' *στέφανος* would be the *second* in order of time. But this is at most a mere coincidence. See 120. — **84. ΨΗΦΙΣΜΑ.** This document has more claims to be regarded as genuine than any which have preceded. Its contents are fairly in harmony with what is on record elsewhere. But the inscription and the date are full of perplexity. The Eubœan affairs to which reference is made occurred in the last six months of B. C. 340. This compliment to Demosthenes would naturally have been paid at the beginning of 339, when, as he says below, the matters were still *νέα καὶ γνώριμα* (85). Of that year Nicomachus was the Archon Eponymus. Chærondas only came into office in 338. The addition of the name Ἡγήμονος is also perplexing. Its natural meaning would be *the son of Hegemon.* But no psephism of the time of Demosthenes ever recorded the name of the Archon's father. Now there was a man of some mark who bore the name Hegemon, belonging to this period (*c. Aristog.*, p. 784; Plut., *Phoc.*, 33), and who would doubtless have been very eligible for the office of Archon Eponymus, though we do not know that he ever held it. Possibly, therefore, some copyist, detecting the inconsistency of Χαιρώνδου, wrote Ἡγήμονος above it, as a conjectural emendation, and subsequently both the names may have been embodied in the text. This, I presume, must have been Dobree's reason for wishing to expunge Χαιρώνδου here, and retain Ἡγήμονος alone. — **Φρεάρριος.** The deme Phrearri is mentioned by Harpocration as belonging to the tribe Leontis, and designated after the hero Phrearrus. — **πολλὰς...παρέσχηται.** A common formula, as Böckh has shown (*Corp. Inscript.*), occurring in documents of this nature. Χρείας = *services*, is rare in the orators: their usual sense of χρεία is *need.* But cf. Antipho (p. 121, l. 11): τῆς χρείας τοῦ παιδὸς ἀποστερηθῶ. — P. 30. **καινοῖς,** 54, note. — **ἀναγορεύσεως.** Post-classical. Plut., *Marc.*, 4. The Greek of the period would be ἀναρρήσεως. — **ἀγωνοθέτην.** General name for the *umpire* or *steward* at any of the public contests, athletic, dramatic, or otherwise: used metaphorically by Æschines, p. 79, l. 29: ἀγωνοθέτης πολιτικῆς ἀρετῆς.

85, 86. DID THIS DECREE, AS ÆSCHINES SUGGESTS, MAKE YOU RIDICULOUS IN THE EYES OF GREECE? THE MERIT OF AN ACTION IS JUDGED AT THE MOMENT. DO NOT ALL THE HISTORICAL CIRCUMSTANCES BELONGING TO THAT SPECIAL EPOCH ATTEST THE VALUE OF MY SERVICES?

85. 2. **χλευασμόν.** *Scoff:* in p. 705, l. 2, we have the cognate form χλευασία. — 4. **νέα καὶ γνώριμα,** *fresh and notorious,* cf. note on ΨΗΦΙΣΜΑ, 84, as to the date. — 6. **ὡς ἑτέρως.** 212, *quite otherwise,* by euphemism for κακῶς, which the preceding καλῶς would suggest as its obvious antithesis. *τὰ ἕτερα ψηφίσωνται οἱ δικασταί*, p. 1175, l. 19. — **ὡς** = *quite*. See lex. See also 34, **ἕτερον**. — 86. 11. **τῷ νικᾶν**. Dative of the instrument: *by the fact of my carrying my measures*. The fuller phrase is *νικᾶν ψήφισμα*. Æschin., p. 63, l. 21. *νικᾶν τῇ ψήφῳ*, *Id.*, p. 39, l. 36; *νικᾶν γνώμας*, Aristoph., *Nub.*, 432.—12. **λέγων καὶ γράφων** limits *νικᾶν* = *in my speeches and motions*. — **τῷ καταπραχθῆναι** and **τῷ...πεποιῆσθαι** are in the same construction as *τῷ νικᾶν*, and Bremi calls attention to the life and vigor which is imparted to these clauses by the omission of the connectives. —14. **προσόδους**, i. e. to the temples = *solemn processions*. — 15. **πεποιῆσθαι**, perf. middlle = *caused to be made*.

87-92. Failing in Eubœa, Philip attempted to cut off our supply of corn, and with this view, to seize Byzantium. Who rescued Byzantium? You, the state. Who advised you? I. That policy secured your prosperity for the time, and gained you the vote of thanks from Byzantium and the Chersonesus.

87. 17. **τοῖς μὲν ὅπλοις, κ. τ. λ.**, *in arms indeed by you, but in statesmanship and resolutions by me*. Here the dative expresses the instrument, while the agent is expressed by *ὑπό* with the genitive. — 18. **διαρραγῶσι**, *burst*, i. e. by straining their lungs to contradict me. *Sup.* 21. Rumpe miser tensum iecur, Juv., *Sat.*, VII., 117. — 20. **σίτῳ ...ἐπεισάκτῳ**. Böckh calculates the amount of corn imported to Athens at about a million *μέδιμνοι*; the main supply being from the neighborhood of the Pontus. *πρὸς ἅπαντα τὸν ἐκ τῶν ἄλλων ἐμπορίων ἀφικνούμενον ὁ ἐκ τοῦ Πόντου εἰσπλέων ἐστίν*, p. 466, l. 24. — P. 31, l. 1. **ἠξίου**. The verb *ἀξιόω*, from its first sense *to think right*, comes to signify *demand* or *claim*, often with a notion of doing so arrogantly or authoritatively, as here. Cf. p. 553, l. 19; p. 570 (*fin.*). — 2. **οὐδ' ἐπί**, *and said that they had not made the alliance on these terms, which assertion was true*. Their refusal was mainly owing to the eloquence of Demosthenes as the envoy of Athens at this time (340 B. C.). Cf. 230, 244. The orator appears to have foreseen the designs of Philip on Byzantium some months prior to this, pp. 93-106, and p. 115. — 4. **χάρακα**. Technically, *vine-prop* or *stake*: here, by synecdoche, for *χαράκωμα*: *stockade, intrenchment*. Bekker reads the latter; but Σ has *χάρακα*, and there is a gloss of Harpocration's *χάρακα* = *χαράκωμα*. On p. 71, l. 20, we have *χαρακώματα καὶ τείχη καὶ τάφροι*. On p. 568, l. 16, *χάρακας* is simply *timber*. — 5. **μηχανήματα**, *having planted artillery*: the expression indicates the severity and formality of the siege. *Τοὺς τὰ*

μηχανήματα ἐφίσταντας, p. 115, l. 7. Grote quotes from Athenæus, *ἐπίδοσιν δὲ ἔλαβεν ἡ τοιαύτη μηχανοποιΐα ἅπασα...κατὰ τὴν Φιλίππου τοῦ Ἀμύντου βασιλείαν ὅτε ἐπολιόρκει Βυζαντίους Φίλιππος* (fragm.), as showing that the siege of Byzantium formed an epoch in the history of besieging enginery. — **88.** 6. **οὐκέτ'**, i. e. he had repeatedly asked the question before: 72, 66, etc. — **τὸ ὑμεῖς.** See C. 522, d; Cu. 379; G. 141, N. 6. — 12. **ἁπλῶς,** *in a word.* This adverb qualifies the whole sentence between itself and *διδούς,* not to be taken in connection with *ἀφειδῶς, unsparingly,* which merely qualifies *διδούς.* The force of the *imperfect* participles should be noted and expressed: *who was it that was all the while speaking and writing* (making motions) *and acting, and in a word giving himself unsparingly to the public welfare.* — **89.** 15. **ἐνστάς,** *which was then upon us.* The aorist participle has the force of a full perfect participle: here we must regard it as a pluperfect, the consecution being historic; lit. = *which had then established itself among us* as a *fait accompli.* War was actually declared in the midsummer of 340, when the Athenians passed a formal decree to remove the column on which the peace of 346 stood recorded. Diodor., XVI., 77. See Grote. — 16. **ἄνευ.** *Besides, præterquam quod.* Non excludit sed una quoque complectitur (Reiske). — 17. **διῆγεν,** *kept you in greater abundance and cheapness of every necessary of life. δραχμῇ καὶ χοῒ καὶ τέτταρσιν ὀβολοῖς, ὥσπερ ἀσθενοῦντα τὸν δῆμον διάγουσιν,* p. 1459 (*fin.*). — 18. **τῆς νῦν.** Sarcastic: *the peace of these days:* that conceded by Alexander. With *τηροῦσιν* sq. cf. 323. — 19. **μελλούσαις,** *with their prospective hopes;* no doubt sarcastically quoting some favorite phrase of the other party. — 20. **ὧν, κ. τ. λ.,** *which hopes may they fail to realize and share those blessings* [instead] *which you with the noblest of aims implore the gods to bestow; and never may they* [the traitors] *impart to you what they have deliberately chosen for themselves,* i. e. may the traitors be disappointed in what they expect to get from Macedon! may they share, however, the common blessings of their native land! but may they never induce you to share in their corrupt proceedings, or to partake the rewards which such baseness aspires to win! The various reading, *μή* before *μετάσχοιεν* and *μηδέ* (for *μή*) before *μεταδοῖεν,* alters the blessing of the former clause into a curse. The reading of Σ (which I have retained) gives the more generous tone to the sentence, but it may be doubted whether the other is not more vigorous and Demosthenic. There is nothing harsh in the asyndeton of *μή—προῄρηνται,* as regards the preceding clause. The entreaty and the deprecation stand side by side, in effective contrast, and the contrast is emphasized by the omission of the connecting particle. — 23. **Βυζαντίων.** Subjective genitive. In 92 he prefixes the *παρά*. — **90.** **ΨΗΦΙΣΜΑ.** This document is suspected of being spurious, partly on account of the mixture of the dialects, partly because it mentions Byzantium and Perinthus as though they formed one united state, which we know historically was not the case. Dindorf is inclined to accept it as genuine; and so are Vömel and Böhnecke, as usual. But Droysen and Ahrens profess to detect "certissima fraudis argumenta." — **ἱερομνάμονος.** The name of the chief Byzantine magistracy, not to be confounded with the Attic use of this name for "envoys to the Amphictyonic council," 148, etc. Whiston suggests that he was a religious officer, perhaps the high-priest of Poseidon, and adds, that this practice of naming the year from a religious officer prevailed in other Dorian states. Kennedy translates *ἐπὶ ἱερομνάμονος*, *in the presbytership of.* — **Βοσπορίχω.** *Dorice* for *Βοσπορίχου*. Ahrens denies that the Byzantine dialect admitted the severer Doric changes, (1) *ω* for *ου* and (2) *η* for *ει*: it was more akin, he says, to the Lesbian and Ionic. In the present document we have eleven more examples of (1) (*βωλά*, *Φιλίππω*, *τῶ*, *τὼς νόμως*, *τὼς τάφως*, *τῶ δάμω*, *τὼς στεφάνως*), and one example of (2) (*ἦμεν* for *εἶναι*). The form *ἀμέ* is Lesbian, and *ἐπιστέωνται* pure Ionic. — **ἁλίᾳ.** The Doric equivalent for *ἐκκλησίᾳ*. — **βωλᾶς.** More properly *γερουσίας*. But see Müller, *Dor.*, II., p. 91. — **ῥάτραν.** The Doric equivalent for *προβούλευμα*. Müller, *ib.*, p. 170. Schäfer, however, takes it = *ἐξουσίαν τοῦ λέγειν*. — P. 32. **διατελέει.** The present tense is much affected in documents of this nature. (*Sup.*, 84, *διατελεῖ εὔνους ὤν*.) The consecution here is all primary. — **συγγένεσι.** Plutarch (*Quæst. Gr.*, c. 57) says that Perinthus was colonized by the Megarians and Samians. DISSEN. Byzantium also was founded by a colony from Megara with a mixture of Argives. — **δενδροκοπέοντος.** This *cutting down of trees* is always noticed as a prominent feature of Greek invasions and raids. Aristoph., *Pax*, 627, 9, *Ach.*, 232, etc. *καίειν καὶ κόπτειν* is the favorite combination in Xenophon. — **ἀμέ.** *ἄμμε* is the Doric equivalent for *ἡμᾶς*. — **91.** **Βυζαντίων καί.** The article *τῷ* should have been repeated before *Περινθίων* to indicate that they were separate states. — **ἐπιγαμίαν.** *Right of intermarriage*, entitling the alien to share the national privileges of the native married. — **ἔγκτασιν γᾶς.** *Right of holding house and land by purchase.* Strictly forbidden to an alien at this period in all the Grecian states.

— **ποτί.** Dorice for *πρός*, as *πόθοδον* for *πρόσοδον*. — **μετὰ τὰ ἱερά,** i. e. immediately on the proceedings being formally opened. They began always with sacrificial solemnities. — **ἀλειτουργήτοις.** *Excused from all public services.* On the *λειτουργίαι* of other states as well as the Athenian, see Böckh's *Econ. Ath.*, Vol. I., Amer. ed., pp. 584, 689. See also Dic. of Antiq. — **εἰκόνας.** The nature of the group of statues to be erected is clear from the context. A figure representing Athens would be sculptured as receiving a crown from two other figures representing Byzantium and Perinthus respectively. Dissen quotes very aptly a similar case from Polybius (V., 88, 8), where Rhodes was sculptured in the Rhodian exchange as receiving a crown from Syracuse. Whiston quotes Pliny (*H. N.*, XXXV., 36, 5), who speaks of Parrhasius' statue representing the *Δῆμος* of Athens. — **92. ΨΗΦΙΣΜΑ.** This document is probably spurious. Droysen, p. 812. — **Χερρονησιτῶν.** The Thracian Chersonese is referred to, in which these four towns had been razed to the ground by Philip 341–340 B. C. — **ἀπὸ ταλάντων ἑξήκοντα.** "*ἀπό* hoc est *ex*, ut Herod., VII., 65." Dissen. So again 102. The general solution of this passage is to suppose the talent here spoken of to have been the small golden talent, equal to six Attic drachmæ (weight) of gold, i. e. sixty of silver. Böckh (*Econ. Ath.*, I., 39). But the question of the value of a talent in the Chersonese and other remote states is in great obscurity. Smith, Dict. Antiq., Talentum. — **χάριτος βωμόν.** *Altar of thanksgiving.* So *βωμοὶ δίκης καὶ εὐνομίας*, p. 780, l. 22. — **παραίτιος γέγονε.** *Hath helped...to obtain* (Kennedy). The phrase is of no uncommon occurrence in similar votes of thanks. — **τῆς Φιλίππου.** We may supply at discretion *ἀρχῆς*, *δυνάμεως*, *χειρός*, or the like. Dissen prefers the last, citing Æschin., *c. Ctes.*, p. 90, *ἐκ τῶν χειρῶν ἐξελέσθαι τῶν Φιλίππου.* But the plural in such a case is more natural than the singular. — **τὰ ἱερά,** i. e. the temples and all thereto appertaining, including the national religion. Cf. Thucyd., IV., 98, *τὸν δὲ νόμον τοῖς Ἕλλησιν εἶναι ὧν ἂν ᾖ τὸ κράτος τῆς γῆς ἑκάστης τούτων καὶ τὰ ἱερὰ ἀεὶ γίγνεσθαι.* — **οὐκ ἐλλείψει.** The subject, *ὁ δῆμος τῶν Χερρονησιτῶν*, is obvious from the context.

93–101. My policy did not merely save these places, and preserve the freedom of Greece, but it also showed the character of Athens in the most brilliant contrast to the character of Philip. And let me also justify my policy by an historical retrospect. Look at the conduct

INVARIABLY PURSUED BY YOUR FOREFATHERS, AND BY THE OLDER AMONG YOU, IN THE TIMES OF LACEDÆMONIAN, AND AFTERWARDS OF THEBAN, SUPREMACY. ATHENIANS HAVE ALWAYS FOUGHT FOR HONOR AND LIBERTY. NO LEAVEN OF MALICE OR REVENGE HAS EVER DEGRADED THEIR FEELINGS.

93. P. 33, l. 1. **οὐ μόνον,** 2, note, *s. v.* — 4. **ἡ προαίρεσις καὶ ἡ πολιτεία.** Dissen calls attention to this as a favorite expression of the orator. See 292, 317. Render, *My policy and administration.* — 6. **καλοκαγαθίαν.** *Spirit of honor.* The combination of high physical and mental qualities, implied in the well-known phrase *καλὸς κἀγαθός*, approximates, in its idiomatic usage, to our own expression "man of honor." Here we have the antithesis *κακίαν*, *baseness.* — **94.** 10. **οἱ μεμψάμενοι ... ἂν** = *οἱ ἐμέμψασθε ἄν.* C. 618; Cu. 595; G. 211; H. 803. — 11. **ἠγνωμονήκεσαν.** *Their acts of trespass* (74), i. e. in the Social War, B. C. 357–355; the then allies included, with Byzantium, Chios, Rhodes, and Cos. — 12. **οὐ μόνον.** *Showed yourselves not merely as bearing no malice and never abandoning the victims of wrong, but even as working their salvation.* *σώζειν* is not simply to deliver from danger, but to restore to a sound condition. — 17. **σύμβουλον...ῥήτορα,** *a counsellor and orator I mean.* He does not mean to deny that the *generals* had sometimes been the means of the state being honored with crowns. — **95.** 20. **Εὐβοέων.** Æschin., p. 65, *περὶ τῶν Εὐβοέων πρῶτον μνησθήσομαι.* The speech of Æschines as published does not contain any allusion to the Byzantines; but the speech, as spoken, we must assume, had done so. — 22. **βλασφημίας** = *defamations,* **συκοφαντίας** = *malignant calumnies.* — 23. **ὑπάρχειν εἰδότας.** *ὑπάρχειν* as an auxiliary verb presents the strongest form of the present tense. Dissen cites as parallels, p. 190, *ὑπάρχειν ἐγνωκότες*, and p. 527, *ἐγνωσμένα ὑπάρχει.* We have another instance in 228. Whiston renders: *Of this I believe you are already well assured.* — 24. **ἀλλὰ καὶ τῷ...χρήσασθαι,** *but also by the fact that it was for your interest so to conduct your affairs as I conducted them.* The clause is dative of means, limiting *ἐπιδείξω.* — 26. **καθ' ὑμᾶς.** *In your time,* literally *in your track,* i. e. in the path of your own lives: on *κατά*, cf. 17: **κατ' ἐκείνους.** — 27. **τῇ πόλει** = *by the state,* dative of the agent after a passive verb. C. 461; Cu. 434; G. 188, 3; H. 600. — P. 34, l. 2. **τῶν ὑπαρχόντων.** *To shape all their future with reference to the best of their present.* He quotes a general *γνώμη* with a somewhat unusual application. The connection shows that *τῶν ὑπαρχόντων* includes their *antecedents* together

with the present. — **96.** 4. **Λακεδαιμονίων.** Vides tempus post Peloponnesiacum bellum describi. DISSEN. — 5. **ἁρμοσταῖς,** 18 : **οἱ πρότερον.** — 6. **Εὔβοιαν.** Captured by the Lacedæmonians B. C. 411. Thucyd., VIII., 93. — **Τάναγραν.** Xen. (*Hell.*, V., 4) mentions that Tanagra remained attached to Lacedæmon after the rest of Bœotia went to war with her. The whole of Bœotia was in the hands of the Lacedæmonians from the close of the Peloponnesian war to the battle of Leuctra. — 7. **Μέγαρα.** Taken from the Athenians by Brasidas, 424 B. C., and attached to Lacedæmon from that time forward. Thucyd. (IV., 66) mentions that the Peloponnesians garrisoned Nisæa for the protection of Megara against Athens. — **Αἴγιναν.** Lysander, in the year 405, restored this island to its original inhabitants whom the Athenians had ejected in 431. Xen., *Hell.*, II. ; 2, Thucyd., II., 27. — **Κλεωνάς.** The date of this city's capture by the Lacedæmonians is not recorded in history. It is singular, as Dissen observes, that the orator should not have arranged the names Κλεωνάς, Εὔβοιαν, Αἴγιναν, τὰς ἄλλας νήσους. But the phrase "the rest of the islands," even standing independently of any island previously mentioned, would always mean to Athenian ears the minor Ægean isles. Plut., *Lys.*, 13, 14. — 8. **οὐ τείχη.** Cf. Plutarch *l. c.* Lysander destroyed the long walls, and limited the Athenian navy to twelve ships of war only : οὔτε ναῦς is therefore not to be understood as literal. — 9. **Ἁλίαρτον.** The scene of the battle in Bœotia, B. C. 395, where Lysander fell. The inhabitants of Haliartus had implored the aid of Athens : Thrasybulus with great energy had led the Athenian forces to the rescue. Pausanias only arrived the day after the battle with the Lacedæmonian reinforcements : he was deterred from further hostilities, made a truce and retired. — 10. **Κόρινθον.** The centre of the Corinthian war, which lasted for eight years after Haliartus and was only concluded by the peace of Antalcidas, B. C. 387. The alliance against Lacedæmon was composed of the Bœotians, Argives, Corinthians, and Athenians. p. 40, l. 20 ; p. 258, l. 13. — 11. **ἂν ἐχόντων.** *Might have borne many grudges* = καίτοι ἂν εἶχον. — 12. **Δεκελεικόν.** The close of the Peloponnesian war was so called from the occupation of Decelea by the Lacedæmonians, its position on the frontier of Attica making it a convenient base of hostilities. — **τῶν πραχθέντων** is genitive of cause. — **97.** 18. **διδόναι.** *To give themselves up.* A favorite use of the word, 80, ἀφειδῶς ἑαυτὸν διδοὺς εἰς τὰ πράγματα. 219, ἔδωκεν ἑαυτὸν εἰς οὐδὲν τῇ πόλει. The continual and customary action expressed by the imperfects ἐποίουν, ἑώρων, προΐεντο, and ἤθελον should be noted. — **πέρας.** *For all mankind have death as their limit of life, even if one shut himself up and keep himself safe in a dove-cote.* This is the meaning Harpocration assigns to οἰκίσκος, and the literal translation seems most vigorous here. Whiston translates *chamber* or *closet.* The passage is greatly lauded by all the ancient critics, notably by Hermogenes, Aristides, and Rufus. Propertius (cited by Dissen) illustrates the sentiment, III., 18. 25 : Ille licet ferro cautus se condat et ære, Mors tamen inclusum protrahit inde caput. — **ὀρθῶς...βουλευόμενοι** in this emphatic position = *and a right and noble decision it was.* — 22. **ἀγαθήν** is separated from ἐλπίδα to point the emphasis of ἀγαθούς above. *Good men and true — taking for their shield good hope and true.* προβαλέσθαι μὲν Εὔβοιαν τῆς Ἀττικῆς, 301. See the same figure in Paul's Epistle to the Ephesians, vi. 16. — **98.** 24. **πρόγονοι.** There was an interval of sixty years at least between these events and the time when he is speaking. — **πρεσβύτεροι,** i. e. when the Athenians under Iphicrates checked Epaminondas in his design of destroying Sparta and compelled him to evacuate Laconia, in the year 369. Xen., *H. G.*, VI., 5. — 25. **ὄντας,** concessive. — P. 35, l. 2. **οἷα πεποιηκότων,** *reflecting what the men had done for whom you were to imperil yourselves.* On relative pronouns used interrogatively, as οἷα here, see Madvig, *G. S.*, 198, b ; H. 825 ; C. 564. As to the interrogative sentence in a participial form, cf. Madv., 198, a. καταμεμάθηκας οὖν τοὺς τί ποιοῦντας τὸ ὄνομα τοῦτο ἀποκαλοῦσιν, Xen., *Mem.*, II., 2 ; H. 826 ; C. 566. — **99.** 8. **ὑπολογιεῖσθε.** *Take it into calculation:* explained by διαλογισάμενοι and the preceding words in 98. ὑπο- implying an underhand (as δια- a thorough) proceeding. — 10. **Εὔβοιαν.** In the year 358 there were two factions in Eubœa, one of which applied to the Thebans for aid, and the other to the Athenians. The Thebans were compelled to yield, and the democratic constitutions of the several states were restored. Diod., XVI., 7 ; Æschin., p. 65. DISSEN. — **Θεμίσωνος.** Themiso and Theodorus, the τυραννοί of Eretria in 366 B. C., seized Oropus which was then Athenian. Peace subsisted at the time. The city was put into the hands of the Thebans, to be held by them until the question, who had the right to it, should be settled. The Thebans subsequently declined to give it up. This is the allusion in Aristot., *Rhet.*, I., 7, where he mentions Callistratus and Chabrias as having been put on their trial. They had commanded the Athenian forces on this occasion. — 12. **ἐθελον-**

τῶν. The first instance of citizens volunteering to act as extraordinary trierarchs. On the general office of trierarch, see Smith, Dic. of Antiq. — 14. **ἀλλ' οὔπω,** *sc.* εἰπεῖν μέλλω. On p. 403, ἀλλὰ μήπω ταῦτα (*sc.* εἴπω). *And indeed though you did a noble thing in saving the island, yet you acted much more nobly in that, when you had become masters both of their persons and their cities, you restored them justly,* etc. καί before τὸ σῶσαι = *also;* it emphasizes the comparison between the two clauses, and can hardly be expressed in idiomatic English. καταστάντες agrees in case with the subject of ἐποιήσατε, which is also the subject of ἀποδοῦναι. — **100.** 18. **μηδὲν ὧν,** *having taken no account of your past wrongs in regard to what you were trusted with:* ὧν and οἷς by attraction for ἐκείνων ἅ and τούτοις ἅ respectively: ἠδίκησθε, as a perfect tense, indicating the complete and serious nature of the wrongs. The sense of the passage is this: You did not take advantage of holding their property so as to appropriate any to yourselves, by way of indemnification for past injuries received at their hands. — 23. **ἐλευθερίας.** Genitive of cause, without a preposition to introduce it. For the principle, see Madv., *G. S.*, 58, a; C. 429. — **101.** 26. **ὑπὲρ αὐτῆς,** *on her own behalf,* p. 74, καὶ (Φίλιππος) πεποίηχ' ὑμῖν μὴ περὶ τῶν δικαίων μηδ' ὑπὲρ τῶν ἔξω πραγμάτων εἶναι τὴν βουλήν, ἀλλ' ὑπὲρ τῶν ἐν τῇ χώρᾳ καὶ τοῦ πρὸς 'Αττικὴν πολέμου. — 27. **βουλῆς οὔσης** is gen. abs. denoting time and cause, *when the deliberation was in a manner in behalf of herself.* — **κελεύσειν** = *urge, move.* — P. 36, l. 1. **μνησικακεῖν.** The irony is obvious. As an example of νὴ Δία, in irony, Whiston aptly cites the c. *Mid.*, p. 527, l. 14, τίς ἀνθρωπίνη καὶ μετρία σκῆψις φανεῖται τῶν πεπραγμένων αὐτῷ; ὀργὴ νὴ Δία καὶ γὰρ τοῦτο τυχὸν λέξει. — 4. **τῶν ὑπαρχόντων...καλῶν,** *glorious antecedents.* WHISTON. Cf. note, 95. — 5. **λόγῳ...τό γε ἔργον.** The favorite antithesis of Pericles, Thucyd., II., 35-46 *passim.*

102-106. I PROCEED, IN MY RETROSPECT, TO MY NEXT POLITICAL ACTION, WHEN I RECONSTITUTED YOUR NAVY, AND COMPELLED THE SECTIONS TO DO THEIR DUTY. HERE IS THE EVIDENCE.

102. 12. **καταλυόμενον,** *in a state of dissolution.* κατάλυσις τριήρους ὁμολογεῖται αὕτη εἶναι πρώτη ὅταν τις μισθὸν μὴ δῷ, p. 1209, l. 11. In that passage there is a play upon the word which would mean *disbanding* as well as *ruin.* The orator was at this time in office as ἐπιστάτης τοῦ ναυτικοῦ, i. e. a Member of the Naval Board. Æschin. (p. 85). — 13. **ἀτελεῖς,** *immunes: exempted,* ἀτελὴς τῶν ἄλλων λειτουργιῶν, p. 565, l. 4. — **ἀπό,** *at a cost of* = the Latin *pro:* ἀπὸ τῶν αὐτῶν λημμάτων στρατιώτης, i. e. at the same pay, p. 38, l. 2. Cf. *sup.* ἀπὸ ταλάντων, 92. Dissen cites ἀπὸ σμικροῦ Aristoph., *Plut.*, 377. The wealthy citizens, when appointed trierarchs, used to contract for the whole expense of the office at a cost of one talent: cf. p. 364. — 15. **ὑστερίζουσαν,** *missing* for want of punctuality. ὑστεριοῦμεν ἁπάντων, p. 49, l. 1. τοὺς ἀποστόλους ὑστερίζειν τῶν καιρῶν, p. 50, l. 11. — 16. **ἔθηκα.** Strictly the active τιθέναι νόμον would only apply to one despotic lawgiver. *Sup.*, 6. Here the orator applies it to himself, as he did before to Solon, to indicate the extent of his influence. The law in question was proposed by him B. C. 340. — **103.** 20. **γραφείς,** *having been indicted for this trial.* The passive γράφεσθαι (in this technical sense) is often constructed with an accusative of cognate meaning (see Madvig., *G. S.*, 26, b.), γραφὴν ὕβρεως γραφεὶς οὐδέπω τούτων δίκην δέδωκε, Isæus, p. 73, l. 75. The accusative ἀγῶνα has to do double duty, depending on γραφεὶς in the above construction and also on εἰσῆλθον which follows. Cf. εἰσῆλθον τὴν γραφήν, 105. — 21. **εἰσῆλθον,** sc. εἰς τὸ δικαστήριον. *I came into court into your presence* is the literal meaning here. Dissen remarks that εἰσέρχεσθαι and εἰσιέναι are used both of the prosecutor (see p. 501, l. 19) and of the defendant (see p. 1081, l. 13). We may paraphrase the passage: On this count I was indicted and appeared before you and obtained acquittal. — **τό,** sc. τὸ πέμπτον, 82 note **ἀτιμώσαντες.** — 23. **ἡγεμόνας.** *The Heads of the Sections.* At this time (from 358 onwards) the expenses of the Navy were provided for on the same system as the Property Tax. Each of the ten tribes at Athens nominated its 120 wealthiest citizens to serve as Subscribers (συντελεῖς) to the Naval Expenses. These 120 were divided into two Sections (συμμορίαι) of 60. Thus a company would be formed of 1200 Subscribers, divided into 20 Sections. By a separate subdivision they were arranged in four classes of 300 each, in reference to the actual amount of their property. The first (i. e. the wealthiest) class were entitled ἡγεμόνες or πάνυ πλούσιοι or οἱ τριακόσιοι. They appear to have served as a general committee of management, and, in the event of any sudden demand for money, it was their duty to pay over the amount at once to the state (*c. Phænipp.*, p. 146) on behalf of the whole Company. The remaining three classes (ἧττον πλούσιοι) would then reimburse the ἡγεμόνες by paying up their shares in instalments at their convenience. By this system every συντελής paid exactly the same amount of tax, whatever the amount of his income. The reform proposed by the orator was, that the amount of tax henceforward should be in proportion to the respective properties. This change, of course, would be a great relief to the lowest class of συντελεῖς, but the ἡγεμόνες, the δεύτεροι, and the τρίτοι would have obvious reasons for objecting. — 24. **δευτέρους,** *the Second Class,* i. e. the second wealthiest 300. For fuller account of the Sections see Dic. Antiq., εἰσφορά and συμμορία. — **διδόναι,** imperfect: *were for giving me* i. e. *offered me:* δραχμὰς πεντήκοντα αὐτοῖς ἐδίδου, p. 542, l. 9. — 25. **μάλιστα μέν,** *if possible,* lit. *as most to be desired.* This antithesis to εἰ δὲ μή is too common to require illustration. — 26. **καταβαλόντα.** I agree with Kennedy in taking this to mean *after having proposed it* (the law), lit. *having entered it* in the public register, kept ἐν τῷ Μητρώῳ, the Temple of the Mother of the Gods. Whiston and others prefer to interpret "having dropped it," as an expansion of ἐᾶν. But I rather doubt this use of καταβάλλειν in the orators. We have, indeed, in Aristotle, πολλοὶ λόγοι πρὸς αὐτὰ καταβέβληνται ("thrown away upon") *N. E.* (3) 5 (*fin.*). — **ἐᾶν κ. τ. λ.,** *to let it drop under an affidavit.* One method of obstructing a proposed law was for its opponent to take an affidavit that he would prosecute the proposer on a charge of παράνομα (13). This affidavit being taken, the piece of legislation had to be suspended until the action for παράνομα should have been settled. Matters being thus in abeyance, there was a famous opening for collusion and compromise: the prosecutor, for instance, might agree with the legislator that the former would proceed no further with his action if the latter would proceed no further with his law. This or the like conspiracy is implied in the present passage. — **ὑπωμοσίᾳ.** Harpocration mentions another technical meaning of this word = "oath of excuse on the part of a defendant," the object, however, being the same in that case also, viz., to "delay the proceedings." τὸ ὑπερτίθεσθαι δίκην προφάσει χρώμενον ἀποδημίᾳ ἢ νόσῳ ἤ τινι τῶν παραπλησίων μεθ' ὅρκου. — 27. **ὅσα.** *An amount that I should be shocked to mention.* Rhetorical artifice. Dinarchus states the amount at three talents, and declares that the orator took it. εἰσί τινες ἐν τῷ δικαστηρίῳ τῶν ἐν τοῖς τριακοσίοις γεγενημένων ὅθ' οὗτος ἐτίθει τὸν περὶ τριηράρχων νόμον; οὐ φράσετε τοῖς πλησίον ὅτι τρία τάλαντα λαβὼν μετέγραφε καὶ μετεσκεύαζε τὸν νόμον καθ' ἑκάστην ἐκκλησίαν, καὶ τὰ μὲν ἐπώλει ὧν εἰλήφει τὴν τιμήν, τὰ δ' ἀποδόμενος οὐκ ἐβεβαίου; c. *Demosth.*, p. 95, 42. — **104.** P. 37, l. 1. **καὶ ταῦτ'.** *And very natural were these intrigues on their part.* ἔπραττον, as the imperfect of uncompleted action. — **ἦν γὰρ κ. π. λ.** *For under the previous laws they had to serve sixteen together, spending little or nothing themselves but grinding down the impoverished of the citizens; whereas, under my law, they had to return the rated amount in each case according to their property, and the man appeared as trierarch of two triremes who previously subscribed a mere sixteenth to one.* — 2. **λειτουργεῖν.** This infinitive and *τιθέναι* which follows are the subjects of *ἦν*, on which *αὐτοῖς* depends as a dative of reference. Madvig, *G. S.*, 38, a; C. 459. — 3. **μικρὰ καί.** An instance of the Greek idiom which introduces the conjunctive particle where the disjunctive would be most natural. *τὸ δυσμαχώτατον τῶν πραγμάτων ὑμῖν καὶ βέλτιστον*, p. 10, l. 9. In such passages *καί* is emphatic=*yes, even.* — 4. **τοὺς ἀπόρους,** i. e. the fourth class of the *συντελεῖς* above described. — **ἐπιτρίβουσιν.** The orator uses *ἐπιτρίβειν* with another sense of *ruin*, p. 288, l. 20, *ἐπιτρίβει τοὺς ἥρωας κακῶς ὑποκρινόμενος.* — 5. **τὸ γιγνόμενον,** *the result produced:* i. e. the amount arrived at by calculating the rate on the whole amount of their property (*κατὰ τὴν οὐσίαν*). By the law of Nausicus (B. C. 378) the rate was one fifth. — **ἕκαστον,** neut. agreeing with *τὸ γιγνόμενον.* Whiston appears to take it as masculine, but this is in defiance of the construction. — 6. **ὁ.** The ratable proportion of such a person's property must have amounted to twice ten talents, according to the second *κατάλογος*, 106. His property would therefore be one hundred talents. *τὸ γιγνόμενον sup.* note. — 7. **τριηράρχους,** i. e. evading the real duties of the *τριηραρχία* they had even dropped the name under the system of *συντέλεια.* — **Οὐδέ**=*not even.* — **ἔτι**=*any longer. For they did not even any longer call themselves trierarchs.* — 8. **ὥστε δή.** *Sooth, to get these reforms suppressed and evade the compulsion to do what was right, there is nothing in the world which they did not offer.* We have to supply *αὐτοί* with the infinitive *ἀναγκασθῆναι.* — 105. 11. **καθ' ὅ,** *in consequence of which I was prosecuted*=that *line* of procedure which led to the result in question. — 12. **καταλόγους.** *Schedules.* The usual sense of *κατάλογος* is a *muster-roll* or *registered list.* We should have expected the documents which follow, as Newman observes, to contain the names of citizens with the respective amount of their properties specified. As it is, they merely contain what appear to be fragments of laws. — **ΨΗΦΙΣΜΑ.** Clearly spurious from its contents. It is not a decree, but a mere historical memorandum. — **Πολυκλέους.** The date of the trierarchic reforms was 340. Theophrastus, not Polycles, is the Archon Eponymus on record. DINDORF. — **τριη-**

ραρχικόν. Several codices insert εἰς τό before this word. The sense would not be affected; only in that case we must render *in relation to the trierarchic department.* The expression would be harsh and unusual. Newman translates εἰς τό κ. τ. λ., "laid a copy of the law before the admiralty"; an interpretation hardly tenable. — **ἐπεχειροτόνησεν.** *Ratified the law.* The ἐπιχειροτονία νόμων is mentioned in p. 706, l. 7. — **ἀπήνεγκε,** *sc.* γραφήν. *Brought a charge;* literally *carried it off to the Archon.* See note 54. — **τὰς πεντακοσίας.** Legitima erat mille drachmarum pœna sed minui poterat a populo. V. Lelyveld, *de infamia,* p. 235. DISSEN. See Smith's Dic. Antiq., Γραφή. Observe the force of the article = *the usual* or *legal.* — **106. 14. καλόν.** *That precious,* viz., the old one. Ironical: καλήν γε ὕβριν ἧμεν ἂν ὑβρισμένοι, p. 128, l. 2. — **καλεῖσθαι.** *The trierarchs to be summoned, sixteen for each trireme,* ἐπί = *per,* distributive. For the use of the infinitive here, see C. 670; G. 271. — **λόχοις.** Usually of a military division, but Aristotle uses it as correlative with φρατρία and φύλη which are civil (*Pol.,* 5. 8). It is generally supposed to be synonymous with συμμορίαις here. Whiston translates, *according to the associations in the classes.* — **ἐπὶ ἴσον,** *to an equal extent,* i. e. share and share alike, *equally.* — **χορηγίᾳ.** *Discharging their office.* χορ. here is not in its strict acceptation, but in the general sense of λειτουργία, which Wolf notices on the *Leptin.,* p. 462, l. 20. — P. 38. **τοὺς τριηράρχους.** *The trierarchs to be taken for each trireme, according to their property by valuation, from ten talents upwards,* ἀπό first of the "origin" for the selection, secondly, of the "point from which" they should begin to reckon. The notion of κατὰ τίμησιν has been already explained: τὸ γιγνόμενον *sup.* 104 note. — **ἐὰν δέ.** *But if their property be rated at a larger sum, let their service be in the same proportion up to three vessels and a tender;* i. e. for every ten talents in the rating let them provide one trireme; but of this the following limit: no one to be called upon for more than three triremes and a small vessel of war. πλοῖον usually of merchant ships, but used as the generic name for any vessel. — **κατὰ τὴν.** *And let it* (λειτουργία) *be in the same proportion for those persons also whose property* [as rated] *is less than the ten talents, forming themselves into a company to make up the ten talents,* i. e. till the rated amounts of their joint properties make up that sum. The use of εἰς here, as of ἀπό above, is somewhat harsh and overstrained; but the meaning is obvious from the context.

107–109. WAS THIS A SLIGHT SERVICE OF MINE? DID IT NOT

TRANSFER THE BURDEN FROM THE POORER CLASSES TO THE RICH? DURING ALL THE WAR, THANKS TO MY DECREE, THERE WAS NO APPEAL FOR RELIEF PRESENTED BY ANY OFFICER. MY POLICY WAS AS BENEFICIAL TO YOU AS IT WAS CONDUCIVE TO YOUR HONOR. AS I DECLINED TO CONCILIATE THE WEALTHY THEN, SO AM I ABOVE SUSPICION IN THE MATTER OF PHILIP'S BRIBES.

107. 4. **τοῦ.** Genitive of the object of the price, or of the purpose. Madvig, *G. S.*, 65, 6; C. 664; Cu. 573, 3; G. 262, 2; H. 781. — 5. **πλούσιοι.** We have to supply δοκοῦσιν from δοκῶ above. — **τῷ.** Dative of cause. σεμνύνομαι more usually has ἐπί with dative, p. 617, l. 5. — **καθυφεῖναι.** *To compromise.* καθυφεὶς τὸν ἀγῶνα, p. 525, l. 26; p. 563, l. 19; p. 652, l. 21; literally *to drop in an underhand manner.* — 6. **οὐδέ,** *and not only,* the force of the μόνον still continuing. Cf. 93 and 2, note. — 7. **πεῖραν δεδωκέναι,** *to have given proof in action.* p. 663, l. 19, πεῖραν ἔργῳ λαβών. — 8. **πάντα τὸν πόλεμον.** B. C. 340 (73) to 338. — **γιγνομένων.** *Being appointed.* — **ἀποστόλων,** *sup.* 80. — 9. **ἱκετηρίαν ἔθηκε.** *Appealed,* literally *deposited a bough of supplication:* the formal method of appealing to the state for relief. The bough was of olive, bound with wool (εἰρεσιώνη). There were two forms of the appeal; one to the βούλη, the other to the δῆμος: in the former case the suppliant deposited his bough as an offering on the altar in the βουλευτήριον; in the latter case on the altar in the Pnyx. — 10. **παρ' ὑμῖν,** *before you,* sc. the people. Observe the emphatic repetition of the negative οὐχ...οὐκ...οὐχ...οὐ without any connective. It may be expressed by *none.* — 11. **Μουνυχίᾳ.** The altar of Artemis Munychia; so called from its being situated in the vicinity of the port. This proceeding was another form of appeal. Soph., *O. T.*, 2, 3. — **ἐκαθέζετο,** *seated himself,* that is, *took refuge.* — **ἀποστολέων.** *The Naval Board* who superintended the affairs of the ἀπόστολοι. They were ten in number (p. 1147). From ἐδέθη which follows it is clear that they had the power of imprisonment. — 12. **ἔξω,** *at sea,* opposed to αὐτοῦ, *in harbor.* Observe the distinction between καταλειφθεῖσα, *abandoned,* and ἀπελείφθη, *left behind.* — 14. **ἀνάγεσθαι.** *To put out.* p. 910, l. 7: the antithesis to κατάγεσθαι, p. 96, l. 27. — 108. **ἐν τοῖς πένησιν.** *Thrown upon the poorer classes.* τὸ αἴτιον is the accusative case. Madvig, *G. S.*, 31, c. — P. 39, l. 2. **βάσκανον, κ. τ. λ.,** *malignant and malevolent and corrupt.* The allusion in the author's favorite words, βάσκανος, βασκαίνω, βασκανία, is always to malicious mischief, the literal sense which refers to the *evil eye* being merged in

the metaphorical. We have *βάσκανος* again 119, 132, 242, 317. — 4. **οὐδὲ ταπεινόν** is emphatic = *no, nor mean.* — 5. **ἔχων...φανήσομαι,** *I shall be shown to have,* that is, *it will be clearly proved that I have.* — 109. 10. **ἀντί.** *In preference to.* ἀντὶ πολλῶν χρημάτων ἑλέσθαι, p. 9, l. 1. This use of the preposition is very common.

110. I WILL NOW REPLY TO THE SPECIAL CHARGES OF ILLEGALITY IN THE MATTER OF THE PROCLAMATION AND THE AUDIT.

13. **κηρύγματος...εὐθυνῶν,** 55. — 16. **τὰ μέγιστα.** He alludes to the sequel of his policy up to the date of Chæronea. — 18. **ὑπολαμβάνων, κ. τ. λ.** *Conceiving as I do, in the first place, that, next in order, I must render the explanation concerning the illegality itself* (with which I am charged); *in the second place, that, although I say not a word about the sequel of my policy, yet I shall equally* (all the same) *have to my credit that consciousness of the facts which is in each of your hearts.*

111–116. I DO NOT DENY MY RESPONSIBILITY TO AUDIT. BUT I DO DENY ON PRINCIPLE THAT A DONOR IS PRECLUDED FROM A VOTE OF THANKS BECAUSE HE CHANCES TO BE AN OFFICIAL. OTHER DONORS HAVE RECEIVED THE THANKS OF THE STATE FOR THEIR DONATIONS THOUGH HOLDING OFFICE AT THE TIME AND THEREFORE RESPONSIBLE AS I WAS. I CITE THE DECREES TO PROVE IT.

111. 23. **ἄνω καὶ κάτω,** *up and down,* the favorite phrase to indicate total confusion, p. 51, l. 2; p. 120, l. 19; p. 424, l. 27. The French *bouleversement* is analogous. — 24. **διακυκῶν,** *jumbling.* KENNEDY. Perhaps the whole may be paraphrased *in a bewildered medley.* — **παραγεγραμμένων.** *Transcribed for comparison.* The clauses of such laws as conflicted with Ctesiphon's proposal Æschines would exhibit in writing side by side with particular clauses of the latter. Cf. p. 640, l. 20, οὐ τοίνυν τούτους μόνον τοὺς νόμους, ὦ ἄνδρες Ἀθηναῖοι, παραβέβηκεν ἀλλὰ καὶ ἄλλους πολλοὺς οὓς οὐ παραγεγράμμεθα διὰ τὸ πλῆθος. — 26. **τοὺς πολλούς,** sc. νόμους, *the majority of them.* — **τὴν ὀρθήν,** sc. ὁδόν. Adverbial accusative. Cf. 322. — 27. **τοσούτου γὰρ δέω.** *For I am so far from disowning my responsibility, as alleged by the plaintiff in his recent imputation and asseveration, that I own myself to have been responsible, my whole life through, for any commission or policy which I have sustained before you.* διωρίζετο describes the minute exactness with which Æschines had defined the illegal acts: ὧν, by attraction, depending on ὑπεύθυνος: διακεχείρικα of special offices, as distinct from general administration. — **112.** P. 40, l. 4. **ὧν μέντοι γε.** *But for* *what I have given to the commonwealth on my own offer from my private property, for that, I say, I am not responsible, no not for a single day.* — δέδωκα in connection with ἐπαγγειλάμενος amounts to ἐπιδέδωκα. On the subject of ἐπιδόσεις (patriotic donations) cf. Smith, Dic. Ant., sub verbo. — 6. **οὐδ' ἄλλον οὐδένα,** sc. ὑπεύθυνον εἶναι : the subject of εἶναι here passes into the accusative, as it is no longer identical with the subject of φημί. Madvig, *G. S.*, 160, 161. — 7. **οὐδ' ἄν.** *Not even if he chance to be one of the nine Archons*; i. e. however distinctly official may be the position which he holds, it would not preclude him from receiving the thanks of the state for his patriotic donations. That would be virtually making him ὑπεύθυνος (forsooth) in respect of the donations themselves. The orator's argument, put more plainly, is this. I gave large donations to the state : true I was a state official at the time, and so far responsible to scrutiny; but the vote of thanks was awarded to me not at all as a state official, simply as a state benefactor. The argument of Æschines had been that the orator's donations must not be allowed to justify a proceeding which was ipso facto illegal, viz. the crowning of a commissioner before the accounts of his commission had been audited (*c. Ctesiph.*, p. 56). — 10. **φιλόδωρον.** *Munificent.* We should naturally expect a word so formed to mean *fond of gifts*, not *fond of giving.* Schäfer. It is the only exception to the rule of words compounded with φιλο-. — 11. **συκοφάντας.** *To take him before the Pettifoggers and set them to audit his donations.* For λογιστάς or εὐθύνους he substitutes, by contempt, συκοφάντας, the acme of opprobrious designation. It would be monstrous, he means, for such a donor to be cited before the Auditors at all; still more monstrous if the Auditors in question happened, as was likely enough, to be a set of pettifogging scoundrels. — **113.** 15. **οὗτος** is subject of φησίν in the next line. — 16. **ἐπέδωκα.** Cf. ἐπαγγειλάμενος δέδωκα, 112, note, and 28. — **ἐπῄνεσεν.** Æschines had said nothing of the kind. See *c. Ctesiph.*, p. 55, where the whole and sole point is μὴ στεφανοῦν. The orator, however, prefers to cite the substance and not the letter of the charge, for obvious reasons. The strength of the charge lay in its letter entirely. — 17. **οὐ περὶ...οὐδενός,** *yes, but not for any of these.* γέ = *yes but.* So γέ, below, l. 20, may be rendered *yes.* — 21. **οὐκ ἐλογιζόμην,** *made no account of it,* that is, did not charge it to the state. — **ὁ μὲν γὰρ λογισμός, κ. τ. λ.,** *for an account requires audits and examiners, but a free gift deserves thanks and praise.* — 24. **ὁδί.** Deictic: pointing to Ctesiphon, who would be standing by. — **οὕτω ὡρι-**

σται = *this is a settled principle.* — **114.** 26. **ἔθεσιν.** This is an almost irresistible correction for the manuscript ἤθεσιν, suggested by Reiske and adopted by Dindorf. The antithesis of ἔθος, *conventional practice,* to νόμος, *legal rule,* is so very constant, p. 414, l. 8, and 275, τοῖς ἀγράφοις νόμοις καὶ τοῖς ἀνθρωπίνοις ἔθεσι. On the contrast of ἔθος and ἦθος, cf. Aristot., *N. E.,* II. 1. So Holmes. The best editors, however, generally adhere to ἤθεσιν, *habits, ethics,* which is equally appropriate. — 27. **Ναυσικλῆς.** His case corresponds to the orator's only so far, that he was ὑπεύθυνος as being in office (στρατηγῶν) and yet received a crown several times in that period. — **στρατηγῶν.** In command of the Athenian contingent which supported the Phocians in 352. Diodorus, XVI., 37. — P. 41, l. 2. **ὅτε.** There is a various reading ὅτι, *because;* but only in b. The alteration seems undesirable, especially as we need a particle of time to explain the change of tense in ἐστεφανοῦντο compared with the perfects which precede and follow. Drake, in his edition of the two Orations on the Crown, says: The perfect (ἐστεφάνωται and τετίμηται) denotes that Nausicles and Neoptolemus were still living, the imperfect (ἐστεφανοῦντο) that Diotimus and Charidemus were dead. But? The last is rather the relative imperfect. — **Διότιμος.** Possibly the same person as is mentioned in the *c. Mid.,* p. 581, where ὁ Εὐωνυμεύς is added. Spalding considers them identical. Arrian (I., 10. 6) mentions a Diotimus as one of the ten orators whose surrender Alexander demanded. *Sup.,* 41 (*fin.*). — 3. **Χαρίδημος.** Probably the same person as appears in the *c. Aristocr.,* 623 sq., a native of Oreus in Eubœa and commander of the mercenary auxiliaries to Cersobleptes in Thrace. — **οὑτοσί.** Deictic, as ὁδί, 113. We have Neoptolemus mentioned in the *c. Mid.,* p. 583, l. 14. — 4. **ἔργων,** i. e. *public works.* See Dic. Ant., s. v. Ἐπιστάτης. — 7. **ἐξέσται.** *Is to be allowed.* The indic. future is more vigorous in this protasis than the natural optative; cf. 63, **κωλύσει.** — **115.** 9. **τούτοις... αὐτά,** *the very decrees which have been passed in honor of these men.* — **Ἄρχων.** This pendent nominative, in lieu of the usual Ἐπὶ ἄρχοντος, at once suggests a spurious document. — **Φλυεύς.** The deme Phlyes was in the tribe Cecropis. Droysen (p. 924) pronounces Demonicus to be "pseudonymus." The addition of the deme to the name of the archon is unusual and marks the document as spurious. — **ἕκτῃ.** *The twenty-sixth.* Usitatior altera numerandi ratio πέμπτῃ φθίνοντος: sed illius quoque exempla attulit Böckh., *de Arch. Pseudep.,* pp. 150, 154. DISSEN. See Dic. Ant., Calendar. — **δοκεῖ.** On the present tense, cf. 90, διατελέει, note. — **ὅπλων.** *Sup.*, 38, note, s. v.: where also διοικήσεως *inf.* is explained. — **Ἴμβρῳ.** Dissen supposes that this refers to the Social war of 355. Diodorus, XVI., 21. There must have been Athenian garrisons at that time in Lemnos and Imbros both. — **κατοικοῦσιν,** i. e. as colonists (κληροῦχοι). — **χειμῶνας.** Referred by some commentators to the Etesian winds. Dindorf takes it of ordinary bad weather. — **εἰσέπραξε.** *Exacted repayment from.* πῶς οὐχὶ καὶ νῦν προσήκει ὑμᾶς τοῦτον εἰσπρᾶξαί μοι τὰ ἀναλώματα; p. 1227, l. 9. — **116. πρυτάνεων λεγόντων.** The expression is without a parallel, and suggestive of a spurious document. It appears to mean *on the motion of the Prytanes.* — **ποταμοῦ.** According to Winiewski (*Comment.*, p. 63) the river Bocarus in Salamis is intended; but there is nothing to substantiate that view. Newman, with greater probability, suspects that the designation ἐπὶ τοῦ ποταμοῦ is derived, by a blunder, from 216 (*inf.*), where the river meant is certainly the Cephisus, and where there is no allusion to Salamis whatever. — **σκυλευθέντων.** *Stripped of their arms,* which would necessitate fresh supplies in the armory department. Cf. Lys., p. 143, l. 44. — **τοὺς νεανίσκους.** A strange term for στρατιώτας. WHISTON. — P. 42. **Παναθηναίοις.** A time when there would be a great concourse in the city, as in hypoth. 2, ὅτε πλήθη συντρέχει. On the Panathenæa and the Dionysia, see Smith, Dic. Ant., s. v. — **γυμνικῷ,** i. e. on the day of the gymnastic contests, which would appear from this to have been the special attraction of the Panathenæa. — **θεσμοθέτας.** The six junior Archons, besides their judicial functions, were ex officio presidents at the Festivals and on similar public occasions. ἀγωνοθέτας, 84 (*fin.*). See Dict. Ant., s. vv.

117. THESE PERSONS WERE NOT HELD DISQUALIFIED. THEREFORE I MUST NOT BE. I WAS NOT LIABLE ON ACCOUNT OF MY BENEFACTIONS. I HAVE PASSED THE AUDIT OF MY OFFICE. WHY DID YOU NOT OPPOSE MY PASSING AT THE TIME?

3. **οὐκοῦν,** strictly speaking, is always interrogative, equivalent to *nonne igitur* in Latin, and requiring an affirmative answer. In its practical use, however, the interrogative form disappears, and the particle becomes inferential only, but stronger than the simple οὖν. The interrogative force, however, is always present though latent. For instance, the literal translation here would be: Am not I therefore myself also [οὐχ ὑπεύθυνος]? — **ταὐτὰ γάρ.** *For I have, I presume, the same rights as other people about the same things.* The sarcastic

tone of the platitude is obvious. — 4. **τοῖς ἄλλοις**, dative after *ταὐτά*. C. 451; Cu. 436, b; G. 186; H. 603. — **ἐπαινοῦμαι.** *I receive a vote of thanks:* historical present; and the *ὧν* which follows is the same. — 4. **ὑπεύθυνος**, i. e. disqualified by official responsibility from receiving the vote of thanks. The platitude, of course, is again sarcastic. — 6. **ἦρχον.** *I* WAS *in office at the time, no doubt.* And so far he admits that he was *ὑπεύθυνος*. — **καὶ δέδωκά γε**, *yes, and I have given account for that, not for what I gave as patriotic donations.* — **ἐκείνων**, as emphatically distinct from *ὧν ἐπέδωκα*, *sup.*, 112, note on *οὐδ' ἄν*. He could not, he admits, *qua* officer receive any public vote of thanks; but *qua* benefactor he contends that he could. The argument might be defended in equity, but in law it is certainly no reply to Æschines. The reply should have shown either that the orator had ceased to be *ὑπεύθυνος* when the vote was proposed, or else that the law made a special exception in favor of benefactors. — 7. **νὴ Δί'.** *But, forsooth, I did wrong in office. Then why did you not appear to accuse me when the auditors had me up? νὴ Δία* (*you will say: at enim:*) in its constant ironical use to preface a supposed assertion of the opponent. *εἰσάγειν* here has its technical sense of the magistrate presiding in court; see Dic. Ant., *Δίκη*. — 8. **λογισταί.** For a full account of these officers, see Smith's excellent article *Εὐθύνη*, Dic. Ant. The conciseness, vivacity, point, and vigor of this passage are remarkable even in Demosthenes.

118-120. NOW READ THE WHOLE BILL, THAT I MAY PROVE MY OPPONENT'S MALIGNITY BY HIS OMISSIONS AS MUCH AS BY HIS SPECIFICATIONS. HE DWELLS ON THE INIQUITY OF PASSING ME A VOTE OF THANKS, BUT HE QUITE FORGETS TO MENTION WHAT I HAVE DONE TO DESERVE IT.

118. 12. **τούτοις.** Dative of the instrument: antecedent to **οἷς** which is the object of *ἐγράψατο* but attracted into the case of its antecedent. *By the points of the bill which he did not indict, by these very points, I say, his charges shall be proved calumnious.* The usual construction of the verb *συκοφαντεῖν* is with an accusative either of the person or of the thing: I can find no instance of it with a dative, and therefore have deviated from the usual translation, which connects *τούτοις* with *συκοφαντῶν* here (*calumnious in those points which he does attack*) as a contrast to *ἃ οὐκ* above. The dative in this case must be taken as a dative of relation, but the construction will not be so satisfactory. The sense, however, is excellent in either case: cf. *ταῦτ' ἔσθ' ἃ διώ-*

κεις, 119. — **ΨΗΦΙΣΜΑ.** Another spurious document. The date of Ctesiphon's psephisma was 337 B. C. Euthycles was not the Archon: for the first six months Chærondas was in office, then Phrynichus. Again, this document is clearly not ὅλον τὸ γραφέν, for we find in the speech of Æschines, p. 87, that the genuine προβούλευμα began with an allusion to τάφρους as distinct from τείχη. Lastly, the document has no particular connection with what goes before or comes after in the argument. See Böhnecke, Vol. I., p. 581. — **ἐνάτῃ ἀπιόντος,** the twenty-first. See Calendar in Dic. Antiq. — **προσαναλώσας.** Observe the force of the πρός, *in addition* to the public moneys, thus corresponding with the ἐπί in ἐπέδωκε. — **θεωροῖς.** This is Schäfer's, Jacob's, and Dindorf's accepted emendation. They understand θεωροί here to be commissioners who were to superintend the public sacrifices, e. g. the Eleusinia. There is, however, no authority for the existence of such an office at Athens. There is an equally ingenious interpretation of the MS. reading θεωρικοῖς — *the theatrical funds of all the tribes* — assuming that each tribe had a separate fund for this purpose, and that Demosthenes gave 100 minæ to each. Considering that the whole document is spurious, it is a matter of surprise that so much ingenuity should have been lavished upon this single word. — **ἀρετῆς κ. τ. λ.** *Sup.*, 54 note. — **119.** P. 43, l. 5. **παρανόμων γράφει,** *you indict for illegality.* παρανόμων genitive of the crime; γράφει, middle voice to express the act of the prosecutor in *getting* the name of the defendant *entered* (written) by the magistrate. — 7. **ποῖός τις.** *In heaven's name what* WOULD *be the ideal of an utter villain, God-detested and calumnious thoroughly?* ὄντως qualifies the whole sentence, whether we take it with the three epithets or with the verb. πρὸς θεῶν is only used in questions, adjurations, and entreaties; never to strengthen an affirmative oath or assertion. — **120.** 8. **θεάτρῳ.** The peculiar honor of this proclamation *in the theatre* has been already discussed at 83. As regards the number of times (μυριάκις...πολλάκις) besides rhetorical hyperbole, there is also another explanation. We learn from Æschines (pp. 58 sq.) that these proclamations in the theatre in the first instance were made without requiring the sanction of any law whatever: that they then became so frequent as to be a positive nuisance: that their publicity made them to be regarded erroneously as a greater honor than the legally sanctioned proclamations in the Boule or Ecclesia: that on this account the Dionysiac law (83) was ultimately passed to limit them. We may well suppose that the orator refers to the period before the Dionysiac law when he talks of *μυριάκις* and *πολλάκις*, as well as referring to the period after the Dionysiac law was passed when the occasions would naturally be more rare. — 12. **οὐ δύνασαι.** There is another reading *οὐ δύνασθαι*, which would be the same in translation, and but slightly different in meaning. When *ὥστε* is followed by the indicative mood the consequence is described as a certain fact, either in the present or in the past, *coincident in time* with the tense of the verb on which the consecutive sentence depends (33, *μισθοῦται*): when *ὥστε* is followed by the infinitive, the consequence is described as a probable result, *future in time* to the tense of the verb on which the consecutive sentence depends. The former construction is a strong and indisputable assertion; the latter is less strong and less indisputable. Supposing the consequence to be of a negative shape, that negative in the stronger construction will always, of course, be *οὐ*, in the weaker construction it will usually be the weaker negative, *μή*. But if the result is future in time, yet also certain in fact, the two constructions are so far fused that the mood is the infinitive on account of the futurity, and the negative is *οὐ* on account of the certainty. Two examples may be cited at once: —

(1) *οὐ μακρὰν γὰρ τειχέων περιπτυχαὶ*
ὥστ' οὐχ ἅπαντά σ' εἰδέναι τὰ δρώμενα.
EURIP., *Phœn.*, 1357, 8.

Here the knowledge obtained was future to the time when the walls were built, and yet certain, for Creon possessed it.

(2) *ὥστ' οὔτε νυκτὸς ὕπνον οὔτ' ἐξ ἡμέρας*
ἐμὲ στεγάζειν ἡδύν.
SOPH., *Elect.*, 780, 1.

Here the consequence was future to the threat and yet experience had made it a certainty to Clytemnestra. See, however, Mr. Shilleto's admirable note (*de F. L.*, p. 203), and Whiston's note on this passage. C. 671; Cu. 565, 617; G. 266; H. 770, 771. The force of *τὰ οὐ καλά* compared with *τὰ μὴ καλά* is somewhat analogous. — 13. **τὸν αὐτὸν ζῆλον.** This answers Æschines' remark p. 60, *ἀπεῖπη μὴ κηρύττεσθαι τοῖς τραγῳδοῖς ἵνα μηδεὶς ἐρανίζων στεφάνους καὶ κηρύγματα ψευδῆ φιλοτιμίαν κτᾶται.* Demosthenes contends that the greater publicity enhances the benefit, not to the man who receives the crown, but to those who confer it or see it conferred. — **ΝΟΜΟΣ.** Clearly not a genuine document. It does not correspond with the account of the Dionysiac law given by Æschines (p. 58 sq.), nor with the words of Demosthenes in the next section (*πλὴν...ψηφίσηται*), which are obviously a verbal citation. Nor would it at all strengthen the orator's argument here, but quite the contrary. Judging from the two conflicting orations, the law must have run in substance thus: "No crowns are to be proclaimed in the theatre, except the Demos or the Boule sanction them by a special decree. And these crowns let the herald proclaim." Æschines interprets the word "crowns" in this law as limited to *ξενικοὶ στεφανοί* absolutely (*εἴ γέ σέ τις ἄλλη πόλις στεφανοῖ*). Demosthenes interprets the word as including any and every species of "crown." He cites *usage* in confirmation of his view. Æschines cites *law* (the other law about crowns) in confirmation of his. So far as the law goes Æschines seems to be right; but his interpretation could not have been familiar to his audience, or else he would not have required to enforce it with such prolixity (p. 58 sq.). So far as usage went Demosthenes must have been right, or else his audience would never have tolerated his saying what he does. No doubt both interpretations of the Dionysiac law were possible; one was elaborate and strict, the other familiar and lax. There is no need, so far as I can see, to impute insincerity to either view: but in this I differ from former editors. — **121.** P. 44, l. 3. **ἀναγορευέτω,** i. e. *ὁ κῆρυξ.* Reiske however supplies *ἡ βουλή* or *ὁ δῆμος.* Surely the act of proclamation could not be attributed to the corporate body. — **ἐλλεβορίζεις.** *Take a course of hellebore;* the supposed cure for madness. Cf. Horace, 2 *Sat.*, iii., 82, 3; 166. *De A. P.*, 300. — **φθόνου,** gen. of motive; *ἀδικήματος,* of crime. So in English the relation in both may be expressed by *for*. — 8. **ὀμωμοκόσι.** On the oath of the Dicasts see 6, note *οὐ μόνον*; and 2, *τὸν ὅρκον.* — **122.** 10. **δημοτικῷ.** *Patriot.* This is in answer to the passage in Æschines, p. 77, where he draws the picture of the ideal "demotic," attributing five qualities as essential; to be (1) free born, (2) of patriotic family, (3) of high morality, (4) able and eloquent, (5) courageous. The "oligarch," he says, is the antipodes to this; and it is needless to say under which head he classes Demosthenes. — 11. **ἐκδεδωκώς.** *Given out: quasi locavisses faciendum:* cf. p. 522, l. 1. — **κατὰ συγγραφήν.** *To be made by contract.* Dissen cites p. 916, *καὶ οἶδε μὲν πρός σε δύο συγγραφὰς ἐποιήσαντο ὑπὲρ τοῦ συμβολαίου.* The *συγγραφή* was always in writing, the *συμβόλαιον* might or might not be. — **εἶτ...κομιζόμενος,** *and then had it delivered to you deficient in what it ought to have had under the contract.* WHISTON. — 14. **γιγνωσκομένους.** *Or as if patriots were known by their words, and not by their deeds and measures.* *ὥσπερ...γιγνωσκομένους* = tanquam noscerentur; on the construction of this acc. absol. see Madvig, *G. S.*, 82. — 15. **ῥητὰ καὶ ἄρρητα.** *With promiscuous scurrility.* A phrase as common as *dicenda tacenda* in Latin. More exactly rendered by Whiston, *you shout, and call me all sorts of names mentionable and unmentionable.* — **ὥσπερ ἐξ ἁμάξης.** *As if you were on the top of a wagon* taking part in the riot of the *χόες*, the second day of the Anthesteria. See Dic. Ant. Dionysia. Cf. Aristoph., *Ran.*, 416 sq. *Equit.*, 544. *πομπείας*, *sup.*, 11 note. *Billingsgate,* as the Londoners would say. KENNEDY. — 16. **καίτοι καὶ τοῦτο,** sc. *ἐνθυμητέον*. The same phrase is found p. 43, l. 15; p. 442, l. 7; p. 568, l. 12. So *ἐπεὶ κἀκεῖνο*, p. 1097, l. 5, etc. — **123.** 19. **ἔχειν.** *Implies wrongs* (really received by the person who brings the accusation, and who is merely seeking for legal redress). — 20. **βλασφημίας.** *Slanders which enemies come to speak of one another as their own spirit dictates* (although no wrong has really been inflicted, and there is no claim for redress at law). All the editors quote in illustration the notorious passage from Cicero *pro Cœl.*, c. 3: aliud est maledicere, aliud accusare, etc. — 23. **οὐχ ἵνα.** *Not that we might get you together in court* (*εἰς ταῦτα*, sc. *δικαστήρια*), *and then abuse one another with abominations in the way of private scandal*, *ἀπὸ τῶν ἰδίων* : *ex vita privata.* Dissen, who cites aptly p. 1335, *λοιδορουμένους καὶ πλύνοντας αὐτοὺς τἀπόρρητα.* The phrase *κακῶς λέγειν* is exactly Cicero's *maledicere.* — **124.** 27. **πομπεύειν.** *To blackguard.* Cf. *πομπείας* 11. The Greek requires a colloquial equivalent here. — P. 45, l. 1. **ἔλαττον,** sc. *τῶν λοιδοριῶν*. *ἐνταῦθα* is equivalent to *ἐπὶ τῆς πομπείας*. *And yet not even here* (sc. in blackguarding) *is it right for him to come off with less,* sc. than he gave. *δίκαιός ἐστιν*, personal construction for impersonal. C. 573; Cu. 571; H. 777. — 5. **δῆλον ὅτι,** C. 717; Cu. 633; H. 868. — **οὗ μὲν...οὗ δέ,** *where...but where,* C. 433 c.; H. 590. — 6. **ὑπὲρ τούτων.** *Pro civibus Atheniensibus,* according to Reiske, who understands *ἠδίκουν* to have for its object the same *τούτους*. Possibly, however, *τούτων* is neuter and *ἠδίκουν* absolute: *τούτων* in that case would refer to all the offences which Æschines in his speech had imputed to the orator. The *ὑμᾶς ἀδικῶν* below is in favor of Reiske's view. — **125.** 8. **ἀθῷος ἅπασι.** *Scathless on every* *ground; that of law, that of time, that of limitation, that of constant previous awards, that of my never having yet been convicted of doing you a single wrong;* the protasis goes on to τῆς δόξης, the δ' after τῇ πόλει answering the μέν after ἐγώ, *where I, on the one hand, am scathless, ... while the city, on the other, must needs share more or less in the glory of my public acts, there you have met me face to face.* To oppose Demosthenes on this ground was to arraign the character and conduct of the people, who had not only adopted his policy but shared in the honor of it. Herein lay the strength of Demosthenes in all this trial. On ἀπήντηκας, see 15 note s. v.; and on προθεσμίᾳ see s. v. Dic. Ant. — 9. **κεκρίσθαι.** Dissen understands this as referring to the prosecutions conducted by Diondas against the psephisms of Aristonicus and Hyperides, by Patrocles against the trierarchic law of Demosthenes, etc., etc. Cf. pp. 302, 628.

126 - 131. HAVING THUS REFUTED HIS ACCUSATIONS ON THE LEGAL AND TECHNICAL POINTS, I PROCEED NOW TO RETALIATE HIS PERSONALITIES. LET ME GIVE A BRIEF SKETCH OF HIS PARENTAGE AND OF HIS BREEDING.

126. 15. **εὐσεβής** refers, as before, to the oath taken by the Dicasts, 1 **ὅπερ** (end). — 16. **δέδεικται,** i. e. I have shown you all distinctly what your verdict should be as regards the charges of illegality brought by my opponent against Ctesiphon. δεικνύναι here, as before, means *to exhibit* rather than *to prove,* 4 **κἂν μέν.** A different interpretation has, however, been suggested, assuming that a burst of applause had followed the preceding sentence, and that the orator is pleased to estimate it as a clear indication of the coming verdict. No doubt it would have been easy for the orator to provide this burst of applause as at 52. But we should certainly in that case have found him taking far greater advantage of it and expressing himself with a more clear construction. — 17. **βλασφημίας.** This word, according to strict syntax, would follow instead of preceding εἰρημένας. Similar inversions are noticed by Schäfer, p. 323, l. 13; p. 329, l. 29; p. 347, l. 28; p. 361, l. 25, etc. They may be ascribed merely to the taste of rhetorical euphony, the sense remaining unaffected. — 19. **τἀναγκαιότατ'.** *The barest facts:* the minimum sufficient for the absolute exigencies of the situation: *just what is absolutely necessary.* WHISTON. — 20. **καὶ τίνων,** *and of what parentage.* C. 412; Cu. 409. — 21. **λόγους τίνας,** *certain expressions.* Æschin., p. 77, οὐ μέμνησθε αὐτοῦ τὰ μιαρὰ καὶ ἀπίθανα ῥήματα, ἃ πῶς ποθ' ὑμεῖς, ὦ σιδήρεοι ἐκαρτερεῖτε ἀκροώμενοι; κ. τ. λ.

The whole passage in Æschines is well worth perusal. He derides the extravagance of the orator's language in having used such phrases as *ἀμπελουργοῦσι τὴν πόλιν—ἀνατετμήκασι τὰ κλήματα τοῦ δήμου—φορμορραφούμεθα*, and the like. — **διασύρει.** *Sup.*, 27, **διέσυρε.** — **αὐτὸς εἰρηκώς,** *although he has himself said.* The participle is circumstantial. — 22. **φθέγξασθαι.** Here the protasis ends without any apodosis, which, as Hermogenes rightly interprets, is intended to mark indignation. — **127.** 23. **Αἰακός...Μίνως.** Judges in the lower world (see Plato's *Gorgias,* 524), and so models of dignity and integrity. — 24. **σπερμολόγος.** Schäfer cites Eustathius (Hom., *Od.*, p. 1547, 41) *ὁ δὲ κυρίως φασὶ, σπερμολόγος εἶδός ἐστιν ὀρνέου λωβώμενον τὰ σπέρματα* (Aristoph., *Av.*, 232) *ἐξ οὗ οἱ Ἀττικοὶ σπερμολόγους ἐκάλουν τοὺς περὶ τὰ ἐμπόρια καὶ ἀγορὰς διατρίβοντας, διὰ τὸ ἀναλέγεσθαι τὰ ἐκ τῶν φορτίων ἀναρρέοντα καὶ διαζῆν. ἐκ τούτων δὲ τὴν αὐτὴν ἐλάγχανον κλῆσιν καὶ οἱ οὐδένος λόγου ἄξιοι.* We may translate *babbler,* i. e. a retailer of second-hand and second-rate information. So in the notorious passage, Act. Apost., xvii. 18. — **περίτριμμα.** The etymology of this substantive suggests at once its twofold meaning: "something thoroughly rubbed in contact" would suggest either "conversant," "expert," etc., or "trite," "worn out," etc. Aristophanes (*Nub.*, 447) clearly intends *περίτριμμα δικῶν* as a compliment. The orator here as clearly intends the opposite. In either case we have no English equivalent and are reduced to paraphrase. Whiston translates, *a drudge of the forum;* Kennedy, *a hack of the market.* — **ὄλεθρος.** *A brute of a secretary* or *a wretch of a clerk.* Æschines appears to have acted in this capacity to some of the Athenian authorities judging from 261, *γραμματεύειν τοῖς ἀρχιδίοις.* The substantive used as an epithet in lieu of the adjective is not uncommon in Attic. — 26. **ἐπαχθεῖς,** 10, **εἰ δὲ πολλῷ** (*fin.*). — **πορίσασθαι.** The verb insinuates that the phrases were *far-fetched.* Schäfer cites p. 938 and p. 1392 for similar usage. We may render, *to imagine such offensive expressions.* — 27. **ὦ γῆ, κ. τ. λ.** The citation is almost verbatim from the last paragraph in the speech of Æschines, *Ἐγὼ μὲν οὖν ὦ γῆ καὶ ἥλιε καὶ ἀρετὴ καὶ σύνεσις καὶ παιδεία ᾗ διαγιγνώσκομεν τὰ καλὰ καὶ τὰ αἰσχρά...* Having been taxed by his opponent with using florid language the orator seizes this obvious opportunity for a retort. — **128.** P. 46, l. 4. **κάθαρμα.** According to the Scholiasts, in time of public pestilence or other national diaster the vilest members of the state were put to a violent death as scapegoats for the whole community. Aristoph., *Plut.*, 454, *Ran*, 733,

Eq., 1136, etc. From this the word would naturally become a term of extreme abuse: *You scum of creation.* — 6. **ἧς τῶν μέν.** *Of those who have really enjoyed it not a man would use such an expression about himself, but would even blush if any else were to utter it.* Whiston is doubtless right in taking this to refer to the remarks of Æschines, p. 88. — 9. **τοῖς δ' ἀπολειφθεῖσιν.** *While to those who, like you, have missed education but affect it, the result is, that whenever they speak they pain their hearers by their brutality, but never appear educated men.* On ἀναισθησίας, see 35, **ἀναλγησίας.** — **129.** 15. **Θησείῳ.** See Smith's *Dict. Geogr.*, Athens. This beautiful and well-preserved temple is now the national museum of Athens. — 16. **διδάσκοντι γράμματα.** The school-work of the period consisted in reading, writing, and reciting passages of poetry with explanations. Cf. Plat., *Protag.*, 325 E. In the *F. L.*, p. 419, the father of Æschines is described as himself διδάσκων γράμματα, somewhat inconsistent, though not entirely so, with this passage and that below on p. 313. — 16. **χοίνικας.** *Leg-irons* (Aristoph., *Plut.*, 276), so called from their resemblance in shape to the standard vessel of dry measure. The Scholiast interprets this as merely an insinuation that Tromes was a worthless slave under perpetual punishment. Dissen compares Plaut., *Capt.*, 3. 5. 64 and 75: *crassas compedes.* — **ξύλον.** Here apparently of the wooden *collar* for the neck. Aristoph., *Nub.*, 592, and Plaut., *Capt.*, 2. 2. 107, are cited by Whiston in illustration. Cf. Act. Apost., xv. 24. — 17. **μεθημερινοῖς.** *By daylight.* Coitus qui sunt imprimis flagitiosi. DINDORF. χρῆσθαι μεθημερινοῖς γάμοις est de die in fornice prostare. REISKE. — 18. **κλεισίῳ.** *Hovel:* according to others, *brothel* here. Bekker reads κλισίῳ and Σ κλεισείωι. — **καλαμίτῃ.** The clew for interpreting this is, no doubt, to be found in the *F. L.*, p. 419, where the father of Æschines is described as keeping school πρὸς τῷ τοῦ Ἥρω τοῦ ἰατροῦ. Ingenious commentators show us how καλαμίτης, *the man of splints*, is a natural synonym in a facetious passage for ἰατρός. I think, however, they all omit to notice that the orator intends a pun also on the name *Heros* here. He is affecting to invest the early life of Æschines with supernatural influences, and as he alluded to the Theseum just before, so now by way of ridicule he introduces another *hero.* I have, therefore, with Dindorf, retained the small η, though I quite agree with those who believe that the allusion is to Heros the physician. So Holmes. In a paper read before the American Philological Association at Easton, in 1873, Prof. Goodwin explains the τῷ καλαμίτῃ ἥρωϊ as referring to a Scythian physician, named Toxaris, who came to Athens in the time of Solon, died there and was buried in the Cerameicus, and, his spirit a century later having given the Athenians advice whereby a plague was caused to cease, he was deified and worshipped as the "Stranger Physician." His monument bore on it a representation of a Scythian bowman with a strung bow in one hand and a book in the other. Now καλαμίτης can mean *bowman* (or more exactly *arrow-man*) as κάλαμος very often means an arrow of reed. This monument was a relic of antiquity even in the time of Demosthenes, and he naturally refers to it as marking a well-known locality, which, as recent discoveries show, would have been not far from the Theseum. — **τὸν καλὸν ἀνδριάντα.** Dissen cites from Bekk., *Anecd.*, p. 394, ἐν τῇ συνηθείᾳ λέγουσιν αἱ μητέρες περὶ τῶν υἱῶν, ὁ καλὸς ἀνδριάς μου. He also sees an allusion to the fact, that Æschines avoided all gesticulation in speaking (*F. L.*, p. 421). The author of the *Vita Æschinis* describes him as εὐφυής, "a fine figure of a man." — 19. **τριταγωνιστήν.** *A tip-top actor of third parts:* see Dict. Ant., Histrio. — **ἐξέθρεψε.** To be taken in connection with γαμοῖς...χρωμένη, which denotes the left-handed *means* by which she *reared up* her son, *the beautiful statue and tip-top actor of third parts.* — 21. **τριηραύλης** has no exact English equivalent, but may be rendered *boatswain* as the nearest. The crew of a trireme rowed to the music of a flute-player who marked the time for them. So Aristophanes mentions αὐλῶν κελευστῶν as a prominent feature of the dockyard. *Acharn.*, 554. Kennedy translates it *galley-piper.* — 22. **ἀνέστησεν.** *Raised her out of this honorable trade.* There is a *double entendre* in this sarcasm, depending on the literal meaning of ἀνιστάναι as contrasted with καθῆσθαι, καθέζεσθαι ἐπ' οἰκήματος, which were euphemisms to describe prostitution. — 23. **νὴ τὸν Δία.** Here a simple asseveration, not as above, 117. — 130. 27. **οὐδὲ γὰρ...καταρᾶται.** *For they* (sc. the acts of his life, ὧν αὐτὸς βεβίωκεν) *were not of an every-day sort, but such as the nation execrates.* This sentence in Σ precedes the sentence ταῦτα μὲν οὖν...ἄρξομαι, and in that reading the subject of ἦν would be Æschines and the antecedent of οἷς his parents: *he was not the son of every-day persons, but,* etc. So Schäfer and Jacobs. The arrangement of my text is the same with Dindorf's, and is approved by quite the majority of editors. Indeed the context alone is enough to settle the question. — P. 47, l. 1. **ὀψέ, κ. τ. λ.** *For it is quite lately, — lately do I say? — nay it is yesterday only or the day before* *that he has become at once an Athenian and an orator.* A good instance of the corrective μὲν οὖν (*immo vero*). Æsch., *Eum.*, 38; Eurip., *Hipp.*, 1009; Plat., *Gorg.*, 466. — 3. **δύο συλλαβάς.** Referring only to the change of the name Tromes into Atrometus, of which the former was a fit name for a coward (τρέμω) and a slave, while the latter was suggestive of an *intrepid* freeman. — 5. **Ἔμπουσαν.** As a nickname no doubt. Cf. Aristoph., *Ranæ*, 289, where the Scholiasts explain that it was the title of a malignant goblin. In the *F. L.*, p. 256, Æschines speaks of his mother's brother as Glaucus, whence it has been fairly inferred that his mother's real name was Glaucis. — 6. **πάντα.** Incessant changing of shape and figure is alleged by the Scholiast as the distinctive quality of the goblin Empusa. The coarse *double entendre* here is sufficiently obvious from what has preceded. — **131.** 9. **ἐκ.** *Instead of:* as coming *out of* one state into the other. The idiom is very common. Soph., *O. T.*, 454, *Antig.*, 1093, etc. — 10. **οὐχ ὅπως.** *Not only not.* The idiom involves an ellipsis of λέγω. Fully stated it would mean, "I do not mention your showing gratitude: that would be absurd to expect in your case though it would be merely natural in any one else." Our own idiom "not to speak of" is often similarly used. Analogous are the uses of μὴ ὅτι and οὐχ ὅτι. For examples see Madv., *G. S.*, 212; C. 717, g; Cu. 622, 4; H. 848, c. — 13. **ἄρα.** *It seems* (i. e. in Æschines' representation): ironical, as in 22. — 15. **πράττων.** In strong antithesis to the εἴρηκεν which immediately precedes.

132–134. As a specimen of the atrocious conduct of Æschines let us take the case of Antipho. He was arrested by me as a traitor, but nearly escaped penalty through the intrigues of my opponent. And for this the Areopagus cancelled the latter's appointment as advocate of Athens before the Amphictyonic council, regarding him as a traitor.

132. 16. **Ἀντιφῶντα.** The case is mentioned by Plutarch (*Vit. Demosth.*, 14) and by Dinarchus (*c. Demosth.*, p. 98, l. 25). The latter deplores Antiphon as a victim. The facts seem to have been as follows. Antiphon had been disfranchised, for some reason not recorded. In revenge he attempted to betray his country to Philip, and conspired with him in a design of burning the Athenian fleet. The date, according to Dissen's calculation, would be shortly after the διαψήφισις held in the year 346. Demosthenes denounced Antiphon before the Ecclesia, who, however, acquitted him. Demosthenes then

brought him before the Areopagus, who had the right to take extraordinary cognizance of extreme cases where the safety of the state was involved. They condemned Antiphon; but their sentence (ἀπόφασις) would then require to be formally approved by the Boule and Ecclesia. After this Antiphon would be tried once more before the Heliæa. We know that the result was his torture and execution. He appears to have been one of the family of Harmodius according to Dinarchus (*l. c.*), but we know nothing more of his history. He is not to be confounded with Antiphon, one of the ten Attic orators. — **ἀποψηφισθέντα** = struck off the register of voters: see Smith, Dic. Ant., διαψήφισις. — 21. **ἐν δημοκρατίᾳ.** Plutarch himself describes this proceeding of Demosthenes as σφοδρὰ ἀριστοκρατικόν. — 22. **ψηφίσματος.** *Warrant,* to be granted by a vote of the Ecclesia. The orator seems to have acted so far illegally that he arrested Antiphon in his own house, although he was not justified in doing so either by official position or sanction of the people. — **133.** 24. **᾿Αρείου.** Smith, Dic. Ant., Areiopagus. — 25. **οὐ δέοντι.** Another instance of meiosis: *anything but opportunely.* The absence of the article gives additional strength to the phrase, and is the more appropriate for an antithesis to ἐν δέοντι. — **ἐπεζήτησε.** *Made further inquiry:* the force of ἐπί in composition is here strongly marked. — 27. **ἐξήρπαστ᾽ ἄν.** *Such a traitor as this would have been snatched out of your grasp, and having slipped through the clutches of penalty would have been despatched to freedom by this master of imposing eloquence.* — P. 48, l. 2. **στρεβλώσαντες.** The στρέβλη seems to have corresponded exactly to the *rack* of our own semi-barbarous ages. A list of modes of torture in which this is included will be found in the notorious passage, Aristoph., *Ran.*, 620 sq. Some discussion has been raised as to how a free Athenian could have been put to the torture at all? There are two obvious answers: (1) Antiphon as ἀποψηφισθείς was no longer a free Athenian; (2) The rack was applied, not for his examination under torture, but for this execution under sentence. See Smith, Dic. Ant., sub. Βάσανος. — νῦν = *as it was.* — 3. **γε** intensifies the bitterness of the taunt: *as you* OUGHT *to have done to this creature likewise,* sc. so far *at least* as your duty and his deserts were concerned. — **134.** 5. **σύνδικον.** *Advocate:* i. e. they retained him to plead their case before the Amphictyonic Council. His appointment, however, was afterwards cancelled, as we see, by the Areopagus, on suspicion of his sympathies with Macedon, which naturally, on this as on other occasions, was opposed to the Athenian interests. Hyperides was anti-Macedonian in his politics. — 6. **τοῦ ἐν Δήλῳ.** The question at issue, which had been already long disputed, was whether the Athenians or the Delians were entitled to have the custody of the temple of Apollo at Delos: the date of the case being tried before the Amphictyonic Council was 345. — **ἥσπερ.** By attraction to ἀγνοίας instead of the dative, which would be the natural construction. There is a various reading ἀφ' ἥσπερ but only in a small minority of the MSS. — 7. **προσείλεσθε.** This is Wolf's emendation, adopted by Dindorf, in place of προείλεσθε MSS. Schäfer approves it as especially consistent with the καὶ in κἀκείνην. Translate, *associated to you that body in addition*, i. e. requested the Areopagus to co-operate in their deliberations with the Boule and the Ecclesia, giving them absolute power over the decision to be formed. Those who read προείλεσθε interpret it εἵλεσθε πρὸ ὑμῶν, i. e. *delegated to act for you.* No other instance can be cited of the verb being thus used, but certainly it is a possible interpretation. — 10. **ἀπὸ τοῦ βωμοῦ.** *Tendering their vote from the altar*, i. e. advancing to vote immediately after having taken an oath with the fullest solemnity. Taylor cites p. 1265, l. 6, πρὸς τὸν βωμὸν ἄγοντες καὶ ἐξορκίζοντες. Cic., *pro Balb.*, 5: ut mos Græcorum est, iurandi causâ ad aras accederet. — 11. **οὐδεμία.** The extreme solemnity of the occasion has been mentioned as enhancing the effect of this public censure on Æschines. — 135. **ΜΑΡΤΥΡΕΣ.** Another spurious document according to Droysen and Winiewski, but defended, as usual, by Vömel. The question is not worth discussing. But we may notice as irregular the absence, in each case, of the name of the witness's father; the phrase ὑπὲρ ἁπάντων which appears so redundant and superfluous; and the absence of any details about the voting on which the orator has so strongly insisted in 134. — 14. **λέγοντος.** Σ has μέλλοντος, which would much improve the sense, an ellipsis of λέγειν being easy: b has μέλλοντος λέγειν and adds αὐτὸν after ἀπήλασεν. I believe, however, that Dindorf's text is the most correct, and we must take λέγοντος as imperfect, *when he was going to speak.*

136. Take another instance of my opponent's political conduct in contrast with mine. When Python at the convention was vituperating Athens, I denounced and crushed him, Æschines aided and abetted him.

18. **νεανίου.** Æschines was 45 in the year referred to (345).

Clearly there is no allusion here to age but only to character. The same sense of violence or extravagance is constantly found in *νεανιεύεσθαι* and *νεανικόν*, of which the Lexica give abundant examples. We may here render *this gallant fellow* as spoken in irony. *γε* is also ironical. — 19. **ὅτε.** Either just before Chæronea (Diodor., XVI., 85) or in the year 344 (p. 81, l. 23). The latter view is supported by Winiewski. 'We know nothing about the facts except from this passage and that in the *De Halonneso* (p. 81, *l. c.*). That Python was a famous orator is attested by Demosthenes, p. 1469, l. 18, and Æschines, p. 44, l. 35.— P. 49, l. 1. **ἐν αἰσχύνῃ.** *To plunge in disgrace.* The phrase is exceptional, as Schäfer notices. — 3. **θρασυνομένῳ.** *Bragging and bursting full upon you.* Colloquial phraseology. *ῥεῖν* of eloquence is very common. Aristoph., *Eq.*, 527, etc.; Juvenal, X., 128 : torrentem et pleni moderantem frena theatri. Dissen also cites Hor., 1 *Sat.*, II., 28.

137. ANOTHER INSTANCE. ÆSCHINES WAS CAUGHT CONFERRING WITH THAT NOTORIOUS SPY OF PHILIP'S, ANAXINUS.

11. **Ἀναξίνῳ.** A native of Oreus in Eubœa, who came to Athens in 341 ostensibly to make some purchases for Philip's Queen Olympias (Æschin., p. 85). At this date the Athenians were contemplating the liberation of Eubœa and a despatch of forces to assist the Hellespont. Anaxinus was, rightly or wrongly, denounced and executed as a spy for these proceedings (*l. c.*). Æschines especially taunts the orator with having caused the death of a man who had been his host in Eubœa. — **κατασκόπῳ.** We have here, of course, a brilliant *petitio principii*. Whether Anaxinus was a spy or not, history has left uncertain. But the argument *noscitur a sociis* falls through in the other event, and therefore the orator promptly assumes that he was. — **ΜΑΡΤΥΡΕΣ.** Another spurious document. The witnesses are mentioned without the address of their several demes. No one of the name of Nicias is found in the list of Archons at or near this year (341). — **ἐπωμόσαντο,** *swore to it before the generals.*

138. I COULD ADD MUCH MORE TO THE SAME EFFECT. BUT YOU NEVER FEEL THESE THINGS AS YOU OUGHT.

18. **οὕτω πως,** *somewhat as follows.* Accordingly the following clause is without a connective as being explanatory. *ὧν* would regularly be acc. = in respect to which, but is in the gen. by attraction. — P. 50, l. 3. **τίθεται.** *Stored, deposited, laid on record,* a financial expression in the first instance, p. 1236 (*fin.*), p. 186, l. 10, etc. *Scored*

up is the closest rendering here. — 4. **οὐδ' ἦν...ὀργήν**, *nor for proper resentment*, acc. after εἰς. — **δεδώκατε.** *You have, through a vile custom, given vast license to any one who wishes to trip and slander him who speaks for any of your interests.* In ὑποσκελίζειν we have another wrestling metaphor. — 8. **ἀνταλλαττόμενοι.** *Bartering for.* The sentiment has been already illustrated in 3, note **ἕτερον δέ.** — 11. **τάξιν.** Cf. 13. **τάξει**, note.

139. Before the declaration of war Æschines did his best to help Philip; and after the war began he never proposed a single measure for the good of Athens.

12. **μὲν δή.** The sense of these two particles combined is usually to dismiss a consideration; cf. the notorious phrase τοιαῦτα μὲν δὴ ταῦτα. The δή in itself implies so strong an assertion of the protasis that no further question can possibly be raised about that, whatever may be said about something else. The μέν paves the way for the introduction of that something else, if necessary, in the apodosis. But no apodosis is absolutely required. For examples see Soph., *El.*, 103; Platon., *Polit.*, 287, *Prot.*, 315. — 16. **τὰ πλοῖα.** *Sup.*, 73, **καὶ μήν.** — **Χερρόνησος.** *Sup.*, 92, **Χερρονησιτῶν.** — 17. **'Αττικήν.** The reference is here to the seizure of Elatea in 339 (the autumn) when Philip was appointed by the Amphictyonic Council to command the forces attacking Locris. The excitement caused at Athens by this seizure of Elatea we read 169 sq. — 18. **ἐνειστήκει.** 89, **ἐνστάς**, note. — 20. **ἰαμβειοφάγος.** The Scholiasts interpret this φιλολοίδορος, and so we find in the *Etym. M.*, s. v. 'Ιαμβοφάγος, the Iambic verse being the distinctive metre of lampoon: 'Ιαμβίζειν γὰρ τὸ σκώπτειν ἐστίν. But surely we must also understand an allusion here to that already threadbare topic, the histrionic profession of Æschines. Of course the *double entendre* cannot be preserved by any English. Whiston's rendering, *mouther of iambics*, is as good as any. — 22. **δειξάτω**, i. e. I will sacrifice part of the time allowed me for speaking, to give him the opportunity, if he can take it, forsooth. — 23. **ὕδατι.** ἐγχεῖται γὰρ τὸ μὲν πρῶτον ὕδωρ τῷ κατηγόρῳ καὶ τοῖς νόμοις καὶ τῇ δημοκρατίᾳ, τὸ δὲ δεύτερον ὕδωρ τῷ τὴν γραφὴν φεύγοντι καὶ τοῖς εἰς αὐτὸ τὸ πρᾶγμα λέγουσιν. Æsch., 82. A description of the clepsydra, by which the time allowed to each speaker was measured, is given in Smith's Dic. Ant. Whiston alludes, in this connection, to the joke at the sobriety of Demosthenes, viz., that other men *spoke* by water, he *composed* by it. — 24. **θάτερον.** An obvious ellipsis of ποιῆσαι, or, better, αἱρεῖσθαι.

The construction is very common: p. 113, l. 10. Platon., *Charm.*, 160 c. With an impersonal subject the ellipsis would be of *γενέσθαι*. — **ἢ μηδὲν κ. τ. λ.** *That either he proposed no measures conflicting with mine because he could find no fault in what I was then doing, or else that he did not bring forward better measures than mine because he was studying the interest of the enemy.* The participial sentences are causal. Madvig, *G. S.*, 174, b; C. 674; Cu. 581; G. 277, 2; H. 789; the force of *παρά* is here decidedly *against:* not simply *beside* but *beside, with the object of contesting and obstructing.* — 27. **φέρειν εἰς μέσον** (*proferre in medium*), as usual, is merely the technical phrase for publication.

140, 141. IF HE FRAMED NO POLICY, DID HE AT ANY RATE HOLD HIS TONGUE WHEN MISCHIEF WAS IN THE WIND? NAY, HE MONOPOLIZED THE BEMA. REMEMBER THAT MONSTROUS CASE OF THE AMPHISSIAN LOCRIANS. I MOST SOLEMNLY SWEAR TO TELL YOU THE WHOLE TRUTH ABOUT IT.

140. P. 51, l. 1. **Ἆρ' οὖν.** *Did he then make no speeches either* (*as he certainly moved no measures*) *when it was needful to do some mischief?* The point is this: no single psephism of Æschines' proposing can be found in the records of the war period (139); but he made plenty of speeches, —and he always spoke with a mischievous intent. Reiske and Schäfer are both anxious to limit the clause *ὥσπερ — ἔγραφεν* by understanding either *τότε* or *ἡνίκα ἐργάσασθαί τι ἔδει καλόν*. But they thus ignore the obvious antithesis of *ἔγραφεν* to *ἔλεγεν*. He moved nothing, but he said plenty; and all that he said was bad. — 2. **οὐ μὲν οὖν.** *Nay, no one else had a chance of speaking,* i. e. he let no one else get a hearing. — 3. **τὰ μὲν ἄλλα.** *Other things the state could bear, as it seems, and this man could do without detection.* C. 677, f.; Cu. 590; G. 279, 2; H. 801. — 6. **τέλος,** *finishing stroke.* — 8. **δόγματα,** i. e. the decrees passed by the Amphictyonic Council respecting these Locrians of Amphissa. Schäfer compares *Μεγαρέων ψήφισμα*, "the vote concerning the Megarians": Thucyd., I., 140. — 8. **τό** has here its original force of a distinctive pronoun. See Donaldson, *New Cratylus*, 148, and note **ἃς** *μὲν*, 71 *sup.* — 9. **ἐκνίψει.** *Wash out,* strictly of the *hands.* The middle voice here denotes action on self. On the metaphor, which is frequent and familiar, particularly in dramatic literature, ancient and modern, cf. Eur., *I. T.*, 1223, *ὡς φόνῳ φόνον μύσαρον ἐκνίψω*. — 10. **οὐχ οὕτω.** *You will not talk enough for* THAT, however prominent and prolix you may show yourself as a speaker. The emphasis falls on *οὕτω*. — **141.** 11. **Καλῶ.** This passage may well be compared with the exordium. He justifies the solemnity of the language in the next paragraph. — 13. **πατρῷος.** *Father-god*, and hence tutelary divinity. Apollo, according to Athenian mythology, was the father of Ion by Creusa, daughter of Erectheus, king of Athens, and wife of Xuthus. Ion succeeded to the throne. (Eurip., *Ion*, 1574, etc.) Hence the Athenians had *πατρῷαι θυσίαι* at Delphi. All the Ionian states seem to have worshipped the Pythian Apollo as their *θεὸς πατρῷος*. See Müller, *Dor.*, I., p. 244. — 15. **εἴποιμι καὶ εἶπον,** *if I speak the truth and did speak it then immediately.*

142 - 144. WHY HAVE I MADE THESE SOLEMN ASSEVERATIONS? BECAUSE, WHATEVER STRONG PROOF I ADDUCE, YOU WILL HARDLY BELIEVE ÆSCHINES HAD THE POWER TO DO SUCH MISCHIEF. JUST WHAT HAPPENED IN THE PHOCIAN CASE. I WARNED THE ECCLESIA AND THEY WOULD NOT BELIEVE ME.

142. 23. **ἔχων.** Concessive: and so *εἰδὼς* which follows. Madvig's *G. S.*, 174 b; C. 674, f; Cu. 582; G. 277, 5; H. 789, f. — **δημοσίῳ.** *The Archives:* the word describes any public building: its character is settled here by the context. Herod., VI., 52, 57. — 26. **ἐλάττων.** Minor quam ut conficeret: *incapable of*, literally *less than the mischief*, i. e. unequal to such a magnitude of mischief. Cf. the analogous use of *μείζους* in the *F. L.*, p. 350 (*init.*). — P. 52, l. 1. **Φωκέας,** 18, and *Introduction* II. — 143. 2. **'Αμφίσσῃ.** This city belonged to the Locri Ozolæ and stood on the Phocian frontier. Ingenious Scholiasts have noticed that the words *τὸν γὰρ...'Ελάτειαν* make a hexameter. — 3. **'Ελάτειαν.** Metropolis of Phocis on the frontier of Epicnemidian Locris. — 6. **εἷς ἀνήρ.** *Was the author in his single self of the greatest disasters.* The common use of *εἷς* as an intensive in connection with a superlative. Cf. Soph., *Trach.*, 459, *οὐχὶ χἀτέρας | πλείστας ἀνὴρ εἷς 'Ηρακλῆς ἔγημε δή;* — 6. **τότ',** i. e. when Æschines had just come back from acting as deputy at the Amphictyonic Council, who had declared war on the Amphissians at his instigation. We must compare throughout Æschines' own account of this (p. 71 sq.). — 9. **ἐκ παρακλήσεως.** Dissen aptly remarks that the name *παράκλητοι* was given to the party of friends who would rally round an accused person, or a person in any critical position, the Latin *advocati*. Cf. the use of the word in the New Testament, rendered in the common version sometimes Advocate, and sometimes Comforter. We may paraphrase here: *his clique who were seated by him.* — 10. **οἱ δέ**=*the rest.* — **144.** 15. **ἐκωλύθητε.** But ac-

cording to Æschines (*l. c.*), Demosthenes *did* impress his views on the meeting, and it was owing to him that the Athenians dissented from the Amphictyonic policy instead of joining the attack upon the Amphissians. — 15. **εὖ...συντεθέν.** *εὖ* passim seiungitur a voce ad quam pertinet. See Heind. at Platon., *Charmid.*, p. 111 (Schäfer). — 17. **δεινότης.** *Craft:* calliditas (Schäfer).

145–159. FOR PHILIP'S PLANS IT WAS INDISPENSABLE TO CREATE HOSTILITIES AGAINST US ON THE PART OF THEBES AND THESSALY. HENCE HIS INTRIGUE IN THE AMPHICTYONIC COUNCIL, WHICH LED TO THE SACRED WAR, AND FOR WHICH HE EMPLOYED ÆSCHINES AS AN INSTRUMENT. THE ACCOUNT ÆSCHINES GAVE YOU IS FALSE. THE ATTACK ON THE LOCRIANS WAS UNPROVOKED. PHILIP'S APPOINTMENT AS COMMANDER-IN-CHIEF WAS ACHIEVED BY THE MEAN PARSIMONY OF THE AMPHICTYONS WHO WISHED TO ESCAPE THE EXPENSES OF THE WAR. DIRECTLY HE WAS APPOINTED HE DROPPED THE LOCRIAN BUSINESS AND SEIZED ELATEA. LISTEN TO THE DOCUMENTS WHICH PROVE WHAT I SAY. FOR ALL OUR SUFFERINGS ÆSCHINES, AS A TOOL OF PHILIP, IS DISTINCTLY RESPONSIBLE AND TO BLAME.

145. 24. **λῃστῶν.** *Guerillas.* The orator wishes to deny the regular army any share in such successes as were won (146). The chief damage done to Macedon, he alleges, was the interference with their commere by these irregular marauders. — 25. **ἐκ τῆς χώρας.** By constructio prægnans for *οὔτε γὰρ ἐξήγετο τῶν ἐν τῇ χώρα γιγνομένων ἐκ τῆς χώρας οὐδέν.* C. 704; H. 680. — **146.** P. 53, l. 1. **μήτε διιέντων.** *If they did not allow him a passage* through their territory. The negative (*μή*) has its usual force with a participle, of introducing a conditional clause. — 2. **κρατοῦντι.** Concessive: cf. 142. *κρατεῖν* with the accusative = *to conquer:* with the genitive = *to conquer and hold.* The accusative is that of relation, not of the direct object. Madv., 31; C. 480, b; Cu. 400, c; G. 159; H. 544, a. *Though victorious in war over the generals you were in the habit of sending out, of whatsoever sort they were* (*for I pass this*), *it was his fortune to suffer losses from the very nature of the locality and the circumstances of each party.* — 4. **φύσει τοῦ τόπου.** Dissen compares *Philipp.*, I. 48 (p. 93), *τόπον τῆς χώρας.* He could not attack them by land because Thebes and Thessaly obstructed his approach; and he could not attack them by sea because their navy was superior. — **ὑπαρχόντων ἑκατέροις.** Macedon was strong in land forces, Athens in maritime: but the land forces were useless, as has been just explained: so that Athens had the advantage in point of armament in the aggregate. — **147.** 6. **συμπείθοι.** *Induce to join him.* Hence the element συμ- is introduced. There is a mixture of moods in this conditional construction which may thus be preserved in English: *His idea was that, were he to try and induce either Thebes or Thessaly to join him in attacking you, no one would listen to him; but supposing him elected commander as having taken up their common grievances, then his expectation was that he would, with comparative ease, deceive them partly and partly persuade them.* The imperfect optative συμπείθοι introduces the more improbable alternative (*si persuaderet*), the aorist subjunctive αἱρεθῇ states the very condition which was actually fulfilled afterwards (*si electus fuerit*): the imperfects ἡγεῖτο, ἤλπιζε suggest the duration and deliberate character of Philip's plans. — 11. **'Αμφικτύοσι.** *For the Amphictyons.* Dativus commodi precisely. — 12. **ταραχήν.** *A disturbance at the Pylæa.* The meeting of the Council was called Πυλαία from the place of meeting, Thermopylæ; so also the members were called Πυλαγόραι. See Dic. Ant., Amphictyons. περί here is of time and place both. — 12. **εἰς ταῦτ'.** *For thereupon he thought they would immediately address him with entreaties,* i. e. to co-operate with them in the quarrel. — **148.** 14. **παρ' ἑαυτοῦ.** Philip obtained this privilege as part of his victory in the Phocian war. — **ἱερομνημόνων.** *Religion-commissioners.* An office apparently for life, at any rate superior to that of the Pylagoræ. See Smith, Dic. Ant., for a full discussion of the point. — 15. **ἐκείνου.** Philip: change of pronoun to avoid repeating ἑαυτοῦ. Schäfer recites exactly the same construction from Xen., *Hell.*, I. vi. 14. — **εἰσηγοῖτο.** *Were to introduce this matter.* The optative here of the condition which did not happen, the subjunctive ᾖ of the condition which did. See 147, **συμπείθοι.** — 18. **ὑπεναντίων.** *His* (sc. Philip's) *adversaries.* The element ὑπ- modifies the force of the adjective a little: there was no open war between Athens and Macedon just at this period. Still ὑπεναντίος and ἐναντίος, according to the Lexica, are used almost synonymously. — 19. **λήσειν.** *He* (Philip) *would evade suspicion.* The subject of λήσειν to be taken from ἐνόμιζε which precedes. — **149.** 22. **προβληθείς.** *Was proposed as Pylagoras, and three or four hands having been held up, was declared to be duly elected:* that the whole thing was a job, or an oversight, is what the orator wishes to imply. — 25. **λαβών.** *With all the prestige of the city about him.* Like ἔχων, φέρων, ἄγων, so λαβών is frequently thus used in lieu of a preposition. As the elected representative, Æschines would of course possess all the influence of Athens to his hearers in the Council. — 26. **ἐπέραινεν,** imp. to denote the beginning of a process = *set about accomplishing:* **πείθει** below, histor. pres. — **ἐφ' οἷς.** *The ends for which.* ἐπί here of the basis *in connection with* which the contract was made. See also 16, **ἐπ' ἀληθείας,** note. — 27. **λόγους καὶ μύθους,** *facts and fables.* — **ἀπείρους λόγιον,** *were unused to speeches,* the hieromnemons. This might well be as they were appointed by lot. Whiston. — P. 54, l. 1. **ὅθεν.** *As to how:* the matter being old in history has to be traced *from its origin:* hence ὅθεν rather than ὅπως. — **Κιρραία.** *The tract of Cirrha:* a frequent resort of pilgrims to Delphi. According to Æschines, the Cirrhæans grossly overcharged and plundered these sojourners. Hence the first Sacred War (B. C. 595) was undertaken by the Amphictyons to punish them. Their city, which stood on the Sinus Corinthiacus, close to Delphi, was captured and destroyed in 585, and the ground on which it had stood was consecrated to Apollo. This no doubt is historical fact (Æschin., pp. 68, 69), though it suits the orator here to speak of it as a myth. — **150.** 4. **περιελθεῖν,** *to make a survey,* with the object of inspecting, to see if the sacred ground was being encroached upon. — 5. **οὖσαν.** *As being their own.* The participle constitutes here a causal sentence. Madv., *G. S.*, 174 (*quippe quum sua ipsorum esset*). — 6. **χώρας.** *A portion of the sacred tract.* Genitive strictly partitive. — **δίκην.** According to Æschines (*l. c.*) the Locrian representatives had moved in the Council that a fine of fifty talents be imposed on Athens for dedicating sundry golden shields, in the new Temple of Apollo, inscribed "taken by the Athenians from the Persians and Thebans when fighting against the Greeks." Besides the offensive inscription, there was a further transgression in the shields having been dedicated before the new Temple was fully consecrated. There is no reason to doubt that the Locrians did move this resolution to have the Athenians fined; true, it was not a case of δίκην ἐπάγειν, but Æschines had never said it was; he had only described them as δόγμα εἰσφέροντας. All that Demosthenes could fairly have urged in reply would have been that this Locrian resolution was not worth being noticed by the representative of Athens; or, at any rate, that Æschines, if he did notice it at all, ought to have noticed it in a different way. In this part of the speech the orator's argument is decidedly weak, not to say evasive. — 7. **ἐπαγόντων,** circumstantial part.: *although the Locrians were bringing no suit against us, nor charging* *what this man now pretends, saying what was not true.* Æschines (*l. c.*) had represented that his charge of sacrilege against the Locrians (alleging that they had desecrated this hallowed Cirrhæan territory) was provoked entirely as a countercharge in answer to their charge of sacrilege against Athens. The orator tries to prove that they had not really made such a charge. — 10. **τελέσασθαι.** *To accomplish a prosecution of our state without serving a summons.* *τελέσασθαι* is a little unusual in connection with *δίκην*, but distinguishes the actual bringing of an action into court from the mere threatening to bring one, which is all the orator admits the Locrians to have done. The summons, of course, would be before the court of the Amphictyonic Council. — **δήπου** = *surely*, or *of course.* — **ἐκλήτευσεν.** *Name the man who served the citation.* On *πρόσκλησις* see Smith, Dic. Ant., Dike, and Cleteres. — 11. **ἐπὶ ποίας ἀρχῆς.** Literally, in what Archonship? i. e. *name the year.* — **τὸν εἰδότα.** *Tell us the man who knows of it,* i. e. adduce confirmatory evidence. All this, though strong in rhetoric, is somewhat absurd in logic, as no one had ever alleged that the trial had taken place at all. — 13. **κατεχρῶ.** The element *κατ-* here of *abusing* rather than of *using to the full.* But both senses are implied. — **151.** 14. **ὑφήγησιν.** *Direction.* The word has an interesting technical use in Platon., *Protag.*, 326, D, *ἀναγκάζουσι γράφειν κατὰ τὴν ὑφήγησιν τῶν γραμμῶν.* Some understand that the writing-master traced the letters faintly in pencil, and that the pupil followed the lines so traced. Others understand that the lines were merely ruled to keep the writing straight. See Heind. *l. c.* — 15. **μικροῦ.** Genitive of separation: *within a little, almost.* See *ὀλίγου δεῖν*, note **τί οὖν,** 20. C. 665; H. 575, a. — **κατηκόντισαν.** *Shot down.* *διέξηλθε διὰ τοῦ στρατοπέδου φήμη ὡς κατακοντιεῖ σφέας.* Her., IX., 17. — 19. **Κόττυφος.** *Κόττυφον τὸν Φαρσάλιον τὸν πότε τὰς γνώμας ἐπιψηφίζοντα* ("a native of Pharsalia and president of the Amphictyons," Æschin., p. 71 *fin.*). We know nothing more about him. — 21. **οὐδέν.** Æschines gives a very different account, pp. 71, 72: *καὶ παρελθόντες τῇ πρώτῃ στρατείᾳ καὶ μάλα μετρίως ἐχρήσαντο τοῖς Ἀμφισσεῦσιν, ἀντὶ γὰρ τῶν μεγίστων ἀδικημάτων χρήμασιν αὐτοὺς ἐζημίωσαν...ἐπειδὴ δὲ οὔτε τὰ χρήματα ἐξέτινον τῷ θεῷ τούς τ' ἐναγεῖς κατήγαγον, οὕτως ἤδη τὴν δευτέραν στρατείαν ἐπὶ τοὺς Ἀμφισσεῖς ἐποιήσαντο*: that is, that the Amphictyonic troops invaded the territory of the Amphissians and compelled them to submit to certain conditions, which, however, they did not fulfil, so that it was necessary to make a second expedition against them. It is, however, quite possible, as Whiston observes, that both accounts were true in the main. We have to allow for each of the two orators regarding the matter from such a different standpoint. — **ἐπιοῦσαν.** *The next,* i. e. the autumn meeting of the Amphictyons. See below, ΕΤΕΡΟΝ ΔΟΓΜΑ. — **εἰς** = *for* or *by*. — 22. **ἦγον.** *Were for handing the war over to Philip.* We understand *πόλεμον* as the object of *ἦγον*, which Reiske renders *ablegabant,* and Bremi *mandare studuerunt.* Cf. p. 125, l. 20. — **152.** 25. **εἰσφέρειν.** *They must either themselves subscribe,* i. e. to provide funds for raising an army. The *εἰσφορά* was an extraordinary war tax. See Dic. Ant., sub v. — **ξένους.** *Enlist foreigners,* i. e. as mercenary troops. — 26. **ζημιοῦν,** i. e. to enforce the payment of the subscription. — 27. **ἐκεῖνον,** i. e. Philip, if elected general, would bear the whole expense of the war. — P. 55, l. 1. **ἐκ τούτων,** *from these considerations.* — **εὐθέως.** The capture of Elatea was in the winter of 339; we do not know the exact date, but at any rate within three months of the autumn Pylæa referred to. — 3. **ἐρρῶσθαι.** *Having bid a long adieu,* i. e. having dismissed from his consideration. *ἐγὼ δὲ τρύτοις μὲν ἐρρῶσθαι λέγω,* p. 62, l. 19. The phrase is common in this sarcastic usage. — **153.** 8. **τό γ' ἐξαίφνης.** *At all events for the moment,* sc. though not ultimately. — **μάλιστα μέν...εἶτα μέντοι.** *Chiefly, it is true...but in a secondary degree.* I have already noticed *μέντοι* as an adversative, 12; no adversative was necessary here, as *εἶτα* is itself antithetic. See note on *ἔπειτα,* 1. — 11. **χρόνους.** We are at a loss to understand in what form these *dates* were preserved on record; certainly it could not have been as they appear in the spurious document below. We should have expected the reading of successive *ψηφίσματα* passed at the period in question, with the dates of the day and month attached, and distinct reference to the several events; or else of the particular *ψήφισμα* describing the appointment of Æschines as Pylagoras. Cf. 155, end. — **154. ΔΟΓΜΑ.** The contents of both these Dogmas stamp them as forgeries. They merely embody the statements of Demosthenes, and quite ignore the conflicting statements of Æschines (p. 71 sq.). Of course the indefatigable Böhnecke and Vömel defend both as genuine. But the elaborate criticisms of Droysen and others effectually demolish their validity. The curious will refer to Dindorf's Demosthenes, Vol. V., p. 406, for a *resumé* of the discussion. — **ἱερέως.** Supposed to be an Arch-Hieromnemon corresponding to the Archon Eponymus. — **ἐαρινῆς.** Both decrees are dated in the spring, which directly contradicts τὴν ἐπιοῦσαν, 151. Reiske corrected ἐαρινῆς into ὀπωρινῆς in the Second Decree, which the ungrateful Böhnecke is pleased to style *coniectura infelicissima.* — **πυλαγόροις** is the older form. See Lex. — **συνέδροις.** We know of no such office in connection with the Amphictyonic Council, but of course it may have existed. — **155. τῷ κοινῷ.** Some critics object to this as an unusual term for *the general body*, but it is a most common expression in Attic. Thuc., IV., 78, etc., etc. — **καταvειμάμενοι.** *Having divided among themselves:* the active κατανέμουσιν, in the first dogma, is used less correctly, *treat as pasture for flocks;* νέμουσι immediately below is quite classical, *they send to pasture.* — **'Αρκάδα.** Æschines calls him a Pharsalian: 151, **Κόττυφος.** — **ἀξιοῦν ἵνα.** The infinitive after ἀξιοῦν is the natural and obvious construction, though the final ἵνα is not absolutely ungrammatical here. — **διότι** = *that.* Classical usage would require ὅτι preceded probably by ἀγγέλλειν, unless we are to understand the latter from πρεσβεῦσαι. — **ΧΡΟΝΟΙ.** The most meaningless of all the forgeries; it specifies a date minutely, but omits to mention what happened upon it. — **Μνησιθείδης.** Æschines says he was appointed πυλαγόρας ἐπὶ Θεοφράστου ἄρχοντος, p. 69 (*fin.*). According to the Fasti, the Archon Eponymus of 339 to 338 was Lysimachidas. At any rate it was not Mnesithides (*qui neque archon unquam neque opinor scriba prytaniæ, aut prætor fuit.* DROYSEN.) — **156.** 3. **ὡς οὐχ ὑπήκουον.** *When they refused to comply,* as already stated, 153. — 5. **συμμάχους.** 'Αρκάδας, 'Αργείους, Μεσσηνίους, 'Ηλείους. SCHOL. — 6. **ἀληθῆ πρόφασιν.** This use of πρόφασιν for the *true reason* is rare and scarcely recognized in the lexicons. It is often opposed to ἀληθές (πρόφασιν μὲν...τὸ ἀληθὲς δέ), and is used just below to denote *the pretexts* alleged by Philip and presented by Æschines. — **κοινά.** *The universal interests as specified by the Amphictyonic decree.* The καί has here an intensive force, not a copulative; 3, first note. — **157. ΕΠΙΣΤΟΛΗ.** This document is not so obviously a forgery as most of those which have preceded. The points of suspicion will be noticed as they occur. — **δημιουργοῖς.** So Thucyd., V., 47, οἱ δημιουργοὶ καὶ ἡ βουλή, where the historian is speaking of Mantinea and of Elis. As a designation of *chief magistrate* it very likely existed in other Peloponnesian constitutions also. Compare our *public servants.* — P. 57. **ὥστε συναντᾶτε.** *And so assemble,* etc. This use of ὥστε with the imperative is rare, though not without example both in prose and poetry. — **Λῴου.** It is pretty fairly established that the Macedonian month Lous was not identical with the Athenian month Boedromion (Clinton's *Fasti*, II., 358), but with Hecatombæon. Panemus, which was a Bœotian and Corinthian as well as a Macedonian word, corresponded to the Athenian month Metageitnion (Böckh., *Inscript.*, I., 732). No genuine document would contain such a blunder as this. — **τοῖς δὲ συμβούλοις.** These words and the two which follow Dindorf places in brackets, and Schäfer wishes to erase. The text is hopelessly corrupt, and it seems useless to suggest emendations. Omitting these words the meaning is : *Those who do not assemble with all their force we shall treat as subject to the usual penalties*, i. e. as enemies. — **πανδημεὶ** = *πανστρατιᾷ*. — **158.** 5. **μὴ... περιιόντες.** *Do not then go about and say:* a favorite combination: *περιιόντ' αὐτὸν πυνθάνεσθαί τισι πώποτε συμβέβηκεν ὑβρισθῆναι.* p. 525 (end). — 6. **ὑφ' ἑνός,** sc. *τοῦ Φιλίππου*. — **159.** 9. **μηδὲν εὐλαβηθέντα.** *Without reserve*: i. e. dismissing all delicacy and respect for the hearers. — 12. **τόπων.** Tracts of territory either with or without buildings and inhabitants: *πόλεων*, distinctively of the inhabited. Whiston makes *τόπων* = *χωρίων*, *places*, i. e. *forts*, and compares Virg., *Æn.* II., 573: Trojæ et patriæ communis Erinnys. —13. **παρασχών** = *furnished.* — 14. **ἀπεστράφητε.** The passive *ἀποστρέφεσθαι* is constantly thus constructed with the accusative, without any preposition to connect them. The same remark applies to all verbs of motion. Madvig, *G. S.*, 21, r. 2; C. 472, f; Cu. 398; H. 544, a. Render: *and how it is that you did not turn away from him as soon as ever you saw him, I wonder.* — 15. **σκότος.** The neuter gender of this word is specially affected by Demosthenes (p. 411, l. 25, etc.), but is rare in Attic authors generally. — 16. **πρό.** *Between you and the truth,* lit. abiding with you before the truth.

160-167. IN DENOUNCING THE POLITICAL CAREER OF ÆSCHINES, I HAVE NOW COME TO SPEAK OF MY OWN CAREER AT THE TIME. DISCERNING PHILIP'S OBJECTS, I RESISTED THEM TO THE UTMOST; NOT THAT MY POLICY WAS ORIGINAL; I ONLY FOLLOWED BETTER MEN, WHOM YOU, ÆSCHINES, CRINGED TO LIVING, THOUGH YOU REVILE THEM DEAD. I REPEAT, IT WAS YOU AND YOUR ACCOMPLICES WHO BY THAT POLICY BROUGHT US NEAR TO RUIN.

160. P. 58, l. 3. **εἰ ἐγὼ μέν.** *If, after I sustained on my part the doing of the labor for your sakes, yet you on your part will not have patience to hear the words which describe them.* The common antithesis of *ἔργον* and *λόγος* = *realities* and *reports*. *αὐτῶν* is objective gen. — **161.** 5. **ὁρῶν γὰρ ἐγώ.** *For seeing that the Thebans and, to some extent, you* *also, under the influence of the partisans of Philip and those who were bribed in either state, were overlooking and in no single point guarding against what was dangerous and required much watching, viz., suffering the growth of Philip.* ἑκατέροις *each of the two* (Athens and Thebes) *separately*, opposed, as Dissen observes, to ἀμφοτέροις, *both collectively.* — 14. **Ἀριστοφῶντα,** 70, and Εὔβουλον also. — 15. **πρᾶξαι.** *To achieve this friendship*, i. e. between Athens and Thebes. The ἀντιλέγοντας which follows is concessive, cf. 142, εἰδώς; 146, κρατοῦντι. — 18. **κίναδος,** cf. κύρβις, κρόταλον, κίναδος, τρύμη, Aristoph., *Nub.*, 448. — **οὓς.** This accusative is governed by κολακεύων, but, by an easy zeugma, suggests the dative which παρηκολούθεις requires. Æschines is said to have been secretary to Aristophon. — 19. **οὐκ αἰσθάνει.** *You fail to perceive*, i. e. your stupidity prevents you from perceiving, *that you denounce them, now they are dead.* But the old reading αἰσχύνει gave a better sense: *you do not blush to denounce them, now they are dead,* the imputation of ἀναισθησία is so inconsistent with the epithet κίναδος. However Σ has αἰσθάνει and all the editors seem to have adopted the correction. —22. **δοκιμασάντων.** *Examined and approved, sanctioned.* — **163. ἐκεῖσε,** i. e. to his statements, 147 - 153. — 23. **τούτου μὲν κ. τ. λ.** *It was through his having caused the war at Amphissa and the rest of his accomplices having developed our hostility with Thebes, that Philip contrived to come down upon us.* — 26. **οὗπερ...συνέκρουον,** *the very purpose for which these men were embroiling the states,* lit. knocking them together, cf. 19, and note there. — 27. **προεξανέστημεν.** *Had we not uprisen a little before him, we should never have been able to retrieve our position; to such lengths did these creatures promote the ill-feeling.* — P. 59, l. 1. **μέχρι** is common with an adverb of time or place, as here. So with δεῦρο, ἐνταῦθα, ὅποι, τότε, τὰ νῦν. — **164. ΨΗΦΙΣΜΑ.** The contents of this and the three following documents are sufficient to stamp them as forgeries. The orator introduces them by saying that they will show the state of feeling existing between Athens and Thebes at the time. Now the first psephisma says nothing about Thebes, and the second next to nothing. Both of them are confined to an account of the state of affairs between Athens and Macedon. The same remark applies to the first apocrisis, and the second refers only to Thebes in its relation to Macedon. After the documents have been read, the orator describes them (168) as of a nature to exasperate Thebes against Athens, and encourage Philip to attack Elatea. Nothing in the documents justifies this description. Some other indications of spuriousness will be noticed in their place. — **Ἡροπύθου.** No such person was Archon in the year 339 or 338. But Elatea was captured in the winter of 339, or at latest at the beginning of 338. — **βουλῆς...γνώμη**, cf. psephisma, 37, and note there. — **ὡς μέν**, 71, note s. v. — **κεφαλαίῳ.** *In fine.* τὸ δ' οὖν κεφάλαιον 213 (*inf.*). — **ἐπιβάλλεται.** This use is quite classical: *throws himself upon*, i. e. *desires, purposes.* — **εἰρήνην.** But the peace of 346 had been regularly broken in 340 (89, **ἐνστάς**), and if any subsequent peace had been made, the orator or Æschines would surely have mentioned it. — **δεδόχθαι.** Cf. 29, note. — **εἰ δὲ μή.** *But, failing that* (the constant formula of apodosis to μάλιστα μέν, *above all*), i. e. as the most desirable alternative if it can only be achieved: in the simplest paraphrase = *if possible...but at any rate.* On the construction of εἰ δὲ μή see Madvig's *G. S.*, 194, b; C. 717; H. 754, b. — **ἀνοχάς.** *Inducias.* The usual Attic form is ἀνοκωχή. — **Θαργηλιῶνος.** The next month but one to Elaphebolion, Munychion intervening. See CALENDAR in Smith's Dic. Ant. — **165. πολεμάρχου γνώμη.** There is no authority for supposing that the Archon Polemarch had any distinctive voice or power on these occasions. Droysen notices this as one of the marks of forgery in the document. — **κήρυκα.** It is highly improbable that the herald would be mentioned in any psephisma. Schäfer suggests, as a reason, *quo plus Philippo offerretur religionis.* But a herald would be attached to such a party as a matter of course, and would need no official mention. — **ἐνδεχομένως.** Post-classical: appears in Polybius: "pro ratione temporum, i. q. ἐκ τῶν ἐνδεχομένων." REISKE. — P. 60. **μετρίων**, i. e. under any *reasonable condition, tolerable position.* — **166. χαίρειν.** *Greeting.* Cf. 39, note. — **αἵρεσιν.** Instead of the more usual προαίρεσιν. So Plato, *Phædr.*, 256 C. — **σπουδήν.** *Effort.* — **μή.** Classical Greek would require οὐ, as the sentence is causal, not conditional. — **ἐξ ὑποστροφῆς.** *Reversing the procedure*, i. e. doing the opposite of what the Thessalians, etc., have done. The phrase is quite classical, though somewhat too poetical for its surroundings here. — **πεπλημμελημένοι.** This use of the passive πλημμελεῖσθαι as meaning *to be injured* is quite classical, though rare. — πλημμελούμενος δὲ καὶ οὐκ ἐν δίκῃ λοιδορηθείς. Platon., *Phædr.*, 275 (end). — **συγκατατίθεμαι**, sc. τὴν αὐτὴν δόξαν. And so Plato writes it in full, *Gorgias*, 501, C. *I concur with.* — **παραπέμψαντες.** *Having dismissed.* Post-classical; the usual sense being *to convey* or *to escort.* — **167. ΑΠΟΚΡΙΣΙΣ.** Even if this were genuine, it would be of little value without the Theban resolution which it professes to answer. — **διότι.** *Sup.*, 155. — **προσφέρονται.** *Proffer:* post-classical in this sense: the verb usually meaning *to take* (food or medicine). — **συγκαταίνους.** *Abettors:* a post-classical word. — **κατεγίγνωσκον.** *I was disposed to blame you on the prospect of your being persuaded.* A harsh construction where we should rather expect *ὡς μελλόντων.* — P. 61. **οἴσειν ῥοπήν.** *Bring you no small advantage.* *ῥοπή* as *the critical turn of the scale* is quite classical, and as common in prose as in poetry. However, exception has been taken to the phrase as it stands here by Whiston and others. It is perhaps unsuitable to a purely formal document. — **προθέσεως.** *Purpose:* not used in this sense by the Attic writers, but found in Aristotle, Polybius, etc.

168. In brief this was how Philip broke up our union and won the day. Remember our excitement at the time of Elatea's capture.

4. **'Ελατείαν.** Cf. note 143. It was 78 miles from Athens, and commanded the approach towards that city. — **οὐδ' ἂν εἰ.** This *ἂν* is repeated with *συμπνευσάντων*, Madvig, 138; C. 622. The phrase *εἴ τι γένοιτο* is euphemistic: *even if some awful crisis were to happen.* *οὐδ' εἴ τι πάθοις*, Theocr., VIII., 10. — 5. **συμπνευσάντων** in this participial construction has the force of the optative mood. C. 658, a; Cu. 595; G. 226, 3; H. 803. There is a *varia lectio* *συμνευσόντων*, which, strange to say, has been adopted by Bremi and others. But *πνέω* and its compounds use only the middle form of the future, never the active. — **ἡμῶν.** *As though the Thebans and ourselves would never again co-operate, come what might.*

169—179. At that fatal crisis, when in full assembly Athens appealed to her statesmen for direction, who was it that rose to answer? I alone. If ever there was a demand for true patriotism and sound policy, that was the time. So I moved a resolution that we should co-operate with Thebes in resistance to Macedon; that our envoys should be despatched forthwith, and our army at once make a demonstration.

169. 9. **'Εσπέρα.** This splendid pictorial passage is duly lauded by Longinus (c. 10) and Hermogenes (p. 284): quoted also by Diodorus, XVI., 84. — 10. **πρυτάνεις** who, from their official position, would be the first recipients of all intelligence. *ὡς = πρός.* C. 711, a; Cu. 445; G. 191, 3; H. 614, 621. — 11. **δειπνοῦντες** in the Prytaneum at the public expense: a privilege of their office. Athen., V., p. 186, A. — 12. **ἐξεῖργον.** *Began driving the shopkeepers from their booths in the Agora*, sc. in order to clear the Agora, so that the Ecclesia might be convened with all possible expedition. Aristoph., *Ach.*, 21, 2. — 13. **γέρρα.** *Wicker-work* literally, but used, according to Harpocration, of any covering or roofing, whether it were canvas or leather, or otherwise. All editions seem to understand it here either as *sheds*, or else *coverings of the σκηναί.* I cannot but think myself that it refers to the γέρρα which fenced in the place of assembly so as to exclude strangers (*c. Neær.*, p. 1375). They expected a "monster meeting" under such exciting circumstances, and made every preparation to receive an extraordinary number. To save time they burnt the hurdles instead of carrying them away, and so threw open ample space for all comers. — **ἐνεπίμπρασαν.** To serve as a beacon, according to Schäfer, but, as Whiston truly observes, the Agora was not a likely situation for that purpose. The sole object of burning these articles was most probably to clear them all away as fast as possible. — **στρατηγούς.** At such a crisis of the war a formal conference between the Strategi and the Boule would be necessary; and probably it was desirable that the Ecclesia should be convened by a joint proclamation from the Strategi and the Boule (37) in order to make the summons as impressive and imperative as possible. — 14. **σαλπικτήν.** Perhaps it was a special formality to send out the summons by the σαλπικτής, as well as by the ordinary κήρυκες, whenever the Strategi were responsible for calling the Ecclesia together. The invariable use of σαλπικτής as a military term, and its juxtaposition to στρατηγούς here, combine to suggest this notion. In the spelling of σαλπικτής I have followed Dindorf and all the modern editors, who agree in omitting the γ. But cf. Lidd. and Sc. s. v. — **μετεπέμποντο... ἐκάλουν,** imperfect, indicating the simultaneous occurrence of many exhibitions of alarm. — 16. **ἅμα τῇ ἡμέρᾳ.** *At dawn of day:* there was nothing, however, extraordinary in this: the early hour of these meetings is constantly noticed: Aristoph., *Ach.*, 20, *Eccl.*, 312, 377, etc. — **ἐκάλουν.** These imperfects add to the pictorial force of the description. — 17. **βουλευτήριον.** A brief notice of the topography is here almost indispensable. The Bouleuterion stood in the Agora, probably on the extreme eastern side just below the Tholus or Prytaneum, which was in the northeast corner. Thus they were both immediately at the foot of the Acropolis, which bounded the Agora on the east. — 18. **πρίν.** So eager were they to commence the business that they went and took their seats in the Pnyx long before the Boule had had time to consider and prepare their report. — 19. **ἄνω,** i. e. on the top of the Pnyx, the Bouleuterion being down in the Agora. The Agora occupied the whole of the level valley which was bounded on the west by the Pnyx, on the east by the Acropolis, on the north by the Areopagus, and on the south by the Museum. The members of the Boule, when adjourning to the Pnyx with their report, would have to traverse the Agora from east to west and ascend the hill of the Pnyx. For fuller particulars see the excellent article ATHENÆ in Smith's Dic. Geog., or Wordsworth's Athens. — **170.** 20. **εἰσῆλθεν,** sc. into the Pnyx, having held their deliberations in the Bouleuterion and now proceeding to report the result to the Demus, and put the question to their vote. — **οἱ πρυτάνεις.** It would be only the committee (*οἱ πρoέδροι*) who would actually attend to read the report (*ἀπήγγειλαν*); or perhaps only *ὁ ἐπιστάτης*, as the mouthpiece of the whole body. — 21. **προσηγγελμένα,** sc. *ὑπὸ τῆς βουλῆς.* The report which they had been commissioned by the council to deliver. — 22. **παρήγαγον.** *Introduced to the meeting the messenger who had come.* Cf. Aristoph., *Ach.*, 22-172, for a description of the ordinary proceeding at an Ecclesia. — **εἶπεν.** *Had told his tale;* i. e. told the Demus the details which he had already told to the Prytanes and Boule. — **ἠρώτα.** *Kept asking:* the imperfect sense being here strongly marked. — **τίς ἀγορεύειν βούλεται;** The regular form of commencing the business. Aristoph., *Ach.*, 45. — P. 62, l. 3. **παρόντων.** The force of the participial construction is concessive. — 4. **ῥητόρων** contrasts curiously with *στρατηγῶν*, the latter being officials appointed by the state, the former merely self-appointed professionals, but yet recognized as a class, and a class on a par with the state officers. Our own "Government" and "Press" suggest an analogy. — 5. **τὸν ἐροῦνθ'.** *Some one to speak for the common weal, σωτηρίας,* as usual, of sound condition reconstituted from a state of decay or danger. The absence of the article is noticed by Reiske, but, as Schäfer comments, "articulo facile caremus: p. 146, 11." — **171.** 10. **τὸ βῆμα.** The famous *λίθος*, a cubic platform of ten feet cut out of the rock in the middle of the Pnyx semicircle. — 12. **οἱ τριακόσιοι,** i. e. the first class of the Finance Sections: their arrangement has been already described (10, **ἡγεμόνας**) in the account of the Naval Sections, whose organization was identical. — **ἀμφότερα,** in apposition with *τούς, those who were both* *those things at once, loyal to the state and wealthy.* — 14. **οἱ...ἐπιδόντες,** *those who subsequently gave the great voluntary contributions.* ἐπιδόσεις are gifts after or in addition to their quota of assessed taxes. — **172.** 17. **παρηκολουθηκότα.** *Who had followed up, traced the course of.* ὁ τὰ τούτου πονηρεύματ' ἀκριβέστατα εἰδὼς ἐγὼ καὶ παρηκολουθηκὼς ἅπασι, p. 423, l. 23. Cf. St. Luke's Gospel, c. i., v. 3. — 18. **συλλελογισμένον.** Perf. Midd. *who had concluded: qui collegisset.* — 21. **οὔτ'.** The reduplication of the negatives throughout this clause is very noticeable. — 22. **ἔμελλεν.** *Was no more likely.* C. 598; Cu. 501; H. 711. — **173.** 24. **οὗτος.** *Well, then:* I *showed myself the man,* sc. ὃν ὁ καιρὸς ἐκεῖνος καὶ ἡ ἡμέρα ἐκείνη ἐκάλει. With this emphatic position of ἐγώ cf. 62 (*fin.*). — 25. **ἅ.** The relative must here be paraphrased for the sake of the English: *I spoke before you...and hear what I said, with your best attention, for two reasons.* — P. 63, l. 1. **τάξιν.** *My post,* 138 (*fin.*). Whiston cites c. *Mid.*, 155, λελοιπέναι τὴν τοῦ δικαίου τάξιν. — 2. **ἐξηταζόμην.** *Approved myself,* 197 (*fin.*). — 3. **φοβεροῖς.** *In the very hour of panic.* φοβερός always of *horrors* only, δεινός of *wonders* also. — **μικρόν** in pointed antithesis to πολλῷ. — 4. **τῆς.** The genitive depends on τὰ λοιπά, not on ἐμπειρότεροι: *you will have far greater knowledge for the future of your whole administration.* — **174.** 5. **εἶπον.** So in Philip. II., Demosthenes quotes at length from a speech which he had addressed to the Messenians and the Argives. — 6. **ὑπαρχόντων.** *Were supporting Philip.* So 358, 7, τὸν Φίλιππον ὑπάρχειν αὐτοῖς, they had Philip, i. e. as a substantial basis of support. Cf. ὑπάρξαι in 1 (note). In the older editions φίλων was inserted after ὑπαρχόντων here, but Bekker erased it. See Schäfer's note. — **175.** 14. **ηὐτρέπισται.** Perf. Midd.; the action being for his own interest. — 18. **ἐπᾶραι.** Supply βούλεται, in answer to the question above. — **176.** 22. **δύσκολον.** *Unpleasant,* euphemism for κακόν. The state of feeling between Thebes and Athens has often already been adverted to; 96, etc. — 23. **Θηβαίοις,** dat. of the agent *by* the Thebans, C. 461; Cu. 434; G. 188, 3; H. 600. — P. 64, l. 1. Observe the emphatic position of **ἀμφότεροι.** — 2. **πρὸς τῷ.** Close application to the subject is here the preposition's force. περὶ ὧν ἂν λέγω obviously belongs to both the infinitives. — **177.** 6. **μεταθέσθαι,** sc. τὸν φόβον: i. e. they are to dismiss apprehension for themselves, and to entertain apprehension for Thebes. — 7. **τῶν δεινῶν,** gen. with ἐγγύς. C. 445; Cu. 415; G. 182; H. 589. — 8. **προτέροις.** As a predicate: *the peril is theirs first.* — 9. **ἐξελθόντας.** *Secondly that all* *of you who are of the age* (i. e. for military service, 18 to 60) *and all your cavalry should march out towards Eleusis and show the world that you are yourselves under arms.* The article *τούς* has from the context the force of *πάντας ὑμᾶς* in both cases. The road to Thebes via Eleusis was the most convenient for an army, though not the most direct, as Whiston points out. — 12. **ἐξ ἴσου γένηται.** *May have equal liberty to speak boldly.* Literally : that this *liberty* may arise for them on a par. — 13. **ὥσπερ,** i. e. that both sides will have equal military support. — 178. 19. **κυρίους.** *To give them absolute power in conjunction with the Strategi to settle their time of going there* (to Thebes) *and the campaign.* — 24. **αἰσχρός.** Because they would not be in a position to refuse. Observe the fondness of the Greek for the personal, or subjective form =*it would be dishonorable under the circumstances.* — P. 65, l. 1. **καὶ ἅ.** If *καί* is here *both,* it introduces the apodosis extending to *πράξωμεν*: if *καί* is *and,* the apodosis is not expressed but understood to be *πάντα εὖ ἔχῃ* or the like : a common aposiopesis before *εἰ δὲ μή.* Madv., 194, b, r. The former is to be preferred. — **διῳκημένοι.** The middle voice again with the sense of action for their own interest. — 2. **προσχήματος,** Holmes renders here *magnificence.* But the commentators generally, with better reason, take the word in its more ordinary sense of *pretext,* or apparent motive, sc. of acting disinterestedly. — 3. **ἂν δ' ἄρα μὴ συμβῇ.** *If after all it be not our fortune to succeed.* Having done everything in their own power for success, their failure could only be attributed to *τύχῃ.* — 179. 5. **Ταῦτα.** The extreme ease and simplicity of the orator's language on this occasion has been noticed by all commentators, and is obvious to any reader. It may be very reasonably supposed that the orator at such a crisis would speak his very plainest, dismissing all elaboration and rhetorical ornament. So Lord Brougham appears to understand him. — 8. **εἶπον μέν.** This vigorous climax has been universally admired, perhaps a little beyond its merits, which are due rather to the exquisitely antithetic power of *μέν* and *δέ* than to any intrinsic vigor of thought in the sentence. *I did not speak thus, and yet not move a resolution ; and I did not move a resolution, and yet not serve on the embassy ; and I did not serve on the embassy, and yet not convince the Thebans.* Instead of *yet not,* Drake well renders *οὐκ...δέ* by *then not.* However we render the passage, it will be awkward and clumsy in English. The Latin translators are equally hampered. Aquila Romanus (p. 21) has "et non dixi hæc quidem non autem scripsi, etc." Quintilian (ix., 3), cited by Whiston, "nec hæc quidem dixi sed nec scripsi, etc." The notorious instance of climax in Cicero (*pro Mil.*, 23) is effected by "nec solum...sed etiam" in each clause. — 11. **ἔδωκ'.** *I devoted myself entirely to your interests.* Cf. *τοῖς δεινοῖς αὐτοὺς διδόναι* 97, where the sense of self-sacrifice is yet more prominent. — 12. **εἰς.** *In the face of*, i. e. so as to meet and encounter. — 13. **φέρε.** Apparently the clerk has to search for the document, and while they are waiting for it the orator seizes the opportunity for the following lament.

180. Ay, Æschines, what was my part in the drama, and what was yours? Was your scenic majesty of much service to his country? or was it your derided rival who was hero of the hour?

16. **θῶ**, *ponam: depict, represent.* — 18. **Βάτταλον.** Some MSS. have Βάταλον, but not so well; the α of the first syllable is short by nature, and yet Athenæus in a pentameter (IV., 176, D) quotes the word as a dactyl: *καὶ τὸν ἐν ἀκρήτοις Βάτταλον ἡδυπότην.* As to the meaning of the nickname there are various solutions offered. The Scholiasts on Æschin., p. 17, l. 42, render it *profligate, effeminate*, giving several different derivations, (1) as the actual name of a flute-player or poet Batalus, notorious for his effeminacy: (2) as the name of the *ὑποπόδιον* (instrument for beating time) which the flute-player worked with his right foot; hence metaphorically a term of contempt. They add one or two coarser etymologies. Æschines (p. 41, l. 13) explains the name similarly as given *δι' αἰσχρουργίαν*: and he quotes with derision the explanation of Demosthenes, that it was a pet name given him in infancy by his nurse (p. 17, l. 42). Schäfer, with the approval of Whiston, Drake, and many of the best editors, connects the name with *βαττολογεῖν* and takes it as an allusion to the orator's notorious defect in speech. It is probably onomatopoetic, like our words *stammer* and *stutter.* — **μηδ'...τυχόντα.** *Not even an ordinary hero*, i. e. more than an ordinary; cf. *οὐδὲ γὰρ ὧν ἔτυχεν ἦν*, 130. — 19. **τῶν ἀπὸ τῆς σκηνῆς,** *those of the stage*, i. e. one of the characters so often acted *on* the stage. See Lex., sub *ἀπό*. It was the privilege of third-rate actors to act such tyrants and kings as Cresphontes and Creon. *ἔστιν ὥσπερ γέρας τοῖς τριταγωνισταῖς τὸ τοὺς τυράννους καὶ τοὺς τὰ σκῆπτρα ἔχοντας εἰσιέναι*, p. 418, l. 12. — **Κρεσφόντην.** A play of Euripides bore this name. Aristotle's *Poet.*, 14, 19. Ælian tells us (*V. H.*, 14, 40) that Merope, wife of Cresphontes, was the chief character in this tragedy, and Plutarch (*Mor.*,

998 E) describes her in one of the scenes as taking up an axe to slay her son. Cresphontes, according to early history, was a Heracleid, king of Messenia, murdered in a rebellion by Polyphontes, one of his nobles, who then constrained Merope to marry him. Welcker conjectures that the action of the drama would be all subsequent to the death of Cresphontes, who would only appear to speak the prologue, as a ghost, like Polydorus in the Hecuba. — **Κρέοντα.** In the Antigone of Sophocles; also a subordinate part. — 20. **Κολλυτῷ.** One of the demes where dramatic performances took place during the rural Dionysia, outside the boundaries of the city. The site of Collytus was in the valley between the Pnyx and the Museum. It was the deme where Plato resided, and probably Æschines also, if we can trust at all to the evidence of the spurious letters. Κολλύτου ἐν ᾧ πέντε καὶ τετταράκοντα ἔτη ᾤκησα. [Æschin.] *Ep.* 5. — **Οἰνόμαον.** In the Œnomaus of Sophocles, where the principal part would, of course, be that of Pelops or else Hippodamia. — **κακῶς.** *You murdered by your vile acting.* One MS., b, inserts κακός before κακῶς, greatly improving the sentence, but none of the other MSS. contain it. It is probably the embellishment of some later hand. With ἐπέτριψας we can compare ἐλυμαίνου, 267. Dissen cites *Memnona iugulare.* Hor., 1 *Sat.*, X., 36. — **ὑποκρινόμενος.** The story goes that Æschines, on one occasion, tripped and fell down on the stage while running after Pelops in the character of Œnomaus (*Vit. Æschin.*). Others opine that his fall was only metaphorical, καταπίπτειν corresponding to συρίττεσθαι (*explodi*) = to break down and be hissed off the stage. — 21. **Παιανιεύς,** i. e. he accepts the name of contempt and facetiously adds his own correct address; similarly he bestows on Æschines the name of dignity, attaching also his address in form. "Forsooth I am the miscreant and you the monarch; well, the miscreant on that occasion was the hero of the hour, the monarch of Elis was a mere nonentity." — **181.** P. 66. **ΨΗΦΙΣΜΑ.** Another forgery; the name of the Archon is wrong; the whole document is pointless and ungrammatical, needlessly long, and as feeble as it is verbose. That such a composition should claim Demosthenes for its author is, of course, ridiculous. Even Vömel does not defend it. There is a special absurdity in supposing he could have written the mythical allusions with which the psephisma concludes. — **Ναυσικλέους.** The date is still 339, of which year the real Archon was Lysimachidas. This forgery is also inconsistent with the forgery of § 164, where the Archon's name is given as Hero-

pythes; it must be remembered that both documents, from their contents, refer to the same year, that the former is dated Thargelion, this latter Skirophorion (the next month later), between which months no change of Archon would naturally occur. — **ὁ Μακεδόνων βασιλεύς.** Philip in an Athenian document would usually be called ὁ Μακεδών. And so one MS. reads: another merely omits βασιλεύς. — **συνθήκας.** According to Böhnecke, the peace of Philocrates, B. C. 346. Cf. 20. — **πόλεις.** On the Thracian coast (27). — **προάγει.** Post-classical for προέρχεται (cf. p. 29, l. 18). — **182. ἐμφρούρους.** Post-classical in this sense: φρουρὰν εἰσήγαγεν εἰς... Æschin., p. 532. — **οὐδέν.** This censorious observation is quite out of place in a public resolution, and is only worthy of so poor a forgery as this. — **κατακόρως.** Post-classical for ἀσελγῶς (cf. p. 120, l. 10). — **183. ἰδίας.** *Proprias nostras;* Athenian; whereas βαρβάρους means the Thracian πόλεις οὐδὲν προσηκούσας in 181, distinct from τινάς καὶ Ἀθηναίων. — **αὐτόν,** sc. τὸν δῆμον: meaning that Athens was indifferent so long as the aggression was merely on their own colonies; but when it came to be on Ἑλληνίκας πόλεις, then Athens could refrain no longer. — **184. διό.** There is no apodosis to the long sentence ἐπειδή...καταδουλουμένους. Schäfer, however, considers this as Demosthenic and compares 126. Grote (XI., 673) remarks on this psephisma, that it implies that Athens was now about to pass out of pacific relations with Philip, whereas, on the contrary, they had for some time been at war, a fact which made the seizure of Elatea all the more formidable and significant. — **εὐξαμένους.** This passage is apparently adapted from the beginning of Xenoph., *Cyrop.*, II., προσευξαμένοισι θεοῖς καὶ ἥρωσι τοῖς Περσίδα γῆν κατέχουσιν (which Schäfer cites as an illustration). Dissen, however, takes it seriously as a natural preparation for a "bellum gravissimum futurum." — **ἥρωσι,** sc. ἐπωνύμοις, whose ten statues stood in the Agora. — **διότι.** Post-classical for ὅτι as in 155, 167. — **ναύαρχον,** 73, note s. v. — **185.** P. 67. **ἀλλότριον.** By euphemism; as δύσκολον, 176, which section illustrates this whole clause. — **ἀλλοφύλου.** The Macedonians were a mixture of Illyrians and Pelasgians. The orator disregards the claim of their kings to be descended from the Argive Temenidæ, Her., V., 22, VIII., 137. He always speaks of Philip as βάρβαρον (p. 35, p. 119, etc.). — **οὔτε...τῷ ὁμοφύλῳ,** *neither in connection by families nor identity of race.* ὁμοφῦλοι, of course, as Hellenes, and συγγενεῖς, as is conjectured, through the Gephyræi, an Athenian gens originally from Thebes. WHISTON. —

ἀποστερουμένους. By Eurystheus, according to traditional history. Cf. Müller, *Dor.*, I., p. 54. — **Οἰδίπουν.** Œdipus had been a connecting link between Thebes and Athens, as we see in Soph., *O. C.*, 91, 1521. — **ἕτερα,** e. g. at Haliartus, 395 ; in the recovery of the Cadmea at Thebes, 379 ; in the alliance between Thebes and Athens, 378, etc. The reference is to services rendered by the Athenians, which would serve as a precedent for their rendering similar services now. — **187. ἐπιγαμίαν,** 91. — **πρέσβεις.** Only five names are given, yet in 178 we read *χειροτονῆσαι κελεύω δέκα πρέσβεις.*

188-191. THIS DECREE PROVED OUR SALVATION. IF THERE WAS ANYTHING BETTER WE COULD HAVE DONE, WHY DID NO ONE POINT IT OUT AT THE TIME? OR WHY DOES NO ONE POINT IT OUT EVEN NOW? IT IS JUST THE DIFFERENCE BETWEEN STATESMANSHIP AND FACTION, THAT THE FORMER COMMITS ITSELF TO RESPONSIBILITIES, THE LATTER SIMPLY CARPS AT EVENTS AND RESULTS.

3. **ὑπὸ τούτων,** i. e. by the Athenian political party who favored Macedon. — P. 68, l. 1. **ὥσπερ νέφος.** Why this trite simile should be so much admired by Longinus, Hermogenes, Demetrius, etc., is not so easy to understand. To say, as they do, that the rhythm of the sentence is perfect, is only the same as saying it is Demosthenic. But I cannot see that in this passage the orator has at all surpassed himself. — 2. **μὴ νῦν ἐπιτιμᾶν.** Observe the force of the pres. inf. in contrast with the aor. (*δεῖξαι*) : *not to be censuring now.* — **189.** 3. **ὁ γάρ.** *For the Statesman and the Sneak, though alike in nothing, differ from each other most in this; the one speaks his mind before the event and commits himself to the mercy of those who have believed him, of fortune, of occasion, of any one that chooses; while the other holds his tongue when he ought to have spoken, and afterwards, if anything unpleasant results, comes girding at that.* The word *συκοφάντης* (118) is quite untranslatable, but had come to be synonymous by this time with *πονηρός*, cf. Æsch., *F. L.*, 105 : *ἡ τῶν πονηρῶν κοινὴ ἐπωνυμία.* Whiston translates it *caviller* or *common accuser;* Lord Brougham, *partisan;* Kennedy, *pettifogger;* while all agree that no English word renders it exactly, since the *thing* exactly does not exist out of Athens. The redundant *τῶν ἄλλων* disappears in English. By *τοῖς πεισθεῖσι* we understand the members of the state who have accepted the policy suggested by the *σύμβουλος*, and who hold him *responsible* accordingly ; the success or failure of his policy depends on circumstances, in which sense he is also *liable* to these. *βασκαίνειν* in the sense of *reviling* takes an accusative either

of the person or thing (p. 94, l. 10). By *τῷ βουλομένῳ* is meant any member of the state who may choose to rise and speak against the statesman after his policy has been proved a failure; such a member is distinct from *οἱ πεισθέντες*, inasmuch as he may have opposed the policy at the time, or may have passed it in silence without expressing approval. — **190.** 10. **ἐκεῖνος** in strong contrast to *νῦν* which follows. — **φροντίζοντος.** *Who has a regard for the state and for saying what is right:* λόγων in reference to *σιγήσας* above. — 12. **ὑπερβόλην.** *I make such a superabundance of concession*, i. e. I show a generosity which is simply extravagant in giving my opponents another chance of attacking me. Demosthenes specially affects the word *ὑπερβόλη*. (p. 35, l. 18; p. 553, l. 12, etc.) — 13. **ἐνῆν.** *Was practicable*, lit. *was admitted by* the circumstances of the crisis. — 16. **μὴ λαθεῖν,** *this ought not to have escaped* ME. The *me* is emphatic. — 17. **μηδέπω,** *not even to this day: καὶ* again intensive. Another good example of the reduplicated negative. Cf. 139. — 18. **φαινομένων.** *Visible:* illustrated by *δεῖξαι* and *ἑόρακεν* above. — **191.** 21. **οὐ.** The amusing sarcasm is sufficiently explained by the context *τοῦτο βασκαίνει*, 189; *ὑπεύθυνον τῇ τύχῃ* (*ib.*). — 22. **ἐγγυᾶσθαι.** *To be answerable for. ἐὰν ἄρα μή τινες ἐθέλωσιν αὐτὸν τῶν φίλων ἐγγυᾶσθαί τε καὶ συνεκτίνοντες ἀπελευθεροῦν*, Plat., *Leg.*, 955, B. — 25. **ἀλλά.** *Yet*, introducing the apodosis, *ἔδειξας* being of course supplied in the protasis. This use of ἀλλά, though common in conditional sentences, is rare in causal. — 26. **τίς** in an indirect question, 73, note. By the slight trajection of *ἤ* this *τίς* is made to refer to *λόγος* and *καιρός* equally. — 27. **τῇ πόλει.** Dative of relation, here decidedly in the category *in commodi*. — P. 69, l. 1. **συμμαχία.** Combined also with *πρᾶξις* above, 22. — 2. **τουτουσί.** Deictic: he would point to his present hearers, the Athenian nation in assembly.

192–195. LOOK AT THE PRINCIPLE OF MY POLICY, NOT AT THE ISSUE OF EVENTS. OF COURSE, NO ONE CAN COMMAND SUCCESS, BUT DID I OMIT ANY MEANS TO DESERVE IT? THE STORM WRECKED OUR VESSEL, BUT DID THE CAPTAIN NEGLECT HIS DUTY? IF WE FARED THUS BADLY EVEN WITH THE THEBANS FOR ALLIES, WHAT SHOULD WE HAVE DONE WITHOUT THEM?

192. 3. **τὸ μὲν παρεληλυθός.** "Let the dead past bury its dead"; "Let bygones be bygones." — 4. **ἀφεῖται.** The perfect gives the force of *utter* and *thorough* dismissal. — 6. **ἀπαιτεῖ.** *Demands the office of a statesman*, i. e. requires the statesman to be at his post and taking his proper part. See 13, **τάξει**. — 8. **προαίρεσιν.** *Principle,* 12. Cf. also 93. — **μὴ...συκοφάντει.** *Do not be continually carping at the events.* *πέρας,* which follows, corresponds exactly to *exitus* and *end.* So also *τέλος* in the next sentence. — **193.** 15. **λογισμόν.** *Calculation,* i. e. forecasting of the future and preparations to meet it. — 16. **ὑπὲρ δύναμιν.** *With an industry above my power;* i. e. an extraordinary and amazing effort. — 17. **ἐνεστησάμην.** To be taken with *οὐ,* which belongs to the verb entirely here, not to the adjectives: *that I did not institute.* — 18. **τότ' ἤδη.** *Tum demum: then but not before,* 47 (last note). — **194.** 19. **σκηπτός.** Most MSS. add *ἢ χειμών,* but Reiske and Bremi concurred in expunging those words as a gloss. So also Dindorf. The word *σκηπτός,* as its etymology indicates, would equally describe *a squall* or *a thunderbolt.* The gloss would limit it to the former sense, whereas the latter is more appropriate here. With the metaphor Bremi compares *χειμάρρους,* 153. — 20. **μείζων.** So *ἐλάττων* (142) in the converse meaning (Madv., 90, r. 4): *too strong for.* — 21. **ὥσπερ ἂν** introduces the implied answer to the question which precedes. Do just as you would in the case of the captain of the vessel, that is, not censure him, nor hold him responsible for the shipwreck when he has done all he can to prevent it. C. 662 d; H. 754. — **ναύκληρον.** *Ship's captain:* originally the captain was always the owner of the vessel, so that the two senses were embodied in *ναύκληρος*; afterwards the sense of ownership disappears, and that of seamanship, or supreme direction, predominates. — 22. **σωτηρίᾳ,** *for a safe voyage.* This technical sense of *σώζεσθαι* as applied to a ship is notorious (cf. p. 883, l. 15, etc.): so *σωθήσεσθαι* which immediately follows would strictly mean *to arrive safe in harbor.* — **κατασκευάσαντα,** *after he had fitted up:* another nautical phrase, and so *σκευῶν* (*tackle*) which follows. — 24. **χρησάμενον,** *usum. Having met with,* or *experienced.* The verb *χρῶμαι,* like *utor* and our word *experience,* applies to any material or influence, whether beneficial or pernicious, with which the subject is brought in contact. Cf. *ἀπλοίᾳ χρῆσθαι.* Eur., *I. A.*, 88. — **πονησάντων,** *labored,* in the nautical sense, i. e. *suffered.* *λαῖφος ὅταν λάβῃ πόνος θραυομένας κεραίας.* Æsch., *Eumen.*, 526. — 25. **συντριβέντων.** Another nautical phrase: *wrecked:* *φυλασσομένους τῶν νεῶν μὴ ξυντρίψωσιν.* Thuc., IV., 11. — 26. **ἐκυβέρνων.** There was nothing to prevent a *ναύκληρος* from steering his own vessel. But the orator, of course, cites an instance where the *κυβερνήτης* has been left in sole charge of the helm. — 27. **ὥσπερ οὐδ',** *just as I too myself was* *not in command.* The force of *οὐδέ* is to emphasize the parallel, where the case of a *σύμβουλος* differs from that of a *ναύκληρος*: in the next sentence the cases are identical and the negative becomes *οὔτε*. See Madv., 208, [illegible]; C. 701, 1, c; Cu. 625; H. 858. — **195.** P. 70, l. 3. **εἵμαρτο** sums up the effect of *τύχη, ὁ δαίμων, ὁ θεός.* — **οὕτως...πρᾶξαι,** *to fare thus.* — 4. **μηδέ,** *not even:* i. e. a different policy would have left us without *even* that advantage. — 5. **ἐκεῖνος,** sc. Philip. Æschines would have been *οὗτος.* — **ἀφῆκε,** *sent forth* letters, messages, *addresses* (literally *voices*) *of every kind.* Reiske and Schäfer render: nihil indictum reliquit, left nothing unsaid. Cf. 277; *οἵας τότ' ἠφίει φωνὰς Φίλιππος.* — 6. **εἰ νῦν.** *If, as it was, when the battle was fought three days' march from Attica.* *ὁδός* is constantly used to estimate distance, and *ἡμερῶν* is here a genitive of quantity. *νῦν* is used with the same force in the next sentence, opposed to *τότε, in the other case.* — 8. **τῆς χώρας,** partitive, depending on *που.* — 10. **στῆναι,** *to stand, to concentrate, to take breath, to do many things that conduced to the preservation of the state.* The asyndeton is especially vigorous, implying rapidity of thought and action at the crisis. — **καὶ δύο.** The conjunctive particle where English requires the disjunctive. 104. *μικρὰ καί.* — 12. **τότε δ'.** The common aposiopesis to express horror. Quintil., IX., 3, 61. — **ἅ γε μηδέ.** The negative *μή* distributes the force of the relative, to which it entirely belongs in this clause, having no reference to the verb. — 13. **πεῖραν ἔδωκε.** Cf. note, 107. The verb has no subject according to the reading of my text, which is Dindorf's and also that of the majority of editors. Only one MS. reads *εὔνοια...τό.* The rest all agree in reading *εὐνοίᾳ...τῷ.* Two explanations may be suggested: (1) that this is a mixture of constructions not inappropriate in a moment of agitation (Madvig, 216); (2) that we understand for the subject of *ἔδωκε* the Supreme *Δαίμων,* as in the elliptical phrases *ὕει, νίφει, σείει κ. τ. λ.* Render: *It is not worth while to mention those things of which we have not even been suffered to undergo the experience through the kindness of some one of the gods, and by reason of the state having shielded itself with this alliance which you inveigh against.*

196-198. I ONLY DWELL ON THESE DETAILS FOR THE INSTRUCTION OF YOU WHO ARE MY HEARERS. ÆSCHINES KNOWS THEM ALL FULL WELL, AND FOR HIM I SHOULD HAVE FEW WORDS. HE IS THE VILEST AND MOST PERNICIOUS OF ALL YOUR POLITICIANS, AND, IF THINGS WERE RIGHT, NOT I, BUT HE WOULD BE THE PERSON ARRAIGNED BEFORE YOU THIS DAY.

196. 16. **ταυτὶ...τὰ πολλά.** *All this my long story.* τί τὰ πολλὰ ἂν λέγοι τις; p. 886 (*fin.*). — 17. **ἔξωθεν.** *Outside the bar,* or wooden railing (δρύφακτος) by which the court was surrounded. Aristoph., *Eq.*, 675, etc. — 19. **ἐξήρκει,** *were enough.* The same use of the imperfect and pluperfect obtains in Latin (e. g. Hor., 2 *Od.*, XVII., 28, and Verg., *Georg.*, II., 132). The imperfect without ἂν is used to denote what would be an immediate and easily foreseen consequence of anything. Cf. Madv., 118, b, where numerous examples are given. This was probably the original form of the conditional apodosis of past time, and ἄν, the particle of futurity, would come to be added to the verb merely for the sake of greater precision and exactness. C. 631, f; Cu. 542. — 22. **προῄδεις.** ᾔδεισθα or ᾔδησθα are the more common Attic forms in the simple verb, as Whiston observes in his excellent note, citing Lobeck (*Phryn.*, 237). — 23. **τοῖς ἄλλοις** depends on τῆς αὐτῆς. Madv., 37, R. 2; C. 451; Cu. 436, b; G. 186; H. 603. — **197.** P. 71, l. 3. **οὐ γάρ,** 47 note οὐδὲν γὰρ ἄν. The passage implies a high compliment to the people. — 5. **τῇ πόλει.** This dative belongs both to the clause which precedes it and to the clause which follows it, referring as much to τοῦτο πεποιηκώς as it does to φαυλότατος and δυσμενέστατος, and being in each case *dativus incommodi*. — 7. **'Αρίστρατος.** It would appear from the context that Aristratus and Aristolaus were working for Philip's interest in their respective localities. History, however, leaves us in the dark as to their operations. The sense of κρίνουσι is the same as κρίνει in 15, and καθάπαξ resembles our colloquial phrase *out-and-out*. — **198.** 11. **ἐνευδοκιμεῖν,** *to be distinguished in,* that is, *to found a reputation upon.* The inf. may be explained as an acc. of respect (Holmes), or as an inf. of *result* with which ὥστε is usually expressed. Dobree notices that 'Ελλήνων...ἀπέκειτο is hexametric. — 15. **δηλοῖς δὲ καί,** *and you show this too.* — **ὧν ζῇς.** Cf. ὧν βεβίωκεν 130, note. — 16. **οὐ πολιτεύει.** Kennedy preserves the contrast aptly: *your political action and your political inaction.* — 17. **ἀντέκρουσε.** οἱ στρατηγοὶ εὐθὺς ἐν ἀθυμίᾳ ἦσαν ὅτι αὐτοῖς τοῦτό τε πρῶτον ἀντεκεκρούκει. Thuc., VI., 46. — 19. **ῥήγματα καὶ σπάσματα.** Cf. *Olynth.*, 2, p. 24. ὥσπερ γὰρ ἐν τοῖς σώμασιν ἡμῶν ἕως μὲν ἂν ἐρρωμένος ᾖ τις, οὐδὲν ἐπαισθάνεται τῶν καθ' ἕκαστα σαθρῶν, ἐπὰν δὲ ἀρρώστημά τι συμβῇ πάντα κινεῖται, κἂν ῥῆγμα κἂν στρέμμα κἂν ἄλλο τι τῶν ὑπαρχόντων σαθρὸν ᾖ. — 20. **κινεῖται,** *are disturbed,* i. e. the limb originally fractured or sprained gives symptoms of the old weakness returning.

199–205. Supposing we had adopted any other policy than that, supposing we had demeaned ourselves to submit to Macedon, how could we have faced the disgrace of our position? How could a nation like ours with its spirit and traditions and renown have endured such a degradation? Surely in our estimation death is better than dishonor.

199. 21. **ἔγκειται,** *incumbit in: lays great stress upon:* cf. sup. μὴ τὰ συμβάντα συκοφάντει, 192. πολύς is used in the same way (adverbially) by Herodotus, VII., 158, and Thucydides, IV., 22. — 24. **εἰ γάρ,** i. e. if all had been going on as Æschines falsely represents it to have been. On the imperfect tenses, cf. 9, note. — 27. **ὅς.** *You who did not so much as make a sound, did not even open your mouth.* — **οὐδ' οὕτως.** *Not even then ought the city to have abandoned this course, if it had any regard for its honor, or its forefathers, or its future.* By τούτων is clearly meant προεστάναι τῶν ἄλλων, 200. — 200. P. 72, l. 2. **ἀποτυχεῖν,** *to have failed:* a good instance of the aorist retaining its preterite sense in the infinitive mood. Madv., 172, a. — 4. **ἀξιοῦσα,** *after claiming continually to be the leader of others,* i. e. to lead the rest of Greece in their opposition to Philip. Observe the difference between the imperfect in ἀξιοῦσα and the aorist in ἀποστᾶσα, the former denoting a continued, and the latter a momentary action. — 7. **προεῖτο.** Pluperf. midd. *had she thrown away.* The adverb ἀκονιτί, *without a struggle,* occurs in Thuc., IV., 73, καὶ αὐτοῖς ὥσπερ ἀκονιτὶ τὴν νίκην δικαιώς ἂν τίθεσθαι. Vocabulum ex palæstra desumptum. Bremi. — **οὐδένα... οὐχ,** *every conceivable peril.* On οὐδεὶς ὅστις οὐ, see Madv., 105, b, R. — 9. **μὴ γάρ.** Subin. εἴπω: i. e. you, Æschines, would alone have been to blame; not the state; not I; heaven forefend I should name either as responsible. A similar ellipse of εἴπω in the phrase μὴ ὅτι has been already noticed. The genitives πόλεως, ἐμοῦ are, of course, governed by κατέπτυσεν. — 201. 10. **ἑωρῶμεν ἄν.** *With what face, pray, could we have looked on any one visiting our city, had matters converged to their present crisis, and Philip been elected leader and lord of all, and had the struggle to prevent this been fought by others without ourselves, and that though our state has never yet, in all her former ages, preferred dishonorable safety to peril for the sake of honor?* The whole sentence from εἰ τά to ᾑρημένης is one sustained protasis, of which, however, there are two branches, slightly distinct, the first ending with ἁπάντων, and the δέ of τὸν δ' ὑπέρ answering to the μέν of τὰ μέν: i. e. the facts are

put as the first consideration, the omissions are put as the second. — **202.** 18. **τίς...Ἑλλήνων, τίς...βαρβάρων,** i. e. who in the wide world. — 19. **Θηβαίων,** whose supremacy extended, from the date of Leuctra to that of Mantinea (18), nine years. — **πρότερον,** i. e. between the establishment of the Thirty, and the battle of Leuctra; thirty-three years. — 20. **Περσῶν.** Tracing history backwards he arrives at the strong point of Athenian history, the period of the Persian wars. Dissen cites in illustration here Herod., VIII., 136 - 144; IX., 1-5; and *Philipp.*, II., p. 68. — 21. **χάριτος.** That is, they would have been thankful to secure at any sacrifice the resignation by Athens of her post as the champion of Greece, it being assumed that the strength of Greece in reality depended solely on the fact of the Athenian supremacy. — 22. **βούλεται.** The indicative again in an historic consecution. Madv., 130, b. The primary tense is here also the more vigorous. — **λαβούσῃ.** *That she should take whatever she pleased, retaining also whatever she possessed, provided she would submit to dictation, and allow some other power to hold the supremacy of Hellas.* A striking example of the participial clause dominating over the principial clause to which it is in form subordinate (Madv., 176, b). We must notice λαβούσῃ, the aorist, of single acquisition, ἐχούσῃ, the imperfect, of permanent possession. Cf. ἀξιοῦσα and ἀποστᾶσα, 200. By τὸ κελευόμενον ποιεῖν is meant simply a state of submission and subjection, the exact opposite of προεστάναι. So again 204. — **203.** 25. **πάτρια,** *national:* i. e. the feelings which the Athenians, as a nation, inherited from their forefathers. — 27. **μὴ δίκαια.** The negative is μή to make the designation indefinite and hypothetical. C. 686; Cu. 618; G. 283, 5; H. 840. It is trajected from its true position (which should be immediately after δέ) in order to keep it close to δίκαια. Translate: *those who are powerful, it is true, but who do what is wrong.* — P. 73, l. 1. **προσθεμένην** denotes the manner or means, *by attaching herself to.* — 2. **ἀλλ' ἀγωνιζομένη,** *but in her struggle for pre-eminence, for honor, for glory, she has persistently imperilled herself through her whole history.* ἀγωνίζεσθαι, of a severe and protracted effort, as in 20. αἰῶνα accusative of duration of time. — 3. **διατετέλεκε,** cf. C. 677, e; Cu. 590; H. 798; G. 279, note. — **204.** 5. **ἤθεσιν,** *character* as the result of manners and habits. ἦθος = a prolonged and strengthened ἔθος. ἡ δὲ ἠθικὴ ἐξ ἔθους περιγίνεται, ὅθεν καὶ τοὔνομα ἔσχηκε μικρὸν παρέκκλινον ἀπὸ τοῦ ἔθους. Aristot., *Eth.*, II., 1. — 7. **ἀγάσαιτο.** *Who would not admire the valor of those heroes?* It is pretty clear, as Dissen remarks, whom the orator intends for the Themistocles of his own period, and whom for the Cyrsilus. — 8. **καὶ τὴν χώραν καὶ τὴν πόλιν,** *not only their territory, but even their city.* — 10. **τὸ κελευόμενον,** i. e. to submit to the terms dictated by Persia. — 12. **ἀποφηνάμενον.** We have had the full phrase *ἀποφαίνεται γνώμην,* 189. — 13. **Κυρσίλον.** A question arises here on a small historical point. Is this Cyrsilus the same person whom Herodotus (IX., 5) calls Lycidas? If not, there was a singular coincidence in the fate of these two unfortunate men. Each of them is represented as having advocated submission to Persia, and being stoned to death in consequence. But the dates differ. The death of Cyrsilus, according to the orator, took place when the Athenians had only just resolved to abandon Athens and take to their wooden walls. The death of Lycidas, according to Herodotus, took place immediately after the capture of Athens by Mardonius, who then made overtures of peace to the Athenian government who were with the fleet at Salamis. This difference of date is almost conclusive against the identity of the two cases. And surely it is very possible that in this exciting year there were two victims to the patriotic fury of the populace, both of whom died under exactly similar circumstances. The first case would be only too likely to serve as a precedent for the second. Cicero clearly accepts it as a true history, judging by his context in the *De Off.*, III., 11, 48. The commentators, however, generally consider the two cases as one, with a discrepancy in the names. — 14. **τὴν γυναῖκ'.** In the case of Lycidas not only the wife but the children also were murdered. Herod. (*l. c.*). — 205. 16. **δουλεύσουσιν εὐτυχῶς,** *who would secure them a comfortable slavery.* Here the indicative again in the historic consecution adds to the force of the picture. So also *ἐξέσται* in the following clause. Besides adding to the vivacity, the indicatives here "identify the Athenians of the two different ages, and represent the liberty and independence of one epoch as the unbroken continuity of the freedom asserted in another." WHISTON. — 18. **οὐχὶ τῷ πατρί.** Cf. [Platonis] *Epist.*, IX. (translated by Cicero, *De Off.*, I., 7, 22), *ἕκαστος ὑμῶν οὐχ αὑτῷ μόνον γέγονεν, ἀλλὰ τῆς γενέσεως ἡμῶν τὸ μέν τι ἡ πατρὶς μερίζεται, τὸ δέ τι οἱ γεννήσαντες, τὸ δὲ οἱ λοιποὶ φίλοι.* BREMI. — 22. **περιμένει.** *Awaits his appointed and natural end: εἱμαρμένης,* as distinct from suicide; *αὐτόματον* as distinct from death by external violence. — **καὶ τῇ πατρίδι,** sc. *γεγενῆσθαι νομίζων, while the other deeming himself born for his country also.* — 23. **ἐπιδεῖν** in its very frequent sense of *living to see evil.* Æsch., *Ag.*, 1246, Soph., *Trach.*, 1206, etc. — 24. **τὰς ... ἀτιμίας,** *the outrages and indignities.* Observe the emphatic position of τοῦ θανάτου = *death itself.* WHISTON.

206–210. SUCH HAS BEEN ALWAYS YOUR SPIRIT. I DO NOT PRETEND THAT I INSPIRED IT, BUT I DO MAINTAIN THAT I MINISTERED TO IT MOST EFFECTIVELY. IF YOU CONDEMN MY FRIEND, YOU CONDEMN YOUR OWN CONDUCT AT THAT PERIOD. YOU ATTRIBUTE YOUR FAILURE TO MISJUDGMENT, NOT TO MISFORTUNE. BUT OH! BY THE MEMORY OF OUR ANCESTORS, YOUR CONDUCT WAS RIGHT BEYOND QUESTION. IT WAS PERIL FOR THE SAKE OF FREEDOM. THE IDEA OF ÆSCHINES SPEAKING AS HE DID ABOUT NATIONAL TROPHIES AND HONORS, AND THEN EXPECTING THAT YOUR STATESMEN SHOULD DIRECT YOU OTHERWISE THAN WAS WORTHY OF THESE PAST TRIUMPHS! IN PUBLIC LIFE WE ARE ALL OF US BOUND TO FOLLOW THE FOOTSTEPS OF OUR NOBLE FOREFATHERS, AND TO ACT IN ACCORDANCE WITH OUR NATIONAL SPIRIT. YOU, GENTLEMEN, IN YOUR JUDICIAL CAPACITY FEEL THIS, I AM SURE, AS I DO, AND ACT UPON IT WITHOUT FAIL.

206. P. 74, l. 3. **ὑμετέρας.** The predicate is put first for the sake of emphasis. — 5. **τῆς μέντοι διακονίας.** *In the execution, however, of every single thing that has been done, I say that I also have had a share.* On the primary sense of ἐπί see 17: here we might render it *connected with.* — **207.** 6. **τῶν ὅλων.** *The entire business,* i. e. both τὰς προαιρέσεις and τὰ πεπραγμένα, both our policy and its execution. τοῖς ὅλοις 39. — 9. **τιμῆς.** *My honor,* sc. τοῦ στεφάνου. — 10. **ἐγκώμια.** *Your triumphs.* Aristotle (*Rhet.*, I., 9) defines ἐγκώμιον as special laudation bestowed for particular and brilliant actions, ἔπαινος signifying praise in general. — **τῆς μὲν ... τὰ δ'.** These particles mark and emphasize the comparison between the less injury done to the orator and the greater wrong inflicted on his country: *seeks to deprive me, indeed, of my honor for the present, but robs you of your triumphs for all future time.* — 12. **τουδί.** *If you condemn my friend Ctesiphon, on the plea that I have not advised our state for the best, you will adjudge yourselves to have done wrong, and not to have suffered those results merely through the perverseness of fortune.* He means that in condemning his policy and action they would practically condemn their own, as he had been merely the mouthpiece and instrument of the national will. Thus their failures would be deserved, not accidental. On the participial construction see Madvig, 175, 176. With ἀγνωμοσύνῃ Schäfer compares Soph., *O. C.*, 86: Φοίβῳ τε κἀμοὶ μὴ γένησθ' ἀγνώ-

μονες: also p. 1468, l. 15. In *δόξετε* here there is much of the technical meaning *to be formally decreed* which *δοκεῖν* so often possesses. — 208. 17. **προκινδυνεύσαντας.** *Who bore the brunt.* The compound *προ-* is of locus here, i. e. the forefront of the battle. The expression is probably adopted from Thucydides (I., 73), who says that, we alone, sc. the Athenians, at Marathon bore the brunt of battle with the barbarian, *προκινδυνεῦσαι τῷ βαρβάρῳ*. This apostrophe is deservedly admired by Longinus (c. 16), Hermogenes (p. 260), Aristides (p. 170), Quintilian, XI., 3, etc. —18. **παραταξαμένους.** *Who stood in the ranks:* Thuc., I., 29. It has been well observed by all critics that the orator carefully avoids in this description any allusion to the *victories* of Marathon, Platæa, etc. He is citing examples, not of *success*, but of *intrepidity*, else of course his parallel would fail. And he justifies his parallel most happily by the words at the close of this sentence *οὓς ἅπαντας...μόνους*. See Longinus, l. c., Lord Brougham (Works VII., 124), Whiston in loc., et al. — 20. **μνήμασι.** *Τιθέασιν οὖν ἐς τὸ δημόσιον σῆμα, ὅ ἐστιν ἐπὶ τοῦ καλλίστου προαστείου τῆς πόλεως* (the Ceramicus) *καὶ ἀεὶ ἐν αὐτῷ θάπτουσι τοὺς ἐκ τῶν πολέμων.* Thuc., II., 34. He excepts the heroes of Marathon who were buried on the spot where they fell. — 24. **δικαίως.** Cf. *εἰκότως* 23. — 209. 27. **γραμματοκύφων.** Derived, according to *Etym. Mag.*, either from *κυφός* (*ὅτι οἱ γραμματεῖς προκεκυφότες γράφουσιν*) or else from *κύφων* the pillory (*ἐπεὶ οἱ ἀγοραῖοι τῷ κύφωνι μαστιγοῦνται*)! We have no English equivalent. Perhaps *you scribbling scoundrel* would be sufficiently abusive. — P. 75, l. 2. **ἔλεγες.** Æschines, p. 79 sq. *πότερον ὑμῖν ἀμείνων ἀνὴρ εἶναι δοκεῖ Θεμιστοκλῆς ὁ στρατηγήσας ὅτε τὴν περὶ Σαλαμῖνα ναυμαχίαν τὸν Πέρσην ἐνικᾶτε, ἢ Δημοσθένης ὁ τὰς τάξεις λιπών; κ. τ. λ.* — **ὧν**, i. e. they were, he alleges, irrelevant in the present action against Ctesiphon. *And yet what of these were required for the present trial?* — **τίνος.** We must resolve this, in English, into an interrogative principal sentence, Madv., 198, a. — 4. **τὸν περί.** *And I who was coming forward to advise the state about her supremacy, in whose spirit ought I to have mounted the Bema? The spirit of a man who would say what was unworthy of the past? πρωτείων*, i. e. to suggest a policy by which she should retain her primacy, 66. The masculine gender of *τίνος* is clear from the context. The gender of *τούτων* is neuter, and it must include the notion of *τρόπαια, μάχας, κ. τ. λ.* which he has specified above. So Holmes. But Westermann, Whiston, Kennedy, Leland, and the commentators generally, take it to be masculine, and refer it to the Athenians, *unworthy of the people.* — 210. 7. **δικαίως.** *Nay, but I should not have been fit to live;* strictly, *I should have deserved to be executed.* We have to supply εἰ φρόνημα τοιοῦτον ἔλαβον. — **ὑμᾶς,** τοὺς δικάστας as distinct from himself τὸν σύμβουλον. — 8. **ἀπό.** *Starting from,* i. e. *in:* διανοίας *spirit.* — 9. **τὰ μέν.** *But to judge the affairs* (lit. *contracts,* συμβόλαια) *of every-day life, on the one hand with a view* (σκοποῦντας) *to special laws and acts, but public measures on the other hand looking only,* etc. **συμβόλαια** is object of κρίνειν. — **ἰδίων.** *Special.* In ordinary cases, civil or criminal, they would be bound to form their decision according to the definite statutes of their code, applied to each individual case. But in a political trial they might frame their sentence according to traditional spirit and precedent, rather than by any letter of written law. The orator's drift is clear. He wishes the jury to overlook the formal illegality of Ctesiphon's proposal, in consideration of the great political services which that proposal was intended to remunerate. — 12. **ἀποβλέποντας.** Observe the force of the preposition, looking *back,* or looking *away.* ἀξιώματα = *worthy examples,* strictly, the obligations imposed by the illustrious deeds of their ancestors. Compare Whiston's note. — 13. **τῇ βακτηρίᾳ.** *His staff and his ticket,* i. e. his official paraphernalia. On the *staff* which each dicast received was painted the letter indicating the court in which he was to serve. The *ticket* he delivered to the prytanes after the sitting, and thus received his fee of three obols. See Dic. of Ant., Dicastery, and Dicasts.

211, 212. BUT I HAVE BEEN DIGRESSING AND MUST NOW SUPPLY AN OMISSION. YOU MUST TAKE THE LETTER WE WROTE AS YOUR AMBASSADORS AT THEBES. ÆSCHINES GIVES ME NO CREDIT FOR OUR DIPLOMATIC SUCCESSES, BUT ONLY FOR OUR MILITARY FAILURES. YET WITH THE LATTER I HAD NOTHING TO DO, AND WITH THE FORMER EVERYTHING.

211. 17. **Ἀλλὰ γάρ.** 42. On ἔστιν ἃ see Madv., 102, b., and Liddell and Scott's Lex. — 19. **ὁπόθεν,** i. e. ἐκεῖσε ὁπόθεν 66. — 22. **τῶν ἄλλων.** Puta Ænianorum, Dolopum, Phthiotarum, Ætolorum. DISSEN. — 23. **πρέσβεις.** See Plutarch's *Vita Demosth.,* c. 18. Amyntas and Clearchus are named as the Macedonian envoys. — 25. **νῦν.** At this present moment (while the story told at the time of the embassy was very different). He appeals to the records of the actual period to confirm him. — **212.** 27. **καίτοι.** *And, I assure you, my opponent has adopted such an extravagance of calumny that, if, on the one* *hand, any of our objects was achieved, he says it was thanks to opportunity not to me.* Cf. Æsch. c. Ctes., 141, p. 76, l. 1. On ὥστε with the indicative see 33, 120, and on ἑτέρως see 85. ὡς adds emphasis = *quite otherwise,* strictly as different as possible. C. 711; Cu. 631; H. 664. — P. 76, l. 6. **συναίτιος,** i. e. he does not give me credit for even a share in the good, while he imputes to me the whole of the evil. **συναιτίας** 64. Render: *so it seems I, the counsellor and orator, am judged by him to have no share in any of the results of argument and counsel, but to be the sole author of the misfortunes that have attended our arms and strategy.* — **ΕΠΙΣΤΟΛΗ.** At this point the forgers' ingenuity or perseverance would seem to have been exhausted, and to the great relief both of reader and commentator we are troubled with no more spurious documents in the rest of the oration.

213–217. The Assembly was held: the allies of Philip spoke first; we made our reply. I need not weary you with details. Thebes accepted our proposal and called upon us to aid them. They could not have paid us a higher honor. And we acted with Thebes throughout the campaign in a manner which showed we deserved that honor. Remember our public rejoicings at the time. Did Æschines take his part in them? Then what does he mean by his present denunciation? Did he take no part in those public rejoicings? Then what a wretch he must have been!

213. 11. **ἐποιήσαντο,** sc. the Thebans. — 12. **ἐκείνους,** the ambassadors of Philip and the Thessalians. — 16. **τὸ δ' οὖν.** *And in fine they required them to show their gratitude for the benefits they had received from Philip and to take satisfaction for the wrongs which they had received from you.* κεφάλαιον is another adverbial accusative, Madv., 31, d; Cr. 483; Cu. 404; G. 160; H. 552. The imperfect ἠξίουν refers to the whole tenor of their speech; as also ἐδημηγόρουν above. — 19. **ὁποτέρως.** They demanded either that Thebes should join in the invasion, or at any rate that they should give the invaders free passage. They promised a share of the spoil in either event, and threatened the devastation of Bœotia in any other. — **διέντας** and **συνεμβαλόντας** agree with αὐτούς in the previous line and denote the two ways, either of which they (the Thebans) may choose. — 21. **ἐκ τῆς,** i. e. *plundered from.* Constructio prægnans. C. 704; H. 618, a. — 23. **ἐκ δὲ ὧν...ἔφασαν,** *while as the result of what they said we should advise, property in Bœotia would be plundered by the war.* τὰ...διαρπασθη-

σόμενα, like βοσκήματα...ἥξοντα is governed by ἐδείκνυσαν. — P. 77, l. 1. **συντείνοντ'.** *All aiming at the same result.* — **214.** 2. **ἀντείπομεν.** Absent from Σ, but found in all the other MSS. Its ellipsis, though quite grammatical, would not at all improve the sentence. — **ἐγὼ μέν.** *I myself would give my very life to repeat.* The transposition of τοῦ βίου is for the sake of emphasis. The meanings of ἀντί seem to pass through the following steps, (1) over against, (2) a counterbalance, (3) an equivalent, (4) a substitute. — 4. **ὑμᾶς** with **δέδοικα** is emphatic for ὑμεῖς with νομίσητε. μή is *lest* governing νομίσητε. — 5. **κατακλυσμόν.** *A deluge had swept over the events,* i. e. all sign and trace of them had been obliterated: on ὥσπερ ἂν εἰ see Madv., 139, c; C. 622, d; H. 754. — **215.** 9. **Μετὰ ταῦτα.** With this we must compare throughout the corresponding passage of Æschines (pp. 73–75) where he represents that the Thebans begged for the aid and alliance of Athens, simply under the pressure of their alarm at the seizure of Elatea by Philip, and prior to "a single syllable of any decree being proposed by Demosthenes." The Athenians then having marched in force to Thebes, Philip, according to Æschines, was afraid to continue the war, and wished to make peace. So, he says, did the Thebans: and the latter requested the Athenian troops to retire to Athens, and the Ecclesia to be convened for discussion of Philip's proposal. It was only at this later Ecclesia, says Æschines, that Demosthenes urged the policy of carrying on the war against Philip, and over-persuaded the Thebans into the same course, for fear the latter should make peace independently, and get pay from Philip for doing so, from which pecuniary benefit Demosthenes would be excluded. Perhaps Æschines believed all this when he said it; the historical records of the period seem to have been in the greatest confusion; and it was impossible to prove distinctly why or when Thebes joined with Athens against Macedon. But the account given by Demosthenes in the description of that Ecclesia (169 sq. Ἑσπέρα μὲν γὰρ ἦν) is so circumstantial, and appeals so directly to the memory of those amongst his hearers who had been present on that great occasion, that if he had not been speaking the truth, exposure and ruin must have followed. In explanation of this confusion in the facts and of the discrepancy between the orators, it will be remembered that eight years had elapsed between the battle of Chæronea and the delivery of the speeches on the Crown, and a still longer interval (it is not known how long) between that battle and the revised edition of Æschines's speech. Whiston agrees with Dissen that Æschines's statements, so far as they differ from the narrative of Demosthenes, were *inserted* in the *revised* edition, and are "manifesta mendacia." — 10. **ἐξῆτε, ἐβοηθεῖτε.** This simple asyndeton is much admired by Bremi, as descriptive of rapid action. — 11. **ὁπλιτῶν.** The *Theban* infantry and cavalry were encamped outside, while the Athenian forces were admitted within the walls. The compliment to Athens is obvious, and the nature of the confidence so displayed receives illustration from the sentence *εἰς τὰς οἰκίας...τιμιώτατα.* Dissen objects to this the absence of the proper pronouns, *their* and *your.* But the articles take the place of the pronouns and emphasize the distinction which is evident from the connection. Render: *while their infantry and their cavalry were without the walls they received your army,* etc. — 15. **πᾶσιν.** *In the eyes* of *all mankind.* Dative of relation, Madv., *G. S.*, 35. — **καθ'.** *Upon.* A good example of *κατά without* its sense of hostility preceding the genitive case (cf. 17 note). So p. 135, *μέγιστον καθ' ὑμῶν ἐγκώμιον.* — 20. **πᾶσι δ'.** The particle *δέ* connects the sentence *καίτοι...ἔδειξαν* with the sentence *καὶ γάρ...Φιλίππου.* As examples of *δέ* standing further on in a sentence than its usual place of second word the Lexica all quote Soph., *El.*, 1117; Xen., *Hellen.*, V., 2, 37, etc. The translation of *καὶ τὰ παρ' αὐτοῖς καί* thus becomes, *both with them and.* — 22. **σωφροσύνης.** *Showed they had confidence in you, as regarded your morality.* The Greek is literally *belief in morality as regarded you.* No single English word can render *σωφροσύνης.* Whiston translates it *self-command,* and Kennedy *good behavior.* The connection shows that self-command is especially intended, although something more is also comprehended. — 24. **ἐφάνησαν,** *were shown* by the facts in the case. —**216.** P. 78, l. 3. **μάχας.** Accusative of time, Madv., *G. S.*, 30. Others take it as a sort of cognate accusative, Madv., 26, a; C. 477; Cu. 400; G. 159; H. 547. — **τοῦ ποταμοῦ.** The Cephissus. The first battle was fought in the valley of the Cephissus between Elatea and Thebes. — 4. **χειμερινήν.** *In the winter,* according to Grote, who supposes a ten months' interval between October of 339 and August of 338. On the other hand Thirlwall prefers to render *of the storm.* The Lexica all concur in asserting that this latter idea would in Attic be usually expressed by *χειμέριος,* not by *χειμερινός,* which generally beyond question means *in the winter.* In the great obscurity of the history concerning this period, it is quite impossible to settle such minor details with precision. I prefer the view of Grote, as being the best in regard to the language here, and also quite consistent with the other history. But I cordially agree with Reiske also when he says, "hæc tanti non est quærere. Quod sciri nequit de eo ne quærendum quidem est. Multa sunt in vetustis auctoribus obscura quæ nulla vis ingenii, nulla investigandi industria, nulla dies unquam aperiet." —217. 9. **ζήλου.** *Bliss.* οἵας λατρείας ἀνθ' ὅσου ζήλου τρέφει. Soph., *Aj.*, 503. So Holmes. Better, *emulation*, or *admiration*. — 13. **ἐξητάζετο.** *Was proved to have been along with the rest*, i. e. taking a share in the general rejoicings. — 14. **μᾶλλον...ὅσια,** *or, rather, does he not act impiously even.* — 15. **εἰ ὧν...θεούς,** *if what he himself called the gods to witness as being most excellent, this he now expects you to condemn as not most excellent, you who have sworn by those gods,* sc. the very gods to whom he then appealed for just the opposite. — **μάρτυρας,** i. e. by means of the θυσίαι καὶ πομπαί 17. He means that nothing can more effectively put a national success on record than the circumstance that it has been the subject of national thanksgiving to heaven. — 16. **ψηφίσασθαι,** i. e. by condemning Ctesiphon they would condemn the orator's policy and its results, among which would be included the particular triumph referred to here. — 17. **ὀμωμοκότας.** τὸν ὅρκον 2. — **εἰ δὲ μή.** The dilemma is merely rhetorical, as Lord Brougham well observes ; Æschines could easily have answered that he saw the fallacy of those rejoicings, though no one else at Athens did so ; that therefore he declined to share them, and stayed at home in seclusion and sorrow. At the same time, his Lordship admires the rhetorical excellence of the dilemma and the exquisite beauty and force of the passage.

218. SO THEBES AND OURSELVES WERE REJOICING AND GIVING THANKS : AND PHILIP WAS IN A STATE OF ALARM AS HIS LETTERS PROVE. THIS WAS ALL MY DOING.

218. 21. **ἦμεν ἐν.** *We were full of thanksgivings.* The preposition of place introduces the *status in quo.* — 22. **νομίζειν.** *Belief:* the awkwardness of the construction is redeemed by its antithetic success. — **περιειστήκει.** *It had come about that those who seemed likely to need succor, owing to the conduct of these men, were themselves sending succor to others in consequence of following my counsels.* There is no difference of translation between ἀφ' ὧν and ἐξ ὧν in this sentence ; the change is merely for variety. — 25. **ἠφίει.** The double augment is peculiarly Attic. "In Demosthene id deesse nusquam notavi." BREMI. — **φωνάς.** *Strong expressions.* Cf. πᾶσαν, τὸ λεγόμενον, φωνὴν ἱέντα,

Plato, 890, D, 530, etc. Cf. 222. — P. 79, l. 4. **συνέχεια.** *Persistence; pertinacity.* From the context, which is sarcastic, we must rather take the word in its bad sense. — **πλάνοι.** *Rovings,* i. e. *πρέσβειαι*: the derisive tone is very marked both in this and the two next phrases. — **ταλαιπωρίαι.** *Tribulations.* — **τὰ πολλά.** *Those numerous.* Cf. *τὰ πολλὰ γράμματα*, Act. Apost., xxvi., 24, where the same irony is underlying. These nominatives are the subjects of *ἀπειργάσατο*, which is singular to agree with the neuter plural *ψηφίσματα*, and to sum them all up together = *what it all accomplished.*

219-221. ATHENS HAS HAD A HOST OF GOOD STATESMEN BESIDES MYSELF, BUT NEVER ONE WHO WORKED SO HARD OR DEVOTED HIMSELF SO ENTIRELY. NOT THAT I HAD ANY EXTRAVAGANT OPINION OF MY OWN POWER. BUT I THOUGHT THE CRISIS EXACTED THE UTMOST PERSONAL EFFORTS, AND THAT NO ONE'S PERSONAL EFFORTS COULD BE MORE EFFECTUAL THAN MINE.

219. 7. **πολλοί.** Compare the exactly parallel passage, p. 436, l. 12, *De F. L.* — **ἐκεῖνος,** *that famous.* C. 542, b. — 9. **Καλλίστρατος.** *μετὰ Καλλίστρατον τὸν Ἀφιδναῖον τῶν ἄλλων μάλιστα εἰπεῖν δύνασθαι*, Æschin., p. 44 (*med.*). Mentioned as an exile endeavoring to return illegally in Demosthenes *adv. Polycl.*, p. 1221. Honorably mentioned by the orator, pp. 1187, 1353, 1359, if those orations are genuine. Cf. Plut., *Dem.*, 5. Libanius (*Vit. Dem.*, p. 503) says that the orator when a boy heard Callistratus speak on the Oropus question, and thence conceived his own passion for rhetoric and public speaking. — **Ἀριστοφῶν,** 70. — **Κέφαλος.** A leading statesman in the political crisis of 403. Although so prominent, he seems to have never committed himself, 351. Æschines speaks of him with enthusiasm, p. 81. So does Dinarchus, pp. 95, 100. — **Θρασύβουλος.** The hero of the revolution in 403. Dinarch., p. 93 (*med.*); Lys., p. 124; Isocr., p. 375 (*fin.*); Æschin., p. 82, etc. All the Attic orators concur in the praises of this *Θρασύβουλος* (*Λύκου Στειριεύς*). There were four Thrasybuli in the same period, but no other of the same reputation. We need have no doubt as to which of the four the orator speaks of here. — 11. **εἰς οὐδέν.** Closely connected with *διὰ παντός.* Whatever movement they took up they did not (so the orator alleges) persevere in supporting it through every phase and department, as he professes to have done himself. — 12. **ἂν ἐπρέσβευσεν.** Frequentative: like our idiom *would not,* though literally *would not have.* Cf. Aristoph., *Pax,* 640-644. — 13. **ὑπελείπε.** *Al-*

ways reserved for himself. The ὑπ- describes the *underlying* motive. The force of the imperfect is here strongly marked. A parallel expression is in Æschin., p. 41 (*fin.*), αὐτοῖς κατέλιπον τὴν ἀναφοράν. — 14. **ἅμα μὲν...ἅμα δ'**, *at once...and*, or *not only...but also.* — **ἀναφοράν.** *Resource, something to fall back upon.* — **220.** 17. **οὕτως.** *So thoroughly:* referring, I think, to the whole sentence, though Whiston limits it to μέγαν, as in 163. — 19. **χώραν.** *To allow any place or even forethought for my personal safety.* χώρα seems to be very rare in this sense. The Lexica only quote Aristot., *H. A.*, X., 3. 4, χώραν παρέχειν (*locum dare*), which is not an exact parallel. The orator means that he did not give his personal safety a thought, or reserve himself any avenue of escape from the consequences ; that he risked all without exception. — 20. **ἀγαπητόν.** *Must be thankful if one could do one's duty without a single omission,* i. e. man's sole aim at that crisis should have been to do his duty thoroughly, reckless of personal considerations, and then to take the consequences be they what they might. And a man should have been thankful even to have the opportunity of so doing his duty ; whatever the personal peril which might be involved in the deed. Others take ἃ δεῖ πράξειεν *to meet his fate,* but, I think, not so well. — **221.** 22. **τυχόν.** *It may be; perhaps.* Adv. Acc., Madvig, *G. S.*, 182 ; C. 483 ; Cu. 401 ; G. 160 ; H. 552. — 23. **μήτε γράφοντ', κ. τ. λ.** The participle here and in the following clauses denotes the condition : *neither if he proposed measures would any one propose them better, nor if he tried* (imperf., C. 594 ; Cu. 489 ; G. 200 ; H. 702) *to execute them,* etc. βέλτιον is to be supplied with πρᾶξαι. — 26. **ἔταττον.** *I always in everything put myself at the post.* For ἐν πᾶσιν we should rather expect ἐπὶ πάντα according to the usual construction of τάσσειν : but the sense is not altered, for we supply the ἐπί out of the proleptic ἐν.

222. SUCH WAS THE RESULT OF MY POLICY. FOR THIS IT WAS RIGHTLY PROPOSED THAT I SHOULD RECEIVE A CROWN.

P. 80, l. 1. **Εἰς ταῦτα,** *to such a state.* — 2. **ταύτην τὴν φωνήν,** *such the voice he uttered, although accustomed to vaunt.* The participle is concessive. The middle voice expresses the personal motive from which boasting must proceed. — 4. **ἐστεφανούμην.** *Was to be crowned.* On this use of the imperfect, see Madv., *G. S.*, 113, r. 1 ; C. 594 ; Cu. 489 ; G. 200, N. 2 ; H. 702. — 5. **γραψάμενος.** *Who indicted the proposers* (Demomeles and Hyperides ; see 82, δευτέρου). The full phrase would have been ὁ γραψάμενος τὸν Δ. καὶ τὸν Ὑ. παρανόμων.

On γραφή, cf. 3, note ἑλεῖν. — 6. **Διώνδας.** Διώνδου μανία, 249. — **τὸ μέρος.** 103, and 82 ἀτιμώσαντες. — 7. **ἀποπεφευγότα.** *Which were then legally confirmed,* lit. *acquitted.* He means that they passed through the ordeal of a public prosecution against their proposer, and as he was acquitted, their justice and correctness were thoroughly vindicated.

223-226. WHY DID NOT ÆSCHINES OPPOSE THIS DECREE WHICH WAS IDENTICAL IN TERMS WITH CTESIPHON'S? BECAUSE HE KNEW HE HAD NO CHANCE OF GETTING A VERDICT ON THE FACTS AS LONG AS THE FACTS WERE FRESH IN PEOPLE'S MEMORIES. HIS ONLY CHANCE WAS TO WAIT TILL THE FACTS HAD BEEN FORGOTTEN, AND THEN TO CONCOCT A FRAUDULENT PROSECUTION DEPENDING ON QUIBBLES OF LAW AND RHETORIC.

223. 13. **τότε.** For the date, see 82. — 15. **μᾶλλον εἰκότως,** *with more reason.*—16. **τόνδ'.** *My friend here:* deictic. So τῷδε = *my client.* He means, that to prosecute Ctesiphon, after omitting to prosecute those who had done exactly the same already, was an irrational proceeding. Whether Ctesiphon's act was right or wrong, at all events it had precedents. If *he* was to be prosecuted now, why were not the former offenders prosecuted in *their* time? — **224.** 17. **ἀνενεγκεῖν** is exactly the Latin *referre ad* and our own *refer to* (as precedents). — **γνώσεις.** The decision pronounced in the Demomeles case. No other is meant. The plural only introduces the idea of the abstract. — 18. **αὐτόν.** If Demomeles was prosecuted, at any rate it was not *Æschines* who was the prosecutor. Why does *he* bring an action now, whereas he did not bring any then? — 20. **πραχθέντων.** *Settled:* like our colloquial use of *done.* He claims that the verdict on his policy was pronounced once for all in the Demomeles case, and that the question cannot be reopened legally. — 21. **αὐτό.** *The actual fact would have been tried per se, before it had contracted any of these precedents.* The bare question, whether Demosthenes was a good statesman or not, would have been put before the court, without legal or rhetorical complication. — **225.** 23. **οὐκ ἦν.** *There was no opportunity* or *it was not possible.* — P. 81, l. 1. **ἐκλέξαντα** has for its object the sentence ἃ μήτε — ῥηθῆναι; but this sentence represents also the cognate accusative after διαβάλλειν. Translate: *picking out what no one knew before, nor supposed would be said to-day, to calumniate them, by changing dates and substituting false motives for action instead of the true ones, to appear to speak to the purpose.* — **τι λέγειν** is the opposite of οὐδὲν λέγειν. Compare our *something to say* and *nothing to say.* Plato is particularly

fond of these phrases. — 3. **προφάσεις.** Very nearly *motives* in our common use of that word. — 5. **πεπραγμένοις** is the dative of the remote object after *μεταθέντα*. — **226.** 6. **τῆς ἀληθείας.** 17 first note. The article adds to the emphasis: *the truth par excellence;* i. e. *real truth, absolute truth: μόνον οὐκ, only not = all but, almost.* — 9. **παρ' αὐτά,** 13, note, s. v. — 10. **ῥητόρων ἀγῶνα.** *An oratorical arena.* Whiston aptly cites Thucyd., III., 67. — 12. **λόγου κρίσιν.** *A decision on power of speaking.* This objective use of the genitive is well illustrated in Madv., *G. S.*, 48.

227 – 231. I MUST NOTICE HERE AN INGENIOUS SOPHISM OF MY OPPONENT'S. HE SAYS YOU OUGHT TO CAST UP MY SERVICES AND REWARDS ARITHMETICALLY, AND SEE WHETHER THERE IS ANY BALANCE IN MY FAVOR; OR RATHER, HE SAYS, YOU WILL SEE THERE IS NONE. NOW I DENY ALTOGETHER THAT PUBLIC SERVICES CAN BE TREATED LIKE SUMS IN ARITHMETIC. BUT YOU MAY SET FACTS AGAINST FACTS, SET WHAT HAPPENED AGAINST WHAT WOULD HAVE HAPPENED HAD IT NOT BEEN FOR ME. I AM QUITE CONTENT TO ABIDE BY THAT CALCULATION.

227. 14. **φησί.** It is indispensable to quote in full the passage of Æschines here referred to, viz., p. 62, 59: *εἰ δέ τισιν ὑμῶν ἐξαίφνης ἀκούσασιν ἀπιστότερος προσπέπτωκεν ὁ τοιοῦτος λόγος, ἐκείνως τὴν ὑπό- λοιπον ποιήσασθε ἀκρόασιν, ὥσπερ ὅταν περὶ χρημάτων ἀνηλωμένων διὰ πολλοῦ χρόνου καθεζώμεθα ἐπὶ τοὺς λογισμούς. ἐρχόμεθα δή που ψευδεῖς οἴκοθεν ἐνίοτε δόξας ἔχοντες κατὰ τῶν λογισμῶν. ἀλλ' ὅμως ἐπειδὰν ὁ λόγος συγκεφαλαιωθῇ, οὐδεὶς ὑμῶν ἐστιν οὕτω δύσκολος τὴν φύσιν ὅστις οὐκ ἀπέρχεται τοῦθ' ὁμολογήσας καὶ ἐπινεύσας ἀληθὲς εἶναι ὅ τι ἂν αὐτὸς ὁ λογισμὸς αἱρῇ. οὕτω καὶ νῦν τὴν ἀκρόασιν ποιήσασθε.* — 15. **οἴκοθεν... ἀμελῆσαι,** *to forget the opinion concerning* US *which you have brought from home.* The phraseology, it will be seen, is borrowed from Æschines. — 17. **λογίζησθε.** *Cast up accounts under the impression that a man has a balance.* The commentators differ as to the question whether the illustration is drawn from the auditing of official accounts by the *Λογισταί*, or from the settling of accounts in trade and at the bank; Holmes, Kennedy, and others insisting on the former, Dissen, Whiston, etc., preferring the latter view. Perhaps the passage in Æschines favors the former. But the language of Demosthenes, *οἰόμενοι περιεῖναι χρήματα*, certainly accords better with the latter. Perhaps we may say with Westermann that while Æschines seems to have in mind the auditing of official accounts, Demosthenes makes it *general.* — **καθαραὶ...ψῆφοι,**

if the sums are even: i. e. if the amount on the credit side is exactly the same as the amount on the debit. The expression arose from a primitive method of keeping accounts with pebbles (ψῆφοι), literally, *if the pebbles are clear*, with no balance left on either side. —18. **συγχωρεῖτε**, *you acquiesce in that result;* the acquiescence involves *concession* of the previous idea that there was a balance in hand, and *concurrence* in the correctness of the accounts examined. The verb συγχωρεῖν combines both these meanings. — **οὕτω**, i. e. if they found no balance in the orator's favor, however much they expected beforehand to find it, Æschines had begged they would act upon that finding, not upon their previous and misconceived idea. προσθέσθαι depends on προσήκειν and means *consent to, accept.* — **228.** 22. **ὑπάρχειν**, *that we are, to begin with* (§ 1), *thoroughly convinced in ourselves* (perfect tense, middle voice). ὑπαρχούσης which follows is exactly our *preexisting.* — 24. **οὐ γὰρ ἄν**, 47, second note. — **229.** 26. **οὐ δίκαια**, 18, s. v. — P. 82, l. 1. **τιθεὶς**. *Not by casting accounts*, literally, playing pebbles. The ἀβάκιον contained a number of parallel columns, the extreme right-hand column being reserved for the units, the first on its left for the tens, the next for the hundreds, and so on. Each number in each column would be represented by actually placing on the board in that column the same number of pebbles; for a debit and credit account two ἀβάκια would be required. If their columns tallied exactly, then the ψῆφοι were καθαραί. This was usually ascertained by examining the two ἀβάκια side by side, and column by column, and taking off (ἀντανελεῖν) a pebble from the one ἀβάκιον for every pebble in the other. See Smith, Dic. Ant., for a diagram of the Abacus. — **οὐ γάρ...λογισμός**, *for this mode of reckoning*, sc. the arithmetical, *does not belong to public affairs.* — **230.** 10. **ἡμᾶς**, the object of φέρειν καὶ ἄγειν, is placed before them for emphasis. So ἐν εἰρήνῃ, the predicate of εἶναι, precedes even the subject of the verb for the same reason. —12. **ἐκ θαλάττης**. AT *sea* is exactly the equivalent of this proleptic use. — **231.** 15. **ψήφοις**. *Sums in arithmetic.* His retort relies on the technical character of the method for casting up accounts. Facts, *deeds*, cannot, like pebbles, be taken up and laid aside. — 16. **ἀντανελεῖν**, *or that we ought to clear these off*, that is, balance them against our misfortunes. — 18. **προστίθημι**. This arithmetical term is, of course, introduced *avec intention* = *add to the account.* — 21. **φιλανθρωπίας**. The *clemency* with which Philip treated Athens after the battle of Chæronea was in marked contrast with his *severity* to *others*, particularly the Thebans. Demades writes (Fragm. 1), ἔγραψα καὶ Φιλίππῳ τιμάς· οὐκ ἀρνοῦμαι. δισχιλίους γὰρ αἰχμαλώτους ἄνευ λύτρων, καὶ χίλια πολιτῶν σώματα χωρὶς κήρυκος, καὶ τὸν Ὠρωπὸν ἄνευ πρεσβείας λαβὼν ὑμῖν ταῦτ' ἔγραψα. — 22. **περιβαλλόμενος**, *investing himself with.* The phrase is common enough, but meant to be sarcastic here, as though Philip *draped* himself in royal and lordly generosity to produce a *fictitious* impression on the mind of Greece. — **καλῶς ποιοῦντες.** *Fortunæ beneficio: happily.* The distinction between this and καλῶς πράττοντες is illustrated in the notorious passage, p. 490 (*med.*), ὅτε δ' ὑμεῖς, καλῶς ποιοῦντες, καὶ κατὰ τὰς κοινὰς πράξεις καὶ κατὰ τἄλλα πάντα ἄμεινον ἐκείνων πράττετε.

232, 233. AND REALLY I MUST NOTICE HOW UNWORTHY IT WAS OF MY OPPONENT TO MIMIC MY LANGUAGE AND GESTURES. HIS BUSINESS WAS TO EXAMINE OUR PUBLIC HISTORY: AS HE HAS NOT DONE SO, I SHALL DO IT MYSELF.

232. 25. **συκοφαντεῖν** may be paraphrased here *to libel.* Cf. 118, 188. So below 233 = *to make a wilfully false and censorious accusation.* — 27. **παραδείγματα πλάττων**, *fabricating illustrations*, such, for example, as that of striking the balance by counters. Compare Whiston, in loc. — P. 83, l. 1. **μιμούμενος.** Æschin., p. 77 (*med.*), οὐ μέμνησθε αὐτοῦ τὰ μιαρὰ ῥήματα...καὶ πάλιν ὅτε κύκλῳ περιδινῶν σεαυτὸν ἐπὶ τοῦ βήματος ἔλεγες, κ. τ. λ. — **παρὰ τοῦτο.** *All in consequence of this, (don't you see?) the affairs of Greece have turned out as they have.* — **εἰ**, *if*, instead of ὅτι, *because.* Madv., *G. S.*, 75. Cf. Cic., *Orat.*, VIII. — **233.** 5. **ἂν ἐσκόπει** continues the apodosis: *would have considered in detail* (imperfect). — **ἐπ' αὐτῶν τῶν ἔργων**, *in view of the simple facts*, or *on the basis of* them. Whiston renders: *keeping to* them. — 6. **εἰσῄειν.** *Entered into public business*, cf. 60. — 11. **πέφευγας.** *Have shirked*, i. e. avoided putting the matter on its true issue. Cf. 116.

234–239. OUR STRENGTH CONSISTED OF THE MINOR ISLANDS ONLY, BESIDES OUR HOME RESOURCES. ALL OUR NEIGHBOR STATES WERE HOSTILE. PHILIP ON THE OTHER HAND POSSESSED DESPOTIC POWER, TRAINED ARMIES, AMPLE MONEY, AND INDEPENDENT PERSONAL ACTION. WHAT HAD I, HIS ANTAGONIST? NOTHING, EXCEPT THE PRIVILEGE OF SPEAKING, AND THAT HIS ATHENIAN SUPPORTERS SHARED ALONG WITH ME. STILL, EVEN THUS, I GOT YOU ALLIES, ARMIES, FUNDS. IT IS ABSURD TO DISCUSS NOW WHETHER THOSE FUNDS WERE RAISED IN FAIR PROPORTIONS FROM EACH CONTRIBUTING STATE. WE NEVER OURSELVES PUT THAT

QUESTION ABOUT OUR SHARE IN SALAMIS. SMALL THANKS WILL ANY OF THESE STATES GIVE YOU FOR BRINGING THIS CHARGE AGAINST ME NOW, INSTEAD OF WATCHING THE CASE FOR THEIR INTERESTS AT THE ACTUAL TIME.

234. 15. **Χίος.** This and the other two islands had won their liberty in the Social War of 355. — 16. **σύνταξιν.** *A subscription.* This term was invented as a euphemism for *φόρος* tribute; see Harpocration, s. v. The subscription here alluded to was paid under the arrangement of the new confederation formed in 377. Cf. Dinarch., p. 92. These changes of the relation between Athens and the islands are fully described in Grote. See also Böckh, *Pub. Econ.*, II., 162. — 17. **προεξειλεγμένα.** *Collected beforehand, anticipated.* So Xenophon (*Œcon.*, IV., 9) uses *ἐκλέγουσιν*. DISSEN. — 20. **οὗτοι.** Æschines and his associates. — 21. **ἔχθρας...ἐγγυτέρω.** More enmity than friendship. C. 445; Cu. 415; G. 182; H. 589. — 25. **πῶς,** sc. *ὑπῆρχεν ἔχοντα*, supplied from above. Concise and pointed. — **235.** 26. **αὐτοκράτωρ.** Compare *Olynth.*, I., p. 10. — 27. **ὅπλα...ἀεί.** Compare *Ol.*, II., p. 24; *Phil.*, III., p. 124. — P. 84, l. 4. **οὐδ' ὑπὸ, τ. σ. κ.** These words are only found in one MS.; but otherwise there is nothing in them which would suggest their being spurious. On the contrary, they are quite Demosthenic and add to the force of the sentence. — 6. **ἁπλῶς...πάντων,** *absolutely master, leader, lord of all.* The climax is made more lively and forcible by the asyndeton. — **236.** 9. **οὗ μόνου.** *My only privilege.* The force of *μετεῖχον* cannot be translated; he means that his privilege, such as it was, was not exclusively his own, but shared to the same extent by Philip's Athenian supporters. — 10. **προυτίθεθ'.** *You extended.* Thucyd., VI., 14. — 13. **ἣν... τύχοι.** *On whatever pretext each* (of their successes) *might happen.* — 14. **ἀπῆτε,** sc. *ἀπὸ τῆς ἐκκλησίας*, *in these points you took counsel in the interests of your enemy and so went home.* WHISTON. — **237.** 14. **ἐκ.** Proleptic: we should say *under;* these defeats were not the cause of his success, but he had to start in each instance *out of* the positions into which they had sunk him. — 17. **μύριοι.** The same numbers are given by Plutarch, *Vit. Demosth.*, 5. Their insignificance for purposes of modern warfare is sufficiently striking. — 18. **ἄνευ.** *Independently of the national forces of the several states,* i. e. these foreign mercenaries were an extra army altogether. Each state had its own army of native troops as well. — 20. **συντέλειαν.** *Joint-contribution;* a much more emphatic term than *σύνταξις*, 234; but the *συντέλεια* was voluntary, the other compulsory. — **238.** 20. **λέγεις.** Æschines, p. 74, *τῶν εἰς τὸν πόλεμον ἀναλωμάτων τὰ μὲν δύο μέρη ὑμῖν ἀνέθηκεν οἷς ἦσαν ἀπωτέρω οἱ κίνδυνοι, τὸ δὲ τρίτον μέρος Θηβαίοις.* — **τὰ πρὸς...δίκαια,** i. e. what would have been just on the part of Athens to Thebes, etc., in reference to their respective shares of the expense. — 22. **Βυζαντίους.** Æschin., p. 90. — **Εὐβοέας,** pp. 66, 67. But nothing in Æschines' speech corresponds to this exactly. — 24. **ἐκείνων.** *Those famous.* The allusion is, of course, to the battle of Salamis. Cf. Æsch., *Pers.*, 341; Herod., VIII., 48; Thucyd., I., 74. — 25. **τάς.** "Where parts of a whole are stated in numbers, the article is sometimes prefixed to the numeral (to denote the definiteness of the relation)." Madv., *G. S.*, 11, r. 6. — **διακοσίας.** It is sufficiently amusing that in the speech *de Symm.*, p. 186, the orator states this number at *one* hundred. It suits his argument there to depreciate; not so here. The number of the whole fleet is stated by Æschylus as 300, by Herodotus as 378, by Thucydides as 400. The Athenian contingent is stated by Thucydides to have been two thirds; and by Herodotus to have been 180 ships. Compare Whiston's note *de Symm.*, 35. — 26. **ἐλαττοῦσθαι.** *To be defrauded,* i. e. made to do and to pay more than the fair share. — P. 85, l. 2. **εἰ,** *that,* Madv., *G. S.*, 194, c; cf. note, 232. — **239.** 4. **εἶτα κενάς, κ. τ. λ.,** *and after all they are but poor favors which you are conferring on those persons by calumniating me.* Whiston. — 5. **τουτοισί.** Θηβαίοις, Βυζαντίοις, Εὐβοέσι, 238. If they had been defrauded (as alleged), it would be but a poor satisfaction to them to see Demosthenes libelled; they would have been more thankful for a policy maintained at the time, to save them from being defrauded. — 8. **παρά.** Of time: as in 10 (*fin.*), 13 (*med.*), etc., *at the moment of,* — implying that there was no leisure for deliberation, or discussion of abstract right; the action had to be instantaneous on the emergency: they had to secure, not all they wanted, but all they could get. Whiston, however, takes *παρά* as in 232 = *under the existing circumstances.* — **ὅσα.** This word is definite with *ἐβουλόμεθα* and hence takes the indicative, while with *δοίη* it is indefinite and so takes the optative. Compare Whiston's note. — 10. **ὁ ἀντωνούμενος,** *he that was bidding against us.* Philip was ready to buy up for himself any allies whom the Athenians alienated from themselves. — 11. **καὶ...προσδεξόμενος καὶ...προσθήσων,** *not only to receive them, but also to pay them money into the bargain.*

240-243. Supposing I had hesitated in doing what I did,

HOW IMMEDIATELY PHILIP WOULD HAVE GAINED ALL: AND THEN WOULD NOT MY OPPONENTS HAVE LAID THE BLAME ON ME? THERE IS NOTHING SO VILE AS SLANDER. ÆSCHINES OF ALL SLANDERERS IS VILEST, BASE IN THE WHOLE OF HIS LIFE AND HABITS, AND WITH TALENTS UTTERLY PERVERTED TO WORK YOUR RUIN.

240. 14. **τί ἄν,** sc. ποιεῖν below: a reduplicated question, the full phrase being reserved for the end of the sentence, where the ἄν is repeated. — **ἀκριβολογουμένου** = λέγοντος τὰ δίκαια, διαλεγομένου περὶ τῶν ἴσων. 238. Whiston: *while I was refining about these points.* — 19. **ἐξεδόθησαν.** *Given up:* here, of an opportunity thrown away, not of a right surrendered, nor of a trust betrayed. — **241.** 20. **τοῦ μέν.** We must supply inverted commas from here to γέγονεν, as the next sentence explains, i. e. *and then,* would they not have said, "*he has got the command of the Hellespont by means of the Byzantines*"? etc. — 21. **σιτοπομπίας,** 87. The same region in the southeast of Russia is now a great corn-growing country. — 24. **ὁρμωμένων,** 71, τὴν Εὔβοιαν κατασκευάζων ἐπιτείχισμα. — 25. **καὶ...γε** = *yes, and.* — **242.** 26. **πονηρόν.** *A vile thing:* the neuters are contemptuous. The same strain of vituperation is kept up in the diminutive τἀνθρώπιον, *monkey.* — P. 86, l. 1. **φύσει κίναδος.** *A born beast.* The meaning of κίναδος is not limited to *fox,* as the Lexica abundantly testify. καί = *even.* — 2. **ἐξ ἀρχῆς.** *Never in his life.* The idiom cannot be rendered literally. — 3. **αὐτοτραγικός.** *The ideal Tragedy-baboon.* The form αὐτοτραγικός is after the Platonic αὐτοαληθές, αὐτοαγαθὸν κ. τ. λ., the eternal archetype (ἰδέα) as distinct from the human counterpart (εἶδος). — **ἀρουραῖος.** *Œnomaus of the country.* The epithet is easily understood as referring to rough and rude country theatricals in the demes adjoining the city. ἐν Κολλυτῷ Οἰνόμαον, 180. — 4. **παράσημος.** *Counterfeit,* lit. mis-stamped. The adjective is a common epithet of bad money, p. 766, l. 6 (cited by Harpocration), but signifies a *counterfeit* in any and every sense. No true and genuine orator, he means, would have so spoken and acted. Cf. Æsch., *Ag.*, 760; Aristoph., *Ach.*, 517 sq. — 5. **νῦν.** *To-day* = *only now at last.* The position of this word at the beginning of the sentence gives it all that emphasis. And it retains the same in 243. — **243.** 6. **ὥσπερ ἂν εἰ.** Cf. 194. The parallel passage in Æschines, p. 86, runs thus: εἶτ' ἐπερωτᾶν με, ὡς ἐγὼ πυνθάνομαι, μέλλει τίς ἂν εἴη τοιοῦτος ἰατρὸς, ὅστις τῷ νοσοῦντι μεταξὺ μὲν ἀσθενοῦντι μηδὲν συμβουλεύοι, τελευτήσαντος δ' αὐτοῦ ἐλθὼν εἰς τὰ ἔννατα διεξίοι πρὸς τοὺς οἰκείους ἃ ἐπιτηδεύσας ὑγιὴς ἂν ἐγένετο.

It is suggested with some reason that Æschines inserted this in his oration after hearing the orator's reply. — 9. **νομιζόμεν'.** *οὔτ' ἀποθανὼν τῶν νομιζομένων ἠξιώθη* Isocr., p. 391. Our word *solemnities* is exactly parallel. The sense of *φέροιτο* (*were being performed*) alludes to the funeral *procession.* And *αὐτῷ*, *in his honor,* is another example of the Dative of Relation. — 10. **τὸ καὶ τό.** *So and so,* another instance of the article (or relative) used as a demonstrative pronoun. 71. Donaldson's *New Cratylus,* 148. — 11. **ἐμβρόντητε.** *Lunatic,* lit. *thunder-stricken.* Cf. *τετύφωμαι* (note), 11. — 12. **εἶτα νῦν λέγεις.** *So then, you speak at last, do you?* *νῦν* = *nunc demum* as above. *εἶτα* expresses irony and indignation.

244-247. WHAT CHANCE HAD I AGAINST PHILIP? HE HAD MIGHT ON HIS SIDE, AND I HAD ONLY RIGHT: I COULD BEAT HIS SIDE IN ARGUMENT, BUT THEY COULD WIN BY ARMS. ALL THAT A SINGLE STATESMAN COULD DO I DID. AND OF THIS I CHALLENGE THE FULLEST INVESTIGATION.

244. 13. **ἧτταν.** Chæronea. The dilemma is again merely rhetorical (cf. 217). Æschines might deplore the calamity, and yet feel satisfaction in his rival's policy having been proved a mistake. — **οὐδέ** = *not even.* — **γαυριᾷς.** *Exult:* strictly of a spirited horse. The present tense here includes the imperfect = did and still do: on the other hand *προσῆκεν* refers back to a past issue which might have happened but never did; precisely "imperfect." — 14. **ἐν ουδενὶ τῶν παρ' ἐμοί,** *you will not find it* (the defeat) *to have befallen the city in any one of my measures,* literally, *the things pertaining to me,* i. e. Athens was victorious *in* its embassies and plans which were managed by Demosthenes, and defeated only in battle where he was not responsible. *ἐν*, not *by*, as rendered by some, but, as usual, *in.* — 20. **βασιλέων,** e. g. Cersobleptes who is so prominently mentioned in the speech *c. Aristocr.* (see also p. 160, etc.) and Teres (*ib.*). — 21. **τελευταῖα.** Here follows *πρῴην* in one MS., and *νῦν* in all the other MSS. But Σ reads as above: and either adverb looks very like an interpolation. — 22. **ταῦτα.** *These points he* (Philip) *came and carried by force of arms.* — **245.** 25. **μαλακίαν.** Æschin., p. 74 (*fin.*): *οὐ γὰρ ῥήτωρ ἀστράτευτος καὶ λιπὼν τὴν τάξιν αὐτοὺς ἐνουθέτησεν.* — **τὸν αὐτόν,** *the same man,* sc. Demosthenes. — 26. **καὶ ταῦτα,** *and that too,* sc. *κρεῖττω γενέσθαι.* *τοῖς λόγοις*, dat. of means. — **246.** P. 87, l. 4. **πᾶσαν.** *Make any and every examination:* 5, *πάντων.* — 7. **πέπρακταί μοι.** Grote thoroughly indorses the orator's opinion here, referring especially to the Olynthiacs and Philippics, above all to the First Philippic. — 8. **πολιτικά.** If we render πόλεις *states*, perhaps *constitutional* is the best translation of πολιτικά. Whiston well renders: *which are found in all states as constitutional and necessary defects.* — 11. **ὁρμήν.** *An impulse to do their duty.* — 13. **οὐδεὶς μήποθ'.** The construction is the common οὐ...μή with the subjunctive where we supply δεινόν or δέος ἐστι, between the two negatives, simply amounting to a future with the very strongest negation. See Madv., *G. S.*, 124, a, 3; C. 627; Cu. 620; H. 845. — **247.** 18. **οὔθ' ἡγεμών.** The phraseology in this passage is a reiteration of 21, 24, 60. The senses of πρός are noticed 17. — **οὐδ' ὁ λόγος...πρὸς ἐμέ.** *The question does not even pertain to me.* — 20. **ἢ μή.** These words are omitted in one MS., which inserts μή between τῷ and διαφθαρῆναι to the great detriment of the sense. But Σ and the rest read as above. Translate: *And really as regards being bribed or not, I have beaten Philip* (i. e. in the game of *corruption* where one party tries to bribe and the other to resist the bribe): *for as the bidder has defeated the acceptor if he buys him up, so the refuser, the uncorrupted, has defeated the bidder.* Whiston cites Herod., I., 68, 69.

248–250. That Ctesiphon is justified in speaking of me in these terms is sufficiently proved by the fact that after Chæronea, in the serious crisis of our fortunes, I was elected again and again to serve on our most important commissions, and though attacked by incessant prosecutions on the part of the Macedonian faction, I was always acquitted honorably.

248. 24. **ἃ μέν.** *The materials then with which I supplied my friend* (Ctesiphon) *to enable him to write these words with truth about me.* Here γράφειν has its technical sense, referring to the psephisma which proposed the vote of the crown. The real primary meaning of δίκαιος is always *right* or *righteous:* the narrower senses *true* or *just* are merely secondary notions of the word. As one good instance, see Soph., *Trach.*, 348. — 26. **ἃ δ'...ὑμεῖς,** *but those which you, the whole people, supplied.* — P. 88, l. 3. **ἐμβεβηκώς.** *In the very midst of its perils and alarms*, lit. *walking in them.* Whiston. It agrees with δῆμος. — **ἀγνωμονῆσαι.** Cf. 207. The state had reason to feel provoked then if ever at the orator's policy. — 4. **ἦν** with the force of ἦν ἄν, as so often. See 196, note ἐξήρκει. — **σωτηρίας.** *Salvation*, i. e. deliverance from impending destruction and restoration to perfect soundness. The use of the word to describe political successes is incessant in the

Attic orators. — 7. **αἱ τάφροι.** See the parallel passage in Lycurgus (*c. Leocr.*, p. 154), *ἐπεμελοῦντο γὰρ οἱ μὲν τῆς τῶν τειχῶν κατασκευῆς, οἱ δὲ τῆς τῶν τάφρων, κ. τ. λ.* — 9. **σιτώνην.** *Corn commissioner.* Besides the regular *σιτοφύλακες*, who had the charge of the public granaries (*σιτοδόκαι*), there were appointed in any crisis of scarcity (*σιτοδεία*) special commissioners to procure an extra importation of foreign corn. See Dic. Ant. SITOS. — **249.** 11. **γραφάς.** See 3, note on *ἑλεῖν*. On *εἰσαγγελίας*, see 13. On *εὐθύνας*, 55, 117, etc. — **συστάντων,** *having combined* (aor.); **ἐπαγόντων,** *continually bringing* (imperf. part.). — 12. **οὐ δι' ἑαυτῶν,** i. e. they suborned persons to make these accusations and carry on these prosecutions, taking care to keep their own share in the proceedings out of sight, and choosing such instruments as were least likely to be suspected of connection with themselves: *subornabant alios quorum nomine sperabant fore ut ipsi laterent.* BREMI. — 14. **πρώτους,** sc. *μετὰ τὴν ἐν Χαιρωνείᾳ μάχην* (Schol.). In 338, when the triumph of Macedon was assumed, there would naturally be a great opening for the Macedonian party at Athens to persecute the Opposition. — 16. **Σωσικλέους.** Only mentioned here: the same remark applies to Melantus. — **Φιλοκράτους** of Eleusis (*c. Aristog.*, p. 783): not the person mentioned above (21), who was of Hagnus. — 17. **Διώνδου.** 222. — 18. **τοίνυν.** There is an anacoluthon here. After the long protasis and parenthesis the speaker takes breath and starts as if with a fresh sentence. Translate: *well, through all these troubles.* Whiston renders: *on all these occasions, I say.* — 22. **εὔορκα.** *Who had taken their oath and gave their verdict on oath,* i. e. who gave a conscientious verdict. On the contrast of tenses in these participles cf. the parallel passage, 6; on *ὑπέρ* = *to the honor of,* cf. 1 and 8; and on *εὔορκα*, 2. — **250.** 24. **τὸ μέρος.** 222. — P. 89, l. 1. **ἐπεσημαίνεσθε.** *Continued to sign and seal,* i. e. to approve officially as correct. Æschines uses the word metaphorically, *de F. L.*, p. 34, *indorsing.* — 2. **προσωμολογεῖτε,** *you further certified.* WHISTON. — 4. **ὄνομα.** *What name was it proper or right for Ctesiphon to assign to my actions, — was it not that name which he saw the public assigning?* etc.

251. BUT, IT WILL BE SAID, A MAN OF HONOR WOULD NEVER HAVE BEEN PROSECUTED AT ALL. IF SO, HAPPY THE MAN! YET HOW IS HE BETTER THAN THE ACCUSED, WHO IS HONORABLY ACQUITTED? I TOO MAY SAY I HAVE NEVER BEEN PROSECUTED — AT LEAST BY ÆSCHINES.

8. **τὸ τοῦ Κεφάλου.** *That remark of Cephalus was fine: never to be put on public trial.* More exactly: *that affair of Cephalus was beautiful: never in any instance to have been prosecuted: yes, indeed, and fortunate too.* The passage in Æschines runs thus (p. 81, *fin.*): Ἀλλ' οὐχὶ ὁ Κέφαλος ὁ παλαιὸς ἐκεῖνος, ὁ δοκῶν δημοτικώτατος γεγονέναι, οὐχ οὕτως ἀλλ' ἐπὶ τοῖς ἐναντίοις ἐφιλοτιμεῖτο, ὅτι οὐδεμίαν πώποτε γραφὴν πέφευγε παρονόμων. We have had Cephalus already mentioned, with the other eminent statesmen, 219. — 12. **πρός γε τοῦτον,** *so far as he* (Æschines) *is concerned at least.* — 14. **ἐγράψατο,** sc. Αἰσχίνης. Another taunt on the *indirect* attack (15, 16). γράφεσθαι describes the mere commencement of the action, διώκειν its prosecution. — 15. **ὡμολόγημαι μηδέν.** Although the normal construction would be οὐδέν we more usually find the negative to be μή after verbs of assertion or concession. If οὐδέν had been written here the negative would not have had so close a connection with εἶναι. Whiston agrees with Schäfer that μηδέν, not ουδέν, is used to express the admission of *Æschines.*

252-255. NOW FOR HIS ARGUMENT REGARDING FORTUNE. ANY ARGUMENT FOUNDED ON FORTUNE IS WEAK, BUT HIS PARTICULAR ARGUMENT IS WRONG IN PRINCIPLE. HOW CAN THE FORTUNE OF ANY PRIVATE CITIZEN AFFECT OR IMPAIR THE FORTUNE OF THE STATE? HOWEVER, LET US EXAMINE HIS PRIVATE FORTUNE AND MY OWN, SIDE BY SIDE, IN DETAIL.

252. 17. **ἀγνωμοσύνην.** *Unfairness,* 207. Cf. ἀγνωμονῆσαι, 248. μεγάλην δὲ θεοῖς ἀγνωμοσύνην [θέμενοι], Soph., *Trach.*, 1266, *injustice.* — 19. **ὅλως μέν,** *in general.* It is correlative to ἐπει δὴ δέ. — 20. **προφέρει.** Cf. p. 576, l. 13, καίτοι πῶς ἐστι δίκαιον τοὔνομα μὲν τοῦτο ὡς ὄνειδος προφέρειν ἐμοί. So *objicere* in Latin. — 21. **ἣν** refers to **ταύτης** below: *how is it proper to speak of that, or how reproach another for that which,* etc. — 27. **ἀνθρωπινώτερον,** lit. *more humanly,* i. e. with a more *just* apprehension of human life: *with how much more truth, and the moderation befitting the nature of man.* — **253.** P. 90, l. 3. **Δωδωναῖον.** He assigns this ancient and venerable title here to Zeus, because he wishes to represent him as the Lord of oracles and prophecies, whose estimate of Athenian fortune once declared oracularly must be always true; the fortune of Athens is therefore intrinsically good; though not exempt from sharing in the common distresses of the world, when such distresses are universal as they are at the present crisis. The good fortune of Athens, involving also the favor of the gods, is a favorite theme with Demosthenes. Compare Phil., I., 12, where he says, "fortune always takes better care of us than we do of ourselves." — **ἡμῖν.** After this word one MS. inserts *καὶ τὸν Ἀπόλλω τὸν Πύθιον*. Dindorf, following Σ, reads as above. But Bremi, Bekker, and Whiston retain the insertion. If retained it weakens greatly the force of *καὶ* before *τὸν Δία*, *Zeus himself*, and weakens somewhat the force of the whole sentence. — 4. **ἐπέχει,** *obtains, prevails.* — **254.** 7. **τὸ μὲν τοίνυν.** *Now the fact that we chose the noblest policy and the fact that we are in better case than those very Hellenes who expected that their position would be constant prosperity, provided they threw us over — this I set down to the state's good fortune.* — 9. **διάξειν,** i. e. that they would live their lives out in a state of perfect happiness. — 10. **τίθημι** is in its technical sense of recording in a valuation or estimate under a particular item. — **τὸ δὲ προσκροῦσαι.** *But that we have met with reverses and that events have not all turned out as we wished, — this I consider the state has participated as our allotted share in the fortune of the rest of the world.* The infinitives are the direct objects of *μεταλαμβάνω* which like *μετέχω* and *μεταδίδωμι* is often constructed with an accusative, as well as with a partitive genitive, and *τὸ...μέρος* is in apposition with these infinitive clauses. In *ἐπιβάλλον* we have an example of the intransitive use of that verb: so Herod., II., 180, *τοὺς Δελφοὺς δὲ ἐπέβαλλε παρασχεῖν*. Id., IV., 115, *τῶν κτημάτων τὸ ἐπίβαλλον*. — **255.** 14. **ἰδίαν.** *Personal,* i. e. Æschines has no right to say that my sins bring a curse on the state (Æsch., p. 73): a man's personal fortune only affects his own personal affairs and extends no further; any estimate of it must be made within that limit. — 18. **κυριωτέραν.** *More supreme than:* i. e. more potent in producing effects. Cf. Æsch., p. 73, *l.*

256. As he has made personal reflections on me, I am obliged, however reluctant, to retaliate.

25. **ψυχρότητα.** *Ungenerous feeling:* a lack of that human warmth of heart and sympathy which would naturally produce great tenderness of word and deed towards the unfortunate. This use of the word *ψυχρότης* is unexampled; but the context explains it. The Lexica, however, and the editors translate it otherwise: *indifference, puerility, absurdity.* But L. and S.: *coldness of heart, indifference.* — 26. **ἐγὼ γάρ,** *for I* (emphatic) do not consider any one wise who insults another for being poor, nor prides himself for being brought up in affluence. — P. 91, l. 3. **ὡς ἂν δύνωμαι.** The full form of the

adverbial expression which is usually elliptical. Cf. 4 throughout. — **ἐκ τῶν ἐνόντων,** *under* (lit. out of) *existing circumstances.*

257-264. I HAD THE EDUCATION OF A GENTLEMAN FROM CHILDHOOD UPWARDS, AND I TOOK THE POSITION OF A GENTLEMAN IN PUBLIC LIFE AND BUSINESS. ÆSCHINES BEGAN LIFE AS AN ERRAND-BOY OF VERY DUBIOUS PARENTAGE, WAS THEN ENGAGED IN A SUCCESSION OF MENIAL AND VULGAR OCCUPATIONS, FINALLY EMERGED AS A STATESMAN, BUT WHAT A STATESMAN! — WITHOUT HEART AND WITHOUT CHARACTER!

257. 6. **φοιτᾶν** has here its common technical sense *to go to school.* *παῖς ὢν ἐφοίτας ἐς τίνος διδασκάλου*; Arist., *Eq.*, 1235; Plat., *Prot.*, 326, C, etc. The course of school education is fully described in the *Protagoras*, p. 325; it consisted of (1) *γράμματα* (language spoken and written), (2) study of authors, (3) music, and (4) *εὐκοσμία* (good principles and good behavior). — **καὶ ἔχειν, κ. τ. λ.,** *and to have what* (i. e. such an inheritance or allowance as) *one must have who is to do nothing mean through indigence,* i. e. I was exempt from the necessity of earning my bread in any menial way, 258. The vulgarity of this "odious comparison" requires indeed all the apology of 256, and even so is intolerable. — 8. **ἐξελθόντι,** i. e. when I became an *ἔφηβος* and was entered in the *ληξιαρχικὸν γραμματεῖον* as now *τελῶν εἰς ἄνδρας*, and of ripe age to hold office. Cf. *c. Mid.*, pp. 564, 565; *c. Aphob.*, p. 857; *c. Onet.*, 865, etc.; Dic. Ant., *Ἔφηβος*. — **ἀκόλουθα,** *suitable, the natural sequel:* i. e. undertaking those state offices which only the wealthier class, 104, were required to serve. The Choregus volunteered, as the accepted representative of his tribe, to bear the whole expense of putting one of the selected Dramas on the stage. We have a full account in the *Midias* of how the orator served the Choregia and the Trierarchia (pp. 540, 564). The duties of the Trierarch have been already noticed, 104-106. The system of the Eisphora (extraordinary *Property Tax*) was identical with that described 103, note, *ἡγεμόνας*. For fuller particulars on the various technical allusions in this paragraph, see Dic. Ant., s. vv.: and with all this account of the orator's early life compare the speeches against *Aphobus*, p. 811 sq. — 10. **φιλοτιμίας.** *Fell short in no point of duty either public or private.* Bremi says: "officia ex quibus honorifice præstitis laus redundat in eum qui præstiterat: hic etiam officia complectitur amicis præstanda." Though *φιλοτιμία* is literally *honorable ambition,* we cannot but paraphrase it here. — 16. **καλά γε,** *honorable at any rate,* whatever may be

said of their utility. — 258. 17. **συμβεβίωκα** with the next seven words happens to make a Hexameter. — **πόλλ' ἂν ἔχων**, *though I could say many other things about it*, sc. if I would. — 19. **ἐν οἷς.** *By dwelling on what I am proud of.* The sentiment is exactly the same as in 4. The unexpressed antecedent to *ἐν οἷς* is *τοῖς πράγμασι*, dative of the cause (i. e. the cause of their probable annoyance), in immediate connection with *λυπῆσαι*. — 20. **σεμνός.** *Imposing:* here false assumption is implied in contrast to just pride (*σεμνύνομαι*). On *σεμνός*, cf. 35, *τὰ ῥήματα*. — 21. **πρὸς ταύτην**, *in comparison with this.* — **ποίᾳ... τύχῃ**, *what kind of fortune you have experienced.* — 23. **προσεδρεύων.** *Sitting in attendance on;* i. e. not a member of the school, but only there as errand-boy and drudge. — **μέλαν.** We know little or nothing about the ink used at this period; but from this passage we must infer that it was prepared like our Indian ink by rubbing from a cake. See Dic. Ant., Atramentum. — 24. **βάθρα.** *Subsellia scholastica.* Cf. Platon., *Protag.*, 325, E, *παρατιθέασιν αὐτοῖς ἐπὶ τῶν βάθρων ἀναγιγνώσκειν ποιητῶν ἀγαθῶν ποιήματα.* — **παιδαγωγεῖον.** Synonymous with *διδασκαλεῖον*. The word *παιδαγωγός* has the general sense of *tutor* as well as its particular sense of the *slave who escorted the boy on his way to school.* — 25. **οἰκέτου.** Exactly our own *domestic:* an in-door servant only. — 259. 26. **τελούσῃ.** Suidas calls Glaucothea a *τελέστρια*, the orator styles her *τυμπανίστρια*, 284. In these initiations, which were of Phrygian origin, Glaucothea as high priestess would play the cymbals, and Æschines would read the requisite passages out of the mystic books. The deity worshipped in these solemnities seems to have been Sabazius, a Phrygian god, afterwards identified with Dionysus Sabazius. Aristoph., *Av.*, 875, *εὔχεσθε καὶ φρυγίλῳ Σαβαζίῳ*, where *φρύγιλος* is a wretched pun on *Φρύγιος*. — 27. **συνεσκευωροῦ.** *And helped in all the other business* (*ceremonies*, Kennedy; *impostures*, Whiston), i. e. all the technical performance connected with the rites, as the context explains. — P. 92, l. 1. **τὴν νύκτα**, *during the night.* *μέν* is correlative to *δέ* with *ἐν ταῖς ἡμέραις*. — **νεβρίζων.** A coined word, contemptuous in its form; so *κρατηρίζων* also: *working away with fawn-skin and bowl.* The wearing of the fawn-skin in Dionysiac rites is sufficiently notorious; here it is probably meant that the business of Æschines was to robe the candidates for initiation, as well as assuming the dress himself. See Harpocration (s. v.). The *κρατήρ* would be indispensable, both for libations and for the orgies which followed. — **καθαίρων.** Dissen cites here the excellent explanatory note of Wyttenbach on Plutarch, *de Superstit.*, 166, a. "Lustrationis pars erat ut corpus lustrandum circumlineretur et quasi circumpinseretur imprimis luto, πηλῷ, tum abstergeretur, quorum illud est περιμάττειν hoc ἀπομάττειν, *sed utrumque promiscue de tota lustratione dicitur.*" See also Harpocration, s. v. ἀπομάττων. As here described, the clay was first smeared all over the skin and then rubbed off with bran. The total operation is meant by καθαίρων, the details by καὶ...πιτύροις. — 3. **ἀνιστάς** is transitive, *raising*, or *making* them *rise*. — 4. **ἔφυγον.** *I've escaped the bad; I've found the better.* The idea of initiation is to consecrate and purify the nature of the initiated. Hence the candidate is told to describe himself as renouncing sin and cleaving to good *forever*. Cf. the notorious passage of Isocrates (*Panegyr.*, 28) concerning the origin and conception of the Mysteries. Also Cic., *de Leg.*, II., 14. Eurip., *Bacch.*, 900, is compared by Elmsley. The same formula of devotion, as Dissen notices, was used at Athens in certain nuptial ceremonies: Suidas, s. v. ἔφυγον. — 5. **ὀλολύξαι** is the *howling* in the orgies. — **καὶ...νομίζω,** *and for my part I believe it,* sc. that no one ever did howl so. — 6. **οὕτω μέγα.** Cf. 285, εὔφωνον; 313, λαμπροφωνότατος. Also, p. 449, *de F. L.*, where the voice of Æschines is fully criticised. — **260.** 8. **θιάσους** has here its technical sense of a *Dionysiac procession* or rather *riot*, —Ἴακχε ἐλθὲ τόνδ' ἀνὰ λειμῶνο χορεύσων ὁσίους ἐς θιασώτας. Arist., *Ran.*, 326. — 9. **μαράθῳ.** *Fennel*, the Attic form of μαράθρῳ. The plant was supposed to have magic powers. Ælian, *H. A.*, IX., 17, cited by Dissen. — **λεύκῃ.** The white poplar was supposed to grow in the infernal regions. Harpocration cites Hom., *Il.*, XIII., 389; XVI. 482. That this Dionysus of the Mysteries was one of the χθόνιοι is sufficiently clear from the *Ranæ* of Aristophanes (*l. c.*). — 10. **παρείας.** *Squeezing the big-cheeked snakes.* Like, if not the same as, the "puff adder." W. The serpents were so called from the puffed shape of their heads; they were not venomous. Cf. Aristoph., *Plut.*, 690. On their use in Bacchic rites, cf. Eurip., *Bacch.*, 697: καὶ καταστίκτους δορὰς | ὄφεσι κατεζώσαντο λιχμῶσιν γένυν. — 11. **εὐοῖ σαβοῖ.** *Evoe Saboe.* The joyous interjections εὐοῖ, εὖα, εὐάν (said to be of Eastern etymology) were specially appropriate to Dionysiac revels. Σαβοῖ is understood to be the abbreviated vocative of Σαβάζιος. — **ὕης ἄττης.** The words of the song put to represent the tune of the dance — Hymen, Hymenæe, is always cited as a parallel. The ancient lexicographers explain ὕῆς ἄττης as being mystic names either of Dionysus or of Atys; and support the former view by fanciful derivations, — ὑῆς from ὑετός, ἄττης from ἄτη. We have no other information as to the meaning or origin of the words. — **ἐπορχούμενος** = *dancing to* the song. — 12. **ἔξαρχος** applies to the music, προηγεμών to the procession, = *præcentor, leader of the dance.* The meanings of κιστοφόρος and λικνοφόρος are somewhat disputed. But it is pretty well established that the κίστη referred to was the chest in which the mystic articles were shut up and carried in procession (cf. the proverb ὄνος ἄγων μυστήρια, Aristoph., *Ran.*, 159, Schol.): and that the λίκνον was a fan-shaped basket containing first-fruits and all necessaries for the sacrifices, Dionysus having, among other epithets, the γέρας of λικνίτης. — 14. **ἔνθρυπτα.** ψωμοὶ οἴνῳ βεβρεγμένοι οὓς ἐποίουν εἰς σκάφην ἄρτους διαθρύψαντες — καὶ φακῆν ἐπισκεδάσαντες (Ulpian), i. e. bits of bread soaked in a bowl of wine and sprinkled over with pulse. It may be rendered *sweetmeats.* — **στρεπτούς**, *twists.* — 15. **νεήλατα,** according to Harpocration were *rolls* of *fresh-ground* barley-meal steeped in honey and studded with raisins and chick-peas. Lobeck, however, derives the word, with much more probability, from ἐλαύνω, citing the use of ἐλατήρ for pastry in Aristoph., *Equit.*, 1181. — 261. 17. **ἐνεγράφης.** *Enrolled on the list of your deme.* The presiding officer in every deme (δήμαρχος) kept a register of all citizens of full age who could be counted among its members; this was called the ληξιαρχικὸν γραμματεῖον, and was the necessary record to prove citizenship. — **τοῦτο,** i. e. the difficulty you had to get your name put on the list, on the ground of your parentage. — 18. **οὖν.** *After all.* Here οὖν has its full original force already noticed (23) as an accusative absolute of the neuter participle of εἰμί — *this being so,* i. e. the point being assumed to be true, though not worth discussing. Compare our *I say,* and *however,* in their resumptive use. — 19. **γραμματεύειν.** 127, ὄλεθρος γραμματεύς. *De F. L.*, p. 371, l. 20, etc. The diminutive ἀρχιδίοις is sarcastic and contemptuous = *petty magistrates.* Aristoph., *Av.*, 1111, κἂν λαχόντες ἀρχίδιον εἶθ' ἁρπάσαι βούλησθέ τι. — 262. 23. **βαρυστόνοις.** *To those actors nicknamed the Lugubrious,* doubtless because they overacted the pathetic. We know nothing of them from other sources. In the *de F. L.*, p. 418, we find Æschines acting as tritagonist to a different pair of artistes, Theodorus and Aristodemus; but that was at Athens, not in the rural (or, as we should say, "provincial") performances. — 26. **ὀπωρώνης.** *A costermonger,* lit. a small fruiterer who would purchase a stock of fruit from the market-gardens and sell it on his own account. The rustic audience, according to the orator, pelted Æschines so freely for his bad acting, that he might have set himself up in the olive and fig trade with the quantities which they threw at him. — 27. **τραύματα.** The remark is meant to be facetious: i. e. Æschines received more wounds from figs and olives in his desperate and deadly battles with the audience than he ever did in the state's service. With Dindorf I prefer to retain *τραύματα* here, though Σ omits it; all the other MSS. have it, and Schäfer retained it, though with a different interpretation; according to his view Æschines robbed the orchards and got caught and thrashed while doing so. But the other explanation is simpler and better. So Holmes. But *τραύματα* is probably a gloss, and is omitted by most editors. And *ἀγώνων*, especially with the relative clause which follows, can hardly mean anything else than the *dramatic* contests *in which* Æschines and his associates *were continually battling* (imperf.) *for dear life.* The result was, Demosthenes means to say, that they *got more* (both kicks and coffers) in this way than from acting in the plays. — P. 93, l. 2. **ἄσπονδος καὶ ἀκήρυκτος,** *an implacable and unceasing war,* where there is no mention of a treaty and no suspension of hostilities on the appearance of a herald with a flag of truce. W. — 4. **σκώπτεις.** As Æschines charged Demosthenes with cowardice in the battle of Chæronea, e. g. p. 76, *καταγαγούσης δ' αὐτὸν εἰς τὴν πόλιν τῆς ἀπροσδοκήτου σωτηρίας τοὺς μὲν πρώτους χρόνους ὑπότρομος ἦν ἄνθρωπος, καὶ παριὼν ἡμιθνὴς ἐπὶ τὸ βῆμα εἰρηνοφύλακα ὑμᾶς αὐτὸν ἐκέλευε χειροτονεῖν.* — 5. **ὧν...αἰτιώσαιτ',** *which might be imputed to his poverty,* lit. for which one might blame his poverty. C. 431; Cu. 422; G. 173, 2; H. 577, b. — 6. **αὐτὰ...κατηγορήματα,** *the actual charges against your character.* — 8. **ποτε.** *At last:* continuing the taunt that Æschines was *long* excluded from political life by his low origin and occupations. — 9. **λαγὼ βίον.** Herod., III., 108, *ὁ λαγὸς ὑπὸ παντὸς θηρεύεται θηρίου καὶ ὄρνιθος καὶ ἀνθρώπου.* "Lepus," says Bremi quaintly, "omnibus gentibus et ætatibus imago est timiditatis, quippe qui ne dormiens quidem audeat oculos occludere." — **264.** 12. **χιλιῶν.** Diodorus (XVI., 86) returns the loss in the battle of Chæronea at more than a thousand killed and quite two thousand taken prisoners. — 13. **ἐθάρρησε.** *Was in high spirits,* i. e. was absolutely and obviously exhilarated and emboldened by the circumstance.

265, 266. I RECAPITULATE AND SUMMARIZE THE COMPARISON OF OUR PRIVATE FORTUNES.

265. 21. **ἐδίδασκες.** This passage has been universally admired by a host of critics from Hermogenes downwards; but I cannot myself admire it at all, except for the neatness with which the "antitheta" are balanced. It appears to me not only vulgar but fallacious. In what respect is the school-boy superior to the pupil-teacher, or the candidate for initiation to the acolyth who initiates him, or the audience to the artistes? The utmost the orator says against Æschines is this, that owing to inferior birth and poverty he had no social advantages, and had to fight his own way in the world. The more honor to him for having successfully achieved it. — **ἐτέλεις...ἠκκλησίαζον.** *You performed initiations, and I was initiated; you danced in the choir, and I was choregus; you were a clerk in the assembly, and I was a member.* — 24. **ἐξέπιπτες.** *You were hissed off the stage, and I hissed you: for the enemy has all your policy been, mine for my country.* It may be heterodox to say so, but all this antithesis seems to me studied and unnatural, and not at all consistent with the honest indignation which Demosthenes affects. But no doubt it would be very effective as oratory. With ἐξέπιπτες compare *de Fals. Leg.*, p. 449. Mr. Kennedy quotes from Milton's Apology for Smectymnuus an imitation of this passage. Speaking of the young divines and students at college, whom he had so often seen upon the stage acting before courtiers and court ladies, he proceeds thus: "There while they acted and overacted, among other young scholars, I was a spectator; they thought themselves gallant men, and I thought them fools; they made sport, and I laughed; they mispronounced, and I mimicked; and to make up the Atticism, they were out, and I hissed." W. — **266.** P. 94, l. 2. **κινδυνεύεις,** *you are on trial whether you are still to continue doing this* (the work of an informer) *or forthwith to be silenced;* and you are sure to lose in either event: if you get your verdict, you go on with your established but degrading profession of traitor and informer; if you do not get a verdict, you 're a ruined man and even that career is closed to you. Accordingly, Æschines is said to have left Athens, even before Demosthenes had concluded his speech, and gone into exile at Rhodes. — 5. **οὐχ ὁρᾷς.** Parenthetical as in 232. *Good, indeed, — don't you see? is the fortune in which having passed your life,* etc. W. — **267.** 9. **ἐλυμαίνου.** *Murdered,* or *used to murder,* cf. 180. The first iambic cited is Eurip., *Hec.*, 1; the author of the second is unknown. On the word *κακαγγελεῖν to be bearer of wretched tidings* the point of the next sentence turns : *and wretch as you are, may you come to a wretched doom,— by the judgment of heaven, if so it may be, if not, by the judgment of all here present.* ἔπειτα (1) answers μάλιστα μέν with a little more force than εἰ δὲ μή (103), respresenting a closer and more immediate alternative. The Greeks were fond of paronomasia, like this : κακὸν κακῶς ἀπολέσειαν, cf. Plutarch., *De Sera,* VII. ; Mat., XXI., 41. See also the Latin : malos male perdere.

268, 269. I WILL NOT MENTION MY PRIVATE BENEFACTIONS. IT IS MEAN OF A MAN EVEN TO RECOLLECT HIS OWN GOOD DEEDS OF THAT KIND.

268. 18. **σιωπῶ, κ. τ. λ.** This rhetorical figure "I will not say," "I will not mention," is alike frequent and plausible in ancient and modern oratory. — 20. **ἐλυσάμην.** *Ransomed.* Cf. *de F. L.*, p. 394 ; *adv. Nicostr.*, p. 1250. — 21. **συνεξέδωκα.** *Helped to dower*— ἔτι τοίνυν καὶ ἰδίᾳ τισι τῶν πολιτῶν ἀπορούσι συνεξέδωκε θυγατέρας καὶ ἀδελφάς. Lys., *de Aristoph., pec.*, 59. — **269.** P. 95, l. 4. **μικροῦ δεῖν,** *almost.* C. 665 ; Cu. 564 ; G. 268 ; H. 772. — **ὀνειδίζειν,** sc. with ingratitude and forgetfulness. Compare the well-known sentiment in Terence, And., I., i., 16 :—

Nam ist hæc commemoratio
Quasi exprobratio est immemoris benefice.

— 7. **ἀρκεῖ μοι.** *Whatever may be my general reputation as to this, that is enough for me.*

270-275. IS DISASTER LIMITED TO US AT ATHENS? IS IT NOT UNIVERSAL, EVEN WHERE MY NAME HAS NEVER BEEN HEARD OF? BLAME BAD FORTUNE : DO NOT BLAME MY BAD STATESMANSHIP. WHY DID NOT ÆSCHINES SUGGEST A BETTER POLICY? BECAUSE THERE WAS NO BETTER. WHEN A MAN HAS DONE HIS BEST TO WIN, LOSING DESERVES NOT CENSURE BUT SYMPATHY.

270. 11. **ἀθῷος,** *unscathed of* or *by*, followed by a gen. of source or cause. — 12. **νῦν,** i. e. the year 331-330. So in 253, τύχην ἣ νῦν ἐπέχει. The supremacy of Alexander was at its height ; the news of his Asiatic triumphs was constantly reaching Greece, and his lieutenant Antipater had just crushed the Peloponnesian secession at Megalopolis. — 14. **τὴν ἐμὴν...βούλει,** *my fortune or ill-fortune, whichever you choose to call it.* — **271.** 20. **φοράν** is rendered by some here as in the corresponding passage, 61, *crop;* but most editors take it here, if not also there, in the sense of *rush, current, torrent.* οὐχ οἵαν ἔδει is

an adj. clause and may be rendered, *lamentable, intolerable,* lit. *such as ought not to have been.* πραγμάτων has here its frequent sense of *troubles.* 272. 22. **τὸν παρὰ τουτοισί** clearly means, *me whose political career has been at home among my own citizens.* W. — 273. P. 96, l. 4. **οὐ γὰρ ἐπ' εὐνοίᾳ γ' ἐμοί,** *for it was not out of good-will to me, assuredly, that you resign d to me prospects, and admiration, and honors...but because you were compelled by the truth, manifestly, and because you had nothing better to say (advise).* Surely you did not sacrifice these in order that I might win them. The fact is, my policy was so good that it was impossible to suggest anything better. As to the construction of the Greek: ἐμοί is the dative of relation (Madv., *G. S.*, 35, a), ἐλπίδων the genitive of privation (57, b). — 274. 12. **ὀργήν.** The accusatives are in apposition to διωρισμένα the object of ὁρῶ. — 15. **οὐ κατώρθωσε.** *Failed in common with all, failed with a failure which all shared.* The orator, here as throughout, imputes the failure of his own policy not to bad judgment but to bad luck, — not to his own bad luck, but to the bad luck of the universe at this particular epoch. On the distinction between ἀτυχήματα, ἁμαρτήματα, and ἀδικήματα, cf. Aristot., *Rhet.*, I., 13 cited by Dissen. On unwritten laws, see Soph., *Antig.*, 452, and Xen., *Mem.*, IV., 4, 19, cited by Whiston. — 276. 27. **δεινόν.** *A man of art, and juggling, and sophistry.* We find the same contemptuous collocation in Plato's *Symp.*, 203, D. On the difference between σοφιστής and ῥήτωρ, cf. Aristot., *Rhet.*, I., 1 (*fin.*). — P. 97, l. 1. **ὡς** here, like ὥσπερ just above, marks its clause as subjective, that is, expressing the view of Æschines, C. 680; Cu. 588; G. 277, N. 2; H. 795, e; and the participle ἔχοντα is in the accus. although it is not impers. C. 675; G. 278, N; H. 793. Render: *as though when one is the first to say things about another which belong to himself, these, forsooth, must also be true.* — 277. 6. **κἀκεῖνο...δεινότητα,** *that also I know well, that in regard to my skill as an orator* (but let this pass), — *for be it so,* i. e. if it be admitted: he completes the sentence here interrupted with the words εὑρήσετε πάντες, κ. τ. λ., l. 12, below. He admits that there may be some truth in imputing to him professional talent as orator; but he argues, pretty correctly, that an orator's professional success depends on his being found to meet the sympathies and to serve the interests of his hearers. The very imputation, therefore, of oratorical success is a sort of guaranty of patriotic service. — 9. **ὡς γὰρ...οὕτως,** *for as* (according as) *you may accept and feel kindly towards each, so* (and so only) ***does the speaker seem to be wise*** (have credit for wisdom). His reputation both as a statesman and orator rests entirely on the verdict of his audience. For *οὕτως = so only, only to that extent*, compare 7, note in *τὰ δίκαια*. — 11. **οὖν**, resumptive, 261. — **ἐμπειρία** here takes the place of *δεινότητα* above, and shows what it means. — 13. **ἐξεταζομένην**, *proved* by the test and examination of facts, 173. — **278.** 19. **τὸν καλὸν κἀγαθόν.** Both these adjectives are attributes alike to the mental, the moral, and the physical, — *καλός* implies the beauty of goodness and *ἀγαθός* the integrity. In their present common juxtaposition they mean pretty nearly what we call *the man of honor*, and what Cicero calls *honestus*. — 20. **τοὺς...δικαστάς,** *thou who have come into* the court *as judges for the public weal*. — 21. **ἀξιοῦν αὑτῷ βεβαιοῦν,** *to require them to secure to himself*, that is, to *gratify his own* personal resentment and enmity. — 26. **ἐν οἷς.** *In cases where the people have to deal with their enemies*, i. e. to defend themselves against their enemies' attack. On this dative of relation depending on the impersonal *ἐστί*, see Madvig's *G. S.*, 38, a. — **279.** P. 98, l. 1. **μηδενὸς δὲ ἀδικήματος.** Translate: *But that without ever having claimed to get satisfaction from me for any public nor, I will add, even any private wrong either on the state's behalf or his own, he should now come forward having gotten up an accusation against my being crowned and honored*, etc. WHISTON. — 5. **συνεσκευασμένον.** Perfect middle. This sense of *συσκευάζειν* as *concocting* and *conspiring* is abundantly illustrated by the Lexica. — **280.** 10. **φωνασκίας.** Æschines speaks of the orator's voice as *ὀξεῖαν καὶ ἀνόσιον* (*de F. L.*, p. 49, 157). Here Demosthenes retorts that Æschines *had chosen to take up this contest from a wish* (*βουλόμενος* denoting the motive) *to make an exhibition of oratory and vocal practice* (*λόγων καὶ φωνασκίας*), *not to get satisfaction for any wrong*. — 14. **ὁ τόνος.** *Raising of his voice*. Æschines had taunted him as *ἐντεινάμενος τὴν φωνήν* (*de F. L.*, l. c.) and had asked *τίς ἡ κραυγή; τίς ὁ τόνος τῆς φωνῆς*; p. 84. Cf. Cic., *Or.*, XVIII. Quintilian, XI., 3. — **281.** 19. **τῆς αὐτῆς.** We understand *ἀγκύρας* from the context *ὁρμεῖ*. This genitive has been already discussed 17 (*first note*). The meaning of the proverb *not to ride at the same anchor* is obvious; here alluding to Æschines's Macedonian proclivities. As one of many illustrations we may cite p. 1296, l. 1, *μηδ' ἐπὶ δυοῖν ἀγκύραιν ὁρμεῖν αὐτοὺς ἐᾶτε*. Cf. Eurip., *Or.*, 68; Plat., *Phæd.*, 227. Bremi, however, understands it to mean "im gleichen Schiffe mit den andern fahren." — 21. **ὁρᾷς**: 266. — **ἐγώ**, sc. *ἔχω, I have*. — **282.** 24. **ἐπορεύου,** *wished to go*. See Grote, XI., 699; Plutarch, Phocion, c. 10. W. — 26. **ἀρνούμενος.** Imperfect tense, — *although be-*

fore he always refused this service (of going on embassy). By πάντα χρόνον he probably means only from 346 to Chæronea. The statement any way is quite inconsistent with the spurious psephism (29) which mentions Æschines among its πρέσβεις. — P. 99, l. 2. **καταρᾶται.** A general imprecation of all who were ἐχθροὶ τῇ πόλει was a formal part of the proceedings in every ἐκκλησία. Cf. Dic. Ant., s. v. The orator implies that his opponent was that worst of all foes, a traitor. — **283.** 10. **μηδὲν...πραγμα.** Compare the familiar expression: τί ἐμοὶ καὶ σοί, *what have I to do with thee?* John, ii., 4. — **284.** 18. **ξένος ἢ φίλος ἢ γνώριμος,** *guest-friend, or friend at all, or acquaintance.* Compare 51, 52. "The repetitions, the enforcement again and again of the same points, are a distinguishing feature of Demosthenes, and formed also one of the characteristics of Mr. Fox's great eloquence." LORD BROUGHAM. — **τυμπανιστρίας,** cf. 259, note. — 21. **εἰλημμένος** and **γεγονὼς** are concessive = *although you have yourself been manifestly found* (lit. caught) *a traitor,* etc. C. 674, f; Cu. 582; G. 277, 5; H. 789, f.

285–291. THE CITY HAS BEEN GRATEFUL TO ME FOR MY MANY SERVICES, AND AS AN INSTANCE OF IT, I WAS APPOINTED TO MAKE THE FUNERAL SPEECH OVER THOSE WHO FELL IN THE BATTLE. MANY OF YOU EMINENT ORATORS ASPIRED TO THE HONOR. BUT THE STATE KNEW HOW YOUR SYMPATHIES AND FRIENDSHIPS LAY, AND THEREFORE REJECTED YOU ALL AND TOOK ME. THE EPITAPH ON THOSE WHO WERE SLAIN CONFIRMS MY ASSERTION THAT THEIR FALL WAS DUE TO EVIL FORTUNE, NOT TO EVIL POLICY.

285. 26. **τὸν ἐροῦντ᾽.** The nature of these funeral orations is sufficiently explained by Thucydides (II., 34). Compare also Platon., *Menex.*, p. 236; Demosth., *c. Leptin.*, p. 499; Aristid., *Panath.*, I., p. 331; Cic. *Leg.*, II., 24, 62; *Orat.*, 44, 151. — P. 100, l. 2. **Δημάδην.** This person was no less remarkable for eloquence than for corruption (Plutarch., *Phoc.*, 1): he was a bitter enemy of Demosthenes (Id., *Demosth.*, 28) and an ardent supporter of Philip, whose good graces he secured when a captive after Chæronea (Diod., XVI., 87): he maintained the same influence with Alexander, and was bribed by the friends of Demosthenes to use it for the preservation of the anti-Macedonian orators when Alexander demanded their execution. Eventually Demades was put to death by Antipater, who detected him playing a double game between himself and Perdiccas (Diodor., XVIII., 48). For further particulars see Smith, Dic. Biog. — 3.

Ἡγήμονα. This orator and Pythocles were both put to death by order of the Athenian Assembly in the year 317, sharing the fate of Phocion whose supporters they had been. Plut., *Phoc.*, 35. Pythocles is mentioned by the orator, pp. 411, 442. — 7. **ἔτ' ἄμεινον.** Dissen comments thus: "*etiam studiosius et luculentius.* Similis usus adverbii καλῶς de quo vide Schæferum ad Soph., *Œd. R.*, 1008." We may render the phrase *yet the more.* The passage in Sophocles runs: καλῶς εἶ δῆλος οὐκ εἰδὼς τί δρᾷς. "'T is all too clear thou know'st not what thou dost." **286.** 11. **εὐθενούντων,** a rare word in Attic Greek and of doubtful etymology, but used repeatedly in the Eumenides of Æschylus: *for what you denied upon oath when affairs were prosperous, this you confessed in the misfortunes of the state.* — 13. **ὧν...ἄδειαν.** Schäfer understands this to mean *freedom to express their feelings without reserve.* But the phrase will hardly bear this extension. Rather: *secured impunity for their designs.* So Whiston also takes it. The context would fit either translation. — **287.** 17. **μήθ' ὁμωρόφιον,** literally, *under the same roof. Should have neither shared the dwelling or the meal:* as these acts would be typical always of sympathy and association. The phrase γεγενημένον εἶναι instead of γεγενῆσθαι seems to be only for variety, the latter form having occurred so instantly before. This usage of the auxiliary εἶναι is not at all uncommon, as Reiske supposes. Cf. Soph., *O. R.*, 580, 1146; Plat., *Tim.*, 26; *Phil.*, 39; *Soph.*, 217, and Madv., *G. S.*, 180, d. — 19. **ἐκεῖ,** in the court of Philip. He seems to be speaking here of the Macedonian rejoicing after the defeat of the Phocians. Whiston. — **κωμάζειν.** All the editors cite the parallel from the *de F. L.*, p. 380; οὗτος εἰς τἀπινίκια τῶν πραγμάτων καὶ τοῦ πολέμου ἃ Θηβαῖοι καὶ Φίλιππος ἔθυον, εἱστιᾶτο ἐλθὼν καὶ σπονδῶν μετεῖχε καὶ εὐχῶν ἃς ἐπὶ τοῖς τῶν συμμάχων τῶν ὑμετέρων τείχεσι καὶ χώρᾳ καὶ ὅπλοις ἀπολωλόσιν ηὔχετο ἐκεῖνος, καὶ συνεστεφανοῦτο καὶ συνεπαιώνιζε Φιλίππῳ καὶ Φιλοτησίας προὔπινεν. — 20. **ὑποκρινόμενον.** *Acting his part.* The orator reiterates his taunt on Æschines's original profession, 15. — **288.** 27. **ὁ μὲν δῆμος.** Another good instance of the really subordinate sentence being introduced by μέν and the principal by δέ. Cf. 3. Paraphrase: *and it was not the case that while the people voted thus, yet the parents,* etc., *voted otherwise.* — P. 101, l. 2. **περίδειπνον.** *The funeral banquet,* called also νεκρόδειπνον. Lucian *de Luctu*, c. 24. — **ὡς.** Fully expressed this phrase would run παρ' οἰκειοτάτῳ ὡς δυνατὸν ἦν. Cf. 4. Render: *with the nearest possible relative.* The addition of ὡς always intensifies the superlative to this maximum degree, and if a preposition is connected with the superlative it naturally comes between it and the ὡς. Abundant examples are cited : p. 309, l. 2, p. 585, l. 3, etc. See also Madv., *G. S.*, 96; C. 553, c; Cu. 631, a; H. 664.—6. **ᾧ γάρ.** *For he who had the deepest interest in their life and fortune, surely he had the largest share of the anguish felt for them all, when they had met that fate, which, oh! that they never had.* With μήποτε we obviously supply παθεῖν. The argument is this : the statesman holds as most precious to himself the life and welfare of every single citizen ; therefore he feels most keenly the blow of their loss in every single instance. Kindred would only feel for their individual kin ; but his own grief is universal. "The sentiment is like that which Œdipus expresses in the beautiful lines of Sophocles (Œd. Rex, 88)." KENNEDY. — 289. **ΕΠΙΓΡΑΜΜΑ.** Göttling contends ingeniously, but strangely, that Demosthenes himself was the author of this Inscription. He relies especially on the parallel passages in this oration, pp. 297 and 322. Bekker contradicts him. We have no historical evidence on the subject; but if Demosthenes was the author, why does he not say so here? And if he was the author himself, what becomes of his argument in 290? To the many verse translations which have been already published of this, I venture to add the following paraphrase:

Here lie the dauntless, for their country's right
Who drew the sword, and crushed the foeman's might.
Death, in the fray, they set by common claim —
(Their lives they spared not in the thirst for fame) —
As umpire of their glory or their shame:
And this for Hellas' sake; that never thrall
Nor curse of bondage on her neck should fall.
Sore had they toiled: their mother earth hath pressed
(So heaven decrees) their bodies to her breast.
Heaven's the unerring aim, th' eternal power:
For man no respite from his destined hour.

— 14. **εἰς δῆριν ἔθεντο.** Literally, *set their weapons to the fight*: a ponderous yet feeble expression : θέσθαι as applied to *arms* being properly to *pile* them, and only bearing the former sense when applied to *troops*, not to weapons. — 15. **ἀπεσκέδασαν.** Here, with brilliant rhetorical facility, the will is put for the deed. — 16. **δείματος.** I must differ (for once) from Dindorf in the reading of this ill-expressed and confused passage, which no amount of emendation will make even tolerable. He reads λήματος; but the MSS. all agree in δείματος. I think we may interpret it thus: *in the fighting — a game whose stakes are courage and fear* (i. e. display of courage is tantamount to winning the game; display of panic is tantamount to losing the game) — *they spared not their lives; but took Death as their common umpire.* In other words they fought till they lost their lives, and thus appealed to the Lord of the Unseen World to decide whether they had been brave or cowards, winners or losers, in the game of battle. On the construction of ἀρετῆς here without περί or any similar preposition, see Madv., 56, Genitive as Object of the Verb; and 53, Genitive of Reference. Soph., *Trach.*, 1122; Plat., *Rep.*, V., pp. 459, 470. It is quite true that ἀρετῆς is meant to be governed by βραβῆ also, but not, as some editors contend, by βραβῆ only. In translating, however, we cannot avoid taking it exclusively with the latter: we might say in English they *fought for death or victory*, but we really could not say *fought for shame or glory*. Whiston translates thus: *In their contest they did not save their lives, but of timidity and courage they made Hades the impartial umpire.* — 23. **ἔπορεν.** The subject is clearly ὁ θεός, and nothing can be more awkward than the ellipsis. The δέ after μοῖραν is perhaps meant to have the intensive force of δή. So Dissen takes it. But among the many defects of the poem such a trifle as δέ coming the fourth word in the sentence, and yet acting as conjunctive, may surely pass unchallenged. Why this inscription has ever been admired I am quite at a loss to discover: to me it seems a tissue of platitudes very clumsily expressed in language, by no means original. And the sentiment is false throughout it. These heroes fell *not* as victors but as vanquished, — they did *not* avert the doom of Hellas, — and their defeat was due *not* to destiny, but to the vacillating policy of the country for which they fought so hard and so well. The orator is probably conscious of this last opening being left for his antagonist, and he tries to close it up accordingly in the next sentence, straining the simple sense of the epitaph to suit his purpose. — 24. **καὶ ἐν αὐτῷ τούτῳ,** *in this very epitaph also*, as well as from me. — **290.** 26. **ἀνέθηκε,** the attributes. This use of the aorist is just parallel to the Epistolary imperfect in Latin, the time of action being restricted to the very time of writing, i. e. a past time; whereas our own idiom looks on the thing written, as an agency, on the part of its writer, which is present as well as past. — P. 102, l. 3. **τρέψειαν.** Strictly optative: i. e. to express a prayer.

291–300. YOUR UNDISGUISED SYMPATHY WITH OUR ENEMIES BRANDS YOU, ÆSCHINES, AS A TRAITOR. IF IT WAS MY DOING, AS YOU ALLEGE, THAT WE OPPOSED THE DESPOT, I GLORY IN THE DEED. BUT YOU TAUNT ME WITH BEING A PARTISAN OF PHILIP. SURELY IT IS YOU, AND THE LIKE OF YOU IN OTHER STATES, WHO DESERVE THIS IMPUTATION. I AND MY STATE UTTERLY DISCLAIM IT. IN WORD, THOUGHT, AND DEED I HAVE PROVED MYSELF PHILIP'S UNCOMPROMISING FOE. I APPEAL TO FACTS FOR CONFIRMATION.

291. 7. **ὡς ἄν.** Supply ἔσχε, *would have had,* not, as Schäfer says, ἔχοι. — 9. **ἐπάρας,** *with his voice raised and in exultation and with a screech.* λαρυγγιῶ τοὺς ῥήτορας (i. e. *screech them down*), Arist., *Eq.*, 358. More literally: *raising his voice and exulting and straining his windpipe.* — 12. **τοῖς γεγενημένοις.** *In the miseries that had come to pass he had no feeling in common with the rest* (of his fellow-citizens): i. e. he stood alone in his glee, every one else being in despair. This is mere repetition of 244, 217. — **292.** 13. **καίτοι.** *And yet one who professes regard for the laws and constitution, like my opponent at present, should at any rate have this attribute if nothing else, that he sympathizes in sorrow and in joy with the nation, and never in his public policy bands himself with the party of their foes.* τοῖς πολλοῖς is the natural dative following an expression of identity; τετάχθαι as a perfect tense suggests entire and complete partisanship; κοινῶν depends on προαιρέσει, which is a *dativus modi.* — **293.** 21. **ἐπεί.** *For if you were to grant me this, that it was through* MY *instrumentality you utterly opposed that despotism over Hellas which was being organized, you would grant me a greater boon than all which you have given to the rest.* ἐμέ is emphatic both by its form and its place in the sentence; by ἄλλοις are meant any other statesmen who have received public votes of thanks or emoluments. — **294.** P. 103, l. 5. **φιλιππισμόν.** Lord Brougham compares "Jacobinism." We have already had φιλιππισάντων, 176. — 7. **ἐπ' ἀληθείας,** 17. *If laying aside falsehood and all malicious speech you ought to inquire on the basis of truth who they are in reality on whose head all would naturally and justly lay the blame of what has happened* — 11. **κεφαλήν,** einem etwas auf den Kopf schuld geben (Schäfer). — **295.** 17. **ὑπάρχοντας.** Schäfer explains *belonging to them,* i. e. *of their own faction:* Dissen, *available,* i. e. *open to being led away:* Westermann, like Schäfer, *their own severally,* and so Whiston. But the word must surely mean a little more than a mere possessive pronoun. Transl. *who were in their*

hands: i. e. who were subordinate members of the states in which these others were leaders, and who blindly trusted to their leadership. — **διαφθείροντες.** The orator always divides the Greek world into two classes: those who sympathized with his own Athenian policy, and those who did not: to the latter he gives the sweeping designation of traitors. Against this Polybius (XVII., 14) makes a very proper protest: *πικρότατον ὄνειδος τοῖς ἐπιφανεστάτοις τῶν Ἑλλήνων εἰκῇ καὶ ἀκρίτως προσέρριψε.* — 18. **Δάοχος.** Harpocration, under the name *Μύρτις,* mentions a number of these revolutionists, quoting the lost history of Theopompus where further particulars seem to have been given. No historical interest attaches to any of the names: some of them we have had already in 48, 69, 71 cited with the same application. Hipparchus is mentioned by the orator, p. 125. And Demaratus is named by Plutarch (*Alex*, 9) as a friend of Philip, and companion of Alexander in his expedition to the East. Cicero imitates this passage, in his oration against Verres, II., 4. — 296. 27. **ἐπιλείψει** suggests at once the obvious parallel in the Epistle to the Hebrews, xi., 32. — P. 104, l. 4. **ἀλάστορες.** *φανεὶς ἀλάστωρ ἢ κακὸς δαίμων ποθέν,* Æsch., *Pers.*, 354. *τοῦδ' ὁ παλαιὸς δριμὺς ἀλάστωρ,* Id., *Ag.*, 1501. The orator speaks of these persons as if they were sent for divine visitations on the sins of their respective states — *national curses.* Whiston renders the three epithets, *foul and fawning and fiend-like.* — 5. **ἠκρωτηριασμένοι.** Perfect middle. *καὶ τῶν νηῶν καπρίους ἐχουσέων τὰς πρῴρας ἠκρωτηρίασαν.* Herod., III., 59. Here exactly *crippled,* as Kennedy translates. — 6. **προπεπωκότες.** According to the Scholiast whom Dissen quotes (Pind., *Ol.*, VII., 5), *προπίνειν* strictly is to present the drinking-cup as a gift to your guest at the banquet where he drinks from it. That it means to *pledge a health* (propinare) we have abundant evidence in the Lexica. The orator (p. 284) dwells on the fact that Philip *προὔπινεν ἐκπώματ' ἀργυρᾶ καὶ χρυσᾶ αὐτοῖς.* And on p. 34 he uses the phrase *προπέποται τὰ πράγματα* in a sense exactly the same as here: *toasted away.* So Lord Brougham. — 10. **ὅροι καὶ κανόνες,** *normæ et regulæ: standards and rules.* — **ἀνατετροφότες.** *While they have subverted liberty and independence* (lit. the having no master over themselves). The similarity of form in the perfects of *τρέπω* and *τρέφω* is sufficiently noticed in all grammars and lexica. The later form in each case was *τέτραφα,* and some editions here read *ἀνατετραφότες.* I have followed Dindorf in retaining the omicron. — 297. 14. **εἰ δεῖ μὴ ληρεῖν,** *if we* *must speak in earnest,* lit. *not trifle.* — 17. **καὶ ἐγὼ παρ' ὑμῖν,** *and I before you,* sc. have been made guiltless (sub. ἀναίτιος γέγονα). — **ἀντί,** followed by the genitive of price, *for, in return for.* The answer to this question which follows is greatly admired by Lord Brougham. — 298. 25...27. **οὐδὲ...συμβεβούλευκα,** *nor in all the advice that I have ever given to my hearers, have I ever, like you* (Æschines and the other hirelings just mentioned) *advised as if I were the tongue of a balance inclining towards lucre.* If this reading of Dindorf (ὡσπερανεὶ τρυτάνη) be correct, the orator compares himself to the tongue of a balance, but disclaims any bias or leaning in one direction, that direction being private advantage. The common reading is ὥσπερ ἂν εἰ ἐν τρυτάνῃ, *with an inclination towards lucre, as if set on the scales* [with a bias]. ῥέπων in either reading would be intransitive, describing the speaker's own bias, not the direction he gives to that of others. The passage in *De Pace*, 12, is an excellent illustration: ὅταν δ' ἐπὶ θάτερα ὥσπερ εἰς τρυτάνην ἀργύριον προσενέγκῃς οἴχεται φέρον καὶ καθείλκυκε τὸν λογισμὸν ἐφ' αὑτό, καὶ οὐκ ἂν ἔτ' ὀρθῶς οὐδ' ὑγιῶς ὁ τοῦτο ποιήσας περὶ οὐδενὸς λογίσαιτο. — P. 105, l. 1. **ψυχῆς.** Here follow in most editions the words τὰ πάντα μοι πέπρακται. They are not found in Σ, and look very like an interpolation. — 299. 5. **μου.** There is not, I think, the emphasis on the pronoun here which Whiston conceives. It would in that case be ἐμοῦ. The passage in Æschines is p. 87. εἰ μὲν γὰρ λέγεις ὅθεν τὴν ἀρχὴν τοῦ ψηφίσματος ἐποιήσω, ὅτι τὰς τάφρους τὰς περὶ τὰ τείχη καλῶς ἐτάφρευσε, θαυμάζω σου, κ. τ. λ. For the agreement of ἄξια, see C. 496; Cu. 366; G. 138, N. 2; H. 511. — — 6. **πόρρω,** i. e. *far below.* So πρόσω δικαίων Æsch., *Eumen.*, 414. — **που** = *perhaps.* See Lex. — 7. **οὐ λίθοις.** This is the passage quoted at the beginning of Libanius's Hypothesis. The idea, though not quite original, is clothed in good and bold language by the orator, and comes in as a most effective repartee on his opponent. The well-known ode of Sir W. Jones, "What constitues a state?" is cited by Whiston in illustration. — 9. **μέγιστον φρονῶ.** *I feel most proud.* The genitive τῶν ἐμαυτοῦ depends on the superlative: lit. *most of my doings.* Fully expressed the phrase would have run ὡς μεγίστοις οὖσι τῶν ὑπ' ἐμαυτοῦ πεπραγμένων. But the compression gives it thrice as much force. — 11. **τόπους, κ. τ. λ.** The allusions are clearly, as Dissen remarks, to Eubœa, Bœotia, Megaris, Corcyra, and Leucadia (see 227–237). These accusatives have all to be understood afterwards as the object of ἀμυνουμένους, τούτων being the whole body of the citizens supposed present in their public assembly which the speaker is addressing. — **καὶ πολλοὺς...ἀμυνουμένους,** *and many to defend them for us.* πολλούς, however, is not in the best MSS. and edd. — **300.** 17. **τοῖς λογισμοῖς,** *calculations,* i. e. *tactics.* He means that his own political calculations were the best humanly possible; that he cannot admit Philip to have been his superior in political judgment, but only in successful fortune. Observe the emphatic position of ἐγώ in contrast with Philip and his tactics. — 18. **στρατηγοί.** Tamen Athenienses post cladem Lysiclem prætorem, accusatore Lycurgo, capitis damnarunt, conf. Diodor., 16, 88. DISSEN. — 19. **δυνάμεις.** The singular is more usual in speaking of military forces. But the plural may be justified here by the fact that several states were combining their respective forces.

301 - 323. Conclusion: I MYSELF HAVE ALWAYS ACTED AS A TRUE STATESMAN.

301. 23. **οὐκ...προβαλέσθαι,** sc. χρῆν: *was it not his duty to place Eubœa as a defence before Attica on the side of the sea?* — 26. **ὁμόρους.** He means Achæa, Corinth, and Megara. — **σιτοπομπίαν,** 87 sq. As to the construction, Schäfer cites a very happy illustration, p. 1262, l. 16, *οἱ μὲν γὰρ νόμοι καὶ τὰς ἀναγκαίας προφάσεις ὅπως μὴ μείζους γίγνωνται προείδοντο.* — 27. **φιλίαν.** Supply γῆν, according to the very common Attic ellipsis: πολεμία is used in exactly the same way. — **παρά** = *along.* — **302.** P. 106, l. 2. **ὑπαρχόντων,** *of what we have already,* i. e. subject allies: a very similar use of ὑπάρχειν to that already noticed in 295. — **ἐκπέμποντα** agrees, of course, with πολίτην, which is understood together with χρῆν in all these clauses: *by sending out succors* from time to time; the imperfect participle denoting a continued or customary action. — 3. **Προκόννησον,** in the Propontis, originally a free colony from Miletus; then subjected to Athens; and ultimately to Cyzicus, the modern Marmora. In the speech against Polycles, p. 1207, the orator speaks of Proconnesus as an ally of Athens. The dates of its history are uncertain. — 4. **τὰ δ',** constructed like σιτοπομπίαν above, that is, after πρᾶξαι, with τὸ Βυζάντιον, κ. τ. λ., as appositions. — 7. **ὧν.** The genitive of privation depending on ἐνέλειπε, which is here impersonal. ὧν ἐνέλειπε as opposed to ὑπαρχουσῶν represents ἃ οὐχ ὑπῆρχε. — **303.** 10. **ἃ καί.** The καί = *both,* emphasizes the connection of *plan* and *execution,* for *both* of which the orator claims equal approval. — 13. **παρεθέντα,** i. e. he disclaims any sin of (1) omission, or of (2) ignorance, or (3) treachery. — 15. **ἧκεν,** *were dependent on,* — a favorite Attic use of the verb. ὥστ' εἰς ἐμ' ἥκει τῆς πόλεως τὰ πράγματα. Aristoph., *Plut.*, 919. — 18. **ἐλυμαίνετο...ἀνέτρεψαν,** *went on* (imperf.) *damaging our cause till they ruined* (aor.) *all.* W. Holmes makes τοῖς ὅλοις adverbial. But better dative after ἐλυμαίνετο, which, as Drake with the approval of Whiston observes, here takes the dative because it has the notion of successive attacks *upon* or *against.* See also Lex., s. v. — **304.** 23. **ἐμοί.** Dative after ταὐτά. Cf. ἄλλοις, 291 ; πολλοῖς, 292. — 24. **ἐκέχρητ' ἄν,** *would have experienced.* — **305.** P. 107, l. 2. **ἐλάττοσι** in its position here as a predicate requires us to paraphrase instead of translating : *That ye may know that the words I employ are far less than the deeds I refer to.* Drake well renders ἐλάττοσι, *falling far short of.* — 3. **εὐλαβούμενος.** Cf. 3, 4. — **λέγε.** See 28, last note. The words from τὸν ἀριθμὸν to ψηφίσματα are put in brackets by some editors, and have indeed something the air of an interpolation, but Dindorf retains them, and Schäfer defends them. — **306.** 7. **κατορθουμένων.** Here follows ὦ γῆ καὶ θεοὶ in most editions. Dindorf omits the words and they are not in Σ. Render with Whiston : *in the event of the success of which indeed, beyond a doubt, we might have been pre-eminently great.* — **μεγίστοις** agrees obviously with ἡμῖν, which we supply as the dative depending on ὑπῆρχεν. The use of these imperfects without ἄν in a conditional apodosis of past time has been already noticed, 248. — 9. **τὸ δικαίως.** *The attribute of justice would have been ours as well:* i. e. we should have been justly supreme as well as unquestionably. — **ὡς ἑτέρως** is euphemistic = *quite otherwise,* that is, *adversely.* See note, 212. — 10. **περίεστι,** in connection with the rest of this sentence, gives the idea of something saved from a wreck. Whatever we have lost, at any rate we have saved reputation and honor. *And although they have turned out quite otherwise, there remains at any rate a good reputation.* — **307.** 12. **οὐ μὰ Δί' οὐκ ἀποστάντα,** (thus should a patriot act) *and not, no not by any means, deserting the interests of the state and hiring himself to its enemies, cherish the opportunities of the enemy instead of those of his country, and malign the man who has undertaken both to advise and propose courses of action worthy of the state, and who has made it a principle to abide by them.* ὑποστῆναι, of putting one's shoulder under the burden, in contrast to ἀποστῆναι above ; the genitive with ἐπί has been discussed in 17. — 18, **ἂν δέ,** *while if any such person annoy him* (τὸν βάσκανον) *at all individually, he lays it up in his memory and keeps an eye upon the person.* The δεῖ at the beginning of the paragraph is carried all through this long sentence, and the *οὐδέ* following *θεραπεύειν* has to be carried on to *μεμνῆσθαι* also. — 19. **οὐδέ γ'**, *at any rate he ought not to maintain an unrighteous and hollow silence.* The epithet *ὕπουλος* suggests a festering sore of which, however, the surface is healed and gives no symptom of mischief. So Æschines, as the orator alleges, holds his tongue and looks pleasant, although his heart is full of venom. The alleged sins of Æschines are threefold in this paragraph : (1) treachery to his own state, (2) malignant envy of her true statesmen and private malice against them, (3) affectation of being perfectly satisfied at the time, and subsequent show of great indignation. The first of these is introduced by *οὐ μὰ Δί'*, the second by *οὐδέ*, the third by *οὐδέ γ'*. — **308.** 22. **ἁπλῶς**, *honestly*, as distinct from *ὕπουλος*. All this is in answer to Æschines, p. 84. — P. 108, l. 1. **τοῦ συνεχῶς**, *sated of the man whom you hear incessantly:* our idiom requires this amount of paraphrase : he alludes to the fact that the prominent statesman must needs be always making public speeches. — 2. **δύσκολον**, *provoking*, euphemistic, like *ἑτέρως*, 306. — **309.** 4. **ἡσυχίας**. *Suddenly he comes out as a speaker from his silence,*— like a gale after a *calm*. *ἐφάνη* is the gnomic aorist. C. 605 ; Cu. 494 ; G. 205 ; H. 707. *ἡσυχίας* must be taken also in close connection with *πνεῦμα*, the *ἐκ* being transitional only, as in *τυφλὸς ἐκ δεδορκότος* (Soph., *O. T.*, 454), etc. — 5. **πεφωνασκηκώς**, *with well-trained voice and words and phrases collected*, 279. — **συνειλοχώς**. *στωμυλιοσυλλεκτάδη*, Arist., *Ran.*, 866 ; *συλλέγων μονῳδίας*, 874 ; *ἐπύλλια*, *Ach.*, 405. — 6. **συνείρει**, *he strings them together with distinct utterance and without drawing breath.* — 13. **ἐμπορίου**, *provision for commerce* between Athens and any particular foreign city, which would require a commercial treaty, etc. to be arranged. — 15. **ἀποδειχθεῖσιν**, *declared*, i. e. open and undisguised. — **310.** 16. **ἐξέτασις**, *opening*, lit. *a process of examining :* hence *an open examination*, where any competitor may enter and distinguish himself. — 17. **ἀποδείξεις**, *opportunities :* lit. *displays* of ability ; i. e. occasions on which a man might display it. — 18. **οὐδαμοῦ**. The metaphor is still from a competitive race. On the auxiliary use of *φαίνεσθαι*, *φανερὸς εἶναι*, *δῆλος εἶναι*, see Madv., *G. S.*, 177, b ; C. 657, k ; Cu. 590 ; H. 797. — 20. **ὁποστοσοῦν**, *the any-eth whatever.* The termination *-οστός*, commencing with the ordinal twenty, is common to all ordinal numbers above the twentieth. The correlative *οὖν* corresponds to the Latin -cunque. Donaldson's *G. G.*, 245. Dissen thinks the orator is here alluding to the notorious oracle addressed to the Megarians: ὑμεῖς δ' ὦ Μεγαρεῖς οὔτε τρίτοι οὔτε τέταρτοι οὔτε δυωδέκατοι οὔτ' ἐν λόγῳ οὔτ' ἐν ἀριθμῷ, Schol., *Theocr.*, XIV., 48. — **ἐπί γ' οἷς**, *at any rate not in anything which led to the advancement of your country.* As οἷς here is neuter, I take the οἷς before οὐδαμοῦ to be neuter also (meaning *in which competition*), not masculine, as Reiske interprets. — **311.** 23. **διακονία** would include home government and policy, while πρεσβεία would be limited to foreign. — 25. **ξενικῶν**, e. g. Thrace and the Bosporus, 244. — 26. **ποῖαι** with its usual sense of sarcasm, as in each of the questions where it follows. Dinarch., *c. Demosth.*, p. 102, ποῖαι γὰρ τριήρεις εἰσὶ κατεσκευασμέναι διὰ τοῦτον, ὥσπερ ἐπὶ Εὐβούλου τῇ πόλει; ἢ ποῖοι νεώσοικοι τούτου πολιτευομένου γεγόνασι; πότε οὗτος ἢ διὰ ψηφίσματος ἢ νόμου ἐπηνώρθωσε τὸ ἱππικόν; κ. τ. λ. — 27. **τί τῶν ἁπάντων**, *in what possible department?* πάντων, 5. — P. 109, l. 1. **εὐπόροις** are the ἡγεμόνας of 103, as ἀπόροις are the πένησιν of 107. — 2. **πολιτική...χρημάτων**, *financial relief for the state and the public.* W. **312.** 3. **τᾶν**, *my good friend:* the colloquial appellative, which, however, occurs once in tragedy (Soph., *Philoct.*, 1373). Buttmann has argued with great probability that it is an archaic vocative τα of τυ (σύ) with ν ephelcusticon added. The old derivation made it the vocative of ἔτης. — 6. **ἐπεδίδοσαν.** There were special patriotic funds started directly after Chæronea, and again to assist Thebes in the revolt against Alexander. But, indeed, during the whole period B. C. 338 to 335 there would be constant opportunities for wealthy persons to show their public spirit in this form. — 7. **ἐπιτιμίαν**, *restoration to civil rights*, cf. 15. He appears to have been disfranchised by the imposition of a heavy fine. His friends then subscribed to pay the fine for him. But he handed over the money so collected to be used not for his own restoration, but for the expenses of the state. It is suppesed that this Aristonicus is the same mentioned in 83, etc. — 11. **ἔρανον.** *A contribution of two talents as a present from the Heads of the sections, for which consideration you murdered the trierarchic law.* The word ἔρανος only implies that the sum was raised by joint subscription among the ἡγεμόνες (103) as a retaining fee to Æschines for taking up the case in support of their vested interests. How far he succeeded in the "slaughter of the innocent," and when, we have no historical information. Others render ἐφ' οἷς, *for the damage which you did*, taking οἷς as the (cognate) object of the verb, attracted into the dative by the preposition. Either translation is possible and makes equally good sense. Compare Whiston in loc. and Grote, XI., 645.

— **313.** 14. **ἐκκρούσω,** *put myself off,* lit. *adjourn myself,* ἐκκρούσας εἰς τὴν ὑστεραίαν, p. 385 (*fin.*). Dissen wrongly quotes ἐξέκρουόν με, p. 348, where it means they *hissed me off* (*explodere*). The orator means here that if he goes into every detail one after another, he will lose the time for arguing his present and immediate point. Render: *that I may not by speaking of one thing after another cut myself off from the matter in hand.* — 16. **φυλάττων** is opposed to δι' ἔνδειαν: *it was not for want of means that you did not contribute, but from your care that no act of yours should be opposed to those for whom you manage everything in your public life.* — 17. **τούτοις οἷς.** Masculine: i. e. Macedon and the Macedonian party, οἷς being the dative of relation in the category *commodi.* — 18. **νεανίας,** *vigorous.* Youth as the type of (1) *vigor* or (2) *violence* appears in the uses of νεανίας and all its derivatives, as the Lexica abundantly testify. The context will always show whether the good or bad sense predominates. Cf. p. 37, l. 10; p. 557, l. 25; Aristot., *Eth.*, I., 1 (*fin.*), etc. — 19. **λαμπρός,** *brilliant,* a favorite combination with νεανικόν, as in the passages above cited. — **ἡνίκ'... δέῃ,** *whenever you must needs speak against the people here.* — 21. **Θεοκρίνης.** Harpocration informs us that this person was a συκοφάντης, as indeed the speech [Demosth.], *c. Theocr.*, would lead us to infer. There is no other interpretation of the sarcasm than Dissen's, viz., that Theocrines, like Æschines, affected to deplore the fate of those who fell victims to his intrigues (cf. Æsch., 72, 76). — **314.** 25. **προλαβόντα,** *having drawn upon the good-will which subsists on your part towards the dead* (the good feeling which you cherish to the memory of the departed), *to examine me and compare me with them, — me who am still alive among you.* Æschines had done this in his peroration, p. 79, alluding to Miltiades, Themistocles, Aristides. The orator justly protests against any comparisons of "virtus incolumis" with "virtus sublata ex oculis." The language (εὔνοιαν, κ. τ. λ.) is closely parallel to that of 1. — **315.** P. 110, l. 2. **φθόνος.** Cf. Thucyd., II., 45, φθόνος γὰρ τοῖς ζῶσι πρὸς τὸ ἀντίπαλον, τὸ δὲ μὴ ἐμποδὼν ἀνανταγωνίστῳ εὐνοίᾳ τετίμηται. The sentiment is too notorious to need further illustration. — 4. **κρίνωμαι.** *Am I to be put on trial and examined?* The subjunctive in questions paves the way for the imperative in answers. For examples, cf. Madv., *G. S.*, 121. The sense of θεωρῶμαι is made plain by ἐξετάζειν in 314. — 6. **ἄλλον.** *Any one else you please of those whose policy is identical with yours, and who are now alive.* The orator only challenges comparison of merit with the living, not with the dead; and only with the opposition party, not with those whose policy had been his own. — **316.** 9. **ὑπερμεγέθεις**, *which are colossal — nay more; one could not express their magnitude.* A good example of *μὲν οὖν* in its corrective force, which is quite as common in prose as in poetry. Plat., *Gorg.*, 466, etc. — 12. **ἄγειν**, *to expose to thanklessness and insult such services as are being done for the present period.* The sense of *ἄγειν* suggests a speaker dragging something out of its existing position into another to which it does not belong. — **317.** 14. **ἄρα**, *as it seems*, i. e. judging by my opponent's argument. — 18. **κατ' ἐκείνους**, *all through their time* (17, note, *κατ' ἐκείνους*) as *ἐπ' ἐκείνων* would mean simply *in their time.* In some texts *τοὺς χρόνους* is added here, but it is not found in Σ, and I follow Dindorf in excluding it. — 19. **διέσυρον**, 27, 218, 323. — **318.** 23. **ἀδελφός.** Philochares, one of the ten *στρατηγοί*, reappointed three successive years (Æschin., p. 48). He had also a younger brother, Aphobetus, who served in distinguished civil capacities. But the former is probably alluded to here. — 26. **τοὺς καθ' αὑτόν**, *and with those of his own age.* — **319.** P. 111, l. 1. **Φιλάμμων.** Mentioned by Harpocration as a distinguished boxer and athlete. Cf. Aristot., *Rhet.*, III., 11; Eustath., *on Hom. Il.* ψ., 686. — **Γλαύκου.** Mentioned as having won the prize for boxing in the twenty-fifth Olympiad. Cf. Pausan., VI., 10; Lucian, *de Imagin*, c. 19. Æschines (p. 81) replies to the orator's argument here, having obviously inserted the reply for the first time in this published oration, though he so phrases it that it might seem a part of the original speech; but the coincidence is a little too remarkable. — 6. **ὅρα.** Cf. 315 (end). — 7. **οὐδένα.** *I shrink from none*, i. e. I will stand side by side with any, to be looked at and compared. Of this accusative, Madvig (*G. S.*, 23, a) states the principle thus: "Many intransitive verbs, which denote a motion, on composition with a preposition, assume a transitive signification"; e. g. *μετέρχομαι, περιΐσταμαι, ὑφίσταμαι, ὑποδύομαι.* But we see that *ἐξίσταμαι* also retains its force as an intransitive verb, for it is constructed quite as often with a dative of reference. Soph., *Aj.*, 673, is an example of the latter; and *ib*, 82, is an example of the former. In translating any verb of this twofold construction, we must be careful to observe the context and to modify the English accordingly. If the reading *οὐδένι*, which many MSS. give here, were taken for our text, we should translate: *I yield to none*, i. e. consider myself the equal of any. Cf. p. 460, l. 2; p. 617, l. 15, etc. —

320. 8. **ὧν** = *of whom*, part. gen. after ἐγὼ κράτιστα. — **ἐφάμιλλον.** *Open* (for competition). This use of the adjective is peculiar to the orator: so p. 488, 13. The more usual sense is *equal, a match.* — 13. **μήποτ'.** We supply συμβαίνειν. The euphemism is too common to need illustration. — 17. **ἕτερον,** sc. Φίλιππον. — **ἐξέτασις.** Ironical; he draws a picture of the Macedonian party at Athens, looking out for leaders and members; they would hold, he suggests, an *inspection* of the public men, to pick out not the best advisers for state, but the most venal and treacherous and ready supporters of Philip. Cf. 310, ἐξέτασις. — 18. **ἐν τάξει.** *At your post,* i. e. you were exactly the sort of people whom this inspection would cause to be selected for office. — 19. **ἱπποτρόφος.** Schäfer and Dissen agree in understanding this to be typical of luxurious and wealthy position, comparing p. 1046, l. 8; Xen., *Œc.*, 2. 6, etc. In Attica, as in Palestine, *keeping horses* was a sign of wealth and luxury. Isocr., 16. 33. Reiske and others understand it of volunteer cavalry, but with no authority to support their view; which, however, if supported, would give by far the best force to the passage. We may paraphrase, *a great man, and famous for his stud.* — 321. 21. **μέτριον** = *respectable, fair.* Cf. note 10, where it is used in the same way as here, with the same reason for choosing the word, viz. to avoid envy and odium. φύσει, as we see from the use of φύσις just below, means *according to the measure of human capacity*, as opposed to the superhuman and the supernatural; that which is within the compass of human attainment or control in distinction from that which is controlled by fortune or providence. τὸν φύσει μέτριον, therefore, means *the reasonably good citizen,* or, as Lord Brougham renders, *the citizen of ordinary worth.* This seems to accord better with the signification of the words and the demands of the context, than *the well-disposed citizen,* which is the reading of Kennedy and Whiston, but which is too nearly *identical* with εὔνοια, one of the things that the citizen must *possess.* — 23. **ἐξουσίαις.** *When in power:* as we should say, *when a member of the government.* Cf. Aristot., *Eth.*, II., 3, for an instance of this sense of ἐξουσίαις. I quite agree with Whiston in declining Dissen's translation, *opportuna momenta.* — 25. **εὔνοιαν.** *Good feeling* towards the state here, as in 1. It would correspond to our *patriotism.* He means that, whereas political disasters and misfortunes may destroy a statesman's policy, nothing should ever destroy, or even impair, his devotion to his country: *for,* he argues, *this is in nature's control,* i. e. the man's own spirit is respon-

sible for keeping him a true patriot; *while power and strength are in other hands,* i. e. depend on fortune and chance. — **322.** P. 112, l. 1. **ἐξαιτούμενος.** Alluding again to the demand made by Alexander for the surrender of Demosthenes and the other leading orators in 335. Plut., *Vit. Demosth.*, c. 24. — 2. **ἐπαγόντων,** sc. τῶν Φιλιππιστῶν. Æschines mentions (p. 76) that an attempt was made to arraign Demosthenes before the Amphictyonic Council, apparently on the ground of his having deserted from an embassy. The passage runs thus: *ἐπειδὴ περὶ Θήβας ἦν τὸ στρατόπεδον πρεσβευτὴς ὑφ' ὑμῶν χειροτονηθεὶς ἀποδρὰς ἐκ μέσου τοῦ Κιθαιρῶνος ἥκεν ὑποστρέψας, οὔτ' ἐν εἰρήνῃ οὔτ' ἐν πολέμῳ χρήσιμον ἑαυτὸν παρέχων· καὶ τὸ πάντων δεινότατον ὑμεῖς μὲν τοῦτον οὐ προὔδοτε, οὐδ' εἰάσατε κριθῆναι ἐν τῷ τῶν Ἑλλήνων συνεδρίῳ.* The embassy in question was charged to convey the apologies of Athens to Alexander for the attempted revolt in 336. Demosthenes may have known that his presence would be specially obnoxious to Alexander, and also may have had fears for his own personal safety. But whatever the motive of his desertion, that could not have been made a charge before the court of Amphictyons (see Smith, *Dic. Ant.*), who would have no jurisdiction in the matter. Dissen suggests that the charge was against the orator as having been the open antagonist of Philip when the latter was acting as Amphictyonic general. No better explanation has been suggested. — 2. **ἐπαγγελλομένων,** *when they kept making offers,* i. e. offers of bribes on the part of Macedon. — 4. **προσβαλλόντων,** *when they set these accursed wretches at me like savage beasts.* With this use of προσβάλλειν we may compare its common signification in the middle voice *to make an attack on.* — 5. **ὀρθὴν καὶ δικαίαν** has the predicative force, hence the article with ὁδόν. Render with Whiston: *for from the very first, straightforward and honest was the course of policy which I chose.* — 8. **μετὰ τούτων εἶναι,** *to be on their side,* sc. of the honor and glory of my country. So Bremi, and this gives the proper force of μετά better than the more common rendering: *in these to have my being.* — **323.** 9. **ἑτέρων,** *the other side,* sc. the Macedonians. — 11. **ἐκεῖσε,** to Macedon. — 15. **ὥσπερ.** *Who vilify the state as though, forsooth, they were not thereby vilifying themselves* (as responsible for the state policy) *while they turn their eye abroad* (in admiration), *and where another has triumphed by the ruin of the Greeks, they glorify this, and protest that it must be so maintained forever.* Their sympathies are entirely with Macedon and against Athens: they despise and abuse the latter, they admire and glorify the former.

324. Peroration. HEAVEN CHANGE THEIR HEARTS, OR HASTEN THEIR DOOM, OUR ONLY CHANCE OF SALVATION!

20. **μὴ δῆτ'.** *Never, I implore you, ye powers of heaven, never bestow your sanction on that! But, if it may be, inspire even them with a better mind and heart! Or if, as they seem, they are past repentance, give* THEM *— and them alone — to utter and speedy ruin by land and sea: and to us the rest, grant ye the quickest relief from our imminent terrors, — yea, a salvation that knows no fall.* The force of this would be a good deal destroyed in English if we took literally the *μηδεὶς* with which it commences, — *let no one of you*, i. e. no deity either lower or higher. The sense of *προ* in *προώλεις* implies *before they have finished our ruin;* their doom must be speedy or else our salvation will be past praying for. The commentators all admire the rhetoric of this passage, and confess their inability to preserve either the music or the full meaning of the language in a translation. It is often compared with the conclusion of Cicero's first Philippic.

THE END.

Cambridge: Electrotyped and Printed by Welch, Bigelow, & Co.

www.ingramcontent.com/pod-product-compliance
Lightning Source LLC
LaVergne TN
LVHW020240110826
845151LV00003B/983